MR AND MRS GLADSTONE

Other books by Joyce Marlow

The Uncrowned Queen of Ireland
The Tolpuddle Martyrs
The Peterloo Massacre
The Life and Times of George I
Captain Boycott and the Irish

MR AND MRS GLADSTONE

An Intimate Biography

JOYCE MARLOW

WEIDENFELD AND NICOLSON
LONDON

Published by Weidenfeld and Nicolson
11 St John's Hill, London SW11

ISBN 0 297 77150 7

Printed in Great Britain by
REDWOOD BURN LIMITED
Trowbridge & Esher

ILLUSTRATION ACKNOWLEDGMENTS

The author and publishers are grateful to the following for permission to re-
produce photographs: The Granger Collection for No. 1; The Bettman Archive
for Nos. 3, 4; St. Deiniol's Library for Nos. 2, 11, 12, 26; National Portrait Gallery, London, for Nos. 8, 9, 14, 15, 16, 18; Radio Times Hulton Picture Library
for No. 17; Sir William Gladstone for No. 24; Mrs. Dorothy Parish for No. 22;
Sir William Gladstone and Mrs. Dorothy Parish for No. 6; Clwyd County
Record Office for Nos. 5, 10, 13, 19, 20, 21, 23, 25; Hugh Cavendish for No. 7.

For Janet and Tony Hurrell

Peace, peace of body, soul & spirit, alike
to your sleeping & your waking hours, so says
the ivy to the oak.

CATHERINE GLYNNE to WILLIAM GLADSTONE;
written on the evening of 19 June 1839,
a month before their marriage.

CONTENTS

LIST OF ILLUSTRATIONS

Following p. 116

AUTHOR'S NOTE AND ACKNOWLEDGMENTS

In recording my thanks to the people who have helped me during the research for this book I wish first to acknowledge the gracious permission of Her Majesty the Queen to use material in the Royal Archives at Windsor Castle. I should like personally to thank Sir Robin Mackworth-Young, Miss Jane Langton and the ladies in the Round Tower at Windsor for their generous and knowledgeable assistance while I was working there. To Sir William Gladstone I extend my warmest thanks for allowing me to quote freely from the personal papers of Catherine and William Gladstone and for his courtesy in showing me round Hawarden Castle. To Mr. Geoffrey Veysey (the County Archivist), Mr. Christopher Williams and Mrs. Rolfe of the Clwyd County Record Office at Hawarden I can only say thank you for their unflagging kindness and co-operation throughout the research and writing of the book; to Dr. and Mrs. Raymond Foster, the Warden of St. Deiniol's Library and his wife, my thanks for their similar kindness and co-operation and for making the library such a pleasant place in which to stay and work—the evening when we sat listening to the recording of Gladstone's voice in front of the blazing log fire in the common room is one I shall always remember; to Lord Ponsonby of Shulbrede again my warmest thanks for loaning me the personal correspondence of his grandfather Sir Henry Ponsonby and allowing me to quote freely from the letters; to His Grace the Duke of Devonshire and the trustees of the Chatsworth Settlement my gratitude for permission to quote from the Devonshire MSS, and to Mr. T. S. Wragg, M.B.E., my thanks for his kind help while I was at Chatsworth; to Viscount Harcourt my thanks for allowing me to quote from the Journal of his father Lewis Harcourt (1st Baron Harcourt), and to Mr. John Moberly, C.M.G., for permission to quote from Sir Edward Hamilton's diaries and letters; also my thanks to the staffs of the Reading Room and Manuscript Department of the British Library, the London Library and the Bodleian Library; and to the Clarendon Press for permission to quote from the published Gladstone Diaries. To Professor John Vincent I extend my thanks for suggesting avenues of research and for the benefit of his Gladstonian knowledge; similarly to Dr. Dudley W. R. Bahlman—who edited the early sections of Sir Edward Hamilton's diaries so admirably—for his friendly transatlantic help; and to Dr. Colin Matthew, who, while adhering to the terms imposed by his editorship of the Gladstone Diaries, was generous in his assistance. Finally, my thanks go to Mrs. Dorothy Parish—"Dossie" of the later chapters—for allowing me to quote freely from her mother's diaries and letters, and for recalling the memories of her grandparents both by letter and in a most enjoyable meeting.

NEWCASTLE-ON-TYNE 1862:
A ROYAL PROGRESS

ON 7 OCTOBER 1862 Mr. and Mrs. Gladstone arrived in Newcastle-on-Tyne for a three-day visit to the northeast. Officially they had been invited by the Tyne commissioners to inspect the improvements made on "the coaly Tyne," but the invitation had been extended to Mr. Gladstone and his wife rather than to other members of Lord Palmerston's Liberal Government and their wives because he, as Chancellor of the Exchequer, was the man who had reorganised the nation's finances, who had recently concluded a break-through commercial treaty with England's traditional enemy, France, and who by espousing the policy of free trade had set the economy on a booming course. Apart from the respect accorded by an industrial trading nation to Mr. Gladstone as a rigorous broom in the fiscal and economic cupboards, large sections of the population had begun to feel, from a distance, that he was a special, different breed of minister, one who cared about them and who was "the Chancellor of the people." In three glorious days in 1862 "when the sun harmonised with the nature of the demonstration," the people were given the opportunity to observe Mr. Gladstone at close quarters and to prove that he and his wife had touched a responsive chord within them.

The couple whom Tyneside turned out to see in its thousands had been married for twenty-three years. He was fifty-three, she was fifty, and physically as much as politically they were an impressive pair. William Gladstone was tall—5 feet 10¾ inches in his stockinged feet, as he precisely noted—and slim, as the strenuous life he led had not allowed middle age to bring portliness. His once thick jet-black hair was beginning to thin at the temples but it was only slightly flecked with grey and grew round the side of his face in the fashionable bewhiskered style. The nose was large and fairly prominent but the skin was singularly unlined and the hollows and crevices which later made him resemble the Englishman's version of the Old Testament prophet had not yet appeared. The most remarkable and remarked upon of Gladstone's physical characteristics were his eyes, so dark that at times they seemed to be black, with a piercing and intensely riveting gaze. He was a well-preserved figure for his age but Catherine Gladstone had an almost preternatural youthfulness. She was of average height and she too remained slim—bearing eight children had not thickened her figure. Her luxuriant brown hair was as thick and curling as in former days, her classical features were barely lined, and if her eyes were not as startling as her husband's, they were a particularly beautiful sapphire blue. But Catherine's outstanding characteristic was as much mental as physical: she had a radiant serenity which charmed most people, among whom were to be counted the citizens of Tyneside in October 1862.

The eighth of October was *the* day, what the *Newcastle Chronicle* described as "a royal progress," "the Jubilee Day of the Tyne," "the Festival of Mr Gladstone," and it started at midday when the Gladstones boarded the steamboat *Harry Clasper* at Gateshead quay and set off accompanied by twelve other boats bearing the mayors and other notables from Newcastle, Gateshead and South Shields. The thirteen official vessels steamed line abreast down the river Tyne, followed by a flotilla of smaller craft and barges bedecked with flags and bunting, many especially painted for the occasion in every colour of the rainbow. The banks of the river were lined with thousands of cheering people, and even the tops of the blast furnaces and factories "crowned with clouds of densest, blackest smoke, out of which forks of sulphureous flame darted" were packed with workmen. As the royal progress proceeded slowly on its way, church bells rang out in Newcastle and Gateshead and guns thundered along the banks, and the reporter from the *Newcastle Chronicle* thought that the blackened faces cheering from the tops of the belching blast furnaces, with the cannon booming below them, were "the exultation of pandemonium, when Lucifer ascended his throne"—though he hastened to add that he was not comparing the Chancellor of the Exchequer with Lucifer. (The young reporter was Wemyss Reid, who became the editor of the highly influential *Leeds Mercury*, and was later knighted for his services. But at the time he thought the Gladstones were beings from another world.)

The triumphal progress lasted six hours, calling at the North Pier in Tynemouth and the South Pier in South Shields. As it neared the latter place, a large vessel outward bound for Calcutta passed close by the *Harry Clasper* and the crew swarmed into the mizzen and the main rigging to give Mr. Gladstone three hearty British cheers. He made a speech per hour, Tyneside roared itself hoarse, it was noted that "Every cheer for him ended with one more cheer more for Mrs Gladstone," and when the couple returned to Gateshead in the early evening, people climbed onto every conceivable elevation and projection to say farewell to her as much as to her illustrious husband. She told the crowds that it had been the happiest day of her life, that she had never experienced such a welcome before and never would again, to which a gentleman in the crowd replied, "Do us the honour, Madame, to come to Tyneside again, and you shall be sure of many such welcomes."

Catherine later said, "It was the first time, you know, that *he* was received as he deserved to be," while Gladstone himself considered that the whole fantastic spectacle could only have been truly depicted by the brush of England's greatest artist, J. M. W. Turner. It was of course the sort of spectacle, particularly with its descriptions of a royal progress, that Queen Victoria (then deep in mourning for the Prince Consort) increasingly came to feel should be reserved for her and not accorded to one of her ministers, and Gladstone's inability to appreciate this royal emotion did not improve his relationship with Her Majesty.

Before Gladstone embarked upon his six-hour Tyneside festival, he had revealed another side of his complex character. On the evening of their arrival in Newcastle the Gladstones attended a banquet in the new town hall, and when the famed orator rose to make his speech he was greeted by tumultuous applause. It was expected that he would refer to the American Civil War, particularly to its disastrous effects on another part of the industrial north, his own native Lancashire, whose mills were idle because the North's blockade of Confederate ports had drastically reduced the supply of raw cotton. But what he said was unexpected. For it was in this Newcastle speech that Gladstone announced, "We may have our own opinion about slavery; we may be for or against the South; but there is no doubt that Jefferson Davis and other leaders of the South have made an army; they are making, it appears, a navy; and they have made what is more than either, they have made a nation." This statement, uttered by a leading minister of the Crown in a major public speech, was immediately interpreted as meaning that the British Government was about to abandon its wavering policy of neutrality in the American struggle and recognise the Confederacy. Seismic tremors were registered in London, Washington and other capitals of the world which wondered what their attitude should be if Britain recognised the Confederate States. The North was then at the nadir of its fortunes and the American minister in London, Charles Adams, commented, "We are now passing through the very crisis of our fate"; the South was delighted and the Lancashire cotton trade, about which Gladstone cared deeply, was plunged into even greater confusion and distress. The speech was a gross, irresponsible blunder—as Gladstone himself later fully acknowledged—because the British Government had *not* decided to recognise the Confederacy. Gladstone had spoken of his own initiative and without any passionate feeling for the South. He had been largely motivated by the wrongheaded belief that the North could not defeat the South and that acceptance of this fact and the establishment of two separate American states would cut short the horror of civil war and save further bloodshed. The speech was typical of one side of Gladstone: he was given to impetuous outbursts, frequently failing to appreciate the effect of his utterances and the power of his oratory, and it was a side of him that "the people" rather liked. The speech revealed a man of passion, sometimes only too humanly unaware when it was wiser to remain silent.

On 9 October the Gladstones travelled to Sunderland, Middlesbrough—

where they were given another river reception—and Darlington, ending a non-stop, fifteen-hour day after midnight. Gladstone was momentarily overcome by giddiness while making a speech in Sunderland; he thought that the concentrated labour had been too much for him, but he recorded, "C. again holding out, and indeed she is a great part of the whole business with the people everywhere." Indeed she was, as had been noted in Newcastle, and she became more so. There had long been highly political ladies, famous hostesses who exerted great influence, wives or mistresses who moulded their husbands' or lovers' careers, but these women operated behind the scenes and were rarely known or seen by the general public. Gladstone himself was the first major English politician holding high office to go out into the country and speak personally to the people—another provincial town, the pottery one of Stoke-on-Trent, was shortly overwhelmed by the thought "That a Chancellor of the Exchequer should be able to steal time away from public duties to descant on the virtues and the labour of a man who was but a humble worker in clay." But that his wife should stump the country with him, making contact with the humble labourers (and their wives), was an even greater novelty, and it was again at Newcastle that the vision of Mr. and Mrs. Gladstone as the perfect partnership began to take hold of the popular imagination. What sort of people were Catherine and William Gladstone that they acquired such a grip on popular sentiment and came to reflect the hopes and ambitions of so large a part of the country?

CHAPTER 1

A VERY SUPERIOR PERSON

WILLIAM EWART GLADSTONE and Catherine Glynne were married in July 1839 after a comparatively brief courtship, when neither of them was particularly young; he was nearly thirty and she twenty-seven. Though many years elapsed before their lives merged, they were born within a few miles of each other, she on 6 January 1812 at Hawarden Castle, he on 29 December 1809 at 62 Rodney Street in the city of Liverpool whose deepening pall of smoke could be seen from the hilltop at Hawarden. He was the fifth child of the second marriage of John Gladstone (his first wife had died childless) with Annie Mackenzie Robertson; both his parents were Scots, his father coming from a Lowland family, his mother a Highland lady from Dingwall. Eager genealogists were later to trace the ancestry of the four-time Prime Minister of the United Kingdom of Great Britain and Ireland to the Gledstanes of Gledstane Castle, a noted Scottish Border family in mediaeval times, but the links were tenuous and Gladstone's immediate forebears were unambitious, respectable, God-fearing folk. However, his father, John Gladstone, was cast in a different mould. He came down from Scotland to Liverpool, strongly infected by the thrusting, capitalistic instinct of the men who made the Industrial Revolution. Starting with a capital of £1,500 he traded with the East Indies, the Baltic and the United States, diversified into property, ships and insurance and then became involved in the lucrative West Indies sugar trade, which also meant he was involved with black slave labour. By the time William was born his fortune stood at £145,000. John Gladstone was a prototype of the tough, self-made man.

Gladstone more or less admitted the formidable side of his father's character when he said, "None but his children can know what torrents of tenderness flowed from his heart." There was a less abrasive side, at least for his children, who numbered six: Anne, Thomas, Robertson, John (known as John Neilson to distinguish him from his father), William and Helen. The first five were born at regular intervals between 1802 and 1809, with a five-year gap before the birth of Helen in 1814. Anne was a gentle, pious, loving girl who spent most of her life as a semi-invalid and who—because she bore her illness bravely and without complaint in a true Christian spirit

—exerted a strong influence on her family, notably William (with whom she had a special relationship, being his godmother as well as his sister). Thomas, or Tom, the eldest son on whom consequently the greatest hopes were pinned, suffered most from his father's dominating personality, as he unfortunately inherited the paternal rigidity and stubbornness but lacked the driving force. Robertson, who was a giant, 6 feet 5 inches tall and almost as wide (in maturity he weighed 350 pounds), and John Neilson were also partially suffocated by the paternal ambitions, though the latter escaped to a degree by going to sea as a young man. The real casualty among the Gladstone children was, ironically, Helen, because as a female her father had no plans for her. She had as good a brain as any of them except William, but it was given neither nourishment nor direction; and as she had as passionate a nature as any of them, except William, the consequences were disastrous and caused the famous brother—and his wife—some of their worst moments of anguish.

The young William grew up in a household in which his ambitious, dynastically minded father believed in the virtues of hard work and thrift which led a man by his independent effort to success and power. But power once achieved was to be used judicially in a Christian spirit, to help better the lives of others and to show them how they could attain, within the limits of their abilities, the desired goals of self-sufficiency and self-respect. The earnest sense of Christian endeavour was in his father's case based on the tenets of the Church of England (though John Gladstone had been born a Presbyterian), and William was christened and brought up in the Anglican faith. There was another influence in the household and if she was a less obviously forceful one than her husband, Annie Mackenzie Gladstone's background effect is not to be underestimated. She was a nervous, retiring lady who disliked the role she was expected to play, as social or political hostess, in her husband's life. John Gladstone's reaction to his wife's reluctance to share his burdens underlines the kinder side of his nature: he did not bully her or rant and roar but allowed her to retire from the front line. But her withdrawal from the mainstream of life in the household, her lack of any concrete interests on which to fall back, perhaps enmeshed with feelings of guilt about her inadequacy, turned her into an invalid. Apart from showing a certain tenacity in her determination to be unwell (she lived to a good age), Annie Gladstone demonstrated an absolute tenacity in her religious beliefs, which centred on the Evangelicism that had swept through England as the eighteenth century turned into the nineteenth.

Evangelicism placed an extra emphasis on the deep-rooted, base, vile individual sin which lay in all mankind and which had to be ceaselessly combatted in a personal fight, assisted only by God. This lonely sense of sin was transmitted to the young Gladstone, and the dualism of his nature on which everybody commented, whether it was the more obvious contrast between the iron self-control and the impetuous outbursts or the deeper conflict between mind and matter, idealism and materialism, partly resulted from his family background. It was to an extent imposed by the pull of a dominating, energetic father who had come to terms with *his* religious and materialistic tensions, against the limpet-like hold of an invalid mother who believed in original sin and a personal redemption not to be found through the base ways of this world. But the family environment was only partly responsible, for none of his siblings suffered from exactly the same problems, as no two members of a family, however close, however similarly educated, ever do. What was peculiar to Gladstone was a far wider-ranging, subtler, more enquiring mind than those possessed by the others (including Helen), while deep within him there was a passionate well of emotion. It was on this fertile ground that the scalpel of his mother's beliefs and the hammer of his father's went to work.

Despite the stress, albeit unconscious, implanted by the opposing credos and characters of his parents, despite the lack of open warmth and affection, the background in which Gladstone matured was not an unhappy one. John Gladstone encouraged discussion and argument, and pastimes such as singing, playing cards (the Gladstones were great whist players) and theatricals were permitted, at least on weekdays. The Sabbath had of course to be kept as a holy day, free from worldly activity. William had a pleasant baritone voice and his love of the theatre, not to mention his own innate dramatic instinct, was fostered by the family play acting. The Gladstone brothers had occasional bursts of young animal spirit—at their father's London house, for example, they enjoyed themselves sprinkling water on the coachmen and watching them take precautions against the threatened rain—but generally the children succumbed to the solemn, purposeful atmosphere which pervaded the household. Politics became of increasing importance, and before William was born his father had turned his attention to this important, powerful scene, adopting Canningite/Tory principles. These included fidelity to the old Tory beliefs—no tampering with the constitution, no reform for the sake of reform, no pandering to the dangerous, democratic, levelling spirit which had overtaken France and was pervading certain sectors of the English population; but they also embraced more liberal attitudes towards trade restrictions, Catholic Emancipation and foreign policy. In 1818 John Gladstone bought himself a seat in the unreformed Parliament and built a house at Seaforth, an area which then lay away from the smoke of central Liverpool, at the mouth of the unpolluted river Mersey, with miles of golden sands and with wild roses growing in the hedgerows. This fine house gave the Gladstone children an extra freedom which William especially enjoyed, for though he was born in an urban environment he was not temperamentally a city dweller and always preferred the country.

John Gladstone was extremely self-confident, not to say self-righteous, but he was aware that he lacked education and a wider understanding of the arts and sciences. He determined that his sons should have the benefit of the best possible education and with the exception of the naval escapee John Neilson, they were accordingly sent to Eton. Whether Eton in 1821 offered the best in education is a moot point, because under the aegis of the famous, or infamous, Dr. Keate, it was more renowned for its flogging and bullying than for its academic standards. But the young William managed to thrive in its atmosphere and to the end of his life he retained memories of Eton which were almost as affectionate and reverential as those he had for Oxford; for him it was "the queen of all schools." In an autobiographical fragment of his childhood, Gladstone suggested that he was an undistinguished child, a slow developer who exhibited little interest in learning, who was neither popular nor unpopular with other boys, whose only marked traits were a love of argument and a deep-seated financial thriftiness, and of whom the best that could be said was that he was not vicious. Nevertheless he participated in many Etonian activities, he co-edited a magazine, the *Eton Miscellany*, in which he showed early signs of efficiency and of the penchant for pouring out words without correction or rewriting, and he made friends, including Arthur Hallam, the golden boy of the era, with whom he had as intense a friendship as that shared by Tennyson and immortalised, on Hallam's early death, in *In Memoriam*.

It was at Eton that the first Glynne/Gladstone conjunction occurred. Sir Stephen Glynne, Catherine's brother, was a contemporary of William Gladstone's, but though they struck up a friendship it was not for either of them among the most intimate. It was also at Eton, when he joined the Debating Society, that on 29 October 1825, Gladstone made his first speech to an audience other than his family. He noted that he *"funced* less than I thought I should—by much."* Indeed he was sufficiently impressed by his effort to write to his sister Helen urging her to fix the date and the time—it was "a quarter or half past four p.m."—as the beginning of his oratorical career. His increasing preoccupation with religious matters also affected his oratory, for in his early diaries there are frequent references to the inaudibility and bad diction of the preachers at the many and varied sermons he attended. These were failings which the aspiring orator, already busily practising his accompanying gestures as much as his voice production, took to heart and resolved not to commit himself. By the time he left Eton with the utmost regret and melancholy in December 1827, Gladstone's interesting character and the intimation of future distinction had become a little more apparent. Arthur Hallam said, ". . . he is a bud that will bloom with a richer fragrance than almost any whose early promise I have witnessed"; while John Gladstone had decided that of his four sons the youngest was the most remarkable, presciently announcing in August 1826, "You shall be my biographer, William."

From Eton, Gladstone prepared to follow the well-trodden path to Oxford and he still considered himself to be a vilely idle, undisciplined, run-of-the-mill young man. But even before he went up to Oxford the range of his reading and interests, and the flow of physical energy which took him on twenty-mile walks, were by normal standards phenomenal. His interests ran from theology to phrenology to geology, from visiting the poor to being enthralled by Charles Kemble as Hamlet and Falstaff. His reading extended from Homer to Macaulay, from Dante to Sir Walter Scott, from Corneille to Locke, from Shakespeare to Burke, from Gibbon to a *Journal Through India* and *Deaf and Dumb: or the Orphan* (an historical drama). The range of his reading matter was always wide because as Gladstone solemnly noted, "People say and I think truly that in literature, as in animal food, too much nutrition kills, and that you must have the incumbrance of pulp."

However, it was at Oxford that by its own standards, the Etonian bud began to flower. The university was as open to criticism as the school, and it was in some quarters thought that Oxford had become a stagnant pool rather than a fountain of learning, its atmosphere poisoned by a High Tory intolerance and rigidity of attitude. But even the critics admitted that it was possible to learn something and that Christ Church ranked high among the possible colleges. Before Gladstone took up residence at Christ Church (in October 1828) there had been a reappraisal of the method of studying the classics which were fundamental to an Oxford education, with a re-emphasis on the colossal stature of Aristotle. Much within the young Gladstone responded to this proffered training, and the teachings of Plato and Aristotle became the moorings for his thoughts.

The Platonic freedom of the mind to explore every avenue of knowledge appealed to him, but it was the Aristotelian principle of the harmonic wholeness of the universe, despite the apparent contradictions, which attracted him more, because it reinforced (or preinforced) his Christian belief in the harmony of God's universe. The methods of Aristotle struck a strong chord in Gladstone, the systematic, analytical investigation of matter based on *personal* observation and the ransacking of every available book as an aid to argument (Plato called Aristotle "the Reader," and it was a sobriquet which could also be bestowed on Gladstone). Gladstone always had to discover things for himself, to chart his own course in his own time, and the slowness and thoroughness of his approach came partly from the Aristotelian training. If the subtle ramifications of his thought processes were also encouraged by his study of Aristotle, the endless qualifications in which he wrapped his arguments and which later so infuriated his opponents (and sometimes his supporters) cannot be laid at the master's door, because rigour and precision of terminology and definition are part of the Aristotelian method. In these latter attributes Gladstone was frequently lacking, and the thick woolliness of his language stemmed more from inherent characteristics and the internal conflict between caution and passion.

The core of Gladstone's life was his profound Christianity, and the basic question which involved every facet of his character was how he personally could and should best serve his God. He had not the slightest shadow of doubt that God existed, that He had created the world in His image and for His divine purpose, but how William Ewart Gladstone, as an instrument of God, should implement that divine will while he was on earth was open to doubt. The question which profession he should choose was initially compounded by his father's wish that he should enter the law, for filial piety was a further Christian commandment. On 4 August 1830 he wrote his father a small pamphlet disguised as a letter—it ran to more than 3,500 words—in which he finally presented his conclusion that "the work of spreading religion has a claim infinitely transcending all others in dignity, solemnity, and in usefulness." But on the tortuous route to the conclusion that he wished to become a minister of God he explained how his inclinations had also drawn him towards secular ministerial office and how he had thought himself justified in considering the political arena because of the dignity and grandeur of its ends and means—"the end, the glory of God, the means, the restoration of Man to that image of his Maker which is now throughout the world so lamentably defaced." To the turgidly obscure outpourings of his youngest son's soul John Gladstone replied solemnly but practically, suggesting that he wait until he had completed his studies before reaching the final decision, which his son dutifully did.

It was while he was at Oxford that Gladstone began to reveal to his God by means of the written word—and thereby keep a record for the world at large—the extent of the inner physical passions which tormented his body and soul; though it was while he was at Eton that he actually started to write his diaries, the first entry being made in July 1825, when he was sixteen years old. He himself later said, "You may take three proverbial courses about a journal; you may keep none, you may keep a complete and 'full blooded' one, or you may keep a mere skeleton like mine with nothing but bare entries of time and place." In the early diaries he more or less adhered to this principle, only indulging himself at length for an event such as his Confirmation; but increasingly as he began to appreciate the force of his physical passions, the ending of the year, his birthday, certain holy days and anniversaries became the occasions for bouts of critical, introspective examination. It would seem that the main evil young Gladstone had to combat was a desire to masturbate.* One says it *would seem* because he does not specify why he was "the very first of sinners" nor which were his "most dangerous and degrading temptations," for as he noted (not without a touch of unconscious humour) when again referring to his rankling passions, they were "passions which I dare not name—shame forbids it and duty does not seem to require it." But from the wording of another early diary entry, and as he wrote of "the blackness of my natural (and vigorous) tendencies," one assumes that it was masturbation against which he fought his lonely Evangelical battle. The passage reads: "As to general progress I

* Apart from being regarded as a Christian sin, masturbation was then believed to cause impotence, curvature of the spine, consumption and actual insanity.

would hope some against my besetting sins except one which returns upon me again and again like a flood, God help me for Christ's sake."

The first record of an activity which later became a necessary part of his life, namely the association with young prostitutes, also occurs in his Oxford diaries, and significantly the incident—two nocturnal conversations with a "poor creature" in distress—happened immediately on his arrival in the city, when he was "unsettled and fidgety." In later years it was when he was restless and subjected to severe stress that the urge to consort with "fallen women" overwhelmed him. But equally significantly, from the start it was young prostitutes to whom he directed his stressful attention, not alcoholics or destitute children or any of the other vast driftwood of early nineteenth-century society. Once he settled into Oxford and became engrossed in his studies, the references to conversations with prostitutes are minimal, but the general sense of sin, which is alarmingly persuasive, was heightened by the sad event of his sister Anne's death, which occurred after a prolonged illness in February 1829. For many years the anniversary of her death invoked one of those bouts of self-evaluation, and two years after her death, on rereading her letters, he wrote, "O is it possible that such a saint can have held communion with such a devil?"

Despite the turmoil within him, Gladstone's public persona at Oxford remained that of a solemn, prim young gentleman. One commentator suggested that it befitted him for the company of maiden aunts or for the keeping of tame rabbits. In the era when he was at the university, the open promiscuity and indulgence of sexual appetites which characterised the Regency period still predominated, if only just, and newspapers still carried advertisements on their front page for pills to increase sexual prowess and astonish the bed partner. However, Gladstone was not singular in his conscience-stricken sexual dilemmas, because the Evangelicism which had affected him was also imposing a less hedonistic, more high-minded ethic on the moral climate as a whole. His earnest, serious personality did not prevent him from making new friends at Oxford and by founding an Essay Society which was known by his initials, WEG, he became the pivot of a group. Benjamin Disraeli later said that Gladstone was essentially a prig and that there was a freemasonry among prigs, so naturally a band of them swarmed around him, even in his young days; but by no means were all his friends priggish. One highly negative example was Richard Monckton-Milnes, whom he met on a visit to Arthur Hallam (Hallam having gone up to Cambridge). Monckton-Milnes was an extrovert with a robust wit and a collection of pornographic literature, notably the works of de Sade, that became famous. Whether Gladstone, who later demonstrated some interest in pornography, was shown the famous library on his visits to Monckton-Milnes' Yorkshire home is unclear, but from the earlier days aspects of his more sexual side were perhaps obvious to this friend. But if Monckton-Milnes suspected that the prim exterior hid swirling passions, his first recorded comment emphasised the former rather than the latter because after meeting Gladstone he announced, "I am sure a very superior person." Gladstone was on the whole a gregarious animal and throughout his life he enjoyed company, but he was essentially a private man, his attention focused on his relationship with God and his battles against sinfulness; of the many friends he made few penetrated the inner core of detachment. Later he said how much he needed and responded to the encouragément and plaudits of other people, but this was true only in the mass sense; he required the support and approval of very few individuals. Despite the often-quoted comment of the society lady Emily Eden—"If he were soaked in boiling water and rinsed till he was twisted into rope, I do not suppose a drop of fun would ooze out of him"—Gladstone did not lack the capacity to enjoy himself, nor was he without a zestful sense of fun, as opposed to a sense of humour, wit, levity or irony.

In December 1829 John Gladstone bought, for the sum of £80,000, an estate called Fasque which lay deep in the Highlands, sixteen miles from Stonehaven. The purchase was important in his youngest son's development as it helped to strengthen his Scottish roots. But the main outside event of his Oxford years was the struggle to reform the House of Commons. From the end of 1830 when the Duke of Wellington announced his hostility to parliamentary reform and his Government fell, nobody was more interested than the young Gladstone, who noted his continuing involvement in secular matters: "Politics are fascinating to me, perhaps too fascinating." His attitude to the reform crisis was staunchly High Tory Oxford and Canningite in its belief that to tamper with the existing constitution by extending the franchise to a few more voters and eradicating some of the grosser malpractices and anomalies which had grown unchecked over the years would be to open the floodgates to the illiterate, deceived, swinish multitude who would smash the whole framework of British society and lead the country into revolution and anarchy. When the second reading of the Reform Bill was defeated in the House of Commons committee in March 1831 and Lord Grey, who had reluctantly emerged to lead the reform cohorts, dissolved Parliament, Gladstone campaigned energetically for the anti-reform candidate at Oxford; at Oxford he won but the verdict of such of the country as could vote was, to Gladstone's horror, overwhelmingly in Lord Grey's favour.

Catherine Glynne was in Oxford during the Reform Bill crisis, visiting her brother Stephen, but she did not then make the acquaintance of William Gladstone. That may have been just as well: the Glynnes had both Whig and Tory connections and were nowhere near as vehemently opposed to parliamentary reform as he was, and the passions roused by the controversy were deep and often ugly—on her way home to Hawarden Castle Catherine witnessed many of the riots which were occurring throughout the country. The personal impact of the crisis on Gladstone was that in May 1831 he spoke in an Oxford Union debate on the issue, and his three-quarters-of-an-hour address—obviously in favour of the anti-reform motion on the Whig Government's incompetence—struck all hearers by its power, its eloquence, its marshalling of material and its vehemence. Here was a young man who not only had the oratorical ability to send a thrill through his audience but who also possessed positive enthusiasm, an attribute which was coming back into fashion. As the tension mounted and the Reform Bill fought its way through the House of Commons, Gladstone had other matters to occupy his mind, namely his final examinations at Oxford; from the ordeal of the classical and mathematical schools he emerged with the Oxonian crown but rarely bestowed, a double first.

On 17 January 1832 he again wrote to his father at great length saying he now accepted the advice to enter public service by means of the legal profession (he was admitted to Lincoln's Inn though he was never called to the bar), but in view of the conflict in Parliament and the consequent threat to the fabric of society he reserved the right to change his mind. Having allowed himself to be pushed onto the secular path, he and his naval brother John Neilson departed on 1 February 1832 for a grand tour of Europe. At the end of March the two brothers had reached Rome and it was on entering St. Peter's that Gladstone was first struck by the enormity of the schism which had split the Christian church at the time of the Reformation. Hitherto even his subtle brain and passion for theology had tended to accept that there were Catholics and Protestants; it was only as he entered St. Peter's that he was smitten by "the pain and the shame which separates us from Rome." Then as later, he considered that the fault lay with Rome, not Protestantism or England, but he offered up the prayer, "May God bind up the wounds of his bleeding church." By the middle of May the brothers had reached Naples and it was here that the regret experienced in Rome turned into a vision of the historic Church of Christ that was infinitely wider, broader, loftier and more inspired in its conception than the Bible-reading Evangelicism on which he had been reared. The effect on Gladstone was profound and led him to a fundamental revision of his religious attitude; increasingly he became convinced that it was his duty to try and effect a reconciliation between all the branches of the Christian Church, Catholic and Protestant, Greek and Russian Orthodox. The Italian revelations were also notable as the first major demonstration of the sympathetic receptiveness of Gladstone's mind, showing how open it was to impressions and ideas, how ready to chart a new course, even if the navigation sometimes seemed perversely slow.

In Venice in the middle of June he learned "the disastrous but expected news, that the Reform Bill had passed the Lords." Next month in Milan he received a letter of "extraordinary import." This was an invitation from his Etonian/Oxonian friend Lord Lincoln, to contest his father the Duke of Newcastle's borough of Newark in the next General Election, Lord Lincoln having been among those greatly impressed by Gladstone's Oxford Union speech—he had told his father, "A man is uprisen in Israel." The Reform Bill might have become law but it was the sluice gates rather than the floodgates of popular democracy which had been opened, and the Duke of Newcastle could still rightly claim that Newark was his to do with as he pleased; however, even he felt the need of a new, strong, young candidate with the right Tory ideas. The totally unexpected proposal left Gladstone "in a flutter of confusion," though not as he noted an overwhelming one, and he immediately wrote to ask his father's advice. John Gladstone responded promptly, soothing the inevitable qualms which had enveloped his son's mind and assuring him that he would be serving God by undertaking this bold and terrible experiment. Gladstone promptly cut short his tour and returned to England, where he wrote his initial election address for Newark (of which, untypically, he penned three drafts) and a long memorandum on "The Fulness of Time." This latter incorporated the idea of God's selecting the exact moment for action, and it is an interesting early example of a belief which became crucial in Gladstone's political life.

Towards the end of September he received a summons to present himself at Newark, as his father's position as a slaveowner was presenting problems in the early canvassing. The slave trade as such had been abolished in the British domains in 1807, after a prolonged struggle led by William Wilberforce and other Evangelicals, but the ownership of slaves had not, and it was not until the 1820s that the agitation to remove the last vestiges of slavery regained momentum. To the renewed agitation John Gladstone reacted with the stubbornness which had helped get him where he was but which showed a lamentable lack of the timing so highly prized by his son. He bought more slave-operated estates in the West Indies and became louder in his defence of a system which the Old Testament had supported and which Christ had not condemned in His teachings. Nevertheless in Newark Gladstone managed to overcome the problems created by his father's slave ownership. He proved an excellent candidate, possessed of a startling and powerful fluency of speech, a quick resourceful mind and yet withal a modest demeanour, and on 14 December 1832 he was duly returned at the top of the poll. Thus at the age of twenty-three Gladstone entered the House of Commons, of which he was to remain a member for more than sixty years.

He continued to defend his father's position with maximum filial piety, because, though he did not wholly share his father's views, he remained strongly influenced by the older man and his own mind had not reached a clear conclusion on the issue. He became a spokesman on the subject of slavery in the House of Commons, he was involved in the committees discussing compensation, and when the abolition bill became law at the end of 1833, the final compensation paid out to the slaveowners—amounting to £80,000,000 of which his father received £93,526 for 2,039 slaves—owed not a little to the young Gladstone's skill and patience as a negotiator.

From his early days in the House of Commons Gladstone attracted the attention of the new Tory leader Sir Robert Peel, who was quick to recognise the talents of the member for Newark—the oratorical power, the thoroughness of approach, the attention to detail, the wide-ranging mind and the extra, intangible quality which even then occasionally erupted in a flash of passion or an onrush of vehemence. An older parliamentary colleague noted, "I rather like Gladstone, but he is said to have more of the devil in him than appears." When Lord Grey's Whig Ministry resigned at the end of 1834 and Sir Robert Peel was invited to form a new Government, he offered Gladstone a Junior Lordship of the Treasury which he gladly accepted, and a month later the Junior Lord was promoted to be Under-Secretary of the Colonies. He was considered worthy of this post because of the manner in which he had handled the slavery issue and the knowledge he had gained of West Indian problems, and it was one which carried power, since the Colonial Secretary Lord Aberdeen was in the House of Lords.†

When Sir Robert Peel appointed his Government, Whig newspapers described it as one of the most ridiculous, insulting and abortive ever presented to a free people. While it was not particularly ridiculous or insulting, it did prove abortive, and early in 1835 Gladstone found himself out of office, along with the Tory party. Much as he had enjoyed the taste of power he did not pine; he sat on numerous committees, parliamentary and otherwise, he continued to read prodigiously, he widened his circle of friends to include the ageing William Wordsworth (whom he revered as a poet but found dull as a man) and, after the death of their mutual friend Arthur Hallam, the young Alfred Tennyson. He attended musical evenings (his trained light baritone voice made him a welcome guest), dinner parties and even balls—though he found these latter boring and therefore went in a spirit of self-discipline. Fortunately, he also resumed his visits to the theatre, which for a time he had considered "inseparably allied with vice, and mainly instrumental in its advancement." One says "fortunately" because the stimulation and satisfaction of the theatre was in Gladstone's blood stream and his constant theatre-going was one of the nicer characteristics that always helped to counterbalance his esoteric solemnity.

In the autumn of 1835 Gladstone's mother died at the Scottish baronial home of Fasque. He later wrote of the impression that the cold clear autumnal moon had made upon him at the time of her death and said, ". . . it froze my heart; it told me nothing definite, nothing therefore to my understanding." The cold moon's failure to still his doubts may have been caused by another emotion, because as his mother lay dying Gladstone was suffering from the pangs of unrequited love. The young lady on whom he

† Being a Lord did not necessarily mean that you were in the House of Lords; that depended on what manner of Lord you were. Aberdeen was in fact the Earl of Aberdeen so he sat in the House of Lords, but the eldest son of a Duke sat in the House of Commons until his father died and he inherited the title (Gladstone's friend Lord Lincoln was in this position), while the younger son of a Duke sat permanently in the Commons, unless he was created an Earl in his own right (e.g. Lord John Russell, whom Catherine Gladstone detested so much). Those whose peerages were of Irish origin also sat permanently in the Commons (e.g. Lord Palmerston).

had settled his affections was Caroline Farquhar, the sister of an Etonian friend Walter Farquhar; he had met her in the spring of 1835 at one of those balls which self-discipline forced him to attend. She was an attractive girl, high-spirited and popular but not untinged with the more solemn attitude which was enveloping society, and Gladstone became a frequent visitor at the Farquhars' house at Roehampton, then deep in the country outside London.

Soon he was lying awake at night, thinking about Caroline by his open window, certain that her heart was with God and hopeful that it might be with him, and finally towards the end of August he wrote to the lady's father, Sir Thomas Farquhar, asking for her hand in marriage. Two visits to Roehampton followed, on the first of which he thought Caroline's heart was moved towards him, on the second of which he had "a three hour talk with the mother. We spoke freely of religion; also of the present state of my affairs, and how they will develop. Now, as I trust, we entirely understand each other; and O God, may I be happy." (This entry was written in Italian, the language he usually adopted when he had particularly secret thoughts to commit to his diary; apart from Latin and Greek, Gladstone spoke and wrote Italian fluently, French and German well.) His pecuniary affairs were in a reasonable state, as his father had promised that upon marriage he would provide a house and an income of £2,000 per annum, and Gladstone's political future was already well regarded. Had he been content to press his suit in person he might possibly have succeeded in capturing Miss Farquhar's hand, for throughout his life people commented on how much freer and more entertaining Gladstone was in conversation than in the written word. Unfortunately and inevitably he had to commit his feelings to paper by writing further letters to both Caroline and her parents; they were obscure, daunting dissertations upon his religious views and a code of social conduct such as he hoped his wife would share. They submerged Miss Farquhar, who on 3 September 1835, through the medium of her mother, politely but firmly rejected the offer of marriage. The following January Gladstone stayed briefly at Hawarden Castle as the guest of Sir Stephen Glynne, but he was then hoping that Miss Farquhar might change her mind and he took little notice of the elder Miss Glynne. Gladstone was a resilient optimist and his persistence was matched by a degree of self-absorption which made him insensitive to other people's emotions, but by March 1836 he had finally accepted that his matrimonial hopes were at an end. Four months later Caroline Farquhar married Charles Grey, one of the many sons of Lord Grey, who was a more suitable social match than the son of a Liverpool merchant, and a considerably less overwhelming gentleman.

In the summer of 1837, having been safely returned for Newark during the General Election caused by the death of William IV and the accession of Queen Victoria, Gladstone went north to help his father canvass; the old man, already well into his seventies, had decided that he wanted to be in

Parliament again.‡ John Gladstone was defeated at Dundee by Sir Henry Parnell, the uncle of the yet unborn Charles Stewart Parnell, who figured so largely in William's later political life. But while Gladstone was engaged in his father's Scottish electoral campaign he remet a young woman named Lady Frances Harriet Douglas with whom he had a nodding acquaintance, and within a very short space of time he proposed marriage to her. Lady Frances was very ordinary and immature, less able to cope with the Gladstonian onslaughts than Caroline Farquhar had been, but her initial reaction was one of silent bewilderment, which only encouraged her ardent and by now somewhat matrimonially desperate suitor. Early in November 1837, having heard nothing definite from Lady Frances, Gladstone unburdened his heart to friends in Edinburgh and they promised to make enquiries on his behalf. A week later he received "a crushing letter" in answer to the queries; but it did not crush him entirely and he continued to remain hopeful until the end of January 1838, when he heard conclusively that Lady Frances did not wish to marry him. The effect on Lady Frances of Gladstone's vehement persistence seems to have been the same as on Caroline Farquhar; she too sought refuge in a prompt marriage to another gentleman.

The effect on Gladstone of this second rebuff was fairly disastrous. From March 1838 onwards he was writing of "the icy coldness of my heart," of walking "among the splendours of the world like a dead man," of being "almost perpetually restless and depressed"—and the engagement of his one unmarried brother, John Neilson, in July 1838, did nothing to lessen his depression. However emotionally drained and frustrated Gladstone was feeling, during these months he was researching and writing his first important book, *The State in Its Relations with the Church,* he was in attendance at the House of Commons and in March he made a two-hour speech which attracted a good deal of praise and attention, though it was in the losing cause of the West Indian slaveowners who were fighting to retain a time-scale apprenticeship scheme (it was abolished and with it the last official vestiges of slavery in the British domains). Nor in these depressed months was Gladstone without the solace of real friendship. Two men in particular had pierced the inner detachment and grown close to him during the 1830s—Henry Edward Manning and James Hope (who a decade later married Sir Walter Scott's granddaughter and in 1853 adopted the name of Hope-Scott).

James Hope was an extremely handsome man of a gentle but firm nature who followed the profession of barrister, and like Gladstone he had grown up in an Evangelical background and then moved towards the vision of the historic Church of Christ. If he was not perhaps Gladstone's intellectual equal, Henry Manning was. Manning was then an ordained minister of the Church of England, a more sophisticated man, considerably more inter-

‡ There was no single polling day. General Elections then often spread over a fortnight. Thus candidates already elected could assist other colleagues or relations.

ested in the frailties of his fellow human beings—Manning enjoyed gossip, which Gladstone did not—with a mind as tough and thorough if less passionate than his friend's and possessed of greater wit. He later said, "Mr Gladstone is a substantive and likes to be surrounded by adjectives. And I am not exactly an adjective." But this statement can be regarded as an example of Manning's love for the *bon mot*, for it was never entirely true of Gladstone and it was certainly not true of the two men's relationship in the 1830s or for several years thereafter, as Gladstone tended to lean more on Manning's advice than the latter did on his.

Gladstone had another problem besides Lady Frances at this time, one which had been worsening steadily for the last eighteen months, that being trouble with his eyesight. He had suffered intermittently from eyestrain for years—not surprising in view of the amount of reading he did in an era of poor illumination—and by the middle of 1838 he was not only very shortsighted, he was beginning to fear that he might be doing irreparable damage to his eyes.

One of the reasons he embarked on another continental tour was therefore to rest his failing eyesight, though typically he took with him the proof sheets of *The State in Its Relations with the Church* and kept a voluminous travel diary. However, a secondary reason for the journey was Helen Gladstone's rapidly deteriorating behaviour. From the moment of her sister's death, Helen had nobody to whom she could turn for real comfort or affection; her father was frequently absent and uninterested in involving a young woman in his affairs when he was at home, while her brothers were absorbed in their careers. Helen embarked upon the first of her obsessional, attention-seeking, compensatory activities, which was overeating, but by 1838 she had abandoned gluttony and was showing too much interest in that favourite but little understood Victorian drug, laudanum. She had also become interested in the Roman Catholic Church, and her family thought it might be a good idea if she had a complete change of environment. Part of Gladstone's mission was to see his sister safely settled with a companion, in the suitably different, wholesome Germanic atmosphere of Ems.

Suffering from bad eyesight, deep worries about his sister's erratic behaviour and an increasing sexual frustration—he was almost certainly still a virgin in his twenty-ninth year—it was not in a particularly joyous mood that Gladstone sailed for Rotterdam. But the much-needed key to unlock the door of the ivory tower that Gladstone had built around his inner self, to relieve the lusty heterosexual instincts and release the tide of affection within him, had already been thrown forth. For before he left London, on 23 July 1838 he noted in his diary that he had breakfasted with the Miss Glynnes.

CHAPTER 2

THE BEAUTIFUL MISS GLYNNE

THE GENEALOGISTS had little difficulty tracing Catherine Glynne's ancestry to illustrious roots on the Plantagenet Roll and beyond those to Charlemagne. From the seventeenth century her paternal forebears had owned some seven thousand acres of land in the ancient Welsh border village of Hawarden, which stands above the Cheshire plain, looking across the marshes of the Dee estuary to the Wirral peninsula and Liverpool, with the line of the North Welsh mountains to the west. In the early part of the eighteenth century the Glynnes built a pleasant Georgian house on the outskirts of the village; at the beginning of the nineteenth century it was enlarged by the addition of an extra wing, turrets and towers. Although the ruins of a Celtic castle lay in the grounds, as Hawarden Castle the castellated residence was henceforward known and it was this house in which Catherine was born which became the home of Mr. and Mrs. William Gladstone, which he fought to save for so many years and which remains in the possession of Gladstone descendants.

Catherine was the elder daughter of the marriage of Sir Stephen Glynne and the Honourable Mary Neville, a daughter of Lord Braybrooke's. Through her mother she was related to some of the great political families in the land (the two William Pitts and the two Grenvilles, four Prime Ministers, were among her maternal connections). Her father she hardly knew as he died suddenly in 1815 when she was only three years old, and as her mother never remarried her immediate family was comparatively small, one sister and two brothers. The boys were Stephen, who inherited his father's baronetcy as a small child, and Henry. Stephen was very handsome and precociously clever but there was a detached quality about him, an apartness from the mainstream of life. From an early age he was interested in topography, antiquities, architecture (particularly ecclesiastical) and uninterested in riding or sporting activities, parties or balls. Later accusations that he was a homosexual, if repudiated by the Gladstones as ludicrous, may have had something to do with the apartness, the dislike for the sporting life and feminine company. About Henry there is not a great deal to be said; he was the plain, stolid, ordinary member of a handsome, witty, original family, though Catherine was fond of him and preferred him to

Stephen. He later became a worthy rector of Hawarden. The youngest child was Mary, Catherine's junior by little more than a year, and from their earliest days "the two Pussies," as they were known in the family circle, so alike in looks with their classic features, abundant curling hair, vibrant complexions and beautiful blue eyes, had the closest and most affectionate bond, though Catherine was always the dominant personality. As Mary grew older the "Pussy" nickname was dropped, but it clung to her sister all her life; to her Glynne relations Catherine was always thus known, and to a generation of nieces and nephews she was "Aunt Pussy."

Lady Glynne was a vague lady, with a depressive strain exacerbated by the early death of her husband, and though she took an interest in her children's welfare and they were devoted to her, she followed the custom of the time in aristocratic circles and allowed herself to be frequently parted from them without undue maternal regret. Consequently, though Hawarden was the Glynne family home, the children spent most of their early years being looked after by relations, notably at Audley End in Essex, which was the Braybrooke seat. They gained as much as they lost from their mother's intermittent attention, however, as the wider family circle was affectionate and close-knit. The atmosphere in which they matured was relaxed and secure but it was based on deep Christian principles. The Glynne children were brought up on the doctrine that privilege entails responsibility. They were not expected to be perpetually solemn—English upper-class tenets did not extend to a puritanical fear of pleasure, and balls and firework displays and amateur theatricals were regular events—but they were exhorted to do their duty to God and their fellow men, particularly the less fortunate.

The pattern of Glynne life followed the customary one for their class; the girls were educated at home by governesses and relations, the boys were sent away to boarding schools. At the age of six it was noted that Catherine "reads and writes nicely, learns a page of Bible History by heart," but also, "She has been in several passions lately." "Pussy's tantrums" were well-known within the family circle, but Catherine had an innate sense of duty and learned to control and discipline herself, temporarily anyway. Her early diaries are an example of training over character. They are neatly written in a legible hand, they list the books she had read, and when she travelled abroad she filled them with details of paintings and buildings, their precise colouring, height and circumference, with suitable pictures accompanying the text. They are in startling contrast to Catherine's scrawled, untidy adult diaries when character emerged triumphant. At a later date in her childhood it was noted, "fewer passions, and in general good and affectionate. A nice little voice, and a true ear. She is a very good horsewoman." Catherine was an excellent rider; she also adored archery and until the end of her life was a fanatical swimmer, mainly in the cold coastal waters of the British Isles. She was fond of music too—Handel was a particular favourite—and was a talented pianist who on one occasion in Paris received lessons from the musical prodigy of the era, Franz Liszt.

Lady Glynne's description of her elder daughter sums her up thus: "one of the most thriving, magnificent children that can be seen, with a remarkably animated, pretty expression of countenance." In the confident, affectionate, outgoing security of the Glynne family circuit Catherine continued to thrive magnificently. As the children grew older their education was extended by visits to the Continent, and in Paris Catherine attended countless balls, was presented at the French court (Charles X's) and lionised the sights of the French capital.*

The Glynnes had a town house in London, and in due course the two sisters were launched into society. Catherine thoroughly enjoyed her London season, with visits to the opera and more balls, but she was not the most social of creatures and was always happy to return to Hawarden or Audley End, to the country and the intimacy of the family circle. In 1834 Lady Glynne had a slight stroke from which she recovered with her mental and physical powers intact, but it left her with a greater tendency towards melancholy and self-pity, and allowed her to shed the family responsibilities for which she had never really cared. It was Catherine, not Stephen, who became the head of the Glynne household.

The later generally held opinion that Mrs. Gladstone was a disorganised lady, charmingly so to the majority view, irritatingly so to the minority, was to an extent an accurate assessment. Catherine was an ardent, ebullient, instinctive creature with the type of quick, receptive mind which easily grasps the heart of a problem, but which becomes bored and restless if faced with routine and is singularly uninterested in detail. To that extent her mind was usually engaged in the next problem before it had cleared the remnants of the last, and her life consequently tended to appear disorganised. But however jumbled or vague her approach might seem, Catherine had a remarkable persistence and tenacity of purpose, and she also had a basic need to be in the forefront of activity. Many years later her daughter Mary wrote, "You know how she loves being inside the mainspring of history, and all the stress, and strain and throb of the machine is life and breath to her." Mary was referring to her mother's position as wife to the Prime Minister but it was a perceptive observation which had always been true, and the consuming desire to be in the vanguard, charging among the cavalry, may have been one of the reasons why Catherine Glynne was attracted to William Gladstone in the first place, her instincts telling her that this man could be destined for the citadels she longed to storm.

Consciously and personally Catherine was not ambitious; she did not question the Christian creed which placed women as wives and mothers and to which the Victorians gave an extra suffocating wrapping. Notions of her as an early feminist can be dismissed, but she had a strong will and an independent strain that she herself never quite recognised, and uncon-

* "To lionise" as a verb to describe sight-seeing has unfortunately died out, but it was in common use for much of the nineteenth century.

sciously she unlocked several barred feminine windows. It was perhaps the unrecognised female independence, together with the longing for the widest horizons, which kept her from the designated matrimonial state until the fairly late age of twenty-seven. She was graceful, charming, attractive, she and her sister Mary were widely known as "the two beautiful Miss Glynnes," and when Disraeli first met her (as the young wife of Mr. Gladstone) he thought she was one of the loveliest women in England. She had many admirers—Gladstone asked her for a list of their names which she duly provided thus, "Seymour Newark Hill Vaughan Egerton Anson Harcourt Lewis Mordaunt"—only one of whom had rejected her rather than the other way round, yet she had not married.

It was in the summer of 1838 that Gladstone first began to show an interest in the elder Miss Glynne and she in him, and in November they both managed to find themselves in Naples. The Glynne party had made its way south in leisurely fashion but Gladstone had included a thousand-mile walking tour of Sicily in the company of his friend, Arthur Kinnaird. In Naples, he dined frequently with the Glynnes and accompanied them on trips to Vesuvius, where as Catherine recorded, "we and Mr. Gladstone sallied forth alone." At the beginning of December both parties departed for Rome, where the dinner and tea engagements and the sight-seeing multiplied. On arrival in Rome, Gladstone received some startling news which caused him to reel rather than to walk away from the post office, in the shape of a letter from his sister Helen announcing her engagement to Count Leon Sollohub, a young Polish gentleman whose family was insisting that Helen should become a member of the Russian Orthodox Church and live in Russia after the marriage. By this time Gladstone was too enamoured of Catherine to follow the path of duty and gallop to Ems to assist Helen in her emotional crises; the extent of his involvement can be gauged from the fact that his twenty-ninth birthday passed without the usual self-examination and with only the comment, "how solemnly this clock strikes."

On 3 January 1839 Gladstone had the perfect romantic opportunity to declare his love when he and the Glynnes viewed the Forum and the Coliseum by the light of a crystal-clear moon. Though he noted in his diary, "Not only should everyone see these ruins by moonlight but I think perhaps see them first by moonlight," and she noted in hers, "the soft clear light reflected on all around & gave a most beautiful effect," his sense of right timing or his nerve failed him and he said nothing. The social engagements continued. Gladstone introduced Miss Glynne to his friend Henry Manning, who also happened to be in Rome, and she greatly enjoyed his company and his wit. A week after he had failed to declare his love, copies of Gladstone's book, *The State in Its Relations with the Church,* arrived in Rome. He immediately presented one to Miss Glynne, who read it diligently and expressed her profound agreement with its contents and admiration for its author.

Gladstone's preoccupation with the role of the Christian religion was one shared by Catherine and many of his contemporaries. In the last hundred years astounding knowledge had been acquired and development of untapped resources had occurred, opening the gates to previously undreamed-of progress and making it seem that mankind (or at least the Western part of it) might at last be reaching its maturity. There was no lack of people asking the questions: progress whither? to what kind of maturity? and what should be the role of the Christian Church in this restless, changing age? For a few the answer lay in the destruction of the existing Christian bourgeois society and the building of a new social order; for others it lay in a rationalism which took what it wanted from Christ's teaching but discarded the faith; but for the majority of activists the solution lay with a redefined Christianity. In England Evangelicism had offered one answer, with its emphasis on the individual cleansing himself and then participating in the cleansing of society. The Oxford Movement—or the Tractarians, as its disciples became known with the issue of the famous Tracts defining its attitudes—offered another. It placed intellectual emphasis on the Church of England as part of the historic, European Church of Christ whose message was universal brotherhood for all men. Gladstone himself was not unduly influenced by the Tractarians, though his friends Henry Manning and James Hope and his sister Helen were, and if his book was in part a product of the new religious ferment, it was a more idiosyncratic effort. (Had it been written by a Tractarian it would have been called the *Church* in its relations with the *State*, for they unlike Gladstone were more interested in the former than the latter.)

Gladstone had told his father that as a Christian operating in a secular role it was important that he should define his views on religion before the Conservative party (as the Tory party was now known) was returned to office, in the face of the very probable event that he would be offered ministerial office, and his father had agreed. He was then spurred on by dissension within the Church of England to redouble his efforts to clarify the true relationship between the State and the Church. In his book Gladstone came to the conclusion that the State was properly and according to its nature moral and could be defined as a person, a conclusion he based on a mass of dense, not to say at times obscure arguments and a wide range of earlier authorities. In his opinion, as the State possessed a conscience it could not afford to be morally neutral but had a duty to profess and promote a religion which must obviously be specific, as there could only be one moral truth for each State. In the case of England the moral truth had been defined in the Anglican Church at the time of the Reformation, and it was implicit in Gladstone's argument that only those professing and acting upon the established State religion should hold public office. He allowed some measure of historic toleration for the Dissenters in England, he was vague about Scotland, but he was definite if not altogether happy about the Catholics in Ireland; they should be made to see and accept the moral truth of Anglicanism. He did *not* propagate the idea of one moral religious truth for the whole world but declared that each State must by its own process choose the religion which was right for its people. This was an early definition of the principle of nationality which became fundamental to the Gladstonian Liberal creed.

Having presented Miss Glynne with such a formidable book to read (and he admitted to Henry Manning that it was "stern" stuff), perhaps encouraged by the manner in which she sped through it, a week later Gladstone sent her an equally formidable proposal of marriage. It started with the nice simple statement that his heart and his hand were at her disposal but then continued with sentences and sentiments labyrinthine and tortured even by his standards. The second paragraph of the proposal is a classic example of Gladstonian circumlocution and of his ability to extricate himself from his verbal maze (observers in the House of Commons later said that when Gladstone was in his verbose mood, they were on the edges of their seats, biting their nails, wondering how he could possibly emerge from his subclauses). The paragraph ran:

> I seek in a wife gifts better than those of our human pride, and am also sensible that she can find little in me: sensible that, were you to treat this note as the offspring of utter presumption, I must not be surprised: sensible that the lot I invite you to share, even if it be not attended, as I trust it is not, with peculiar disadvantages of an outward kind, is one, I do not say unequal to your deserts, for that were saying little, but liable at best to changes and perplexities and pains which, for myself, I contemplate without apprehension, but to which it is perhaps selfishness in the main, with the sense of inward dependence counteracting an opposite sense of my too real unworthiness, which would make me contribute to expose another—and what other!

Gladstone had not finished explaining how unworthy and presumptuous he was; Miss Glynne had another lengthy, if slightly less involved paragraph to read:

> For the substance of what I write I have no apology to offer which can be effectual. As respects its time, my own mind required no postponement, and I could not presume that it would give me any more reasonable hope of access to your affections. I wait your Command with the humility which I owe to a being so far purer and better than my own, and with other feelings which I have not the right to describe in colours of truth. And, indeed, they are chequered with the consciousness that I ought to wish you a more blessed portion in life than that which alone it is my power to tender. For pardon, for indulgence, I do not ask. Your own nature will yield me, unsolicited, much more than I desire. But I must cease. May you live, and die, it is not less my anticipation than my desire, from day to day more possessed of the peace which passeth understanding, and of the holiness which is its fountain.
> With esteem, with gratitude, suffer me by one more act of boldness to add, with warm and true affection, I am, Yours, W. E. Gladstone.

Fortunately, Catherine Glynne had a fundamentally more serious nature than either Caroline Farquhar or Lady Frances Douglas; she had her ability to grasp the essence and ignore the verbiage and she had a strength of mind which in its way was equal to his. Nonetheless the proposal took her by surprise, Gladstone's conviction that she was the woman he truly desired and admired having not apparently communicated itself. Catherine responded with a concise letter and a personal interview in both of which she said that if Mr. Gladstone wanted an immediate reply it would necessarily be negative, but in which she intimated that she held him in high esteem that given time might ripen into love.

At that point Gladstone had to return to England for the opening of the new parliamentary session (he had not been neglecting his duties—Parliament in those days had a very long recess, often from August until the following January, unless urgent business dictated a recall). From Marseilles he penned another lengthy obscure letter to Catherine in the minute handwriting he tended to use in his personal correspondence when he was suffering from great emotion; in his diaries he used it as a matter of frugal space-saving. One sin of which Gladstone cannot be accused is intellectual snobbery; while it might have helped if he had descended from his lofty intellectual pinnacles more frequently and been more aware that not everybody shared his interests, he always paid people the compliment of treating them as intelligent equals. Back in England he examined his emotions at some length and the examination revealed that he loved Catherine, that he thought he had again been precipitate in his proposal—his friends had earlier warned him that he had been overhasty with regard to Lady Frances Douglas—and that he was in a very low state, deadened and exhausted, like "a sacked and blackened country, seared with a recent conflagration." Apart from the pain caused by yet another apparent matrimonial rebuff, Gladstone was suffering from the strictures of his friend Arthur Kinnaird, who, having walked a thousand miles in his company, had accused him among other faults of "deliberate insincerity." Outside personal criticism always took Gladstone by surprise, as he was too involved in self-criticism to expect others to perform the task, particularly when they arrived at conclusions which had not occurred to him.

He had many other things to occupy his mind, including the reception of *The State in Its Relations with the Church*. He found that he was being praised only in restricted circles and then mainly for the wrong reasons: die-hard Anglican Tories fastened onto the implications of England for the Anglicans but failed to understand his passionate plea for the marriage of a moral State and Church. In most circles, Whig or Tory or new Conservative, he was derided as a bigot, a zealot, adrift in a mediaeval wood, barking up trees that had long since been blasted, or as somebody possessing dangerously Romanish tendencies (this despite the distinctly nationalistic lines of his argument). The most famous criticism was Macaulay's in the *Edinburgh Review*, and it succinctly expressed the views of the majority of lay Englishmen, which were that the State might possess some vague sort of Christian conscience but it was there to deal with temporal matters and its relationship with the established church was one of expediency based on a pragmatic compromise. Macaulay also said that on Mr. Gladstone's premise everything from a gas company to a fox-hunting society should profess and promote a religion; he criticised the "dim magnificence" of the author's languages and penned the famous lines that haunted Gladstone for years, "the rising hope of those stern and unbending Tories." Because of its startling, old-fashioned ideas the book was a success. Gladstone enjoyed himself making corrections for a reprint and replying to his critics, pointing out that there were primary and secondary classes in his view of a moral society, and while the nation and the family came into the first class, gas companies and fox-hunting societies fell into the second and were not subject to the same strictures. He also said that he was aware that the Church of England was a compromise but for him it was an effective moral compromise which should not, and must not, be based on expediency.

Gladstone had another, more personal problem to occupy his mind. His sister Helen's engagement to Count Sollohub was foundering, and the still comparatively young woman—Helen was not yet twenty-five—who already suffered from a lack of purpose in her life, was not unnaturally plunged into a slough of despair and despondency. Gladstone was as sympathetic as he could be, but as he did not believe in the supremacy of circumstance over mind, he had deduced that if women had truly desired a different role in life there would have been "evidence of a struggle in the female mind against the impediments of its condition" and this he had not found. As Helen should therefore have been content with her lot he could not see that her problem was other than a lack of will power, a failure to overcome her various passions in the same manner as he had mastered his carnal temptations. Had Gladstone been able to explain to his sister the sort of temptations to which he was subjected it would have helped but he could not, for even in the secrecy of his diaries he respected the tabus of the age, and his sexual statements were implicit rather than explicit. (He himself recognised the limitations, later noting, "I feel I have not yet learned to confess freely, even on paper.") His approach to Helen was thus an abstract, unhelpful exhortation to exert her Christian will.

By early May the Glynnes had returned to England and were staying at their London town house. Helen's problems temporarily receded before the pleasure of being a welcome guest at 36 Berkeley Square and the encouragement he was receiving from Catherine. On 8 June he and Catherine were guests at a luncheon party at Lady Shelley's house in rural Fulham, in the afternoon they "walked apart" and she agreed to marry him. But it was not until the next day, after he had given her his letter to Caroline Farquhar to read, the one in which he had explained his view on religious and social conduct, and she had neither blanched at the contents nor reacted badly to being presented with a distinctly secondhand document, that Gladstone felt he could absolutely and freely call her his own and thereby kiss her on the cheek. For the next few weeks his sheer joy is touchingly apparent in his writings; he immediately penned thirty-seven letters to his friends and relations, including two to his brother Tom, who having failed to be returned to Parliament at the last Election, was growing increasingly jealous of his youngest brother (the news that William had made such a socially acceptable match could hardly have cheered him). Gladstone became playful in a note to Catherine, "I may possibly while I am there just call at no. 36 to enquire after a certain Miss Glynne with whom I have a kind of bowing acquaintance."

On 17 June, Lord Lyttleton (George) proposed to Catherine's younger sister Mary and was accepted, and a double wedding was immediately planned at Hawarden. On 13 July Gladstone travelled north to Hawarden, where he stayed until the marriage, the superstition of ill luck attendant on the bride who saw her groom before the wedding having not yet entered the popular mythology. The day before the wedding Catherine and William performed their acts of Christian charity by distributing two hundred waistcoats and bedgowns to old men and widows in the Hawarden parish, an act which Gladstone considered "a most interesting sight." The great day dawned fair and at midday on 25 July 1839 twelve carriages left Hawarden Castle, circling the ruins of the old castle on the route through the estate and along the High Street to the mediaeval church where, as the *Chester Chronicle* noted, "the footsteps of the brides expectant were strewn with flowers by beautiful children" (the ugly ones having presumably been banished from sight). The whole scene produced in Gladstone "such a gush of delight as I had not yet experienced. Such an outpouring of human affection on these beloved girls, combined with so solemn a mystery of religion."

The honeymoon was spent at Norton Priory, a house in Cheshire loaned by friends, and one assumes that Gladstone was a virgin when he married from a passage in his diary immediately before the wedding: ". . . but I now know enough to be convinced that not without a fateful providence of God have I been reserved for access to a creature so truly rare and consummate as my Catherine." It is a fairly automatic assumption that Catherine was a virgin and that she had, with the conventions of the age, survived the lack of sexual fulfilment better than he. While Gladstone might have been a more understanding human being had he had a few affairs, the iron will power which had overcome the lusty sexuality has to be admitted. From Norton Priory the couple returned briefly to Hawarden and then went north to stay with John Gladstone at Fasque, a journey which in the days before the cutting of the railway was wearisome, usually undertaken by boat (and Gladstone was a bad sailor who suffered from appalling seasickness) and then by coach. He worried about the first impressions Catherine would make on his family and vice versa but he need not have done so, as she was able to take everything in her stride including the increasingly difficult old man. From the start she and John Gladstone had one shining common interest, William's career. Though she told her mother that "the old father" became awfully cross if anyone was late for prayers, she was more than comforted by "William's petting and kindness." Their pleasure in each other's company was such that in September Gladstone had to remind himself that he and Catherine had not been following the arranged plan of mutual reading of the Bible and other improving literature, and that it was high time they recommenced their application. From the general sense of rapture one also assumes that the Gladstones' sexual relationship was eminently satisfactory. They had pet names—Catherine was the ivy and William the oak—and on their first parting she told him, "I dreamt of you most of the night while looking sorrowfully at your empty place when I laid myself down." The usually formal Gladstone called her "My own dear Cathie" or "My own own" and signed himself "Your own known WEG." A few years later when the tensions within him were seething, he noted that only twice in his life had his carnal lusts been "materially limited" and that one of these occasions had been the period when he first married.

In an unabashed piece of Victorian sentiment Bishop Wilberforce described the Gladstones' marriage as that of "two cherries upon one stalk," but from its inception it was surprisingly modern in its composition. Gladstone may have thought that the female position as a second-class citizen was due to inherent defects in the feminine mind, but he did not regard the role of wife and mother as a secondary duty, nor did he believe that the female should surrender her free will (even if The Taming of the Shrew was among his immediate pre-marital reading matter). In his courtship letters to Catherine there was a great deal about her freedom to choose; he had great respect for her as a human being in her own right, and there was never any question of her subduing her personality to his. Before the marriage the couple agreed to tell each other all their secrets—not that he did, but he probably told Catherine as much as he told anybody—and he begged her to correct and rebuke his failings, which she did occasionally. What Gladstone gave Catherine was a focal point for her unbounding, undirected energies and ambitions, while what she brought into his life was an exhilarating and much-needed gust of unorthodoxy. She told her husband, "What a bore you would have been if you had married somebody as tidy as yourself," but it was not just a question of tidiness. Catherine's bubbling, unpredictable personality saved Gladstone's meticulous sense of order and lack of proportion from crushing or stultifying him.

In January 1840 their first parting occurred when Gladstone had to return for the opening of the new parliamentary session and, as at the time they had no London house, Catherine went to visit her sister Mary at Hagley, the Lyttletons' ancestral home in Worcestershire. She wrote to ask her husband, "Did my Willie miss me as much as I did him?" and whenever they were parted the couple wrote to each other daily, sometimes twice daily. In one of his first married letters Gladstone thanked Catherine for some flowers she had sent from Hawarden, saying, "The violets are nice;

but your letter is all violets," which seems a felicitous description of her epistolary output. Catherine loved writing letters and poured forth her thoughts with minimum punctuation, dashing from comments on the magnolias at Hawarden to the appointment of a bishop to the children's whooping cough to the machinations of that odious little man (Lord John Russell) with uninhibited enthusiasm, in an increasingly slapdash hand on any bit of paper which lay about—"My old thing wont mind a bit of paper with a hole in it," she told her husband. For Gladstone the correspondence was not only an affectionate duty but a regular minor safety valve, because he was an obsessive writer who needed to clarify his thoughts or help purge his soul by committing the ideas and emotions to paper. He did not in fact use Catherine as a medium for real soul-purging, but he kept her informed on a wide variety of subjects and she thanked him for his pretty, happy, unstudied letters. These are not adjectives which one would normally apply to Gladstone's massive correspondence, which has a curious blank, impersonal uniformity of style, for though he was an obsessive writer and an omnivorous reader he had no interest in style; it was the content that mattered, not the way in which it was expressed.

It was appropriate that the first parting should have led to Hagley, because Catherine's affection for her sister and the needs of the Glynne family generally provided one of the reasons why the Gladstones were so frequently separated. From their earliest days together he noted how much the whole family leaned on Catherine, aunts and cousins as much as Stephen, Henry, Lady Glynne and Mary Lyttleton. From leaning on Catherine it was a natural step for the Glynnes to accept Gladstone as a prop, and again from the early days he discovered that though Catherine might have kept the family raft floating, Lady Glynne's accounts were "in a state of considerable confusion from the want of unity and supervision of management." He also soon found that his kind, amusing, intelligent brother-in-law George Lyttleton was an equally bad manager and that Sir Stephen Glynne's affairs were in a tangle. Catherine herself swore that she would cease to be careless—she would not leave Gladstone's letters lying around for anybody to read, nor would unused stamps in future blow about the floor—and she would become a good manager and accountant. These promises, which Catherine effected in fits and starts, were but a drop in the ocean of the Glynnes' financial and managerial problems—Hawarden was quite a large estate and Sir Stephen had already become involved in ultimately disastrous mining operations on the smaller Oak Farm estate on the Staffordshire/Worcestershire border. It was partly because Gladstone assumed the burden of trying to supervise and clarify these problems that not only he and Catherine but also the rest of the family began to regard it as natural that Hawarden should be their country home.

Gladstone soon found a town house, 13 Carlton House Terrace, and after a great deal of anxious consultation, long-distance and then in person, Catherine agreed that its layout and situation were as ideal as possible, in a quiet cul-de-sac with access to Carlton Gardens and within easy walking distance of the House of Commons. On 11 February 1840, with the financial assistance of John Gladstone and Lady Glynne, the young couple moved in. Catherine had quickly become pregnant—in the previous September Gladstone had noted in his diary (in the Italian reserved for secrets), "Today my darling told me what she felt, with the cause of same." On 1 April 1840 she wrote a worried, touching letter to her husband in which she said that there was something awful in the thought of bringing into the world "a being for weal or woe, a being whose happiness here and hereafter may mainly depend upon one!" Should anything happen she wanted William to know that he had given *her* the greatest possible happiness and that she would not worry about the baby's future in his dear hands. Gladstone was in the main sympathetic about this pre-maternity crisis, though he dismissed "that dark spot of peril for your precious life which hangs upon the sky" in somewhat callous if Christian manner by telling her that her possible death in childbirth would trouble him more were he not certain that she was ready to meet her Maker with a "Lord here I am." He also assured his wife that her great and courageous nature would see her through the ordeal and that she was his strong tie with the earth.

Catherine needed every ounce of her courage when she went into labour in the early hours of 3 June, for it lasted until a quarter past eleven at night. The doctor told Gladstone that this was short for a first child, but the last four hours were such that even his belief that it was God's will, and that by such pain women came nearer their Maker, suffered a slight if soon repaired shock. Gladstone was present more or less throughout the labour to comfort his wife, together with Catherine's aunts, Lady Wenlock and Lady Braybrooke (there is no mention of her mother), who in the last stages "encouraged her to scream." As the little boy was brought forth "from under the bedclothes," William noted that "he was declared to be extremely like me; with Catherine's mouth." The next day Catherine was "absolutely melted in the penetrating sense of maternal love and delight, passing all expression," though even she admitted to her husband that the pain had been "awful." This first beloved child set an immediate seal on the Gladstones' marital happiness, and he was christened William Henry after his father and one of his godparents, the Reverend Henry Manning.

CHAPTER 3

TWO CHERRIES UPON ONE STALK

WHEN THE GLADSTONES were in London they entertained a fair amount and were in their turn invited to a good many functions. He was an up-and-coming politician and an excellent conversationalist; she was ardent, beautiful and amusingly unpredictable. Elderly gentlemen in particular found the young Mrs. Gladstone attractive; Catherine was delighted when after a conversation with her the Duke of Wellington "went out of his way to shake hands with William," and not a little relieved when the loquacious Duke of Cambridge fastened onto William instead of her. While Catherine's beauty and spontaneity made her a charming hostess they did not turn her into a socially good one, nor, despite her consuming interest in William's career, into a politically useful one, because in her family circle people understood each other implicitly, had little time for bores and saw no need for outside conventions. In addition, her family had a private language which helped make them even more exclusively self-sufficient and which became quite famous in the 1850s when Lord Lyttleton published *A Glossary of the Glynnese Language*. Catherine therefore tended to invite people she liked to her functions and to ignore the niceties of returning calls because she did not understand the fears or inhibitions or ambitions of those born outside a charmed circle. The number of people offended by Mrs. Gladstone's cavalier social manner grew quite large but fortunately some of those offended met her in other circumstances and were mollified by the charm and spontaneity; even more fortunately, she happened to have known from childhood and to have liked a large number of influential people.

At the time of the marriage Gladstone's political talent had been recognised and if he had not reached his full power as an orator he had an ability to make the unruly House of Commons pay attention—in his speeches, as opposed to his writing, the manner of delivery was as important as the content. Yet he was something of an enigma, for as Macaulay had unkindly but accurately observed, he espoused dead or dying causes and his convictions belonged to another age. It has been suggested that it was Catherine, with her connections to the great Whig families, who first turned her husband towards a more liberal course, but while the association with the illustrious, influential political families did Gladstone's status no harm, he made little overt use of it and consciously Catherine did nothing to persuade him onto a liberal path. In the first place, although she always had a strong social conscience, it did not occur to her to question whether there might be fundamental injustices within the system and she was at that time fairly Tory in her outlook; when Gladstone wrote to tell her that his friend Arthur Kinnaird was taking a more Tory course in political life, she was delighted. In the second place, she was convinced that William was right in his judgements because he was so much cleverer than she was, and she noted in her diary, "How every day that passes impresses me with the treasure I am blessed with but also how far away far I am behind him."

Unconsciously, in all directions, Catherine unwound coils within her husband. If Gladstone was never particularly stern and unbending in his private life, Catherine released and encouraged his childish sense of fun and capacity to enjoy himself, and to that extent she made his mind more flexible. But the first speech in which Gladstone indicated that he was other than a rigid, old-fashioned Tory owed little to Catherine and sprang from his own deeply held convictions. In 1840, under the aegis of its Foreign Secretary Lord Palmerston, the Whig Government became involved in an Opium War with China. Although British nationals had flagrantly been smuggling opium in opposition to the Chinese Government's efforts to stamp out the trade, gunboat diplomacy was used (it was as a result of this unedifying episode that Hong Kong was ceded to Britain). Gladstone made a speech in which he said that the actions of the British Government had been iniquitous; and he showed signs of his impetuousness by suggesting that in the circumstances—as was reported to an astonished Queen Victoria—"the Chinese had the right to poison the wells, to keep away the English!" While such a speech demonstrated that he had an independent liberal strain and was an early indication of Gladstone's passionate belief in the rights of all nations and a justice that transcended national interest, the occasions when he revealed this side of his nature were then rare.

In June 1841 the Whig Government, which had shown a surprising tenacity in retaining office—particularly as its leader, Lord Melbourne, was wont to declare that being Prime Minister was a damned bore—finally resigned. In the ensuing General Election Gladstone was returned for Newark without difficulty, and though Catherine told him "wifie longs to transport herself and her little boy to the scene of the action," she did not do so. She had not been too well and she told her "darling thing" that there was a sea-bathing place called Rhyl about twenty miles from Hawarden which she rather fancied, and there she duly took herself, in the company of her sister Mary Lyttleton and her baby; from Rhyl she contented herself with her husband's letters. As soon as Gladstone had been returned for Newark, Catherine sent him an urgent letter begging him to come and assist her brother Stephen in his efforts to be returned for his native county of Flintshire.* It was during the course of this election campaign that Sir Stephen, who designated himself "a Liberal Conservative," was publicly accused of indulging in buggery (among a long list of other sins). Despite his brother-in-law's attempts to allay the foul slanders and whip up support for his candidacy, Sir Stephen was defeated. Catherine was more upset by the defeat than was her brother, who cheerfully returned his attention to mediaeval architecture.

At the General Election the Conservatives were returned to power and Sir Robert Peel, who had by now reorganised the Tory party and given it its new name after the shock of the 1832 Reform Act, formed one of the most efficient, creative, forward-looking and initially stable administrations of the nineteenth century. Gladstone, who always acknowledged his debt to the great Conservative leader, had many reasons to be grateful to Peel, not least because the older man's shy, reserved, cold exterior hid a warm and sympathetic heart. This was needed in dealing with Gladstone's tender conscience, impetuous outbursts—and vanity. In 1841 just before the Conservative victory, Catherine thought her husband's prospects appeared bright "considering he has the drawback of being a Christ Church man and one or two other things against him." It was the one or two other things that worried Sir Robert Peel more, notably the specific views his young protégé had expressed about the role of the established Protestant Church which made him feel that Gladstone would not be welcome as the Chief Secretary of Catholic Ireland. But the post of Irish Chief Secretary was the job Gladstone had expected to be offered and when Peel suggested the Vice-Presidency of the Board of Trade, without a seat in the Cabinet, the young man was not pleased. Eventually he allowed himself to be persuaded into accepting the lesser post and at the Board of Trade Gladstone blossomed, as Peel had suspected he might, and learned how to present his case in Parliament. In the session of 1842 he spoke one hundred and twenty-nine times and took part in one hundred and fifty-six divisions. Whenever possible Catherine went to the Ladies' Gallery of the House of Commons to hear him speak. In February 1842 she recorded, "I found myself nearly upon Lady John Russell's lap, with Lady Palmerston and other wives near . . . It was quite a pain to me before William rose, but before he had said many words there was something at once so spirited and collected in his manner that all fright was lost in intense delight & interest." Catherine continued to have a certain amount of stage fright before her husband rose to speak but her intense delight in his oratory was usually justified. However, increasingly she was tied down by her domestic and maternal duties and began to complain that life was "a little dreary sometimes" with her husband's constant absences. Gladstone admitted the difficulty of reconciling domestic and political duties but said he had an ob-

* In 1974, after a massive reorganisation of local government in Britain, Flintshire was given the ancient Welsh name of Clwyd.

ligation to carry out the latter to the best of his ability, and his wife agreed. Indeed she had as strongly developed a sense of duty as he had and as *her* absences became more frequent she gave the call of *her* conflicting responsibilities—children or relations—as a reason for not putting him first.

It was while Gladstone was engrossed in learning his job as a junior minister that Helen Gladstone's problems came to their first climax. For two such devout Anglicans as the Gladstones it was shattering: at the end of May 1842 they received "the stunning and awful announcement" that Helen had asked Dr. Wiseman, the head of the Roman Catholic Church in England, to receive her into its bosom, which he duly did. Helen Gladstone can be viewed as the first in a long line of very distinguished converts to Roman Catholicism whom the ferment of the Oxford Movement set into apostate motion. But the suspicion that she turned to Rome as much in defiant revenge against her family as in a desperate search for a meaning to life cannot be dismissed—particularly as a few years later Helen made a great show of hanging pages of books by Protestant divines in her lavatory at Fasque, to be used as toilet paper. The accusation that she became a Catholic convert when her responsibility was diminished is not without justification either, as Helen was already well on her way to being a drug addict in 1842; this was the main straw at which her brother clutched.

Catherine shared her husband's horror, if not with the same tortured passionate intensity, for she too believed that the Church of England possessed religious truth and virtue and could not see why anybody should abandon it of her own free will. To her as much as to her husband, it was obvious that in Helen's case the mind had been clouded and the free will fragmented by opium, and there was therefore no clarity or truth in her apostacy. When Helen's conversion produced no improvement in her drug addiction—on the contrary her intake of opium increased and her behaviour consequently became more difficult and erratic—her brother's attitude hardened: for the sake of her drug-racked body Helen should be removed from the family circle and put under restraint. It was the autocratic John Gladstone who drew the line at this suggestion. Gladstone was again strongly supported by Catherine, whose compassion did not extend to embracing the plight of educated, affluent, intelligent ladies who fell into overdramatised decline; she graphically described Helen's emergence from one of her periods of self-imposed retirement, "dressed as a sort of tragedy queen or soeur-de-charité, with gold crosses dangling at her side." For a period the Gladstones refused to see Helen or allow her to see their children, and it was only when John Gladstone told them that they were behaving with "an over-refinement, scrupulosity, or uncharitableness" of manner and that if they continued to do so he would be forced to refuse to see *them*, that they grudgingly reopened contact. If their reaction seems unduly harsh it should be borne in mind that both Catherine and William believed in free will and both thought that Helen should be removed from access to the drug—living at home with her father it was only too easy for her to obtain supplies of laudanum, as it was sold freely across the counter in dozens of shops. Helen under the influence of opium, alternatively secretive, lucid, paranoic and playing the tragedy queen, cannot have been an easy person to deal with.

It was in 1842, during the long parliamentary recess, that Gladstone suffered one of the few serious accidents of his life. The family was at Hawarden with Catherine only a month away from her second confinement when about two o'clock in the afternoon of 13 September, Gladstone was in the castle grounds cleaning a gun and the barrel fired, shattering the forefinger of his left hand. He was taken to the Hawarden rectory and a doctor was summoned posthaste from Chester. On arrival at the rectory the doctor decided that an operation must be performed immediately. Catherine later recounted how he "took off the finger and then found he had not taken enough off—and had to take a second piece off," this in the days before anaesthetics. While she thought her husband's conduct was remarkable, showing patience, gentleness and cheerfulness and seeming to think only of others, he thought her bearing throughout the incident was beyond all praise, heightening even his admiring love for her. Catherine's physical resilience was the more amazing as she had an organic heart defect, about which her husband consulted a doctor in September 1840 and she herself did likewise a year later. Both doctors' reports said the heart ailment was not too serious and it cannot have been, as Catherine bore eight children, suffered one bad miscarriage, failed to have one in 1842 in the face of her husband's sudden accident, and lived to a very good age.

The second child's arrival into the world, on 18 October 1842, was as painful as that of the first-born Willie; and Gladstone noted that his wife had "the higher gift of elevating this anguish." This time it was a girl, christened Agnes, and a difficulty arose which had not occurred with Willie but which followed the advent of nearly all the others, that being trouble with the milk and feeding. Wet-nursed children were said to suffer a much higher mortality rate than breast-fed, so Catherine struggled to feed the baby; but she developed abscesses and by the end of November 1842 Gladstone recorded that the "gallant contest" was well nigh ended. Agnes was put on ass's milk and as the Gladstones were once again on their travels, an ass journeyed with them.

From Hawarden Gladstone himself returned to London for the new parliamentary session, wearing a black fingerstall to cover the stump on the left hand, a sight which remained familiar but tactfully unremarked for the rest of his life. Later in 1843 he was offered the post of President of the Board of Trade with the desired seat in the Cabinet, but as Catherine airily recorded, "There was a hitch about the church question" which prevented his immediate acceptance. The "church question" concerned the amalgamation of the historic bishoprics of Bangor and St. Asaph which had been proposed by the Whig Government with the intention of giving the extra see thus created to the unhistoric, industrial centre of Manchester. St.

Asaph was on Gladstone's doorstep at Hawarden, thus he had a particular interest in the question and was among the many devout Anglicans pledged to prevent the amalgamation; but Sir Robert Peel refused to commit himself on the subject and Gladstone said he might therefore find himself unable to accept the post of President of the Board of Trade. The long-suffering Sir Robert gave his young lieutenant three days to make up his mind on this tender religious point and Gladstone recorded, "I have to consider with God's help by Monday whether to enter the Cabinet, or to retire altogether." With the help of God, assisted by Catherine, James Hope and Henry Manning, he decided that he would be following the right course by entering the Cabinet. After a long conversation on the subject in Kensington Gardens, Catherine noted, "How thankful I ought to be to be joined to one whose mind is purity and integrity itself . . . in witnessing that tenderness of conscience wh. shrinks at the base idea of any worldly gain could in any way interfere with higher duties." There is the suggestion that at times even the devoted Catherine found the pure integrity of her husband's conscience a trifle irritating, but then she never hid her worldly ambitions for William, nor had she doubts that he would be serving God splendidly by becoming Prime Minister.

It was as Vice-President and then President of the Board of Trade that Gladstone rose to prominence. Under Sir Robert Peel's guidance he was responsible for sweeping tariff reforms, the first attempt in years to clarify and simplify the barnacle-encrusted mass of import and export duties. By lifting so many restrictions these reforms opened the way to the introduction of free trade (though this was not the intention of either Sir Robert or his lieutenant). Gladstone was also responsible for the first Railway Acts, which imposed regulations on the operations of the railway barons whose armies of "navigators" were cutting and hewing and blasting their way across the British countryside; his introduction of statutory, cheap, third-class fares on all lines was the first measure which brought him to the grateful attention of "the people." Interestingly, in the 1844 Railway Bill Gladstone proposed a clause whereby the State could buy out the railway companies if their performance was not to the public satisfaction, a clause which might be called socialistic (it was defeated). But he himself considered that in principle "the most socialistic measure" he, or anybody else, had introduced in the nineteenth century was his Coalwhippers Act of 1843. The coalwhippers were the men who loaded and unloaded coal at the London docks, a filthy ill-paid job made worse because employment was at the mercy of publicans who acted as the owners' agents. Gladstone's indeed socialistic measure was to abolish this practice and institute an official central employment exchange; it was one which again brought him in contact with a sector of "the people"—he went down to the docks to examine conditions for himself—and which both he and they enjoyed.

In the early summer of 1843 Catherine had one of her first moments in the limelight, though the occasion was not of a pleasant nature. A servant in their employment at Carlton House Terrace, a girl named Elizabeth Roberts, had stolen some jewellery from her mistress and had then tried unsuccessfully to pawn it, and Catherine had to attend Bow Street Magistrates' Court to give evidence in the case. She recorded, "It was quite a new scene to find myself there . . . they wd not admit William with me & I felt very shy." William was later allowed to make a short speech in Roberts' favour and he pleaded for mercy for the poor creature, but she was nevertheless sentenced to a term in the Millbank Penitentiary. The comment about how shy Catherine felt in court is interesting because many people remarked upon her abounding self-confidence, while others said she had not a nervous bone in her body and did not know the meaning of fear, but even she had a certain diffidence and at times had to steel herself to act.

In her own milieu Catherine was usually uninhibited and she carried her spontaneity into her relationship with Queen Victoria, though she had a suitable English reverence for royalty. The two ladies had originally met in 1832, when the thirteen-year-old Princess Victoria had visited Hawarden Castle. It was a brief visit and in later years Her Majesty had sometimes to be reminded when she had first met Mrs. Gladstone—but not that she had always liked the delightful lady who had been born Miss Glynne. Apart from Gladstone's official audiences with the Queen on receiving or surrendering his seals of office, the young couple were invited to dine at Buckingham Palace, invitations which owed as much to Catherine's personality and family connections as to William's political position. The Queen's personal affection for Mrs. Gladstone was several times demonstrated when Catherine received invitations to take her children to the Palace or to Windsor Castle to meet the royal children. On the first occasion she recorded, "P. Alice a nice fat baby—Princess Royal about a head shorter than Willie, very engaging & good not exactly pretty but like the Queen—the P of Wales very small & the head not striking me as very good shaped . . . his long trousers tied below the ankle & rather full very unbecoming especially with his height." She also said that the Queen was in fits of laughter at the children's antics and how relieved she was that *hers* had behaved themselves.

Surprisingly, Gladstone himself had entertained doubts about the institution of monarchy, but he had come to the conclusion that there was a qualified testimony in its favour to be inferred from "the circumstances attending the appointment of Saul" and that it was "most nearly analogous to Divine Govt." Unfortunately, by the time he was first introduced to the Queen personally—as opposed to attending official functions—an event which occurred in April 1842 and threw him into an agony of apprehension, he had forgotten the former qualification, and the sight of his Sovereign at close quarters led him to believe "the day is near when with mine eyes I shall behold the King of Kings, when I shall be introduced to thee O my Redeemer." This divinely reverential attitude towards the personage of the Sovereign, if not always or necessarily towards the institution of monarchy, did not help his relationship with Queen Victoria.

By 1844 Sir Robert Peel had turned the attention of his energetic, reforming Ministry to Ireland, specifically to the Catholic college of Maynooth. The college already had a miserly grant from the State (Macaulay said that in contrast to the splendours of Oxford and Cambridge it was a disgraceful Dotheboys Hall). As a gesture towards the better training of the Catholic clergy and thereby, it was hoped, to better government in Ireland, Peel proposed to increase and make permanent the grant. But Gladstone had in *The State in Its Relation with the Church* upheld the view that the State could only profess and promote one religious truth, and from the moment Peel proposed the increased grant he said he would have to resign if it were implemented. The more pragmatic Peel insisted that nobody would hold him to his previous statements (though Peel had considered the book an ill-judged venture for an aspiring politician) but when the Maynooth Bill was introduced at the beginning of 1845 Gladstone indeed resigned his seat in the Cabinet. The resignation was greeted with loud applause from those few who shared his moral views on the State's Christian functions and, less pleasingly, from anti-Catholic factions throughout the country of whom there were still a large number, while his friends shook their heads sadly at the overtender conscience which rendered him unfit for the hurly-burly of political life. But nearly everybody was baffled when Gladstone voted for the Maynooth Bill on its second reading.

For Gladstone the whole business was a nightmare—a word he used himself—but the issues were becoming clearer to him. He had to resign on the question of the principle he had stated in his book; he had to test the courage of his convictions, otherwise people would justly regard him as a mere adventurer. But in the privacy of his heart and in talking and writing to those closest to him—Catherine, James Hope, Henry Manning—he had been moving slowly away from his earlier beliefs. Each day was showing him "more and more that the idea of Christian politics can not be realised in the State according to its present condition of existence," and moreover that on balance he was content to stay in politics because "Government must subsist; and if not (as in strictness) it ought, then as it may!" Therefore, he was free to vote for the Maynooth grant as a question of the better subsistence of good government. But it was a piece of reasoning that to outsiders appeared to be casuistry, sophistry or sheer lunacy, particularly as his work at the Board of Trade had earned him so many plaudits and brought him so firmly to the forefront. The normally reticent Sir Robert Peel had even taken the trouble to write to John Gladstone, "I cannot resist the temptation, if it be only for the satisfaction of my own feelings, of congratulating you most warmly and sincerely, on the distinction which your son has acquired, by the manner in which he conducted himself throughout these discussions [i.e. about tariff reform] and all others since his appointment to office."

When the 1845 session ended, with Gladstone in his self-imposed, high-principled wilderness, the Maynooth question had turned his attention to Anglo-Irish relations in general, and he proposed to James Hope that they go on a walking tour of Ireland "with the purpose of looking at close quarters at the institutions for religion and education of the country and at the character of the people." It would have been an excellent idea and might have produced in Gladstone a trauma as great as Maynooth, for when he examined a problem at close quarters the results were sometimes seismic. Unfortunately by 1845 his sister Helen's difficulties had again come to a head and Gladstone never went on a prolonged visit to Ireland or found the opportunity to examine at first hand what the people thought and felt and how they lived.

In the summer of 1845, as Helen's condition had not improved, her father decided yet again to send her to Germany, in the company of a doctor and companion, to see if the complete change of environment would effect a favourable change. But by the autumn the reports from Germany had become alarming and it was Gladstone who volunteered to go and find his sister and try to persuade her to return to England. It was a mission which he accepted willingly, partly from a sense of family obligation but also because the sexual tensions were again strong within him. While he was in Germany, Gladstone himself noted that absence from home was one of the contributory causes of these tensions, but he might more accurately have said absence from Hawarden, for that was the only place where he was comparatively free from them. It seems probable that he undertook the continental rescue journey in the hope that it would counteract the restlessness of spirit and even more of body. By the early 1830s Gladstone had fought his Herculean battle against his lusty sexual instincts and apparently overcome the desire to masturbate which had caused him so much anguish. In 1839 he married Catherine and was able to taste the sexual fruits of which he had so long dreamed. They were sweet, but Catherine was fairly constantly pregnant; Willie was born in June 1840, Agnes in October 1842, Stephen in April 1844 and Jessy in July 1845. By the end of 1842 an Oxford-type, sin-laden introspection was creeping back into Gladstone's diary entries; he noted that the enigma of his soul was not yet solved and that his inward life was a tissue of self-deceit, and a year later in 1843 he recorded, "fearful is the guilt of sin returning again & again in forms ever new but alike hideous."

At this time the strait jacket for a proper relationship between the male and the female in a good Christian marriage in the new mature civilisation was slowly being constructed. Reversing the process which had descended from Eve the temptress, the early Victorians were turning man into the lustful carnal brute and woman into the pure unsullied spirit. The image of the detached female who corporally happened to produce children but spiritually had no connection with sexual matters was later expressed in the statement, "The best mothers, wives, and managers of household, know little or nothing of sexual indulgence. Love of home, children, and domestic duties, are the only passions they feel." The Gladstones did not subscribe to the general strait jacket and the extraordinary sexual image (nor in reality did all other Victorian married partners), and the cloak of prudery which increasingly enveloped sexual matters was not donned by them. Catherine had not been brought up to be ashamed of her body—there are still people in the Hawarden district who knew somebody who remembered Mrs. Gladstone wandering through the castle in a state of déshabillé or standing naked by a window calmly having a wash—and Gladstone shared (or learned to share) his wife's physical informality. When possible he was present throughout Catherine's labours and at the births, and when her feeding difficulties became acute with the later children he was on all occasions busily engaged in trying to staunch or relieve the flow of milk, as one of his several diary entries on the subject will show: "Much rubbing however (by Mrs S. and me) seemed to keep the right organ from getting into an obstinate state"; "Mrs S." being Mrs. Smith, the midwife.

However, the belief that the prime duty of a Christian marriage was the procreation of children was accepted by the Gladstones, and it was one which enabled Catherine (and other women) to endure the agony of their continual labours. Whether the Gladstones completely accepted the tabus which accompanied the constant bearing of children—for example, that one did not have sexual intercourse once the pregnancy was established or while the baby was being breast-fed as to do so was considered both indelicate and injurious to the foetus or the mother—is less certain. Gladstone himself would not have accepted another hopeful belief—that breast feeding acted as a form of contraceptive and the woman was "safe" as long as she kept feeding—as he was vehemently opposed to any form of birth control. But after the birth of the fourth child, Jessy, he wondered whether their family was large enough, "if ever there is to be a release from the toils which now enclose," though precisely which toils he meant—Catherine's suffering in labour and difficulties with the feeding, his increasing frustration or the awful if joyful responsibilities of parenthood to which he had earlier referred—is not clear. While Catherine's passions were by no means directed solely towards home, children and domestic duties (particularly not the latter), it was true that the constant business of bearing, feeding and caring for children tended to blunt the sexual appetite, or at least engross the attentions. The women were thus comforted or stultified, but the men were not. Apart from the limited number of occasions when Gladstone was able to enjoy the pleasures of the marriage bed, he and Catherine were increasingly separated. He therefore lacked the immediate comfort and support of her uninhibited gaiety and simple assured strength.

Catherine had not yet gone into perpetual motion—as her husband later described her peregrinations—and some of the separations were instituted by his actions, for example the trip to rescue Helen in 1845; but more of them came from hers. She always insisted that she *hated* their horrid separations and *yearned* to be with her "dear old thing," and years later, when they were both into their sixties, she was still writing to her husband, "No words can say how much I miss you." Yet the hatred and the yearning did not keep her by Gladstone's side. If the absences perhaps stemmed from her unrealised independent strain, there were other reasons. Apart from the general Glynne dependence on Catherine she was also an excellent nurse, the sort of calmly disorganised, affectionate person everybody wanted by their bedside when they were ill. With large families and limited medical knowledge there was a great deal of illness in Victorian households, and Catherine was always willing to respond to the calls. Furthermore she did not like London; she was a country girl, born, bred and in the bone, and she usually found the capital too *grubous* for words, *grubous* being "Glynnese" for something dingy or dismal, or for a temporary indisposition. With regard to London it obviously meant the former and Catherine had good reason to wish to take her children to the bracing air of the seaside or to the pureness of Hawarden or Hagley, because the onward march of industrial progress was turning London into a city over which a pall of smoke hung for much of the year, smoke which the natural dampness of the English climate quickly transmuted into thick heavy fog. As her husband's daily letters kept her in touch with political developments there was no need for her to be permanently at the scene of the action, and with her family increasing at a steady pace she was not.

When Gladstone travelled to Germany in the autumn of 1845 he was thus seething with the new frustration of the sexual appetite gratified, but only intermittently, and from the increasing absences of his wife. But however strong the frustrations were, however much they racked Gladstone's soul as much as his body, they did not prevent him undertaking and enjoying half a dozen other activities while he was in Germany (apart from rescuing Helen)—theatre-going, church-going, sight-seeing, letter-writing, dining out, reading. Everybody who knew him well and later wrote about him commented on Gladstone's outstanding, unique ability to shut his various activities and emotions into separate compartments or to switch them on and off like electric light (the similes varied according to the period). It evolved partly from his immense concentration, partly from the capacity to stand back on himself like an actor (and he had many of the traits of the great actor), but basically from the direct Evangelical link with God, for at root and on the Day of Judgement the only being who mattered was God. At the end of 1840 he had wondered, "what if it should be right to arrange for a voluntary periodical confession?" but though by now many people erroneously regarded him as being virtually a Catholic, the sentiment he expressed towards the end of his life was the one he held, with only the briefest doubt, from the beginning of his introspections: "The healthy soul ought to be able to discharge its burdens at the foot of the great throne without the assistance of an intermediate person." What Gladstone was soon to call the chief burden of his then unhealthy soul was thus one he could not share with anybody, least of all Catherine. To have involved her in his sexual torments would have meant contaminating her with his sin; he had to continue to fight his battle alone.

Once in Germany he went first to Munich, where Helen was supposed to be. She had moved on, but he made good use of his visit as it was on this occasion that he first met Dr. Döllinger, the famous German Catholic theologian, and as he himself said, "laid the foundations of one of the most interesting and cherished friendships of my life." Eventually Gladstone tracked his sister to Baden-Baden, where he found that she was taking three hundred drops of laudanum a day and witnessed some horrific scenes with Helen being forcibly held down to have leeches applied. At times she refused to see him even though he had letters of entreaty and authority not only from his father but from her spiritual adviser in England, Dr. Wiseman.

It was while Gladstone was in Baden-Baden that he indulged in an extensive examination of his soul and his besetting sins and, as he later recorded, that for the second time in twenty-odd years his sexual lust was materially limited. In the examination he did not explicitly list his besetting sins but he set out the channels, incentives and remedies. The channels were comprehensive, encompassing thought, conversation, hearing, seeing, touch and company; the incentives numbered among them absence from home, idleness, exhaustion and curiosity of knowledge and sympathy; the remedies included prayer, immediate pain, not deviating, not lingering, not looking in bookshops and "withdrawal from *presumption and first appearance* of any exciting cause." The reference to not looking in bookshops referred to the reading of pornography, a pastime which Gladstone had already adopted, though it should be said that it was pornography by his standards. He does not appear to have indulged in what would be called hard-core pornography, the fantasies of human beings in endless sexual daisy chains, always happy, always satisfied but never reaching any conclusion, which were only too readily available. (This was in the days before the Obscene Publication Acts; much as later generations of British authors· may have cursed them, they were introduced because of the trash which flooded the market and which was regarded as pernicious and corrupting even by such original and socially conscious investigators as Henry Mayhew.) Gladstone confined himself to a higher class of bawdy literature such as Petronius, Boccaccio and the French *Fabliaux*; nonetheless for him it was pornography and therefore sinful. The remedy of pain was not immediately adopted, but he had already wondered "how far pain may become the ground of pleasure . . . pleasure and pain simultaneous & the first superior, but the latter is actually the occasion, the material, the substratum of the former." This particular memorandum on one age-old Christian dilemma had led to the startling conclusion, "For all we know Cranmer may have had the joy in the burning of his hand more than the pain of it";

though Gladstone admitted that this might be taking an example beyond its justifiable limit.

It was also from Baden-Baden in one of his daily letters to Catherine that Gladstone penned some of his most quoted lines: "Ireland, Ireland! that cloud in the west, that coming storm, the minister of God's retribution upon cruel and inveterate but half-atone injustice." These lines have been interpreted as showing a prescient awareness that Irish affairs were increasingly to intrude upon English politics and to dominate Gladstone's own political life in its later years; but his awareness of the coming storm and divine retribution, which did not again assail him for twenty years, should be viewed in the context of Maynooth and the role of the Christian in a secular state. Apart from focusing on his bodily temptations, Gladstone's mind continued to be concerned with the religious crisis.

Catherine assured her husband that she did not mind his prolonged absence in Germany as long as it was helping Helen (which it is doubtful it was) and saving his father extra worry. Eventually at the end of 1845, Miss Gladstone reluctantly agreed to return to England, though more under the threat of the withdrawal of her ample paternal allowance than from her brother's exhortations. Helen's problems had by no means reached their final climax: a few months after her return to England she told her Catholic friends that she was being restrained against her will by her family, and the friends approached the Commissioners in Lunacy (the body which then examined suspected lunatics or to which they could appeal). But one of the commissioners was Lord Ashley, a political colleague of Gladstone's, and this problem was settled by the two men without publicity. Helen later admitted that she was not being unduly confined.

Gladstone himself, and the ever-ambitious Catherine, had the comfort of his returning to office, if only briefly, as Colonial Secretary in the reshuffle of Sir Robert Peel's Cabinet caused by the early Corn Law convulsions. But the acceptance of paid office under the Crown then meant that one had to vacate one's parliamentary seat and stand for re-election (Ministers were paid, if M.P.s were not). With the knowledge that Sir Robert Peel was supporting some lessening of the protective Corn Laws, Gladstone had no hope of re-standing for Newark, still in the control of that most protectionist of aristocrats, the Duke of Newcastle. There was no rush of safe Tory seats offered to a Peelite who in the public eye had the added disadvantage of being associated with the Oxford Movement and its Romanish tendencies (the Maynooth view of Gladstone as anti-Catholic had quickly disappeared when he voted for the second reading of the Bill). Gladstone was therefore left in the peculiar position of having a seat in the Cabinet but none in the House of Commons.

The Corn Laws reached crisis point in 1846 but when they had been passed in 1815 it had been in a House of Commons ringed by troops with fixed bayonets. They restricted the import of cheap foreign grain until the price of the home-grown commodity had reached a certain sum, and they had always been regarded by many sectors of the population as protecting the interests of one group only, the landed gentry. By the early 1840s the Anti-Corn Law League, led by Richard Cobden and John Bright, had roused and organised public opinion to a high pitch of protest, and the issue of cheap bread for the people had widened into the most divisive and bitter controversy of the day—free trade versus protection. Initially Gladstone had moved faster than Sir Robert Peel towards the view that there must be some relaxation of the Corn Laws in the shape of a sliding scale of duty, though he did not then approve of Cobden and Bright, whom he considered to have stirred class hatred by their ridicule of the landlords. The Corn Law crisis was brought to a head by the terrible potato famine in Ireland, and if it was not a major crisis in Gladstone's career—partly for the reason that he had no seat in Parliament and was not therefore able to participate in the bitter debates on the issue of repeal—it had important side effects in that it initiated his dislike of Disraeli and kept him out of office for several years.

When Peel, against the tradition of the Tory party and without having stated his intentions at the General Election, decided on the total repeal of the Corn Laws and thereby the abandonment of protection, Disraeli was already forty-two years old. It had taken him five attempts before he got into Parliament in 1837; Peel had refused him office in 1841. The influential group demanding retention of the Corn Laws had no real leader; Disraeli saw his chance and seized it. The old territorial aristocratic interests had a genuine appeal to the romantic side of Disraeli's cynical nature, but it would also be true to say that he lacked burning convictions either for or against protection and acted from enlightened self-interest. Gladstone, who had little understanding of the ambitions and struggles of men who had to fight against the currents of class, religious or racial prejudice—and Disraeli had to battle against all three—could see only the self-interest. For him Disraeli's attacks on their mutual leader were not only disloyal and vicious, they smacked of those mortal sins opportunism, lack of principle and expediency, and thereafter he entertained a deep distrust of Disraeli's motives and actions.

After carrying the repeal of the Corn Laws, Peel's government was resoundingly defeated. With the Conservative party split in two, the Whigs came back into power under Lord John Russell. Gladstone, left without a seat in the Cabinet or in the House of Commons, did not find a constituency for some time. As a farewell gesture Peel suggested honouring the worthy name of Gladstone by nominating his young colleague's father for a baronetcy, a title he had longed for. It was a suggestion to which Queen Victoria willingly acceded and the old man became Sir John Gladstone, Bart., of Fasque and Balfour, though perhaps too late in the day for him to be fully appreciative, as his faculties were beginning to fail.

CHAPTER 4

IN THE WILDERNESS

THE YEAR 1847 STARTED calmly for the Gladstones, too calmly as he still had no seat in Parliament. In January the whole family went to Hagley to stay with the Lyttletons. There Gladstone helped fill his comparatively idle hours by working on a study of Greek civilisation and Homer, a task which occupied him intermittently but intensively for the next decade. He again indulged his "prurient curiosity" by reading pornography but he also spent a good deal of time playing with "a troop of children" (Mary Lyttleton's pregnancies were even more frequent than Catherine's). However much Gladstone's inner tensions were already fermenting, nobody in that large informal household seems to have been aware of them; they were kept in their sealed compartments, they had no apparent effect on the many other compartments which made up William Gladstone and no symptoms were revealed by displays of bad temper, irritation or moroseness. Gladstone was a proud, devoted and excellent father. He not only quoted Juvenal—*Maxima debetur puero reverentia* (the greatest reverence is due to the child)—he put the maxim into practice. The four children already born by the beginning of 1847—Willie, Agnes, Stephen and Jessy—and the four yet to come—Mary, Helen, Henry and Herbert—all received from their father as much personal attention as he could give them, including hugs and kisses, sitting on Papa's knee, riding on his back and making gigantic snowmen with him, as well as Scripture lessons, prayers and instructions in Latin and Greek. A distant attitude would have been difficult with Catherine around but the physical affection Gladstone showered on his children was perhaps also a reaction to his own childhood, for when his father died he poignantly recorded, "I kissed thrice my father's cheek & forehead before and after his death: the only kisses I can remember." However, the habit which became associated with Gladstone and which he was supposed to have drilled into his children, namely chewing each mouthful of food thirty-two times, did not in fact play a large part in their lives.

Gladstone's sense of his moral transgressions, which was particularly strong in the years when his children were young, made him doubly sensitive about rebuking them for their juvenile sins or disobediences. Both he and Catherine believed in discipline but they thought it should be transmitted by love, example and explanation, and in the rare instances when it extended to corporal punishment they were both filled with anguish. Throughout the years of their children's development the Gladstones consulted each other, and no decisions about governesses, schools, illnesses or improving suspected weaknesses of character were taken without mutual discussion. The amount of time he could devote to his children was limited by his political and other activities and the main burden of rearing them fell on Catherine; she was probably as ideal a mother as could be found. In the first place she gave her children far more personal attention than was then common, and when years later the famous Mrs. Gladstone was invited to write the preface to a book entitled *Early Influences* (a nineteenth-century version of Dr. Spock), in her introduction Catherine insisted that parents must learn to know their children and that this could only be done by personal care and interest (though she also emphasised that discipline was necessary and that overpetting could be harmful). She put her dictums into practice, providing her children with a freedom and gaiety of atmosphere in which they could blossom.

The delightful side of her lack of convention, rules and regulations was exhibited from her earliest days of motherhood—when Willie was a baby she wrote to tell her husband, "A drawer with a blanket doubled in it made him an excellent bed and he slept soundly & told me it was as comfortable as the smartest crib." Obviously she had her faults; a little more organisation and regard for some conventions might have improved her offsprings' confidence, as most children respond to a measure of this sort of security, too. For example, as she was a lady who could throw on any dress and still manage to look beautiful it never occurred to her to bother about her daughters' clothes, and they tended to be given old, unflattering garments to wear. This habit also stemmed from Catherine's erratic attempts at economy (which became necessary from the end of 1847) and from the more general belief that her family must understand the problems and difficulties of life. Certainly none of the Gladstone children grew up to believe that they were special or privileged by virtue of their father's position or their mother's ancestry. With minor reservations the children adored their mother, as did the tribe of nephews and nieces and young second cousins; one of her nieces later commented, "People say there is nothing so warm as a bed in the snow. If that's true, then Aunty Pussy is the snow bed!"

Towards the end of March 1847 Gladstone received a tentative approach from an election committee at Oxford University to stand as a candidate in the next General Election. The university seats were unique: Oxford returned two Members to Parliament who were voted for by members of the colleges, but nothing so demeaning as the candidate making public speeches or indulging in personal canvassing occurred; the campaign was conducted by his election committee and he was then elected (or not) without being present at the count. The Gladstone campaign continued until the General Election at the end of July; its focus was upon the religious views of the various candidates. Gladstone was attacked as an unsound Anglican who had helped undermine the Church's position and influenced his sister's conversion to Roman Catholicism, but on 1 August he received the news—he was then at Fasque—of his election. One of his first acts when Parliament reassembled was to vote for the Bill which proposed that Jews should be allowed to enter the House of Commons by deleting from the oath of allegiance the words "on the true faith of a Christian." The action was in keeping with Gladstone's increasing conviction that the functions of Church and State had separated and that religious toleration should therefore be extended to all British citizens; but it was not one which pleased the majority of his Oxford constituents.

It was while the family was at Fasque that in mid-September the Gladstones' five-year-old daughter Agnes became desperately ill with erysipelas. Popularly known as St. Anthony's fire, it was then a common and frequently deadly disease (it was the one from which Gladstone's mother had died). For a week the child fought against the fever, the spreading inflammation, the consuming thirst and the agony of being touched, with her parents keeping an alternate round-the-clock vigil by her bedside. Her father inwardly raged against her seemingly imminent death, his heart "hard and unquiet & not willing to give my child back, & it rebels even when I say with what strength is given me Thy will be done in earth as it is in heaven." But by 26 September, though Gladstone recorded that the havoc of the disease had been frightful, the crisis was over and he was able to reassure himself that such things were sent to temper men and to assist their capacity to draw near to death themselves. Perhaps the most touching entry in a period when Gladstone's normally impervious writing showed some trace of emotion was one in which he noted that the other children prayed for their sister's recovery, and that little Jessy "behaved like one fit for heaven": for within three years Jessy herself was dead.

Catherine's resilience and fortitude during the dreadful illness was again remarkable because she was only two months away from her fifth confinement, she had been fairly ill with a threatened miscarriage on arrival at Fasque and though her husband shared the agonising vigil the main burden of nursing Agnes fell on her shoulders. The atmosphere of the household itself was not one which lightened the load, because Sir John Gladstone was now very deaf, his eyesight was bad and he was cantankerous, constantly arguing with William about the repeal of the Corn Laws and free trade, both of which he opposed, "as usual at the top of his voice." Tom was more jealous than ever of his youngest brother (and had refused to vote for him in the Oxford-election), John Neilson was resentful because he thought William left the task of caring for Sir John too much to him, while Helen was at the height of her drug addiction (the gigantic Robertson sensibly kept out of the way). Helen was now having serious fits and was suffering from hallucinations—her brother described her as "full of horrible apprehensions . . . She sees people come in through the walls, 'little people' covering her drawers." It has been related that she was refusing to talk to William (if not Catherine), but his own account of these tortured months indicates that the refusal was intermittent. When the Gladstones left Fasque in mid-October, Helen travelled with them as far as Rugby, where she was given into Tom's care to be conducted, at her own request, to a Catholic convent near Leamington. Before he left Fasque, Gladstone noted the many problems of the last few months, including, "My father's illness, C's narrow escape from miscarriage, Helen at worst, Agnes's illness, + Oxford, Tom's disaffection, feud about the chapel, Hampton and his wife." The feud about the chapel referred to the church Sir John Gladstone had built and endowed near Fasque, and the battles between the ministers, the congregation and the patron (and his sons) about how it should be conducted. Mr. and Mrs. Hampton were the Gladstones' butler and maid, and the latter had recently confessed to Catherine that before their marriage they had indulged in unlawful intercourse. The confession caused the Gladstones disquiet, not because they were shocked but because they thought they had exerted a good Christian influence on the Hamptons and had been vain of their apparent success.

A more disastrous problem was soon to descend, and neither of the Gladstones was in a good physical state to deal with it. He had contracted erysipelas while helping to nurse Agnes; temporarily both his arms were crippled and they were still giving him pain in November. On 23 November 1847 Catherine gave birth to her fifth child Mary, with a labour even more severe than usual followed by even more painful feeding difficulties. The disaster—and it may be so designated—was the crash of Sir Stephen Glynne's Oak Farm enterprise. If thus far the emphasis has been on the difficulties created by members of Gladstone's family, those spawned by the Glynnes were not inconsiderable. With the Lyttleton family, relations were on the whole remarkably harmonious, though Catherine, as the manager of the Glynnes, sometimes overplayed her hand and sent her sister instructions how the Lyttletons could economise and how George might exert himself more; they did not always react kindly to the interference. Lady Glynne was something of a trial to both her daughter and her son-in-law (though she spent most of her declining years with the Lyttletons at Hagley), as she grew more melancholic and refused to accept her lot with due Christian endurance; Catherine and William, who were not attuned to melancholy depression, considered she had little to endure. Sir Stephen was the greatest problem even before the Oak Farm crash and Catherine occasionally lost patience with him; her husband had earlier written to tell her that she would "addle" her brother beyond all hope of recovery if she kept on about his responsibilities.

The saga of Oak Farm went back to 1835 when a company had been formed, headed by Sir Stephen, to work the vast deposit of minerals which supposedly existed under the ground of the property. Gladstone was initially drawn into the Oak Farm business—apart from his involvement in trying to untangle the Glynne finances—because on their marriages both he and George Lyttleton were invited to make a modest investment in this seemingly sound enterprise, which they did to the extent of £1,000 each. The management of the company was left in the charge of a gentleman named Boydell who had ideas above his competence and who, in an era of vast speculation and with no check from the owner of the property, indulged in grandiose schemes of expansion. In 1844 there were ominous signs of trouble and a new company was formed with Boydell as general manager but in which neither Sir Stephen, Gladstone nor Lord Lyttleton was directly involved. However, the indirect involvement was immense, as the credit for the company had been and continued to be guaranteed by Sir Stephen and the Hawarden estate, and there was then no limited liability for companies. For a considerable time before the crash Gladstone was occasionally filled with foreboding about the competence and trustworthiness of Boydell and torn with anxiety about the "wretched" Oak Farm enterprise. His fears were justified, for when Boydell had to admit that the company was hopelessly insolvent and that creditors were pressing for payment, Sir Stephen Glynne (or Gladstone on his behalf) found that he was liable for £122,000 on the Oak Farm company, that he had already lost £115,000, that there was a further £118,000 on mortgages and bond debts against the Hawarden estate and that with other debts the grand total liability was £395,000.

Sir Stephen's uselessness in the catastrophe was recognised by his family, and he was allowed to depart for Constantinople in search of antiquities. Henry Glynne was as uninterested as his elder brother in practical measures to salvage the family honour, home and an income from the wreck, and it was Gladstone who paid the penalty for having a sense of responsibility, duty and financial probity. As Catherine struggled with the baby, her husband was engaged in endless family conclaves and meetings with solicitors and creditors. Sir John Gladstone, whose diminishing faculties still functioned at the mention of money and who was involved because he had already provided financial assistance to Sir Stephen in earlier rough times, suggested that the Hawarden estate be sold *in toto* to clear the debts and leave Sir Stephen (and his mother) with an income. The suggestion was rejected, not least by his son, for Hawarden was the Glynne ancestral home. But clamouring creditors had to be met, and it was Gladstone who attended the bankruptcy proceedings in Birmingham and who produced a formula which satisfied them. Sir Stephen Glynne (in his absence) promised to raise £200,000 as quickly as possible to repay the most pressing debts; by earlier family agreement, on Gladstone's suggestion, it had been arranged that this should be accomplished by selling Hawarden land, of which £60,000 worth would be bought by Gladstone and £25,000 worth by George Lyttleton. The latter was unable to raise £25,000 and his portion was taken over by Lord Spencer, one of the Glynne uncles-by-marriage. Sir John Gladstone provided a good deal of the money for his son's share of the burden, the rest Gladstone raised by his own investments and prospects (which also originated with his father), and Hawarden Castle was closed with the intention of letting it to any good tenant (though none was found and the castle was never let).

Gladstone later said that the five years between 1847 and 1852, in which his mind was so concentrated on trying to clear the Oak Farm mess that even his parliamentary duties were neglected, had provided the best possible training for his role as the Chancellor of the Exchequer. In reducing debts of nearly £400,000 he learned the facts of financial life in the hardest of schools (though he had acquired a good knowledge of the country's economic affairs while at the Board of Trade, until 1847 he knew nothing about commerce at ground level). But while he was living through those years he had no assurance that he would ever be Chancellor of the Exchequer, for they were the ones in the Peelite wilderness. After the repeal of the Corn Laws the bulk of the Conservative party remained bitterly opposed to Sir Robert Peel and re-formed under the leadership of Lord Stanley, swearing to reintroduce protection the moment they were returned to office. In practice some Tories genuinely believed that Peel was a Judas who had forsworn his party's principles, but others, while believing that he had acted precipitately, were more equivocal on the subject of protection versus free trade. At least officially the main body of Conservatives had a concerted policy, whereas the Peelites had not. The group which followed Sir Robert Peel after his defeat included Lord Aberdeen, Sidney Herbert, Gladstone and his friend Lord Lincoln. They were notably high-minded but they were united only by their opposition to protection and their loyalty to Peel, the man who for them had put the interests of the country before those of party, and who had preferred to follow his conscience rather than expediency. Gladstone himself later said of Peel that unattached Prime Ministers were as dangerous as great rafts floating unmoored in a harbour, and the presence of Sir Robert, massive even in his decline, surrounded by his able but uncommitted lieutenants, contributed to the instability of parliamentary life in the late 1840s.

Gladstone also admitted, privately in his diaries and occasionally to Catherine, that the whole Oak Farm business was a nightmare and that under no load had his heart sunk more often in despair. But he naturally believed that it was the will of God, that it had been sent to test him, and he assured Catherine that he in no way held her responsible for the burdens which had fallen upon him. Catherine herself made stern efforts to be economical, not to consume such large quantities of food (her husband was worried about the amount they spent on food) and to keep proper household accounts, for her considerable dowry (£30,000) had been swallowed by the crash. During these years the Gladstones were without Hawarden as a base; it was a factor which troubled him more than it did her. To say that

Gladstone was never assailed by his "besetting sins" while he was at Hawarden would be inaccurate, but the serenity and beauty of the estate—the parkland with its immemorial elms, oaks and beeches, its streams and miniature waterfalls with such names as "Niagara," the ruins of the ancient castle, the views from the old churchyard across the Dee estuary—instilled in Gladstone a comparable serenity and he was rarely troubled by the tensions which assailed him in London. During the closure of the estate Henry Glynne remained at the rectory, and in fact Catherine spent a good deal of time there, as her brother's wife Lavinia (née Lyttleton) was constantly ill in childbirth and her children were sickly. But Gladstone's occasional visits to the rectory were small compensation, and without such a comforting home as Hawarden in which he could relax with his family, his frustrations remained unsoothed.

By the middle of 1848, the lack of any clear direction to his political career had meshed with the shocks of the last year and brought Gladstone's inner tensions to their first crisis; he penned an enormously long examination of the state of his soul, which implicitly meant his carnal passions. He wrote of the extraordinary tenacity of evil within him which, despite his efforts to limit it and to keep open the doors of mercy by constant prayer, was showing no signs of lessening its hold; on the contrary his dangerous curiosity and filthiness of spirit were increasing daily, and the corrupt action of his mind was no longer inward nor confined to himself. His most deadly foe he considered to be "corrupt sophism"; for while it was necessary for men to study the depravities of the human heart and body in order to understand them and thereby provide remedies, this task must be undertaken by those who were distinctly *called* or who had controlled their passion and whose holiness was such as to produce no corrupting excitement. For none of these reasons could he without sophism excuse himself, and he must therefore be defiled by the natural law of cause and effect; but he had lost the courage to look his Deity in the face: the overexhaustion of the last few months had predisposed him "to that vague habit of mind which seeks relief in some counterexcitement—a wilful welcoming of the Evil One, a determination to serve God and Mammon." At the end of these several thousand tormented words he wondered whether even this record was for good or evil. Or was it merely another subtle aspect of sophism?

Simply, this self-examination can be regarded as the testament of a man of strong sexual instincts in the prime of his life—Gladstone was thirty-nine years old—who was suffering from severe frustrations. But there was nothing simple about the dilemma for Gladstone, and by the free will which God had given him, he had to find a solution without crashing through the barriers of the civilised society based on defined Christian ethics in which he so profoundly believed, and thereby hurting his sweet Catherine and his beloved children. And he was well aware of the immediate barrier into which he might crash and thereby definitely hurt Catherine, namely adultery, or in his own words, "the allowing and entertaining of positive desire." He had attempted to sublimate his desires by reading pornography but apart from the fact that this also entailed a serious sin and was part of "that which is called *delectatio morosa*" (thinking of evil without the intention of acting) and was adultery in the heart, pornography was not proving a satisfactory counterexcitement. He had already started to fall back on the excitement which had stimulated him occasionally since his Oxford days, namely personal association with prostitutes. Hence the reference in the self-examination to his corrupt actions no longer being solely inward-looking and confined to himself.

Prostitution was a major social problem throughout the nineteenth century but particularly in the middle decades when the effects of industrialisation and capitalism rampant were being experienced by its under-belly—the poor, the proletariat, the working class, whatever appellation one chooses. Recessions, sweated labour (particularly for the females, who formed a large part of the labour force in the cities), further industrial developments—for example, thousands were uprooted by the building of the rail links and termini—made prostitution the only means of earning or supplementing their income for many women. Gladstone noted a conversation with a poor creature who "has a son to support; & working *very* hard with her needle she *may* reach 6/- per week as maximum; pays 5/- for lodging—sends her boy to school at 6d a week." In the early 1850s a figure of 50,000 prostitutes was given for the metropolitan area, and in 1857 *The Lancet* published figures which said that one house in every sixty in London was a brothel of some sort. That equalled six thousand brothels with an estimated labour force of 80,000 prostitutes. When Henry Mayhew published the fourth volume of his investigations into the conditions of *London Labour and the London Poor* in 1862, he also gave the figure of 80,000 and said that the number of disorderly prostitutes in custody had risen from 2,502 in 1850 to 3,734 in 1860.

By no means all prostitutes were disorderly. Mayhew divided them into three categories, the first being the high-class kept women (some of whom became famous) with their villas, carriages and gorgeous clothes, the mistresses of successive or simultaneous rich gentlemen. The second category included the women who rented rooms and maintained themselves, or tried to, in the area surrounding Piccadilly; who met at one of the well-known rendezvous, Kate Hamilton's or the Argyll Rooms; who paraded in the late afternoon up and down the Haymarket or in the Burlington Arcade, "rustling in silks and satins, and waving in laces." The third category included the brothel dwellers and the older, worn-out women who inhabited the warrens off Oxford Street and the notorious Seven Dials area round Leicester Square and Covent Garden, and virtually everybody operating in the East End. Mayhew, who was one of the first to lay the blame on the social and economic exploitation of the female, also stressed how transitory the prostitute population was. At any given time, only a small percentage of the thousands involved were there by choice or intent, and this large floating population provided a fertile field on which social reformers and good Christians—sometimes if not necessarily synonymous—could set to work. The societies to redeem fallen women, to provide them with temporary refuges and to try and find them respectable work (which usually meant domestic service) proliferated. The solution of paying them better wages in their various jobs, including domestic service, was not one which appealed or appeared practical to many reformers, socialist, Christian or otherwise.

Both Catherine and William Gladstone were founder members of a House of Charity opened in 1846 in an old disused workhouse at 9 Rose Street, Soho; she as much as her husband was involved in the attempts to rescue young girls from their lives of sin, if not entirely from the same motives. The establishment was named St. Barnabas and had links with an Anglican sisterhood at Clewer near Oxford, run by a friend of the Gladstones. To Clewer were sent those women who seemed genuinely to wish to reform. One of the first attempts to rescue a young girl was a combined effort by the Gladstones, she being Rebecca Ayscough, who came to their attention while she was in the Millbank Penitentiary in 1842.* It was believed that Rebecca truly repented her past life as a prostitute, and for a period she went to work in the house of the Reverend Henry Manning; but the effort to comply with strict rules and regulations, to be grateful for her current good fortune and continually penitential for her past sins proved too much for Miss Ayscough and eventually after several years it was sadly admitted that the lust of impurity was still within her. The Draconian measures which existed in the various refuges and frequently in the private houses to which the girls were sent were one of the problems that faced their would-be rescuers, but the idea that one must pay for one's sins and that real redemption could only be achieved through suffering held sway. A prostitute told Henry Mayhew that "she knew all about the Refuges. She had been in one, but she didn't like the system; there wasn't enough liberty, and too much preaching, and that sort of thing: and they couldn't keep her there always: so they didn't know what to do with her." This was another problem; the number of people who were willing to take "fallen women" into their employment was limited, and there simply were not sufficient jobs for them other than the underpaid, sweated kind they were already in or had left to become prostitutes in the first place.

At the time Gladstone wrote his lengthy self-examination in the middle of 1848, he told his friend James Hope and noted in his diary that the St. Barnabas House of Charity had become less suitable for acts of charity than it had been. By "suitable" what he meant was that the impersonal, official contact with fallen women was failing to provide the needed counterexcitement, and that he preferred the direct personal action of speaking to prostitutes in the streets near his London home. The Gladstones were now liv-

* Her name is usually printed as Ayscough, though her own signature on extant letters to Catherine looks like Ascough.

ing at 6 Carlton Gardens, a house which had been given them by Sir John, but its position was virtually the same. It lay near the bottom of Haymarket, that notorious promenade for prostitutes, so there was no shortage of young females whom Gladstone could accost or be accosted by. Increasingly, as the shocks and disasters accumulated, it was he who approached them, though at this point Gladstone was still struggling like Laocoön with the serpent to keep his carnal lusts within bounds.

It was in January 1849—before he embarked on his regular associations with prostitutes—that he started to scourge himself, or in his own words, "during the week I made a slight application in a new form of discipline," an application which was henceforward marked in his diaries by a sign resembling a whip. When the information was made known in the publication of Gladstone's 1840s and 1850s diaries that he had indulged in self-flagellation, there was an assumption in some quarters that he was a masochist who enjoyed *"le vice anglais."* But flagellation is a very old Christian discipline, the correlation between pain and pleasure was one to which Gladstone had already given thought and there is no evidence in his diaries that he enjoyed scourging himself. In 1851 he noted that out of "sheer cowardice" he had not recently used the discipline, which *had* proved a beneficial measure against his temptations and impurity; and in 1859 he apparently abandoned it altogether.

Having reached one peak of his sexual frustration in 1848 there was a temporary lull, and that year saw the end of a problem which had caused both the Gladstones anguish over the years—Helen Gladstone's behaviour. By October 1848 Helen was in a cataleptic state, with her hands tightly clenched and her jaw rigidly locked; she was sent to Edinburgh by her father to be under the care of a celebrated nerve specialist, Dr. Miller. What Dr. Miller described as "a bunch of Roman Catholic ladies" was saying prayers by her bedside when her spiritual adviser, Dr. Wiseman, arrived. Shortly afterwards Wiseman advanced upon Helen with a sacred relic—again as described by Dr. Miller, "the knuckle bone of some female saint"—and the miracle was performed; at the touch of the bone Helen's hands and jaw released themselves. Gladstone thought it "dismal that true miracle should be brought into discredit by these notions sheer products of a heated imagination"; his wife agreed and Dr. Miller was equally sceptical, insisting that Helen had been capable of opening her hands and jaw had she wished to do so. However a "true miracle" may be defined, it was a fact that after 30 October 1848, Helen was not only cured of her probably hysterically induced ailments, but she was no longer a drug addict. To throw off an addiction that had lasted nearly a decade almost overnight can be called miraculous whatever the cause, and certainly for the person involved. Thereafter, if Helen was never a well-balanced, fulfilled lady she was no more than eccentric, and a rapprochement with her brother William was effected when in 1849 Catherine invited her sister-in-law to stay in London and she accepted, and the Gladstones allowed their sixth child to be christened Helen in honour of her aunt.

The years of watching his sister under the influence of opium had not only been ones of pain for Gladstone, they had also shown him what could happen when people threw off the bonds of self-restraint. The hurt Helen had inflicted on her family in her wild search for freedom and meaning was a lesson which Gladstone took deep into his heart, and was probably one which restrained him as the urge to shake off some of his own shackles mounted. For the first few months of 1849 he struggled against his carnal desires with a reasonable amount of success, and though much of his attention was focused on the Oak Farm affairs, he was not entirely absent from the House of Commons. In June 1849 a long-standing problem concerning his friend Lord Lincoln reached its head and helped divert Gladstone's mind from his own problems.

Lord Lincoln was one of the more priggish of the band of prigs whom Disraeli said surrounded Gladstone, an intensely solemn, earnest gentleman of strong Tractarian leanings who lacked his friend's elasticity and breadth of mind as well as his capacity to enjoy himself and life to its God-given fullness. Lincoln was also much under the influence of his authoritarian father the Duke of Newcastle—though he had the courage to follow his convictions and defy him on the question of protection. Life at Clumber, the Newcastles' ancestral home in Nottinghamshire, was dominated by the old tyrant and was far from joyous; Gladstone described the "stiff horse-shoe semi-circle" that sat round the fire in the evenings. In 1832 Lord Lincoln married Lady Susan Douglas (a relation of the Lady Frances Douglas whom Gladstone had hoped to marry), a beautiful, highly emotional young girl who sought love, laughter and lightness from life. Both partners tried to understand each other and Lincoln loved his wife to the best of his emotional ability, but it was a doomed relationship and in 1842 Suzy Lincoln left her husband for the first time. In 1843 Gladstone became a guardian to the four Lincoln children, and Catherine looked after them for a while; she recorded, "Oh what an interesting & melancholy sight—poor little Ly. Susan called me 'Mama.'" In 1844 there was a temporary reconciliation but Suzy Lincoln was soon off again, to return home briefly in 1847, by which time she, like Helen Gladstone, was seeking relief in laudanum. In August 1848 she finally cut loose and departed for the Continent in the company of her lover the young Lord Walpole, and Gladstone —to whom her husband unburdened his heart—showed that he had learned tolerance from the years of watching Helen by urging his friend to be understanding and to realise "how laudanum goes to destroy responsibility & unfit people for punishment." By the end of June 1849 Lord Lincoln finally admitted that he had recieved news that his wife might have committed the last act of infidelity.

There was much discussion about the affair privately among Lord Lincoln's Peelite friends, because he was a public figure and a scandal involving one of Peel's high-minded lieutenants was to be avoided if possible. But Lincoln had come to the end of a sad road; his mind was turned towards divorce, and early in July he asked both Gladstone and Manning (by now Archdeacon Manning) if they would travel to Italy on his behalf to beg his wife to return home or, more concretely, to ascertain whether she was living with Lord Walpole and was, as rumoured, pregnant with his child. Wisely, Manning found reasons why he could not undertake the task, but after consultations with Lincoln's lawyers and with Sir Robert Peel, Gladstone agreed to perform the mission. He had Catherine's full support, because she was very fond of "poor Suzy" and laboured under the misapprehension that even at the eleventh hour her husband would be able to persuade her to return home. She sent Lady Lincoln a letter in which she begged her "to follow his advice and listen seriously to what he says. He has no motive but your good: it is that, believe me, dear, which actuates him." Gladstone was probably also actuated by the same reasons that had driven him to Germany in search of Helen three years previously, but in the upper reaches of his mind he set off in search of Lady Lincoln because both she and her husband were his friends and he wanted to save a beautiful woman from her life of shame.

Gladstone sailed for France on 13 July, posting cross country to Marseilles, where he managed to fit in a visit to the opera to hear *Lucia di Lammermoor*. From Marseilles he sailed to Genoa and experienced great difficulty travelling to Naples, where Suzy Lincoln was supposed to be, as Garibaldi's forces had only just retreated from Rome and the countryside was in a state of anarchy. Having finally reached Naples he found that her ladyship had left for Milan so he retraced his steps northwards, only to be told in Milan that she had left for Lake Como. In the city of Como Gladstone had interviews with the chief of police and "Mrs. Laurence's" landlord, but "Mrs. Laurence" (or Lady Lincoln) was said to have moved to a villa at Varena farther along the lake; so he chased there, only to find that she had gone to Bergamo. He bombarded her with letters and at one point managed to approach her but she refused to speak to him. He returned to Como, where he interviewed the doctor who had attended her and received the medical confirmation that she was pregnant. By 9 August he was back in London, having travelled three thousand miles in twenty-seven days without having spoken to Suzy Lincoln.

It was a plot which any farceur would have been proud to have concocted, and it was a mission in which only such a man as Gladstone could have persisted. Despite the only too obvious evidence that Suzy Lincoln had no wish to be saved and returned to her previous existence in England, he continued to hope that he could rescue her, and in the end he collected the proof of infidelity because it was a duty he owed to Lord Lincoln. But it never occurred to Gladstone—or to Catherine—that the mission would be regarded by many as risible, distinctly peculiar or even sordid. He was in some ways guileless, frequently failing to appreciate that he was a public figure and that, as with his speeches, his actions would be judged by their content and effect. While Catherine did not labour under any illusion that her husband was a *Tomkins* (a Glynnese word for a person of no importance), she was little help in guiding his more impetuous gestures or foreseeing the consequences of certain acts. She too had a childlike faith in human goodness, her own disregard for conventions and, after ten years of marriage, a strengthened belief that if her "dear old thing" decided to do something it must be the right course. Sir Robert Peel was among those who shared Catherine's view and who thought that Gladstone had been motivated by feelings of "unparallelled kindness and generosity . . . in the hope of mitigating the affliction of a friend, and conducing possibly to the salvation of a wife and mother." As indicated, it was not an opinion held by everybody, and the full effects of Gladstone's chase from London to Naples to Lake Como had yet to be felt.

Back in England, after reporting to Lord Lincoln's lawyers about his findings, Gladstone decided to go to Hawarden for Catherine's confinement, which was already a fortnight overdue. On 28 August 1849, in the rectory of Hawarden, Catherine bore her sixth child and fourth daughter, a particularly large baby which caused severe pain and some alarm in the last stages of labour. However, Gladstone considered the infant, Helen, to be most promising-looking, and he and Catherine were able to travel to Fasque for the autumn with "6 children in tow." It was while they were at Fasque, enduring rather than enjoying the company of an increasingly excitable and confused Sir John, that early in October they received the news of Suzy Lincoln's confinement. Catherine was spurred into writing one last letter of entreaty to her dearest Suzie (her spelling remained erratic and she would address her son as Willie and Willy in the same letter). The entreaty fell on deaf ears and it is doubtful that the scheme of reformation Catherine had in mind would have appealed to dearest Suzie, for she had already suggested to her husband that Lady Lincoln might go into a penitentiary "where for say a year she could be with a kind, judicious friend and under *good discipline*," somebody for example like Archdeacon Manning, and from which she might emerge "a new woman."

CHAPTER 5

THE CHIEF BURDEN OF MY SOUL

AT THE END OF 1849 Gladstone considered that his inward life was dark, and it grew darker in the next twelve months. The first crisis was already in being as the year 1850 started. It concerned the doctrinal position of the Church of England. The matter went back to 1847 when a clergyman named Gorham was presented by the Crown to a small Anglican living in Devonshire. Gorham had strong Evangelical leanings and did not believe in baptismal regeneration, using the Evangelical argument that if one could be regenerated through baptism, how then were babies with no free will or mind fit to receive it? But baptismal regeneration was one of the thirty-nine articles of the Church of England, fundamental to its creed for the majority of Anglicans, and the Bishop of Exeter refused to institute such a doctrinally unsound clergyman. Gorham first appealed to an ecclesiastical court which found in the Bishop of Exeter's favour, whereupon he took his case to the Judicial Committee of the Privy Council—a lay body, though two Archbishops sat through these particular proceedings as advisers and assessors. The Judicial Committee delivered their judgement in March 1850, and it was a beautiful English compromise which the judges hoped would neither disturb the doctrinally orthodox nor send the Evangelical Anglicans fleeing from the Church. "The Gorham Judgement" stated that the Judicial Committee had no authority to settle matters of faith but only to interpret the legal meaning of certain words in the thirty-nine articles, and in their considered legal opinion the precise meaning of regeneration through baptism had been in doubt since the Reformation, therefore Gorham was entitled to his interpretation and his bishop should institute him.

By its judgement the Judicial Committee had interfered in a matter of faith; it had reversed the decision of the ecclesiastical court and laid open to "interpretation" one of the articles of the Church of England, and the reverberations were immense. As Gladstone told Catherine—their correspondence was filled with the questions raised by the Gorham Judgement—"The issue is one going to the very root of all teaching and life in the Church of England." Indeed it was; protest meetings were held, urging that the Archbishops and Bishops take a stand in rejecting the lay interference, and Gladstone himself attended a meeting at Manning's house. Thirteen men were present and a declaration of protest was signed by all except Judas Gladstone, who was said to have demurred on the ludicrous pretext that he was a Privy Councillor and could not commit himself against a Privy Council decision. Gladstone himself denied the allegation; it was for reasons other than his tender position as a Privy Councillor that he refused to sign. Basically the Judgement had not shaken Gladstone's faith in the essential catholic nature of the Church of England as it had his friends' (notably Manning and James Hope), though he told Catherine that it might force him out of public life forever. Such a crucial Judgement should have produced a stronger reaction and a more vehement public attack, but in effect it was the issue on which Gladstone finally crossed his Rubicon.

At the start of his political life he had been enveloped in his vision of the purified Anglican Church and Tory State acting in Christian unison; Maynooth had brought him to the banks of the Rubicon by demonstrating the impracticality of the idea in present-day politics; he had swum farther from his starting position by accepting that the functions of the State and Church had separated; by his acquiescence in the Gorham Judgement he reached the opposite bank. Thereafter, there was no likelihood that Gladstone the ambitious, supremely able politician would throw over his career permanently or allow his religious conscience to override pragmatic instincts. He continued intermittently to wish to retire into the spiritual life (Gladstone the theologian was always active), but after the Gorham Judgement he concentrated his attention on defining the exact limits of the powers claimed by the Church and yielded by the State at the time of the Reformation, on trying to ensure that these limits were not further eroded and on bringing a Christian influence to bear in political life.

As Gladstone struggled to find the answers to these doctrinal matters, and with the fear that Manning and Hope might secede to Rome, he was summoned to the House of Lords to give evidence in Lord Lincoln's divorce case, what he described as "a most tedious process." (There was then no civil divorce; the applicant had to present a private Bill to Parliament, a costly process available only to the rich.) But the irritation caused by the wretched divorce (Gladstone's own adjective) was swallowed by the far more serious matter of Jessy Gladstone's illness.

For the first three years of her life Jessy was a bright child possessed of a quick, absorbent mind, a large stock of healthy animal spirits and a sweet patient nature—her father wrote, "When there was a question of beds, Jessy was the one who could be knocked out. When there was not room in the carriage Jessy was the one to be left behind." The great delight of Jessy's life was to be with Catherine; she was Mama's girl. In 1849 she started to become so passive and torpid in her behaviour that she was given the nickname of "dormouse"; she clung increasingly to Catherine and then had spasms which developed into convulsions. On Good Friday 1850 Gladstone experienced the first real uneasiness about his daughter's illness, though Catherine had already felt a deeper anxiety, and the deterioration was then rapid, with little Jessy lying in her bed moaning and screaming, her head moving incessantly from side to side. On the following Tuesday the doctors diagnosed "tubercular inflammation of the membranes of the brain" (i.e. meningitis), but the symptoms abated temporarily, giving her parents the hope that she might yet pull through. However, at midnight on 8 April the convulsions restarted, racking Jessy's whole frame, and at two o'clock in the morning of 9 April she died, her last conscious words having been, "I want Mummy." Her father wrote of the last hours, "so many, many gasps, each of which it seemed must be the last; to see her in such an agony of battle, & to be by her side, her parents by her side, and to be powerless to give her visible aid; to feel as we moistened her lips, that it was a mockery . . . this sight was sad, & terrible to flesh and blood."

Catherine bore up until the end and then broke down in passionate weeping, as did the Hamptons and the other servants, and Gladstone was reported as going half-mad with grief, though he gave little hint of it in his personal recollections of those dreadful days. The authority for the statement was his daughter Mary, in a book written many years later, and as she was only two and a half years old at the time she presumably received the information from her mother. In a few lines he penned to Catherine from Fasque, there is the suggestion that Gladstone's grief overcame his iron control and belief in God's will: "not so weak as when I have been with you, and as when therefore I ought to have been strongest"; and there is no doubt that Jessy's death affected him deeply. While he was sharing the last days of the vigil with Catherine, with the obsessive writer's need he kept a journal which he later incorporated into a "Most Private" account of his daughter's brief life and agonising death. It was at Fasque that Jessy was buried, for her father believed that she had loved the place dearly. He travelled to Scotland with the coffin and "no other company than the thought of her who seems incessantly to beckon to me & say 'come Poppy come.'" Catherine had the other children to attend to, and her husband's wish that the body should be buried five hundred miles from the place where it had died meant that she could not attend the funeral. Gladstone sent her a long, detailed account of the interment in the chapel at Fasque and told her how kind and tactful his sister Helen had been in asking his permission to attend the Anglican funeral service (she being a Catholic). Catherine wrote back slightly incoherently, assuring him, "my spirit was with you . . . sweet blessed Jessy your task is now done . . . longing and longing to be there, *at times* feeling cut off from you—but not really 'so safe' 'safe' I hear your voice saying 100 times over . . . it seems a sad silence now more than ever when my heart if it is possible clings so to you—clings doubly, our hopes & fears have been so completely one."

However much Catherine's heart was clinging to Gladstone, and though she told him that she could not bear to be parted from him, as soon as he returned from his sad journey to Fasque they were again separated, for she went to Brighton with the children for several weeks. She had reasons for her visit; her daughter Mary's eyes were in a very bad state and it was feared that she might go blind; to make matters worse the child developed whooping cough (which had been sweeping through the Lyttleton and Gladstone children), and Catherine was convinced that both afflictions were more likely to be cured away from the unsalubrious atmosphere of London. In fact the Brighton sojourn had been arranged earlier; Gladstone had given her carte blanche to rent a house (and she assured him that she had found a nice *cheap* one). But at this moment in 1850 he wanted his wife and children with him, as he indicated in a letter to Catherine: "I am not prepared to question the propriety of your staying in Brighton though the leaning of my wishes was otherwise."

Catherine herself was, not unsurprisingly, in a low state and a relative wrote of her in Brighton, "Dear Pussy looks much worn and sits very silent when there is general conversation going on." She had watched Jessy die in agony, the threat of blindness hung over Mary and there was the heart-rending misery of listening to the other children's chatter, particularly Mary's, as she was not old enough to understand that her sister was dead. Mary, who was a precocious and positive child, kept saying, "I do want to see Detty; I must," and "Naughty people, to take Detty away." In addition Catherine's eldest son had been sent away to school for the first time and she had written, "I do miss Willy sadly even more than I expected really it feels as if I had lost part of myself." As he was a sensitive, conscientious but not overbrilliant child she worried about his ability to cope in the outside world, though the worry did not make her question the convention that upper-class English children should be sent to boarding school. She also fretted about her husband's political position; when there was a parliamentary upheaval early in 1850, then when Sir Robert Peel died suddenly in the summer and the question arose who should lead the Peelites or how they should act, Catherine urged her husband to be decisive: "I would like you to stand up grandly & rally yr members about you! . . . what crude remarks but I have some large ideas." But Gladstone continued to insist that his duty in Parliament was to remain independent, and that there were many obstacles to the formation of a new party with himself as leader, not least of which was his lack of social position and wealth.

Catherine perhaps stayed overlong in Brighton because the fresh breezes and the quietness of the town provided *her* with some much needed relief, but it was while she and the children were on the Sussex coast that Gladstone embarked on his regular street conversations and deeper private involvement with individual prostitutes. One feels that it was partly the sexual frustration, partly the cumulative outside stresses and to a certain extent Catherine's absences which drove him to seek this counterexcitement; when she returned to London the references to the conversations with unhappy women ceased temporarily. Despite the inner stress, Gladstone's ability to concentrate his mind on other matters was in no way impaired and in June he delivered one of his best earlier speeches in the House of Commons, one which underlined his fundamental belief in a transcendental justice.

The occasion was the famous Don Pacifico debate in which Lord Palmerston defended his highhanded actions in blockading the port of Piraeus and demanding exorbitant compensation from the Greek Government on behalf of a Portuguese Jewish gentleman named Don Pacifico whose house in Athens had been attacked during a riot, and who happened to be a British subject (though some people queried whether in fact he *was* a British subject). Palmerston finished a four-and-a-half-hour speech with a rousing appeal to the House in which he asked whether a British citizen should not, like the Romans of old, be able to claim *civis Romanus sum* and to feel that the strong arm of England would protect him against injustice and wrong. Gladstone blasted the Roman principle: "What, then, Sir, was a Roman citizen? He was the member of a privileged caste; he belonged to a conquering race, to a nation that held all others down by the strong arm of power. For him there was to be an exceptional system of law: for him principles were to be asserted, and by him rights were to be enjoyed, that were denied to the rest of the world." Was this how Lord Palmerston viewed England's role in the world? or should England's policy be to mete out justice to the weak as well as the strong? to exert her beliefs by influence rather than by brute force? The verdict, both of the House of Commons and of the country, was in Lord Palmerston's favour, though Gladstone hoped that the strength of the opposition might not be without its effect upon the tone of his lordship's future proceedings.

At the beginning of July, Catherine departed with the children for Hagley, where her sister Mary provided solace and comfort in the still strong grief over Jessy's death. She recorded "awful journey like the Black Hole of Calcutta," and with her departure Gladstone fell back into his own black hole and again began searching for prostitutes. However, from August until February 1851 he was rarely in London, and the stress and temptation were thus temporarily withdrawn. At the end of August he travelled to Fasque by himself, as Catherine had by now taken the children to Rhyl. There Gladstone found that his father was greatly decayed in mental power and "as to corporal and personal matters it is now all but a case of second childhood." In one of his lucid periods Sir John announced that Helen had become everything to him, though Gladstone considered that she did very little for him and the burden fell on his brother John. After a fortnight he told Catherine that his presence appeared to be of little material value to his father and afforded equally little relief to his brother John, and she urged him to come to Hawarden—she was now staying at the rectory—but only if he felt he had done his duty at Fasque.

Gladstone duly went to Hawarden and after a brief visit to London, during which he looked in vain for one of his young prostitute friends and became extremely depressed about "the darkening prospect" of Manning's Anglican faith, he returned to Hawarden, where Henry Glynne's wife Lavinia was being nursed by Catherine in what proved a fatal illness; at the funeral Gladstone again noted that Catherine was "the prop and centre of all the rest." Three days after the funeral, on 18 October 1850, Gladstone, Catherine, Mary and Agnes departed for the Continent. Their destination was Naples and their objective was to spend the winter in a mild climate in the hope that it would benefit Mary's eyes.

The Gladstones travelled to Naples by the cheapest possible means—third class on the new French railways, for example—and when they arrived in the city on 11 November they rented an apartment rather than stay in an hotel, though Gladstone said this was because Catherine preferred the freedom and space. To say that he was financially mean would be untrue, but he had his innate frugality, believing that luxurious living was unnecessary and unchristian (though he had no objection to it among the aristocracy whose homes he frequently visited) and that the individual —and the State—should exist well within their incomes. When writing to Catherine in the months after Jessy's death he could not resist gently reprimanding her careless financial habits: "I am very thankful for your letters and will continue to have them on any terms but I suggest your not letting the habit of sending them unpaid which is now so frequent grow or continue." His own income had of course been reduced by the Oak Farm losses and the endeavours to clear the debts, to the extent of £1,700 per annum or one third of its total, so there was the extra need to be careful. Catherine fully supported, if she did not always put into practice, her husband's views on the comparatively austere life.*

The object of the journey was personal but Gladstone soon found himself drawn into the Neapolitan political scene. In 1850 Italy was a conglomeration of states which were mainly under the suzerainty or direct domination of Austria, with Naples forming part of the Kingdom of the Two Sicilies ruled by the Bourbon King Ferdinand. Two years previously in 1848, the European year of revolution, King Ferdinand had reluctantly agreed to the establishment of a constitution in Naples which granted a minimum amount of civil liberties to its population, but in practice he had arrested those who had tried to implement the constitution or had in any manner opposed his rule. When Gladstone arrived in Naples the gaols were groaning with political prisoners and when he made the acquaintance of James Lacaita—an Anglo-Italian who was the legal adviser to the British

---

* The value of money in nineteenth-century Britain is obviously a vast, complex and variable subject. As a rough guide for the 1850s: at one end of the scale agricultural labourers were existing on £26 per year; the famous protest song "Eight Shillings a Week" still had validity, and that sum (40p in decimalised currency) worked out at less than £26 per annum. In comparison, Gladstone with his income of £5,100, even cut to £3,400, was rich beyond the dreams of avarice. Set against these figures were the incomes of the landed aristocracy and the *nouveau riche* manufacturers. Gladstone several times commented that he was the poorest man in the Carlton Gardens area, where incomes of £20,000 were unexceptional.

legation in the city—his attention was quickly directed to the mockery of justice at the innumerable trials, and to the appalling conditions in which the prisoners then languished. Gladstone visited one of the prisons and saw "16 prisoners confined in a room about 16 palms in length by 10 or 12 in breadth & 10 in height," permanently chained, given no food and dependent on what could be sent in by relatives. When Lacaita himself was arrested early in January 1851, Gladstone wrote, "One grows wild at being able to do nothing." He consulted Lacaita and Carlo Poerio, a leading minister himself under arrest, about what he personally could do to help stamp out these abominations and restore liberty in Naples, and whether public exposure would be helpful (an earlier British attempt to help Poerio had misfired). Poerio told him that as a conservative regime, the Neapolitan one was dependent on the tacit support of the Conservative party in England and strongly recommended that Gladstone should take action on his return home, as nothing could now make the situation worse.

Gladstone's return was retarded by the purpose of the visit, and even if he had felt he could leave his daughter in his wife's care he was restrained by Catherine's condition. She had been unwell since her arrival in Naples; on the evening of 7 January 1851 she was taken ill, and by three o'clock in the morning it became apparent that she was having a severe miscarriage. A month later she was still confined to bed, she then had a bad haemorrhage and she continued to suffer from what her husband described as nervous symptoms. But on 18 February Gladstone left his wife in Naples, still fairly ill and confined to bed, impelled by the resignation of Lord John Russell's Whig administration and a ministerial crisis at home. Some people felt that Gladstone should have returned to London considerably earlier, but Catherine came as near to censuring her husband as she ever did (the Gladstones were always polite in their mutual reprimands). She wrote to him, "I hope you make the world (who are interested) take in that you left me the very soonest you could indeed I am sure it was a very near question whether you were fully justified in going when you did & it ought to be known that Ld Malvern for instance *almost blames* you for going so much for your staying unnecessarily!" Catherine was not left without friends in Naples, and Sir Stephen Glynne arrived in the city before her husband's departure (though the presence of her brother in a trying situation was an arguable benefit).

On his arrival in London Gladstone was met by an emissary from the Conservative leader Lord Stanley, who was trying to form a Government, and the next day he had a long interview with Stanley himself, who offered him any post in the Government (except his own) and possibly the Foreign Office. Gladstone wrote to Catherine saying that when the news of the ministerial crisis reached her he knew that she would feel "like a hunter not allowed to join the hounds," but she must try to restrain her natural affectionate impatience. Catherine had no desire to restrain her impatience, she wanted William back in office. But the Peelite difficulty in supporting Lord Stanley lay in the old question of protection which he still officially if equivocally espoused (and the Peelites remained loyal to the memory of their dead leader, if increasingly divided in their political views). One of Gladstone's personal difficulties lay in the fact that Benjamin Disraeli had recently if unofficially assumed the role of the Conservative leader of the House of Commons, and the idea of serving under such an unprincipled character appalled him. Lord Stanley had informed Prince Albert that he hoped Gladstone would undertake the leadership of the House of Commons but he did not explicitly mention the subject to the gentleman himself, and with the question of the Commons leadership unclarified, Gladstone and the Peelites held aloof and "little Johnny Russell" and the Whigs scuttered back into office (Lord John was minute of stature).

In the spring of 1851 Gladstone was as much interested in telling the world about the Neapolitan horrors as in his own immediate political position. As the Government remained Whig and his affiliations were Peelite, he turned to the new leader of the group, Lord Aberdeen, who had been Peel's Foreign Secretary and was therefore in a good position to make strong internal representations to the Austrian Government, which had over-all power in Naples. Behind-the-scenes pressure was exerted by Lord Aberdeen but by the beginning of July, four months after Gladstone's return, it had produced no results; without consulting his lordship (though he assumed he had his tacit consent) Gladstone burst into print with a *Letter to Lord Aberdeen* which he had in fact penned in April. To say that the two *Letters*—another one quickly followed—produced a sensation would be an understatement, for here was a well-known Conservative politician condemning the actions of a conservative regime in the most trenchant terms—"this is the negation of God erected into a system of Government." The *Letters* were translated into several languages and were read by the high and the low throughout Europe—Queen Victoria urged her Uncle Leopold to read the ". . . melancholy pamphlets. A fearful but perfectly true picture of what he has seen & he has not told half of what he has heard." Gladstone found himself a hero among radicals, socialists and particularly Italian nationalists, and if their approbation of his action did not immediately convert him to any of their causes, it brought him into contact with the forces of the left and helped push him further along the liberal path. (Conditions in Naples improved slightly after Gladstone's onslaughts had aroused the European conscience, but the government remained a repressive autocracy until August 1860 when Garibaldi and his thousand men crossed from Sicily in their drive towards Rome and Italian unification.)

Soon after his return from Naples Gladstone also made a great speech on the subject of religious toleration. At the end of 1850 the Pope had decided to divide Catholic England into dioceses and to appoint Helen Gladstone's spiritual adviser, Dr. Wiseman, as the first Cardinal-Archbishop of West-

minster since the Reformation. There was an immense uproar, fanned in
this instance by the Whigs; cries of No-Popery rang round the country and
the Whig Government introduced a Bill to prevent the Pope from implementing his proposals. Gladstone did not particularly approve of the Pope's
actions but he disapproved more strongly of the religious intolerance which
had been stirred up and which the Bill endorsed. In a marathon speech in
the House of Commons he said, "The character of England is in our hands
. . . if to-day we take this step backwards, it is one which hereafter we
shall have to retrace with pain. We cannot change the profound and resistless tendencies of the age towards religious libe1ːy. It is our business to
guide and control this application; do this as you may, but to endeavour to
turn them backwards is the sport of children, done by the hands of men,
and every effort you may make in that direction will recoil upon you in disaster and disgrace." As in the Don Pacifico episode the temper of the
House was against Gladstone and the tolerant, and the Bill was passed,
though it was a dead letter and was never enforced.

Catherine and the two girls returned to England in the middle of March
(and henceforward, until she was grown up, Mary was known as "Naples
Mary"), but for various reasons their parents were again separated for much
of the year. At the beginning of April Gladstone was briefly in Paris; he
then went north to Fasque, where his father was fast fading. He recorded a
sad conversation, "Who are you?" "William." "Are you William?" "Yes."
Catherine said she *longed* to go with him, not only so that they could be together but because she loved the old man very much; nonetheless she felt it
her duty to take Mary and the other children to Brighton. Gladstone did
not return from Fasque until May and during his absence Catherine attended the opening of the Great Exhibition in the specially constructed
Crystal Palace in Hyde Park—"a sight so dazzling—one's very idea of
Arabian nights and fairy scenes & as glittering & lovely as anything of the
kind could be." (In the view of one of the many political émigrés in England but one with whom Gladstone's leftward progress did not bring him
into contact, Karl Marx, "With this exhibition the world bourgeoisie erects
its pantheon in the new Rome, where it proudly places on show the deities
it has fabricated.") Early in July Catherine departed for Hagley with the
children for the annual summer holiday at the Lyttletons', and there she
stayed until the end of August.

It was during July, while Catherine was away, that Gladstone reached
the crisis in his sexual temptations and intimate personal associations with
individual prostitutes. He himself attributed the final "loss of all *resolution*
to carry forward the little self-discipline I ever had" to the half-expected but
long-dreaded reception into the Roman Catholic Church of Henry Manning and James Hope, which occurred at the beginning of April 1851. He
said that the last two terrible years, culminating in the loss of his closest
friends, his two intellectual and spiritual props, had really displaced him
and uprooted his heart from the Anglican Church seen as a personal living

Church. They had left him unmanned, unnerved and lacerated "and I may say barely conscious morally . . . They may yet succeed in bringing about my ruin, body and soul." Despite the temporary loss of living conviction, Gladstone's essential faith in the catholicity of the Church of England was untouched; but his very faith made the apostacy of his friends more unendurable and incomprehensible. James Hope to an extent he forgave, as he had kept Gladstone well-informed of his spiritual doubts and increasing belief that the Church of Rome was the only true Christian Church (though Gladstone expunged his friend's name as an executor to his will). But it was twenty years before he had contact with Manning and when the relationship was resumed it was on an impersonal, non-intimate level. He felt Manning's desertion deeply; when he was arranging his letters a few years later he noted, "In selecting Manning's through the long years of our intercourse I again go through the sad experience," and over twenty years later a visit to Chiswick brought "mournful recollections. Manning was at Chiswick." The bitterness and completeness of the estrangement was due to the force and strength of Gladstone's and Manning's respective characters; once their views diverged each was convinced he was right; but Gladstone's pain was as much for the Anglican Church which had been rent and sapped by "the loss of its gems" as for himself individually. It is arguable that if Manning and Hope had not entered the Church of Rome, that if they had continued to provide Gladstone with the solace and stimulus of their friendship, he might have turned back from the path on which he had recently set foot. Yet it seems unlikely, because to them no more than to Catherine was he able to reveal the sexual temptations which assailed him, and he would therefore still have had to find a solution by himself.

The solution Gladstone found was to walk the streets at night in the vicinity of Carlton Gardens, up the Haymarket, into Piccadilly and the maze of side streets in Soho, round Leicester Square and sometimes into Covent Garden, accosting and talking to young girls. (He considered that the nature of his political work, with late-night sittings in the House of Commons and the consequent late-night walks home, contributed to his temptations, the suggestion being that if he had been in regular employment with regular hours he would not have been tempted. But this seems a piece of the sophistry he regarded as one of his main sins.) With those young girls who were willing to listen to him he formed friendships, visiting them in their lodgings, giving them money and sometimes inviting them to Carlton Gardens. How far he indulged himself sexually with certain girls, ones such as a beautiful young woman named Elizabeth Collins who figured largely in the temptations of the early years, remains his secret. To date, the only statement that has been published on the subject is a qualified assertion, made by Gladstone to his son Stephen in 1896 (Stephen then being the rector of Hawarden and acting as his father's spiritual confessor), to the effect that he had "not been guilty of the act which is known as that of infidelity to the marriage bed." What else he might have been guilty of was not specified, and all his sons were conscious that their father had limited himself to this negation.

Gladstone himself was aware of the dubious nature of some of his acts and of the ambivalent motives which might underpin them. After he had spent a couple of hours in Elizabeth Collins' lodgings in "a strange & humbling scene" he immediately returned home and scourged himself; two days later he recorded, "Fell in with E.C. & another mixed scene somewhat like that of 48 hours before," and he again returned home to scourge himself. A week later he spent a further two strange and questionable hours with her and after again returning home to scourge himself he wondered, "whether or not I have been deluded in the notion of doing good by such means, or whether I have sought it through what was unlawful I am not clear." With girls other than the beautiful Elizabeth Collins, whom he described as "half of a lovely statue, lovely beyond measure," he wrote of treading on the edge of danger and of being guilty of weakness, "nor can I truly say mere weakness." The period when he was first indulging in his questionable behaviour with Elizabeth Collins was towards the end of July 1851, and on the twenty-fifth day of the month, the anniversary of their wedding, Catherine wrote to him from Hagley. She said, "Thanking God as I do for a twelfth return of this day which made us one, I tremble to think how great have been my advantages how small my trials & I shudder to think how much better I should be having you for my guide—you who do not know half of the evil done in my life, you who were ever ready to make such excuses for me & to view all I do too partially much." Gladstone replied by return of post, "When you say I do not know half the evil of your life you say that which I believe in almost every case is true between one human being and another; but it sets me thinking how little you know of the evil in mine which at the last day I shall have a strange tale to tell . . . Self examination is a mournful task especially in one who feels himself made up, as I do, of strange and sharp contrasts . . . I will not tell you my beloved that you have nothing to strive against; but how gladly I would change with you."

The strange and sharp contrasts troubled Gladstone throughout his life, mostly when he was in London and initially when Catherine was absent. His association with prostitutes can be viewed as a supreme example of canting, humbugging, Victorian hypocrisy, undertaken by a highly sexed gentleman who subscribed to the unnatural sexual conventions of the era, lacked the courage of his natural body urges and therefore had to pretend that he was rescuing girls—young, attractive ones too—from their sinful lives while in fact he was obtaining a prurient voyeur's satisfaction, or perhaps more. But nobody strove harder than Gladstone to be truthful and honest with himself or to strip his soul to the core, and if he perhaps underestimated the basic sexual drive of his activities, he was clear in making distinctions between those conversations and visits which were strange and corrupting and those which were not. There was an early encounter with

Elizabeth Collins, for example, after which he did *not* return home to scourge himself because he thought there had been a change in its content. He always believed that he could help the girls, even if he admitted that from eighty he had spoken to in the first few years, only one had been definitely saved. Years later, a woman with whom he maintained a correspondence (as he did with many of them) wrote to him from Leeds saying that encouragement from *him* was a blessing and that when she next visited London she hoped to be able to see him, as she longed "to hear that soft kind voice again." The hope and the encouragement, if not the final desired salvation, that many of the girls gained from contact with Gladstone was real, however ambivalent his motives. What is apparent about his relationship with females—from Catherine to the Elizabeth Collinses and Lightfoots and Scotts and Reynolds whose progress (or lack of) he so studiously recorded, from the higher class of courtesans with whom he later associated to his daughters and nieces—is that he actually *liked* women and found a real enjoyment in their company. Most men prefer the *companionship* of their own sex and Gladstone's comparatively rare liking for, as opposed to lusting after, the female sex, contributed to his association with young prostitutes.

Catherine was well aware of her husband's one-man rescue operations, if not perhaps of the strong sexual desires which underpinned them. He consulted her about several of the girls; on one occasion he came dashing back from Hagley to London with Catherine's full approval in search of a specific girl; from time to time he took girls to Carlton Gardens to meet Catherine; and he advised Elizabeth Collins to seek his wife's advice. She did much of the donkey-work in arranging for the penitential to go to the Anglican Refuge at Clewer. Catherine seems to have had the feeling that her husband's personal crusade was a trifle strange, once writing to him about "your own *peculiar* night work" (my italics), though it must be admitted that at this time she was worried about his health and thought he might be overtaxing it. Generally, there is little reference in her letters to her husband's prostitute operations; presumably, with her buoyant confidence in him, she accepted them at face value, as a necessary Christian endeavour. Gladstone himself remained highly conscious of the dubious nature of these activities, which he soon regarded as "the chief burden" of his soul. The compromise he allowed himself to effect was indeed an unmapped route, fraught with dangers and hidden rocks.

CHAPTER 6

A MOST RIGID ECONOMIST

By the early autumn of 1851 Catherine had become involved in the sort of charitable scheme which increasingly occupied her attention. While her husband was engaged in rescuing young girls, she directed her less stressful energies to the business of providing further refuges, homes and medical relief for the poor. In this instance it was a plan (though nothing came of it) to convert the old foundry at Hawarden into model lodging houses, and she had also started to raise money for the various charities she supported. At this latter task she proved to be a formidable fund raiser—Lord Palmerston sent her a typically jaunty note in which he said that he was willing to support any charity, particularly if Mrs. Gladstone recommended it. Gladstone himself was at Fasque, as his father's condition was visibly weakening, and on 7 December the old man died, aged eighty-seven. Before and after the funeral there were discussions with his brothers about the disposal of Sir John's estate. It was an immensely complicated business which was not finally wound up for years but it was conducted and completed without *too* much acrimony. Gladstone estimated that the value of his father's estate was £2,000,000 gross, £1,300,000 net. Tom, as the eldest son, inherited £151,000, the title and Fasque; John received £277,000; William and Robertson £151,000 each with property such as Seaforth divided between them; while Helen received £50,000 but with the provisos that she should live on the life interest and could only will £15,000.

Helen was not unnaturally resentful about her share of the spoils and the provisos; it was her brother William who was responsible, because Sir John's last will had been drawn up when he considered her the chief burden of *his* soul (before she became everything to him) and it was William who urged his father to restrict Helen's share, as he thought that she would either squander it or donate it to Catholic charities. That she was entitled to make the choice herself Gladstone did not consider a valid argument. The other main source of friction was Fasque itself, as Gladstone loved the place and Tom (or Sir Thomas as he now was) had never shown much interest in it; therefore Gladstone asked his brother if he would sell it to him, but this was one pound of flesh (or masonry) that Tom could claim as his own and he refused to sell the property. Although Gladstone and his eldest brother never severed contact, with the restraining influence of the authoritarian father gone their relationship was even more strained. Eighteen months after Sir John's death Catherine wrote to her husband, "I never read such letters as Tom's—the last has surprised me even *from him*—that is saying a great deal . . . his mind is completely warped & morbid it seems to render him perfectly unfit to judge decently." This was a view which the tenants of the Fasque estate would have supported, for when Sir Thomas moved in to become laird of the manor he was detested by nearly everyone.

With his father's death Gladstone's financial position was much improved, though he continued to regard himself as being far from rich. If this seems an odd assessment—and a century later when the value of the pound sterling has sunk almost as fast as the cost of living has risen, £151,000 remains a healthy sum—in the context of the vast fortunes which lay in private hands, particularly in the hands of many of Gladstone's ducal parliamentary colleagues, he *was* a man of comparatively modest means. The burden of clearing the Oak Farm debts still hung round his neck, leaving the Gladstones in a position "to be utterly overturned by the first storm," as he told Catherine, but with the money left by his father and with other favourable financial adjustments he was able to make a further reduction in the debts, and in 1852 Hawarden Castle was reopened. It officially became the Gladstones' home as much as Sir Stephen's because the trustees who had been appointed after the crash in 1847 still refused to allow him to reassume the legal ownership, and the Gladstones bore the main cost of the upkeep, with Sir Stephen paying a small proportion.

At the beginning of 1852 Gladstone took his eldest son Willie for the entrance examination at Eton while Catherine was on her travels with the other children from Hawarden to Hagley to her Wenlock relations at Escrick, near York. Willie broke down during the examinations and was extremely unhappy in his early days at Eton, and it is a tribute to the strength of his parents' affection for and understanding of him that he was not completely submerged by the experience. By the end of February Catherine was back in London—during her absence her husband had again been involved with Elizabeth Collins and other "poor creatures"—and in early March it seemed that her latest child would be born prematurely; but the doctor predicted, with a high degree of accuracy, that the baby would not arrive until 3 April. After Catherine had experienced two exhausting and deranged nights—the adjectives are Gladstone's—he returned from the House of Commons in the early evening of 2 April 1852 to find that his wife's labour was in its last fierce stage. At 6:40 P.M. a vigorous little boy was born who was christened Henry. The usual problems with the milk followed, but his wife's presence and maternal difficulties did not in this instance stop Gladstone's almost nightly conversations with and visits to the lodgings of various young prostitutes. In May he wrote, "I am surely self-bewildered," and his self-bewilderment continued to be strong for the rest of the year. Even when he went to Hawarden in the summer, the visit failed to provide him with much solace and he noted an extraordinary and for him very unusual sleeplessness. He was struggling on the edge of the black pit, and his tensions may have been exacerbated by Catherine's illnesses, because the seventh confinement had left her very weak. In July she was feverish, in August she was in great distress and the doctor said she must wean the baby, and throughout the autumn months her husband recorded that she was unwell or poorly.

This was also a period of continuing political unrest and instability; with the old allegiance to the Crown or to patrons gone, with the embryonic party loyalty initiated by Sir Robert Peel broken by him, it was the heyday of individual Members of Parliament, and they were able to unseat a Government, or prevent one's being formed, as groups of them saw fit. In February 1852 it was the turn of Lord Palmerston and his supporters to administer a "tit for tat"—as Lord John Russell had earlier dismissed Palmerston from the post of Foreign Secretary, he then made Russell's position impossible and his shaky administration was forced into resignation. Lord Stanley (by now Lord Derby) was asked to try to form a new Government and the Peelites again had long, anxious discussions as to what their attitude should be. But they were more politically divided than ever—Gladstone recorded four distinct shades of opinion among them—and though Catherine wrote to her husband "of the probable impossibility of Stanley's forming a Govt without *you*" (she still called him Stanley), it turned out indeed to be a practical possibility. The new Conservative administration was mainly composed of politicians who had never held office, and it became known as the "Who? Who?" Ministry because the very deaf and ageing Duke of Wellington (he died shortly afterwards) kept saying "Who?" when being told which politicians Lord Derby had selected.

Gladstone said that part of his difficulty in committing himself to either major party at that time lay in the fact that his sympathies had become liberal but his loyalties remained Tory. If the need for loyalty to his father's beliefs had been removed by death, as the Member for Oxford University he had a duty to follow the Tory line. A great deal of emphasis has been laid upon Gladstone's representation of Oxford University and the extent to which it held back his Liberal development, but it did not in effect prevent him from voting or acting in a Liberal manner when he saw fit. Gladstone's ambivalent position in the late 1840s and 1850s can be attributed to the cautious side of his nature, which always had to make its own way in its own time.

Another difficulty which faced Gladstone was who should lead the Whig/Liberal party if it was decided to turn Lord Derby's Ministry out of office. (The Whigs were already thinking about changing their name to Liberal, to give them a new image and attract a wider base of support, as Sir Robert Peel had done for the Tory party by renaming it Conservative). "Little Johnny" Russell had become unacceptable to nearly everybody and the alternative leader, the man who had dominated Russell's previous administration, was Lord Palmerston. The thought of serving under him was obnoxious to Gladstone. With Russell or Palmerston as the choice to lead a Whig/Liberal Government, Lord Derby's Ministry was allowed to remain in office. By November it had become clear that the Conservatives had no intention of reintroducing protection and another attempt was made to persuade the Peelites to join and thus strengthen the administration. Lord Derby intimated that Gladstone was the stumbling block because he refused to serve under Disraeli and wanted the leadership of the House of Commons. Lord Derby told Prince Albert that he was not prepared to sacrifice Mr. Disraeli and further, "Mr. Gladstone was, in his opinion, quite unfit for it; he had none of that decision, boldness, readiness & clearness which was necessary to lead a party, to inspire it with confidence, & still more, to take at times a decision on the spur of the moment, which a leader had to do." Wrapped in his startlingly wrong judgements Lord Derby decided to try and soldier on without the Peelites; and the test of whether his Ministry would survive became the Budget presented to the House of Commons by his Chancellor of the Exchequer, Mr. Disraeli.

Disraeli had many sterling qualities, but as was maliciously if accurately observed, "his mind was not particularly apt to fasten itself on to details," and this was an aptitude required of a Chancellor of the Exchequer. The Budget Disraeli presented at the beginning of December also tried to placate too many interests. It was Gladstone more than any man who destroyed it. In the early hours of 17 December he rose to reply to Disraeli's final speech—a *grand* one, as he generously noted, though he also thought the Chancellor might be under the influence of alcohol—with the elements dramatically attuned to the scene in the House of Commons (a rare December thunderstorm raged overhead). It was reported that Gladstone *bounded* onto the floor of the House but in fact he was suffering from the acute tension which always assailed him, like an actor's first-night nerves, before he had to make a major speech. His attack on the weaknesses and inconsistencies of Disraeli's Budget proposals was regarded as a masterpiece of lucid trenchant oratory, and the speech established Gladstone as a major political force and an orator of the front rank.

The Budget debate of 1852 was also the first time Gladstone and Disraeli crossed verbal broadswords in the House of Commons in a more personal manner (they had spoken against each other before), as two oratorical giants representing opposing styles and beliefs. Gladstone's oratory was composed of long, rolling sentences; John Bright vividly described their general progress, saying that whereas when he (Bright) spoke he struck across "from headland to headland, Mr Gladstone follows the coastline; and when he comes to a navigable river he is unable to resist the temptation of tracing it to its source." The navigation was not always meandering, nor were the sentences always involved—Gladstone could be extremely *concise*, particularly on financial matters. His speeches were shot through with

fire and passion and delivered in a voice of vibrant clarity which soared upwards with the hanging inflections of the old-style actor, paused and then
swooped down to regather strength for the next attack.* Like many powerful orators he had idiosyncracies of pronunciation; he always said "figyures"
for *figures* rather than the normal English "figgers," and he pronounced
many of his "u" sounds in an American rather than English idiom, "consti-
tootion" for "constitution." At his greatest Gladstone wrung the House of
Commons into breathless silence. Disraeli's oratory was in complete contrast: his navigation was usually more direct than John Bright's (though he
could be long-winded), his style was cool, even languid, but when he attacked it was with the deadly accuracy of the expert duellist or, occasionally, of the spitting cobra. At his greatest Disraeli mesmerised the House
with his pellucid flow and delighted it with his sardonic wit.

When her husband made his memorable speech in December 1852
Catherine was en route from Hagley to Hawarden and she told him of the
frantic eagerness with which she clawed at *The Times* on Stafford station
and how thrilled she was to read it. Gladstone himself was less thrilled by
The Times' report, in fact he was deeply mortified by what he considered
to be a mangled abbreviation of his speech, though he also considered that
such mortification was good for his pride. The result of the debate was
the Government's defeat; reluctantly Lord Derby accepted that he had to
resign and the country was once more thrown into a ministerial crisis. The
solution seemed to Gladstone to be a mixed Government which would be
something different from a fusion of parties, and after an immense amount
of bargaining and manoeuvring this was what emerged, with the Peelite
leader Lord Aberdeen at the head of the Coalition. The post finally
offered to Gladstone, with Queen Victoria's strong endorsement, was Chancellor of the Exchequer and he accepted it with alacrity. Catherine remained at Hawarden during these days of intense anxiety, assuring her
husband that she was with him in spirit and begging him to excuse the
unearthly nature of her letters; *unearthly* being a Glynnese word denoting
strangeness.

Gladstone then had to consider whether to move into the official residence of the Chancellor of the Exchequer at 11 Downing Street or
whether to continue living at Carlton Gardens. Having examined the
official residence he immediately consulted Catherine by letter, informing
her that he had been "agreeably surprised with its goodness both as to accommodation and state," that the number and airiness of the bedrooms was
satisfactory, the servants' quarters varied from fair to good, and there were
stables closer to the house than they were at Carlton Gardens. The information about the airiness of the bedrooms was important as Catherine was
a great believer in a plentiful flow of air, particularly in the sleeping area
(she did not approve of too much furniture or carpets in bedrooms as she
thought they sucked up the available air). The information about the ser-

---

* There is in existence a recording of Gladstone's voice but not of Disraeli's.

vants' quarters was important, as neither of the Gladstones wanted their servants living in dog kennels, while that about the accessibility of the stables meant a good deal to Catherine the enthusiastic rider. On the strength of her husband's description she wrote back to say she was willing to move into 11 Downing Street; accordingly on 3 February the Gladstones took up residence, and on 7 February they gave a housewarming party which was a great success. The move into the official residence was accompanied by a prolonged row with Disraeli about the furniture and the robes of the Chancellor of the Exchequer. The increasingly acrimonious correspondence on the two subjects emphasised the growing animosity between the two men. Both of them later insisted that neither actually hated the other, but from the 1850s onwards there was a widening gap between them which was unbridged as much because of personal style and character as of political differences.

The acceptance of ministerial office meant that Gladstone had to stand for re-election at Oxford; though he was again opposed and half-expected defeat, in fact he was returned with a larger majority, which pleased him more than he thought it would. He then proceeded to fail to please many of his constituents: Gladstone the upholder of tradition, the man who had previously opposed any interference with Oxford's ancient charters and institutions as an attack on the liberty of learning, undertook to prepare a Bill which made the university's structure more democratic, and in February 1854 introduced this Bill to Parliament. His acceptance of the need for reform, once he had examined and weighed the evidence, was a further example of the openness of his mind. In the pre-Crimean War period of the Aberdeen Coalition he also tried to reform the Civil Service by throwing it open to competition—entrance then depended on who you were or whom you knew—but in this he was not successful.

It was in his main role of guiding the nation's finances that Gladstone consolidated the position he had gained at the Board of Trade and emerged as a front-rank politician. He brought his immense concentration to bear on the task of preparing his first Budget, frequently working until two or three o'clock in the morning after a day spent at the House of Commons. On 18 April 1853 he presented his proposals to the Commons in a four-and-three-quarter-hour speech which was hailed as a masterly effort; Queen Victoria said she "must write a line to Lord Aberdeen to say *how* delighted she is at the great success of Mr Gladstone's speech last night—which Lord John describes as one of the ablest ever made." Gladstone shared an ability with an earlier great finance minister and fiscal reformer, Sir Robert Walpole, of making complicated, boring financial matters comprehensible and interesting to the layman. He outlined the recipe thus: "Get up your figures thoroughly and exhaustively, so as to have them absolutely at your fingers' ends, and then give them out as if the WHOLE WORLD was interested in them." His Budget was based on sound Peelite principles—a strict economy in public spending, a further revision of tariffs designed to promote industrial productivity and economic wealth, and the maintenance of a healthy surplus by expenditure never exceeding income. His specific proposals were an extension of income tax for a further seven years, and the introduction of a Succession Duty Bill. The former was a bold measure, because income tax was regarded as an unnecessary evil which grossly infringed the rights of the individual, and previous Chancellors, including Sir Robert Peel who had reintroduced it, had proposed it for a very limited period (it may be noted that the supposed home of capitalism rampant was for many years the only country in the world which had a general tax on the more prosperous). The Succession Duty Bill was extraordinarily complicated but in essence it proposed a probate duty on real property, earning Gladstone the plaudits of "the people" and for the first time making the upper classes regard him with some suspicion and hostility as a renegade of possibly socialistic leanings.

On the night of 10 May 1853 the new Chancellor of the Exchequer became embroiled in the sort of incident to which his activities with prostitutes laid him wide open. Gladstone was on his way home from the opera at Covent Garden when at 11:40 P.M. he was accosted by a girl in Coventry Street. After they had been in conversation for only a few minutes, a man approached them, one William Wilson, who accused Gladstone of making improper suggestions to the young woman. The girl claimed that she was afraid of Wilson and Gladstone duly accompanied her to her lodgings, followed by Wilson. Having left the girl Gladstone proceeded towards his home in Carlton Gardens, with Wilson still following and saying he must expose the Chancellor's behaviour "and thus annoy the whole Conservative party," unless of course Gladstone was willing to give him money or find him a suitable government appointment. In Sackville Street Gladstone saw a policeman, whom he asked to get rid of Wilson, but Wilson was unwilling to go and eventually he was taken to Vine Street police station. The incident was reported in *The Times* on 12 May 1853 when Gladstone appeared at Marlborough Street Magistrates' Court to prefer the charge against Wilson of "following and annoying him through Princes Street, St James's . . . and attempting to extort money by threatening to charge him with immoral conduct in St James's." The case was then adjourned for investigation to be made into Wilson's character, but on 15 June he came up for trial at the Old Bailey, where Gladstone had again to give evidence, and he was duly sentenced to a term in the Coldbath Fields prison. Gladstone kept in touch with him there and used the occasion to inform his colleagues that conditions in the prison were bad and should be improved.

Gladstone's comments on the incident were that his conversations with prostitutes were "certainly not within the rules of worldly prudence," nor was he certain that Christian prudence sanctioned them for a man such as himself. However, he did not feel that his aims warranted the imputations cast against him by Wilson, though he thought that the prosecution speech at the Old Bailey went beyond the *exact truth* in stating the high-minded motives and character of the Chancellor of the Exchequer. It is possible that the incident was a put-up job. Gladstone had been operating on a fairly regular basis in a confined area for over two years, and though the days of his nationwide fame had yet to come, he had recently made an impact with his Budget and it is doubtful that many of those working the Piccadilly beat were unaware who he was. Wilson's plan failed—if plan it was —because Gladstone believed in the basically good intentions of his mission (and in this instance the girl had accosted him), and because he was naïve in the ways of "worldly prudence" and would not therefore be intimidated by blackmail threats. The plan also failed to have any repercussions— those newspapers which reported the incident did so briefly, factually and without editorial comment—because with such a figure as Lord Palmerston one of the strong men of the Government and still prominent in society, it was difficult for the new morality to impose its code vigorously and the moral climate retained a breath of the lax, pragmatic Regency air. Thirty years later when the new morality held most of society in its grip, such an incident could have wrecked Gladstone's career.

Whatever views are held about Gladstone's associations with prostitutes, nobody can accuse him of being secretive about them. From the start he strode about the West End undisguised (and he was always a striking figure), and he also operated mainly on the open streets within a mile radius of his home. From the early days the Duke of York steps, which were almost in his own back garden, were a favourite rendezvous for the girls with whom he retained longer-term contact. The lack of secrecy, taken in conjunction with Catherine's knowledge of the "night work" and the number of letters Gladstone wrote to the girls—a prudent, secretive or ashamed man would not have committed himself to paper—underlines the conviction that a sense of Christian mission at least ran in harness with the personal sexual need, or probably outstripped it. The Wilson incident did nothing to restrain Gladstone's activities; on the contrary with Catherine and the children's departure for Hagley in June he more than doubled them and was out in the evenings as much as four times a week.

In mid-August the whole family met on Stafford station—Catherine and the children travelling from Hagley, Gladstone from London—for a journey to Scotland. It was a strenuous journey, including visits to the Duke of Argyll's at Taymouth, Lord Aberdeen's at Haddo and the Duke of Sutherland's at Dunrobin, and the Gladstones, with six children ranging from the ages of thirteen to just over a year, travelled by public transport; not for them the private coaches or trains hired by other members of their circle. The visits entailed a great deal of organisation for Catherine and as usual she jotted down the itinerary on a scruffy bit of paper—one night here, a week there, a night on the boat here, another few nights there. But she managed to get her family to the requisite places at the required times. Despite his meticulous attention to detail, Gladstone left such matters as complicated family journeys to his wife; indeed he increasingly relied on Catherine to get himself from place to place, and there are frequent queries in his letters asking *which* train he was supposed to be catching and *where* he had to change?

At Dunrobin Castle, perched in its spectacular wooded setting high above the North Sea, Gladstone fell ill with that most unromantic of ailments, a carbuncle, and while he was laid up the Duchess of Sutherland read to him constantly. The Duchess was an intimate of Queen Victoria's, the centre of a powerful social circle with mansions dotted round England and Scotland, a formidable lady of good intelligence and strong liberal political views. (The Sutherlands were not regarded as liberal by the tenants of their vast Highland estates—they owned most of the county of Sutherland—many of whom were evicted, often brutally, to make way for the sheep which were considered more profitable.) The Duchess became one of Gladstone's closest women friends, and until her comparatively early death he confided in her almost as much as he did in his wife. Catherine appears to have accepted the intimate if platonic relationship in a pragmatic manner, particularly as the Duchess was an influential lady who could assist Gladstone's political career.

After the Scottish jaunt Gladstone himself returned to London while Catherine remained at Hawarden; by this time their separations had assumed the right balance, which contributed to the success of the marriage. Catherine continued to insist, without doubt genuinely, that she hated their partings, but the cliché that absence makes the heart grow fonder can have a basis of truth, if there is a real fondness on both sides as there was in the Gladstones' case. There were moments when he would have benefitted from his wife's more constant presence because he had not yet come to terms with his nocturnal activities. But the frequent separations enabled Gladstone to sort out his problems by himself, which was the only method he could follow—and with his strong sexuality he would have had some problems however constantly Catherine had been by his side. They also gave him the freedom to enjoy the company of his close friends, male and female, while Catherine was able to function in the environment she enjoyed most—an informal country atmosphere—and to pursue her independent activities. The Gladstones were together sufficiently for their marriage to have real meaning but the breaks ensured that the antipathetic traits in their characters—her vagueness, untidiness and lack of interest in examining matters in depth, his meticulousness, solemnity and intellectuality—did not grow beyond the point of occasional mutual irritation.

On 10 October 1853 the Gladstones were in Manchester, where he unveiled a statue of his revered leader, Sir Robert Peel (in fact Peel was a native of Manchester's twin city of Salford). This was the first occasion on which the Gladstones appeared as a political duo before a large audience in the industrial North, and they were received with enthusiasm, if not on the same massive scale as that accorded a decade later in Newcastle-on-Tyne. It was an occasion which they both enjoyed. Catherine loved the excitement and the crowds, as they provided a welcome, temporary change from the domestic life, but above all she revelled in the acclaim given to *her* William which vindicated her burning faith in him. Gladstone himself found that he could not only control a large unknown audience but could elicit from them a single response, and there was between them and him the invisible bond which leaps across the footlights or courses through a crowded hall, exhilarating the whole auditorium. It was in Manchester in the autumn of 1853 that the actor and the demagogue in Gladstone joined forces for the first time, and that "the People's William" can be said to have made his debut.

The content of the speech was weighty and serious but it was in a way less important than Gladstone's discovery of his ability to sway a mass audience. He spoke of the recent declaration of war between Turkey and Russia into which the other European powers might be drawn. What became known as the Crimean War was for a long time after its conclusion regarded as the most futile and unnecessary in European history, but in recent decades the view has been expounded that it was in fact an inevitable war. It was the view held by Gladstone at the time, if not later. In his speech he indicated that Britain's involvement was not yet inevitable but should she become embroiled it would be on the grounds of the maintenance of the public law in Europe, as Russia could not be allowed to take the law into her own hands and do as she wanted with Turkey.

In November 1853 the Russian fleet decimated the Turkish fleet and the popular hysteria for Britain to declare war mounted, not because most people were interested in concepts of public law, but because the "Russian bear" was seen as an animal which wanted to crush European liberty in its despotic paws and in particular to grab Constantinople (peculiarly, regarded as the gateway to British India). Early in 1854 Gladstone had a long conversation with the Prime Minister, Lord Aberdeen, on the subject of the war and Britain's involvement. The gentle, peace-loving Aberdeen wanted to resign but Gladstone argued against this step, saying that a longstanding quarrel had been brought into the open by the Russo-Turkish war and Britain's involvement would be a defensive measure. Aberdeen rightly said that all wars were supposedly defensive ones, and how could he possibly align his country on the abominable Turkish side? To this Gladstone replied that Britain would not be fighting *for* Turkey but *against* Russia, thereby warning her off for the future. Having helped persuade his leader that Britain should intervene, at the beginning of March Gladstone doubled the income tax from 7d in £1 to the then staggering sum of ½d in £1, on the principle that if wars had to be fought they must be paid for by taxes, not loans. Fortified by Gladstone's stringent financial measures, on 27 March 1854 the British Government declared war on Russia.

While Britain was sliding towards the edge of the Crimean precipice, on 7 January 1854 Catherine gave birth "to a dear little boy, a pair for Henry" in a labour which, again in her husband's words, was "severe—even relatively to the usual meaning of the word in such matters; which God knows is serious enough." The boy was christened Herbert and it was the last time Catherine had to endure her labour pains and the problems with feeding; she was now forty-two years old, and either she passed through the menopause or both she and her husband decided to call a halt. In the months following the birth of the last child, indeed for most of the year, Gladstone was involved with his prostitutes. To give a random sample, on 31 January he "Saw E. Collins who I believe goes on well: a source of real though I must add ill-deserved satisfaction," on 3 February, "Saw Horton; missed Loader," on 4 February, "one piteous & one shocking yet moving case," on 5 February, "Saw A. Loader," on 7 February, "J. Bywater," on 8 February, "Later saw Griffin: no real good I fear," on 9 February, "Saw in evg another such case as last week," on 12 February, "Jane Bywater reported well of, is rescued, & goes to the St Barnabas Refuge." (Alas, Miss Bywater did not remain long, writing to tell Gladstone that if she had stayed shut up she would have committed suicide.) The entries continued for the rest of the year, if with less frequency, and in his 1854 retrospect Gladstone wrote of his need to escape before long "from a sphere of so much temptation so sorely oppressing me," of the sins of wrath, impurity and sloth which assailed him and of his being "exhausted and smitten down . . . able to do nothing for the discipline of soul & body."

There was little evidence of the sloth of which he accused himself. During the year he was engaged in a prolonged row with the Bank of England about the proposals contained in his emergency war Budget of May, in debating his University Reform Bill, in trying to press his Civil Service reforms and in the controversies which surrounded the sacking of a junior Minister and his own Parliamentary Private Secretary. Both men were dismissed on the grounds that they had brought discredit upon their office, and the Private Secretary happened to be the Honourable F. Lawley, a son of Lord Wenlock's and therefore Catherine's cousin. Gladstone was still not a proponent of democracy, but he believed profoundly that the people had the right to demand of their leaders and public servants the highest standards of probity and integrity. Lawley had been gambling heavily and speculating in government stock but though he had not made use of privileged information, for Gladstone his actions and the fact that he was Catherine's cousin made it imperative that he be dismissed. (Fortunately the Wenlock relations shared his beliefs and the family friendship was not diminished.) It was Gladstone as much as anybody who, by his own uprightness and integrity, crystallised and helped establish the code that British public servants should be just and honest, above bribery and corruption.

Apart from the unpleasantness caused by the Lawley affair, there were other family problems and sadness; in February 1854 two-year-old Henry was taken seriously ill with what seemed like Jessy's symptoms, but fortunately it was not meningitis and as soon as he was better Catherine whisked him off to the fresh sea breezes of Brighton. From there in mid-March she was summoned to Hagley, where Lady Glynne appeared to be dying, but there was a respite and it was not until 14 May that her mother died. After the death Catherine wrote to her husband, "I cannot be selfish enough to *bid* you to come here . . . We all feel you should go there [i.e. the House of Commons] if the business requires your presence . . . George thinks very seriously of your burning the candle at both ends—you who work like a dragon 'furiously.'" While one agrees with Catherine's estimates of her husband's work load rather than his appraisal of sloth, Gladstone would have done well to pay more attention to one matter of business in the House of Commons, namely the conduct of the Crimean War. Despite his role in urging a declaration of hostilities he abhorred war and hated the pomp and hysterical glory which engulfed it. Consequently he had tended to turn his back on what was happening in the Crimea.

Gladstone was not the Minister for War but he was a member of the Cabinet in whose hands its direction lay, and that direction was abominably inefficient. The Cabinet was increasingly divided between what would now be called "hawks" and "doves" and was led by a man who hated the idea of war even more strongly than did Gladstone. By October 1854 the split was widening. Lord Aberdeen had had enough and wanted to resign, but it was felt that to do so in the middle of the war would be unpatriotic; there was, moreover, no agreement on who should replace him; therefore duty kept him in office. Then there was Lord John Russell, who was not as unsympathetic a character as Catherine tended to paint but was alarmingly inconsistent in his behaviour, if not in his basic attitudes. At this moment he was claiming that the Government had no defence against the charges of mismanaging the war and therefore should resign and re-form (under his leadership, he hoped, as Russell was also extremely ambitious). Lord Palmerston wanted to ignore any possible charges and get on with the job of fighting the war, and other members of the Cabinet floated between these views or aligned themselves behind one standpoint.

Catherine was at Hawarden for much of October and then again for most of December, and she bombarded her husband with letters exhorting him to stand firm, to bring Lord Aberdeen up to scratch, to get rid of "Little Johnny" Russell. In one letter she demanded, "What is what and who is who?" which with variations—sometimes it was written as "Who's who and what's what?"—was a favourite piece of Glynnese indicating general bewilderment and suspicion. Just before Christmas she wrote of Russell, "I can only hope that the troublesome little man will cut his own throat at last" and again, "I hope something will turn up sooner or later to alter the present state of sham/unearthly/not human Cabinets." Something turned up sooner rather than later and the Aberdeen Cabinet may have regretted its failure to dismiss Lord John in December 1854, because in January 1855 he suddenly resigned of his own volition. He told his colleagues it was on account of the Radical M.P. John Roebuck's demand for a Committee of Enquiry into the conduct of the war, and said that as in his opinion there was no defence he was taking the only possible course and resigning. After much anxious consultation the Cabinet decided to fight Roebuck's motion —Queen Victoria in any case refused to accept their resignations—but when the motion came up for debate a week later the Aberdeen Government was heavily defeated and the Queen had to submit to the inevitable.

Six days of intense anxiety and manoeuvring followed, with the country left without a Government in the middle of a war. First Lord Derby tried halfheartedly to form a Ministry before abandoning the task, to Disraeli's justifiable fury because the feeble failure at a moment of crisis kept him and the Conservative party out of office for most of the next decade. Then an aged but respected Whig leader, Lord Lansdowne, was asked to try but Gladstone refused to serve with him, not because he did not respect Lansdowne but because his conscience told him that as the Member for Oxford University he could hardly accept office under a Whig having just refused to serve with the Conservative Lord Derby. Next Lord John Russell tried, but nobody wanted him, and eventually if reluctantly Queen Victoria turned to the people's hero, the man who from the start had favoured a vigorous prosecution of the war, Lord Palmerston. On 6 February 1855 he succeeded in forming a Government, mainly because Lord Aberdeen called a meeting of the leading Peelites, obviously including Gladstone, and told them that they must serve with Palmerston for the sake of the country. Thus, having refused to serve under a Conservative, having also refused office under a respected Whig, Gladstone accepted it from a man whose character and principles he detested. His conscience was rightly troubled, and after only a fortnight in office he quarrelled with Lord Palmerston and resigned. The ostensible reason for the resignation was Roebuck's continued demand for the Committee of Enquiry, the issue on which the Aberdeen Cabinet had resigned. Lord Palmerston did not want an Enquiry any more than did Gladstone but the House of Commons was more insistent than ever that the Enquiry should proceed and Palmerston said the Cabinet would have to bow to the demands. Gladstone's argument was that if condemnation was to be meted out it should be by the Government of the day and the motion for a Committee of Enquiry was a constitutional encroachment on the powers of the executive and should be resisted on those grounds.

Catherine was on tenterhooks in the days leading up to the resignation; she wrote to her sister Mary, "I have just been sniffing in William's room & find Prince Albert has sent a box.† I also smelt out letters with 'Immediate' on them from Graham and Sidney Herbert‡ . . . Henry and I are sitting tight in my boudoir from whence we can see when the cabinet breaks up.

† A box of ministerial dispatches.
‡ Sir James Graham and Sidney Herbert were fellow Peelites who had joined Palmerston's Ministry; they both resigned with Gladstone.

Then we shall rush to the House of Commons . . . but oh I am not really to be pitied because whatever William decides will be right." The suggestion that she might be pitied indicates that she had no wish for William to resign, but once he did so she gave him her unquestioning loyalty and support. When the country at large, and some friends, expressed their disapprobation Catherine wrote to one of her closest friends, "To doubt William's sense & judgement seems to me altogether extraordinary. He says that if he is wrong he must be extremely wrong; there is no medium . . . If William has not got sense and judgement I don't know who has." Gladstone himself was more liable to admit that his sense and judgement were not infallible and years later he listed his resignation in 1855 among his "Recorded Errors," then correctly assessing that either he should not have joined Palmerston's Ministry or, having allowed himself to be pushed into it, he should have supported it and tried to effect his beliefs from inside, not outside, the Cabinet. When Gladstone actually resigned he underestimated Lord Palmerston's talent, toughness and ability to survive, and in this view he was not alone. Most people (in power that was, not the general public) regarded Palmerston as a stopgap Prime Minister thrown up by the exigencies of the hour, and Disraeli made his famous, witty but ill-judged assessment: "At the best only ginger-beer and not champagne; and now an old painted pantaloon, very deaf, very blind, and with false teeth which would fall out of his mouth if he did not hesitate, and halt so, in his talk." The "old painted pantaloon," who admittedly was seventy-one years old, amazed everybody not only by pursuing the Crimean War to a victory which satisfied popular opinion, but by remaining Prime Minister, with only a brief disappearance, until his death eleven years later.

CHAPTER 7

A LONG COUNTRY SOJOURN

HAVING ATTRACTED a good deal of opprobrium by his resignation Gladstone proceeded to attract more by launching into a campaign for peace negotiations with Russia. He felt that in the last twelve months the public law of Europe had been vindicated, Russia was now willing to make concessions, the struggle in the Crimea had become futile and appallingly wasteful of human life, and therefore peace should be effected. Gladstone was faced with two major obstacles to a wide appreciation of his stance: public opinion, which wanted its revenge on Russia and in particular the capture of the long-besieged Sebastopol before it would think of peace; and his own behaviour. He had been a member of the Aberdeen Cabinet which had declared war; he had joined Lord Palmerston's Ministry; he had then resigned on a fairly technical point and without stating that he favoured peace. His behaviour seemed at best that of a high-minded gentleman whose scruples of conscience were hard to follow; at worst that of a sophist who had turned tail in mid-flight. His popularity sank to a very low level and some people thought the last had been seen of Mr. Gladstone as a front-ranking politician.

However, there was one result of his emergence as a peace prophet in the comparative wilderness which had beneficial long-term effects, and that was his association with Richard Cobden and John Bright. The most famous partnership in the nineteenth-century English political arena, they had led the Anti-Corn Law League to victory. Both men were strong Radicals, Free Traders and pacifists (for Cobden in particular free trade and peace were synonymous), and they had led the small but articulate anti-Crimean War faction from the start—in 1855 Bright made one of his most famous speeches, proclaiming, "The angel of death has been abroad throughout the land; you may almost hear the beating of his wings." Inevitably Gladstone's newly declared stance brought him into contact with them, and though they did not immediately develop close political relationships, the influence of Cobden and Bright on the final stages of Gladstone's transformation from Tory caterpillar into Liberal butterfly was not inconsiderable.

If her husband's behaviour during the Crimean War was not the happiest or best-arranged of his career, Catherine's involvement in another side of the war was similarly unfortunate. From the start she and her older nieces and daughters—Agnes was by now twelve—were busily engaged in the accepted female wartime activities of knitting mufflers, sewing shirts, collecting contributions and sending off parcels to the front. But as always Catherine longed to be more actively involved, to be of some practical use, and as the conditions in the hospitals became known she threw her energies into raising funds, selecting and equipping a party of volunteer nurses. Unfortunately, the party which Catherine chose to back was led by a lady, Mary Stanley, who had ulterior motives, and it did not have the approval of Miss Florence Nightingale, who had already reached Scutari before Mrs. Gladstone started her efforts. Mary Stanley was supposedly a friend of "dear Flo" but in effect she wanted to steal some of the limelight she considered "dear Flo" was hogging, not only for herself but for the Roman Catholic Church, which she was on the point of entering. Miss Nightingale had more than enough problems in the Crimea dealing with the entrenched hostility of the military doctors without the appearance of another group of nurses led by a rival, and the newcomers received short shrift from that determined and if necessary ruthless lady. Catherine was soon the recipient of indignant letters from Mary Stanley complaining of Florence's behaviour (she was no longer "dear Flo"), and more pathetic ones from innocent members of the party who could not understand why their services were being ignored. Eventually, she received a long explanatory letter from Miss Nightingale herself and as she told her sister Mary, "After all the trouble and all the care here it seems that Miss N. had managed the doctors with enormous tact and had got over all their jealousy *but she had promised that no more nurses should be sent!* Forty-three arrived, and her breath was taken away." Catherine decided that a peace offering was required and she accordingly had sent out to Scutari a thick, warm dressing gown to help protect Miss Nightingale in the bitterness of the Crimean winter. Gladstone frequently placed himself in a difficult position because of the ramifications of his thought processes, which made so many problems not two-sided but hexagonal, but in Catherine's case it was the lack of considered thought or due enquiry which got her into trouble.

The years 1855 and 1856 were among the more domestic of the Gladstones' life, which is not to say that he withdrew from public life, and until a peace treaty was finally signed in March 1856 he was involved in the efforts to end the Crimean War. After two years as the wife of the Chancellor of the Exchequer Catherine found the quieter life unstimulating and unsatisfactory; she wrote to her sister Mary, "What an ebb it all is!," *ebb* being a Glynnese word meaning something low or degrading to a sad and ludicrous degree. Gladstone himself was far from being fully contented, because one matter about which he had no cant or hypocrisy was the desire of public men for office. At this moment, when he held Lord Palmerston in the lowest possible esteem, he said one of the few things he admired about the gentleman was "the manly frankness of his habitual declarations that office is the natural and proper sphere of a public man's ambition, as in that he can most freely use his powers for the common advantage of his country." (The latter sentiment was perhaps more typically Gladstonian than Palmerstonian.) Gladstone was still occasionally assailed with doubts—though less frequently than in former years—about the validity of his public role and whether he might serve God and himself better by retiring into the spiritual life, but while he remained in the political arena he freely admitted that he hungered for office.

Despite the lack of political fulfillment, neither of the Gladstones was given to bewailing their lot; to Catherine introspection was an unknown word and she had the convictions of William's rightness and judgement to comfort her, while he turned his mind to other activities and engrossed himself in them. Towards the end of June 1855 a domestic matter arose which had long-reaching implications, when Sir Stephen Glynne decided to alter his will. Catherine and Gladstone had several long, troubled conversations on the subject because the essential part of the new will was that their eldest son, William Henry Gladstone, would become the heir of the Hawarden estate. Gladstone felt that Sir Stephen was right to prevent the cutting up of the estate after his death (and it was now accepted that Stephen himself was unlikely to marry) but he was worried that Henry Glynne's daughters had been unfairly treated and that no account had been allowed for Henry's male issue. (Not that Henry Glynne had male issue, but there was the possibility that he might remarry and produce a son.) Gladstone thought the whole will touched "both honour and justice very nearly," but for once Sir Stephen was firm that this was the way he wanted matters arranged, Henry Glynne was not perturbed and in September 1855, when the will was legally witnessed, fifteen-year-old Willie Gladstone became the heir to the still heavily encumbered Hawarden estate.

While her husband was involved with her brother's "testamentary arrangements," Catherine herself was at Hagley nursing Mary Lyttleton, who was pregnant with her eleventh child and was in a low, depressed state. Mary was like her sister in many ways; she had the ability to take things in her stride, she was affectionate and disorganised and she was extremely untidy—in the Glynnese language there were two clearly defined types of rubbish, *Offal* and *Groutal*, *Offal* equalling "All Mrs. Gladstone's drawers," *Groutal* equalling "All Lady Lyttleton's drawers." But Mary did not possess her sister's iron constitution, ambition and buoyancy; she had a more passive strain which in times of depression came near to fatalism. By 1855 Mary was forty-two, had borne ten children and was, to use another Glynnese word, *pompe*, that is, pumped out, jaded, exhausted. Catherine arranged for her sister to come to Carlton Gardens for the actual confinement later in the summer, so that Mary could have the best possible medical attention and her presence throughout the ordeal she dreaded, and a baby boy was duly born without disaster. However, after the birth the doctor said that the mother's physical condition was alarming and that under no circumstances should she have another child as it would surely kill her. There is a conflict of evidence as to whom he gave this information—Mary herself, Catherine or the Dowager Lady Lyttleton—but it is certain that nobody told George Lyttleton. Whether he would have believed the information had he been given it is a moot point—he was not, and Mary again became pregnant.

However, it was two years before the tragedy ran its course, and in the early autumn of 1855 Gladstone and his eldest son Willie went on a strenuous holiday in North Wales, on one occasion walking forty miles from Barmouth to Dolgellau and on another falling in "with a self sufficient but benign forward & intelligent pedlar; most warlike," who made the journey considerably more entertaining. The advance guard was soon joined by the rest of the family at Barmouth, though Gladstone noted that "C & co arrived very late after all sorts of miscarriages," which showed that Catherine's organisation of family journeys had their limitations. The whole family enjoyed themselves bathing in the freezing waters of Cardigan Bay and they struggled most of the way up Cader Idris and Snowdon—not that it was a struggle for Gladstone or the older boys to reach the summits but it was for Catherine and the girls—and he wrote of his and Catherine's "rare treasure" in their children. Gladstone was frequently said to have a splendid wide-ranging knowledge of mankind but very little understanding of individual men (or women); in his assessments of his children's characters, wants and needs he showed good judgement. When Mary was hardly more than a baby he commented on her extraordinary responsiveness to music, which was then encouraged; he understood Willie's conscientious sensitivity well; he was appreciative that Stephen's rather withdrawn nature contained "an outright earnestness of purpose" and had a suitably solemn conversation with the boy, who was not yet twelve years old, when he announced that "he would like to be a clergyman if he could see how to manage the sermons." Herbert and Henry were still too young for much assessment and Gladstone had not a great deal to say about Agnes, a placid, beautiful child who caused the minimum amount of problems, but on Helen's seventh birthday he noted that she was "an eminently earnest child, with deep feelings, & rapid & strong perceptions." Gladstone sometimes understood his children better than Catherine—she tended to overestimate her sons' abilities (particularly Willie's) and underestimate her daughters' (particularly Mary's).

During 1855 much time was spent arranging Gladstone's books at Hawarden, already over six thousand of them, some of which had come from Fasque, others from Carlton Gardens. The room which was designated for the library became famous as "The Temple of Peace," his special sanctuary with its long windows looking towards the ruins of the old Celtic castle; with dozens of children around the house—Gladstones and Lyttletons—Gladstone needed a *sanctum sanctorum.* Queen Victoria later commented acidly on the degree to which her Prime Minister allowed his wife and children to be around when he was dealing with political matters, a degree which might be commendably domestic but was hardly business-like. The comment might seem surprising from such a well-known upholder of domestic bliss, except that by the time Her Majesty made it (1881) anything Mr. Gladstone did was bound to be wrong, while in the mid-1850s she still approved of his home and political life.

Gladstone's major preoccupation during 1855 and 1856 was his study of Homer, which he had begun nearly a decade previously, and in August 1855 he noted in his diary, "Began work on the Iliad: with serious intention of working out something on old Homer if I can." His practical approach to the task was interesting: "Worked on Homer: with scissors & otherwise, having obtained waste copies for the purpose," and "Finished my scissor work upon the Iliad." The results, which were presented to the world in 1858 in three volumes as *Studies in Homer and the Homeric Age*, had as the main thesis the contention that the doctrine of the Trinity was foreshadowed in Homer. It was a thesis which caused reactions varying from bewilderment to merriment to contempt; Tennyson thought he was "a little hobby-horsical" upon the subject while another friend if fairly trenchant critic, Lionel Tollemache, said that his invention of "the Athanasian Iliad" was "the sorry refuge of the theologian at bay." Riding the hobbyhorse of the Hellenic Trinity gave Gladstone an immense amount of pleasure and satisfaction, and he was perhaps not so much a theologian at bay as a naturally industrious religious man endeavouring to find an underlying unity in Western man's recorded search for a spiritual meaning to life.

During 1856 the Gladstones moved into a new London house, in fact back into Carlton House Terrace, but this time it was number 11 and it remained their London home for nearly twenty years. There were also long stretches of domesticity at Hawarden, and the children often presented plays, with Catherine as their enthusiastic producer-cum-stage-manager-cum-dresser. Their father thought Willie, Agnes and Helen showed the most dramatic talent in a play called *Where Shall I Dine?* and that they all gave creditable performances in a version of *Blue Beard* performed in French. With the acquisition of an excellent French governess, Madame Bourgeau, French reigned supreme at the dinner table at Hawarden— Catherine spoke and wrote good if slapdash French, so everybody was able to participate in the conversations—and the children's command of the language increased accordingly. (Not all the Gladstones' governesses were such happy acquisitions; a Miss Browne had earlier been dismissed after a series of crises for being far too hard, and other termagants were yet to arrive.) There were some tremors: in July Stephen had two operations which, as was then the custom for the affluent, were performed at the Gladstones' home in London, and in October Catherine received an alarming "telegraphic message" from Hagley which caused her husband to drive her posthaste into Chester to catch the first possible train. The reason for the alarm was of course that Mary Lyttleton was again pregnant and was showing distressing symptoms of exhaustion, with particular concern about the condition of her liver and kidneys.

Catherine herself was not in the best of health at this time, and she probably had the knowledge that Mary was unlikely to survive the strain of the actual confinement. In addition, most of the staff at Hagley was ill, the Lyttleton finances were at an even lower ebb than usual and George Lyttleton was useless at a time of crisis (Catherine wrote of his *unearthly* manners in sickness). However, she managed to get her sister back onto her feet and after a Christmas spent at Hawarden the whole Gladstone family descended on Hagley for the usual New Year visit. It was a particularly happy one and the atmosphere at Hagley was even more informal than at Hawarden. The Gladstone household was far from being stuffy but there was an underlying earnestness of character in the family, whereas the Lyttletons had an insouciant vivacity and a native wit that gave their approach to all subjects, even the ones they took seriously, a positive joy. Matters which they regarded seriously included religion and cricket; they adored playing cricket as much as going to church, and when it was raining cricket matches were frequently held in the long gallery at Hagley with the ball whizzing past the art treasures. It can be said that the Lyttletons represented English amateurism, being intelligent, amusing, confident, inventive, aware of the ridiculousness of life but somewhat casual and indolent, while the Gladstones (with the exception of Catherine) represented English professionalism, being serious, hard-working, efficient but lacking in humour and, to a degree, confidence. (The cult of the amateur has always tended to overwhelm and undermine the professional in England.) After the happy family New Year, Catherine went briefly to London and then Hawarden before returning to Hagley, where on 7 February 1857 Mary Lyttleton survived the birth of her twelfth child and temporarily it seemed as if all might be well.

These two comparatively quiet domestic years did not stop Gladstone's associations with prostitutes. When he was in London he was out in the evenings, sometimes only once a week, sometimes considerably more. When he was at Hawarden he wrote regularly to such of his young friends as were literate (and a surprising number were), and on one occasion when he walked to the old family house at Seaforth he found himself passing through "an extraordinary district" which attracted his attention (though he does not seem to have spoken to any of its inhabitants). His assessment of his character continued to be troubled: on All Saints' Day 1855 he wrote, "how deeply unworthy I am of the company of those whom it celebrates . . . Again I find feebleness & timidity for duty, & a disposition to Epicurian self-indulgence is growing upon me . . . the time for trying to brace myself has arrived"; and in the year's birthday retrospect he prayed to be delivered from the pit of corruption and for his sins to be cast behind his back. When he had to speak seriously to "little Lena" (Helen) he thought, "it seems so hollow to speak to her of her sins and pray with her, & then think of my own." In his 1856 birthday retrospect, while he considered that a long, unbroken country sojourn had been a great spiritual mercy, he also thought, "But my soul is still disturbed by the waves, & divided in the service of many matters; the anchor is not yet surely out." Despite the moral flagellation (physical flagellation was limping towards its end), there was a less desperate edge to Gladstone's introspections, and in the 1855 All Saints' Day entry he also noted, "In the point perhaps of all my worst this year shows perhaps a faint improvement as compared with the last four"; in the birthday retrospect he similarly recorded, "I see amidst a flood of evil some miserable snail paced movement towards what is better."

In the spring of 1856 and then again at the end of the year Lord Derby renewed his overtures to Gladstone in the well-worn groove of his rejoining the main body of the Conservative party, and for a time it looked as if he might actually take the step. Several meetings occurred between Gladstone, Lord Derby and other leading Conservatives and Disraeli even invited his rival to a dinner party to discuss the matter. The same problems remained— Disraeli's personality, the extent to which he was imposing his principles (or lack of them in Gladstone's eyes) on the party and his leadership of the House of Commons—and while Gladstone now fully accepted that Disraeli could not be dislodged from the leadership without his consent, it was the position he wanted. There were also, if less explicitly at this moment, Gladstone's liberal drift and progressive ideas. The overtures were widely bruited—several newspapers decided that Mr. Gladstone would rejoin the Tories, take over the leadership of the House of Commons and make the party a viable machine with which to dish the Palmerston Whigs—and when the parleys fell through yet again there was a loud outcry against the impossible, dithering, conscience-ridden Mr. Gladstone perched on his remote Olympian heights. As the strains of the overture became disharmonious Catherine wrote to comfort her husband and to assure him that she understood his motives; at the same time she indicated that her trust was just occasionally less than implicit by telling him, "I do hope you are not playing tricks while cats away & that you sleep enough."

The beginning of March 1857 saw an unusual parliamentary front opposed to yet another of Lord Palmerston's Chinese ventures, unusual in that it included the Tory Disraeli, the Peelite Gladstone and the Radicals Richard Cobden and John Bright (among others). A Chinese-owned, largely Chinese-manned vessel had been engaged in smuggling and acts of piracy in the Canton River and was seized by the Chinese authorities. But it happened to be flying the British flag (if with doubtful legality), therefore the British representatives in Canton and Hong Kong immediately demanded the release of the vessel and its crew, together with an apology from the Chinese Government. To the former demand the Chinese acceded, but they refused to apologise, whereupon the Governor of Hong

Kong ordered a squadron of the British navy to bombard Canton, which it duly did, in the process inflicting casualties on the civilian population. Most of this occurred without Lord Palmerston's authority but when he learned the full sequence of events he gave it his backing. When the House of Commons learned the news, Richard Cobden moved a resolution censuring the Government's conduct and Gladstone made another of his resounding speeches on the subject of international law and justice—"that justice which binds man to man, which is older than Christianity, because it was in the world before Christianity; which is broader than Christianity, because it extends to the world beyond Christianity; and which underlies Christianity, for Christianity itself appeals to it."

The Commons voted in favour of the censure motion—if only by a majority of sixteen—and Gladstone thought the vote brought immense honour to the House. Lord Palmerston thought he had the approval of the majority of the people and immediately dissolved Parliament and appealed to the country. He also in this instance had the approval of Queen Victoria, who wrote to her favourite uncle, Leopold, King of the Belgians, saying, ". . . that men like Cobden & Bright shld do such things is quite fair & they are perfectly consistent but that men like Gladstone (he is almost mad, I think)" should expect their country to kowtow to every other nation and live like cotton spinners she considered quite monstrous. However, she thought the miscreants would all be punished for their sins during the General Election and that Gladstone would probably lose at Oxford. She and Lord Palmerston were correct in their judgement of the country's feelings; many of the anti-war, anti-Palmerstonian candidates were defeated, including Cobden and Bright, though Gladstone was returned for Oxford University. It was not the first time that Her Majesty had commented on Gladstone's possible madness. She had earlier told her Uncle Leopold that all the good people in her Government were a little mad and at this time she included Gladstone among her good people, apart from such aberrations as censuring the conduct of the British Government.

The result of the General Election and Palmerston's subsequent action in ordering a British expedition to Peking, where it burnt the Summer Palace and forced stringent terms on the Chinese, profoundly shocked Gladstone. He became more convinced that Palmerston's leadership was morally evil and he told Sidney Herbert (by now his closest friend) that henceforward he intended to do his duty "only in the ranks" and that he would no longer become embroiled in party politics. While Gladstone nursed his shock and the temporary belief that he had nothing to offer that the country wanted, Catherine was spending most of her time with her sister Mary. In the spring of 1857 she and George Lyttleton were with Mary in Brighton, where it was hoped that the fresh sea breezes would pump life into the exhausted body, but by the end of June they were back at Hagley and Mary was too weak to get out of bed. Gladstone wrote to his wife, "God bless you and sustain you my dearest; you are about an angel's mission where you are," and as hope rose and fell for Mary he again wrote, "Recollecting what was the favourable reaction produced by calomel in the case of our darling Jessy, and how soon the ray was quenched in deeper clouds, I hold myself in." Catherine was by her sister's side night and day but by the end of July Mary could sleep only under the influence of morphine; on 12 August Catherine wrote to tell her husband that she was "all pulled down and suffering," on 14 August she again wrote, ". . . she will receive the Holy Communion either today or tomorrow . . . I do feel at moments that my heart could break when I look at her . . . I fear the dawn . . . oh may we all be given strength," and on 17 August her sister died in her arms.

Gladstone rushed to Hagley to see his sister-in-law the day before she died, but his period as an onlooker in the parliamentary ranks had been brief and during the weeks when Mary Lyttleton was approaching death he was involved in a matter which he said caused him the gravest and deepest anxiety of his career to date, that being the Matrimonial Causes Bill, which was presented to the Commons at the end of the session. The Bill, which aimed to make civil divorce slightly more available to the general public, was introduced into the House of Lords, through which it passed, not without opposition but with the support of the Archbishop of Canterbury; but when it reached the Commons it was opposed by a small group headed by Gladstone. For him it went to the very root of Christian marriage and was an infringement by the State on the prerogatives of the Church which he had to resist with every fibre in his being. As an opponent of the Bill he was not in the strongest of positions, because he had been a member of the Aberdeen Cabinet which had first considered the measure and had not then made any loud protests, and more damagingly he had been a participant in a noted divorce case—it was at this juncture that his gallop through Europe after Lady Lincoln was resurrected to harmful effect. *The Times* said that "the journals of the House of Lords bore testimony to the fact that the Rt. Hon. Gentleman . . . had tracked the wife of a noble duke, who afterwards obtained a divorce, all through Italy and appeared as a witness to her adultery," while the *Morning Post* denounced him as the man "who would deny to the poor that relief which he was the principal means of obtaining for a noble and wealthy colleague."

To say that the restricted terms of the Bill made divorce available to the poor was somewhat inaccurate, and it was the growing army of the middle class, together with the rationalists, who were demanding that divorce should no longer be limited to the very rich (there was also the practical matter that the existing machinery of presenting a private bill to Parliament was taking up too much time). Worse allegations were hurled against Gladstone that he had actually been paid by Lord Lincoln to chase after his wife, and matters reached such a pitch that he felt obliged to make a personal statement in the House of Commons. This he did briefly and with dignity on 14 August 1857, stating that he had only been called as a witness to prove that Lord Lincoln had tried every possible means to regain his wife's affection and that he had *not* been called as a witness to the adultery. The disclaimer was accepted but it did not alter the fact that Gladstone had been involved in a case of the sort he was now so passionately attacking, nor did it strengthen his position in the public eye. Equally it did not lessen his opposition; divorce was unchristian and morally evil and if it became readily available it would shake the foundations of marriage. Gladstone realised that the Bill would almost certainly become law and he fought as hard to modify it as to stop it, in particular objecting to the clauses which penalised the woman.

It would be unwise to cast Gladstone in the role of feminist, but he always believed in the fundamental female right to exert her free will and in her equality before God. In his personal relationships he put his belief into practice but in his public stance he tended to accept the idea that women would lose their spiritual influence if they involved themselves in the sordid affairs of the world, and to dismiss the argument that their position was man-made. During the Divorce Bill debates Gladstone spoke twenty-nine times; he interrupted constantly and argumentatively, and years later he was accused of having in his tactics instituted the method of obstruction which was used so effectively by Charles Stewart Parnell and the Irish nationalists. However invidious Gladstone's position seemed to his opponents, nobody doubted his passionate sincerity on the subject, and after his prolonged and skilful attacks fewer people regarded him as a spent force or an impractical politician.

That year, 1857, was not the happiest of the Gladstones' life and one of the few incidents to break the general gloom of personal tragedy and political abuse was Willie Gladstone's being invited to accompany the Prince of Wales to Germany in the summer. The two boys were close in age—Willie was born in June 1840, "Bertie" in November 1841—they had been introduced as children and while Willie was at Eton he received further invitations to take tea with the Prince of Wales at Windsor Castle. When it was suggested that Willie might be a suitable companion for the heir to the throne on a journey abroad, both Gladstone and Catherine were delighted at the honour and she wrote to tell her husband, "I keep the details regarding the Prince of Wales (of course) to myself." The "of course" was superfluous because Catherine, for all her bubbling enthusiasm and tendency to rush in without due consideration, could be as tight as a clam, and her husband never had any fear that she would be indiscreet about political matters or subjects that had to be kept secret until officially announced. The visit to Germany was a success, though it was the father, not the son, who became a friend of the Prince of Wales, but Gladstone was dismayed to hear from Willie that the heir apparent had been involved in "a little squalid debauch." He wrote to Catherine, ". . . the Prince of Wales has not been educated up to his position . . . It does not give me a bad opinion of him . . . I fall back upon the teachers with whom I hold the fault to lie.

I rejoice that Willy's whole soul loathes the tuft-hunting." The Prince's education had indeed been unfortunate, not because his parents did not care for him but because they failed so lamentably to understand his unscholarly character, and in their efforts to turn him into a second Prince Albert they subjected him to a bewildering series of regimes and denied him the affection that his nature craved. "Bertie" might have been a considerably happier man, less addicted to the "tuft-hunting" which occupied so large a part of his adult life, had he been blessed with Willie Gladstone's parents and received their warmth and understanding in his earlier years.

By the end of 1857 Catherine was in her own words suffering from "a few tiresome antics," an *antic* being another Glynnese word for something —usually small or unimportant—that it was impossible to define precisely or clearly. But Catherine's illness was not unimportant, in fact she was on the point of collapse; she was forty-five, she had borne eight children and suffered the bad miscarriage in the course of fourteen years, all the confinements had been difficult and she had recently nursed her sister to her self-imposed death. Even Catherine's physical resilience had been sapped, but it was Mary's death that knocked her temporarily off balance. Jessy's death had been agonising and terrible to bear, the death of her sister-in-law Lavinia, Henry Glynne's wife, had been another blow because she and Lavinia had been close, but Mary had been a pivot of her life, the beloved sister known from the earliest conscious moments. Queen Victoria recorded her sympathy for Catherine's loss, "I have felt & thought *so much* of poor Mrs Gladstone—having formerly heard & seen so much of her poor sister, knowing her affectionate tenderness for her." Catherine expressed her own anguish in a letter to her niece, Lucy Lyttleton, "The first Christmas without *her* your darling Mammy—Do you know there are times when I cannot believe I shall not see her again I seem to *yearn* so much for her—I believe I am only beginning to take it in & to know that I must tread the rough journey alone."

It was the sixteen-year-old Lucy who increasingly filled the terrible void left by her mother's death and who became perhaps the dearest and closest person in Catherine's life, after William. Catherine was devoted to all her children but some were more equal than others—the first-born Willie and the last-born Herbert were favourites—and with Lucy she developed a special relationship that was not extended to her own daughters, not even to "Naples Mary," who was her mother's close companion as she grew up. The relationship deepened not simply because Lucy was her mother's daughter (Mary Lyttleton produced other daughters) but because she was so like Catherine in temperament. She was more intellectual than her aunt (or at least she disciplined her brain better), she was more organised and she was an even more devout Christian—friends later said that Lucy regarded church as other people regarded the public house—but she had the same physical energy, the same restless ambition, the same ardent nature and the same social concern. What Lucy also possessed was wit, a Glynne attribute which had largely bypassed the Gladstone children (Mary was the main exception and she had a nice line in humour), and this trait probably appealed to Catherine too. Lucy was both the Gladstones' favourite niece—her life was to be inextricably and tragically linked to theirs—and Gladstone himself had a special regard for the beautiful, ardent girl, but it was Catherine to whom "dearest Locket" meant so very much. (Lucy was sometimes called "Locket" after the nursery rhyme Lucy Locket who lost her pocket.)

During January 1858 Catherine was actually confined to bed at Hawarden, a most unusual occurrence for her and one which underlines the seriousness of her unspecified illness. She wrote to tell her husband—he having returned to London for the opening of the new parliamentary session—that she had had a good night despite *someone* being away, and that she was enjoying the luxury of breakfast in bed, though she emphasised that she was mainly staying in bed because it was so cold and she could give the children their Bible lessons from there without fatigue.

Towards the end of February when a fresh parliamentary storm and ministerial crisis broke, Catherine was still at Hawarden, and she could only tell her husband that his letters made up for so much of the bodily separation and how she thanked God that "our dear England's honour should thus be preserved & how thankful I am that *you* should nobly have borne your part!" England's honour had in this instance been put at risk by the assassination attempt of a revolutionary named Orsini on the life of Napoleon III. The attempt failed, but Orsini was one of the many political refugees who had found a safe harbour in England, the bomb used against the French Emperor had been manufactured in England, and the French immediately lodged a strong protest stating that traditional English asylum was being grossly abused and hinting that more stringent laws were required. Instead of climbing on his usual high horse, Palmerston surprisingly agreed and introduced a Conspiracy to Murder Bill into the House of Commons; but for once his feeling for the popular pulse failed him. The Bill was not only vigorously opposed in the Commons, but opinion in the country was loud in its denunciation of Palmerston's tame capitulation to the insulting, interfering French demands. Gladstone, equally surprisingly, bore his part in the opposition to the Bill, on the grounds that the French had implied that the British favoured assassination, a plant which was "congenial neither to our soil nor to the climate in which we live" and that the Bill would establish "a moral complicity between us, and those who take safety in repressive measures." The Bill was defeated, Lord Palmerston promptly resigned and the Queen duly sent for Lord Derby and asked him to form a new administration.

Gladstone's need for Catherine in moments of stress was touchingly demonstrated in a letter he wrote to her at Hawarden immediately after the defeat of the Whig/Liberal Government: "What would I give to have you here or to come to you this night or rather morning! . . . In hours of great joy as well as great sorrow it is very sad to be away from you—I thought of following by the 6 a.m. train four hours hence—but the crisis is important and I dare not." In trying to form a new Government Lord Derby made the usual offer of a post to Gladstone, but as he was reaching his equally usual negative decision he received a long letter from John Bright which indicated that certain advanced sectors of opinion regarded Gladstone in a more liberal light than he himself did. Bright, who was still not a close friend, apologised for intruding on what must be a personal decision but said he felt he should let Mr. Gladstone know that the whole liberal party in the country disliked Lord Derby (and they disliked Mr. Disraeli even more). He told Gladstone, "If you remain on our side of the House, you are with the majority, and no government can be formed without you. You have many friends there, and some who would grieve much to see you leave them—and I know nothing that can prevent your being prime minister . . . I think I am not mistaken in the opinion I have formed of the direction in which your views have for some years been tending . . ."

Bright was not incorrect in his assessment that Gladstone's drift was towards liberal ideas and the likelihood of his rejoining the Tory fold was remote. However, another determined effort was made by the Tories to effect the juncture in May 1858, and this time a twist was given to the proceedings by Disraeli's entry into the fray. He wrote a personal letter of entreaty to his rival in which he dispensed with the approach of "Dear Mr Gladstone" or even "Dear Sir" and plunged straight into his appeal. He said that their mutual relations appeared to have formed a barrier to the desired result of Mr. Gladstone's rejoining the Conservative party, assured him that he had always been prepared to make sacrifices for the public good which he considered to be identical with Gladstone's acceptance of office in a Conservative Government and asked, "Don't you think the time has come to be magnanimous?" He noted, "Every man performs his office, and there is a Power, greater than ourselves, that disposes of all this," reiterated that the conjuncture of Mr. Gladstone and the Conservative party was critical and said that should his rival enter Lord Derby's Cabinet he would meet many warm friends and admirers, among whom he Benjamin Disraeli could be counted whatever Mr. Gladstone might think.

Disraeli's personal appeal indicates that he was extremely anxious to get Gladstone into the Derby Government, and it can be regarded as a magnanimous gesture on his part, but how much the anxiety rested on the knowledge that the Ministry (and thereby Disraeli's own tenure of office) was almost certainly doomed unless Gladstone joined it and how much on a real desire to oil the joints of the long creaking relationship is difficult to assess. In his reply Gladstone said that he had never considered Mr. Disraeli's retention of office or their personal relationship as the main difficulty of the conjuncture and that there were broader objections than Mr. Disraeli might suppose. He finished his reply by saying, '. . . you have yourself well reminded me that there is a Power beyond us that disposes of what we

are and do, and I find the limits of choice in public life to be very narrow."
One feels that Disraeli's inclusion of God as the bait to trap Gladstone's
high-minded Christian conscience was a mistake, for Disraeli was not noted
for his reliance on God, and if Gladstone was not renowned for his sense of
humour, he was equally unrenowned for being stupid. Disraeli later said
that he had gone down on his knees to try and beguile Gladstone back into
the Conservative party in 1858 but he also said, "We are at all times ready
to take back this deserter, but only if he surrenders unconditionally." Again
one can take one's pick between his motives.

The further rejection of office did Gladstone's general reputation no
good. It was said that he was the strongest orator and the weakest man in
the House of Commons; it seemed a hundred years from his days as the
bold, brilliant Chancellor of the Exchequer, and newspapers again enjoyed
themselves painting verbal pictures of him on his remote heights. Gladstone described his position in a different metaphor; in a memorandum
written to Lord Aberdeen about the reasons for rejecting office he said,
"but a man at the bottom of the well must not try to get out, however disagreeable his position, until a rope or ladder is put down to him." Gladstone
longed for the appropriate ladder to be lowered, one which he could grasp
with a clear conscience, because he was approaching his fiftieth year and he
could no longer be regarded as a rising hope, stern, unbending or otherwise; but Palmerston's antics still prevented the now desired juncture with
the Liberals. During these depressing early summer months Gladstone had
Catherine by his side to sustain him and convince him that all would come
right in the end, but she remained far from well. Her ill-health and the
doctors' suggestion that she would benefit from a winter in a mild climate
are one of the reasons that have been advanced for her husband's acceptance of a peculiar assignment.

The suggestion that Gladstone should go as a special commissioner to the
Ionian Islands was made in October 1858 and came from Bulwer-Lytton,
the Colonial Secretary.* The Ionian Islands had been a British protectorate
since 1815 and many problems—notably their inhabitants' wish to be
united with mainland Greece—were seething. It was thought that a special
commissioner, empowered to investigate the problems and then report back
to Lord Derby's Government on the best course to be followed, would be a
good idea. Gladstone was suggested as a politician of standing who had an
especial interest in all things Greek—his study of Homer had been published that year (and Gladstone displayed an author's interest in his notices, asking Catherine, "Please give particular directions to keep for me
The Times of Aug 12 & 13 & Aug 14. The 2 former have reviews of my
book").

* Lord Derby's ministry had one distinction which is unlikely to be rivalled, in numbering
two first-rate second-class novelists in its ranks: Benjamin Disraeli, who had already written
Sybil, Coningsby and Tancred; and Edward Bulwer-Lytton, the author of The Last Days of
Pompeii, The Last of the Barons, Harold and Rienzi.

Gladstone's friends regarded the offer as a Trojan horse; it might be a comparatively important mission but it was hardly worthy of somebody of his standing; it seemed a more romantic version of the kick upstairs to the House of Lords; should he fail in the mission—and in the welter of Greek politics that was more than likely—his career could end with a ludicrous whimper. Catherine supported the friendly opposition, telling her husband, "My own, I think after much wavering I come to the conclusion weighing pros & cons according to my limited knowledge that I shall be relieved if you do not undertake the mission." Gladstone wanted to go: he was bored and restless out of office; the lure of the Greek islands was Circe-like for such a Hellenist; he thought he might make a useful contribution towards solving the problems; he also wished to make contact with members of the Greek Orthodox Church who might assist in his cherished dream of the re-union of all Christian Churches; and there was Catherine's health which would benefit from a winter away from England. At the beginning of November the Gladstones duly departed for Corfu, accompanied by Agnes and by James Lacaita, who was to act as secretary (since the meeting in Naples in 1850, Lacaita had become a British subject and a friend of Gladstone's). Lucy Lyttleton nicely described the departure, "he as Lord High Commissioner (to I.I.) on some knotty problem."

CHAPTER 8

LORD HIGH COMMISSIONER

THE GLADSTONES TRAVELLED to Corfu via Brussels and Berlin; in the Belgian capital they attended the opening of Parliament and were entertained to dinner at Laeken by King Leopold, who wrote to tell Queen Victoria that Mr. Gladstone was a very interesting man. In Berlin they unfortunately missed the Crown Princess of Prussia (Her Majesty's eldest daughter Vicky), who wrote to tell her mother how much she regretted not seeing Mr. Gladstone. From Berlin they travelled to Trieste and from there they sailed down the Dalmatian coast, past the range of the Albanian mountains (6,030 feet, as Catherine noted) to Corfu, and Catherine started keeping a diary again. Until 1850 she had kept her diary intermittently but she then abandoned it and henceforward it was only the leisure and novelty of foreign travel that prompted her into action. On their first official appearance—at the opera— the Lord High Commissioner Extraordinary and his wife were, as Catherine recorded, "received by 'God Save the Queen,'" and the national anthem became the regular greeting as they visited Cephalonia and Zante and the smaller islands. (Fortunately, nobody wrote to tell Queen Victoria about the royal receptions.)

The weather was not particularly kind, gales blew, rain lashed down in torrents, thunder roared and lightning rent the sky, and when they later visited Athens (walking twenty-two miles round the Greek capital during the day), the Acropolis was wreathed in icicles. But Catherine recorded at least one fine day when they hired a boat and went "gliding through the various islands . . . all attired in their loveliest clothing, so green and garden like." Catherine thoroughly enjoyed herself and she told Lucy Lyttleton, "You would die to see me at our dinners the only woman surrounded by 10 Greek men all buzzing Italian." Her husband enjoyed himself when they visited Albania, were entertained by a female chieftain and spent the night in the communal hall, sleeping on the floor surrounded by beautiful Albanian ladies. As indicated by Catherine's ability to walk twenty-two miles in Athens, the change of climate, the beauty of the Greek islands, the respite from domestic worries and probably being at the heart of the activity effected a remarkable recovery in her physical and mental condition. At

least Catherine left the Ionian Islands a new woman, her batteries recharged.

Otherwise the mission was not a success. It got off to a bad start when a
despatch written by the resident Lord High Commissioner, Sir George
Young, was stolen and leaked to the press. This document advocated the
union of the smaller islands with Greece and the outright annexation by
Britain of the largest island, Corfu; it had in fact been written months be-
forehand and in the meantime Sir George had changed his mind and decided that the *status quo* should be maintained. Few people were aware of
this, however, and the public reaction, in England and on the rest of the
Continent, was that Gladstone must have been sent to implement the proposals. At home this was largely regarded as another betrayal and abnega-
tion of Britain's responsibilities, and abroad it was seen as a British plot to
seize an important island (Corfu was then viewed as a vital defence position for British India). Gladstone was greeted by hostility on nearly every
side—by many of the inhabitants of Corfu as the man who would force
them to become British subjects, by the British garrison as a Hellenist who
sympathised with the thieving, idle, unstable islanders and might recom-
mend anything. In fact, Gladstone's Greek sympathies were slightly impaired when he found that few people on the islands had read Homer or
even knew much about him, and by what he sadly regarded as the gross exaggeration and inattention to detail of the inhabitants. However, he was
not the person to be deterred by hostility, he always believed that a job was
worth doing to the utmost of his ability, and he accordingly set about inves-
tigating the situation with his meticulous attention to detail.

By the end of the year he had decided that the solution was not union
with Greece but a complete reform of the constitution the Ionian Islands
had supposedly been granted in 1815, with Britain exercising her proper
responsibilities as the protecting power and steering the excitable islanders
to political maturity. The resident Lord High Commissioner, Sir George
Young, seemed the man least likely to propose and implement the reformed
constitution, so Gladstone suggested to London that *he* be temporarily appointed to that position to present the new constitution to the local Assembly and gain the approval of the inhabitants. His suggestion was enthusi-
astically accepted by Lord Derby's Government and by Queen Victoria,
who, like many of her subjects, was always loathe for Britain to give up
anything, even some small islands off the Greek coast. Then a serious snag
became apparent; by accepting the official paid post of Lord High Commissioner, rather than the special unpaid roving commission, Gladstone auto-
matically had to vacate his Oxford seat and stand for re-election. And if the
writ for the election were moved before he had completed his task he could
be in a very difficult position. To complicate matters the telegraphic system
broke down at this point, leaving Gladstone in limbo, and when the news
of his appointment broke in London the uproar was immense. He was accused of supplanting that fine British diplomat, Sir George Young, and the

jokes spread that he intended to make himself King of the Ionian Islands (these were flimsily based on the fact that the Gladstones had rented a house in Corfu rather than stay in the residency; but the reason was, as Catherine recorded, that the residency was "a miserable house in the midst of much stagnant water"). The sort of jibes were made that his friends had dreaded when he accepted the mission—that he had been tricked by an insidious rival (i.e. Disraeli) into accepting a fifth-rate job and he was no longer a politician whom anybody could take seriously.

Gladstone's friends managed to extricate him from the Ionian mess by getting a new Lord High Commissioner appointed and sent posthaste to Corfu (and though there had to be a by-election at Oxford, he was returned unopposed). Before Gladstone left Corfu in mid-February 1859, when nobody was sure whether he was Lord High Commissioner Extraordinary or otherwise, he continued to do his utmost to get the new constitutional proposals accepted by the Assembly, but they were defeated by an unholy alliance of nationalists and British-oriented place seekers (the latter having thrived under the old corrupt system).

Having accomplished nothing in the Ionian Islands, with his reputation in England sunk to a new low level, Gladstone returned home. Perhaps one should let him have the last, more hopeful, typical word on the mission: "Whether it was right that I should come, I do not feel very certain. Yet (stolen dispatch and all) I do not regret it; and I really do not know for what it is that political life is worth living, if it be not for an opportunity of endeavouring to redeem in the face of the world the character of our country, wherever, it matters not on how small a scale, that character has been compromised." As the final word on the Ionian Islands, it may be noted that three years later, calmly, without much fuss or opposition, Lord Palmerston's Ministry—of which Gladstone was a member—agreed to surrender the British protectorate and the islands were united with mainland Greece. To Gladstone's friend and revered ex-leader Lord Aberdeen may be given the final assessment of his position after the extraordinary Ionian mission; when Aberdeen was asked whether he concurred with the verdict that Gladstone's career might now be finished he replied, "Ah, but he is terrible on the rebound."

On their way home the Gladstones witnessed the signs of impending war in Italy—the final struggle against Austrian domination for a united sovereign Italy was about to erupt—and Gladstone had a long conversation with one of the doyens of Italian nationalism, Count Cavour. Since his days in Naples, when his outlook had been essentially conservative in supporting the maintenance of the *status quo* and liberal only in the horror against the way it was being implemented, Gladstone had moved towards a more general liberal stance by accepting the idea of Italian unification. He had always supported the nationalist impulse, nationalism in its practical form had begun to equal Liberalism, and the outbreak of the Austro-Italian war polarised attitudes.

However, on his return to London Gladstone found that Lord Derby's Ministry had become interested in parliamentary reform rather than the Italian Question. But the proposed Reform Bill was defeated by the Whig/Liberals and Radicals because they were suspicious of the Tory motives and thought the terms were too tepid. Lord Derby dissolved Parliament and appealed to the country, and despite John Bright's contention that he lacked wide support the Conservatives were returned with a slightly increased majority. Nonetheless the Conservatives still remained a minority Government and could be defeated *if* the opposing Whig/ Liberal/Radical factions could unite; and a strong new Government could be formed *if* Mr. Gladstone could be persuaded to join it. (Despite the Ionian mockery Gladstone's talents were recognised and coveted, but again *if* they could be firmly harnessed.) Throughout May 1859 political circles in London were in a ferment, gossip flared like a lighted gunpowder trail and Catherine added a few sparks to the speculations. One set of gossips said Mrs. Gladstone had indicated that her husband was in favour of a strong Liberal Government and was willing to join one, but another observer noted in his diary, "Saw Mrs Gladstone, who did not seem to contemplate a junction with Palmerston but rather that he should join Derby." Matters came to a head on 6 June when a meeting was called in Willis's Rooms in St. James's Street, attended by all those M.P.s whose allegiance was loosely Liberal. Working from the common ground of a disposition towards Italian nationalism, the hatchet was buried between those two dreadful old men—as Queen Victoria described Lord Palmerston and Lord John Russell—and each agreed that he would support the other, whichever should be called upon as Liberal leader. John Bright pledged the support of the Radicals for a broad-based Liberal administration, and his moderation helped convince the patrician Whigs that they might all be able to work together. Thus the deadlock of rival personalities and factions was broken, thus the Liberal party and the two-party political system came into existence, for henceforward there were only two major parties to which M.P.s could commit their loyalties. The only question mark remained that wandering Ishmael, William Ewart Gladstone.

The Liberals had coalesced, and they immediately decided to move a vote of no confidence in the Conservative administration. The honour of introducing the motion was given to a most patrician Whig, the twenty-six-year-old Lord Hartington, eldest son and heir of the Duke of Devonshire. When the House of Commons divided on the vote Gladstone's position was, as Lord Derby told Queen Victoria, "said to be unknown, even to himself." As it was, not approving of the no-confidence motion, he went into the division lobbies on the Conservative side, but the Government was nevertheless defeated. Her Majesty tried hard to avoid having either of the two dreadful old men as her Prime Minister again but eventually she accepted the lesser of the evils, or rather, the one who had the most support. At the age of seventy-five, with his customary gusto, Lord Palmerston reassumed the mantle of first Minister in the land. He immediately offered Mr. Gladstone any post he cared to choose and without hesitation Gladstone chose his old job as Chancellor of the Exchequer.

While rejoicing with Aunt Pussy that darling Uncle William was back in office, Lucy Lyttleton nicely summed up the reaction which greeted Gladstone's acceptance: ". . . why, if he can swallow Pam, couldn't he swallow Dizzy, and, in spite of him, go in under Lord Derby?" The reasons why Gladstone was ultimately able to swallow "Pam" and not "Dizzy," having denounced the actions of the former as loudly as those of the latter, were that he did not dislike and distrust Palmerston quite as strongly as he did Disraeli; he was longing for office both to fulfil himself and to serve his country's interests; and because the ladder had been lowered to him in the guise of the Italian question. He told a friend that he was "in real and close harmony of sentiment with the new premier" upon that issue.

Having climbed up the ladder and set his feet on firm ground, Gladstone galloped off with the ardour and enthusiasm of the long-restrained race horse or, as Lord Palmerston described his appearances in the Cabinet, ". . . charged to the muzzle with all sorts of schemes for all sorts of reforms which were absolutely necessary in his opinion to be immediately undertaken." The first scheme of reform Gladstone presented to his mainly reluctant Cabinet colleagues and then to the country was his Budget. If he, like his hero Sir Robert Peel, may be accused of being an implementer of other people's ideas rather than a true originator, those who co-ordinate and implement ideas may also be called innovators. Gladstone's Budget was his own in that he worked it out himself and he proposed further sweeping tariff reform and the abolition of the Paper Duty. (This tax inhibited the production of cheap newspapers, books or magazines and had long been called by the Radicals "a tax on knowledge"). But the axis of the Budget was the Commercial Treaty with France, and its battle cry was free trade.

Richard Cobden was the great proponent of free trade; he saw in the free-trade principle "that which shall act on the moral world as the principle of gravitation in the universe . . . I believe the effect will be to change the face of the world . . . I believe that the desire and motive for large and mighty empires, for gigantic armies and navies, for those materials which are used for the destruction of life and the desolation of the rewards of labour, will die away." It was the moral principle which obviously if somewhat belatedly appealed to Gladstone, the concept that war must inevitably wither away if all the nations of the world could be persuaded to trade with each other freely for their mutual benefit, each selling what it had to offer. One of the problems was that some nations had more to offer than others; in the 1860s Britain retained her Industrial Revolution lead and had a great deal to offer, and not all supporters of free trade were in it for moral reasons. In the twentieth century the concept of free trade has been torn to shreds as an example of imperialistic, bourgeois greed masquerading under a cloak of morality, and even in the 1860s an American commentator said, "free trade was a system devised by England to enable her to plunder the world." But that was not how Richard Cobden saw it; for him it was a great principle, and if Gladstone the economist appreciated its economic virtues for England, for him too it was a force for moral good in the world.

In September 1859 Richard Cobden visited Hawarden and put forward the idea which he and John Bright had long entertained of a Commercial Treaty with France, introducing a small free-trade area in which both countries would lower some tariff barriers. It was in fact Cobden who negotiated the treaty, but it was Gladstone who persuaded his Cabinet colleagues to accept the deal and who then wrapped it so skilfully in his Budget that it was an inextricable package. When the moment came for Gladstone to present his Budget to the House of Commons he was quite seriously ill with congestion of the lungs, the strain of preparing it, working on the average a fourteen-hour day, sometimes as much as eighteen hours (including all his activities), having taken a toll of even his magnificent constitution. The Budget consequently had to be postponed, but Gladstone's physical resilience was as great as his wife's and after only five days in bed, on 10 February 1860 he delivered a four-hour speech which even his opponents considered a *tour de force,* one of the greatest feats of eloquence ever heard in the English language.

In his Herculean efforts he was assisted by a concoction prepared for him by Catherine which consisted of raw egg beaten with sherry and poured into a container, and as his strength ebbed or his throat became dry Gladstone took a sip of the mixture. Thereafter, whenever he had an important speech to make he used the pick-me-up, also which became the subject of much speculation and occasionally black comedy; for example, "there are some conscientious Conservatives who believe it is obtained by boiling down a healthy infant selected from the bosom of the family of a Conservative elector." The dexterity with which Gladstone uncorked the top of the container, took a quick sip of the concoction and replaced the cork without pausing in the flow of his oratory also attracted comment, though on one occasion it was noted, "an ill-fitting cork baffled the frenzied efforts of the orator to replace it!"

The Budget as a whole was hailed as a masterly effort and the free-trade kernel was accepted, but Gladstone hit stormy waters with his Bill to repeal the Paper Tax. The Bill scraped through the Commons but it was then thrown out by the Lords because at that time each new tax proposal was dealt with as an individual Bill and the Budget was not accepted (or rejected) as a whole. Gladstone's blood was up—he was not only determined to get his Bill passed, he was equally determined to prevent the unwarrantable interference by the House of Lords in a financial matter from occurring again. In his fight against the Lords, he had little support within the Cabinet and virtually none from Lord Palmerston.

Indeed Gladstone was at loggerheads with many of his Cabinet colleagues on many issues, notably the question of defence, because despite the Commercial Treaty there had been a war scare against France and it was considered essential to strengthen Britain's south coast defences. Gladstone said the scare was nonsense, rightly pointed out that England was a very difficult country to invade and declared he had no intention of allowing large sums of government money to be spent on the unnecessary strengthening or building of forts along the south coast. Throughout July Lord Palmerston was sending Queen Victoria memoranda about Mr. Gladstone's capricious and trying behaviour and his continual threats of resignation. (There was a joke that the chimneys at Broadlands, Palmerston's country seat, were constantly smoking with the innumerable resignation letters.) On the question of the defences Palmerston said that if he had to choose between losing Portsmouth, Plymouth or Mr. Gladstone he would, albeit reluctantly, choose the latter. Earlier in the year he had sent a confidential memorandum to Her Majesty in which he had said he "would think himself giving better service by recommending the H of Lords for Mr Gladstone than for Lord John Russell." (Lord John had decided that he wanted an Earldom, his official reason being that it would give his daughters a title; he duly became Earl Russell in 1861 and moved to the House of Lords.)

Palmerston's lighthearted approach to his Chancellor of the Exchequer's trying behaviour was at the heart of the two men's inability to work in harmony. Thus far the emphasis has been on Palmerston's highhanded attitude toward foreign affairs, as this was the area in which Gladstone initially clashed with him, but even in this field Palmerston had Liberal sympathies. He was not an arch-proponent of gunboat diplomacy, he was more an exponent of what is now called brinkmanship, or as Richard Cobden said, "P. likes to drive the wheel close to the edge and show how dexterously he can avoid falling over the precipice." He was an extremely hard-working old gentleman—there was no aristocratic indolence about "Pam"—with a constitution as tough as Gladstone's, a much thicker skin and an expert knowledge of the House of Commons and how to handle it. But Palmerston was a patriotic pragmatist; for him there were no eternal allies or perpetual enemies, and in foreign affairs he saw his duty as furthering British interests without stamping too hard on other people's, but if one had to stamp, that was life. His attitude can be summed up in observations he made to Richard Cobden: "It would be very delightful if your Utopia could be realised, and if the nations of the earth could think of nothing but peace and commerce, and would give up quarrelling and fighting altogether. But unfortunately man is a fighting and quarrelling animal."

To Gladstone these attitudes were anathema; for him life was a serious business and he could not understand how people could treat serious matters flippantly; for him man was not a quarrelsome brute but one imperfectly made in the image of God who must constantly search for perfection; and for him it was England's duty as the leading nation of the world to guide others by her shining example of liberty and justice. Apart from the antipathetic figure of Lord Palmerston at its head, Gladstone had other problems within the Cabinet because it was basically Whig and the Whigs were the most exclusive body in England. Traditionally they were more progressive than the Tories but in respect of social mobility and accepting outsiders they were decidedly more conservative; it was said that one could no more become a Whig than one could become a Jew. It was also said, by a Whig, that Gladstone was Oxford on top and Liverpool underneath; thus despite his wife's connections he did not belong.

On the matter of the defences Gladstone agreed to a compromise but on the matter of the control of the nation's finances he completely dished the House of Lords. He presented them with a package deal in his 1861 Budget (including his Paper Bill) which they had either to accept or reject as a whole, and faced with the prospect of the storm their total rejection of the Chancellor's Budget would create their lordships capitulated. Henceforward it became the accepted practice for the annual Budget to be presented to Parliament as a single measure. Another of Gladstone's innovations was the introduction of long-term financial measures, and he has rightly been called the father of all five- or seven-year plans. His espousal of free trade earned him the plaudits of the commercial middle classes and increased prosperity, so that Gladstone could justly claim that during his tenure of office as Chancellor from 1859–66 while the rich might have grown richer, the poor had also grown less poor. For Gladstone his "figyures" were not boring strokes and curves on pieces of paper, they were living symbols which affected the lives of every man and woman in the country, and his enthusiasm and conviction were so infectious that his Budgets in the early 1860s were awaited with the same eagerness as much-publicised films in the heyday of Hollywood.

The only measure which was greeted with opposition from all sides, including his own family, was contained in his 1863 Budget. It was that charities should be subjected to income tax. Gladstone's argument was that a great deal of money was left to charity as a means of avoiding income tax rather than assisting the deserving cause, so he suggested that a grant be given to charities such as hospitals from government funds. The proposal was another interesting example of the socialistic leanings of the man who believed in individual effort and detested state intervention; and it was defeated.

The two measures which made large sectors of the population begin to regard Gladstone as their lodestar were the Paper Bill, together with the fervour with which he defended it against the House of Lords, and his Savings Bank Bill. This latter measure introduced a Government-backed bank into which people could put their savings, however small they might be, with complete security; it showed that Gladstone cared about the needs of ordinary people in the new hard-working, thrifty economy. The repeal of the Paper Tax opened the floodgates to the popular press and, as the upper classes had suspected it might, led to the spread of democracy. The effect of the Savings Bank Bill can be judged from a beautifully brief letter Gladstone received from a lady who lived in the small town of Keswick in the Lake District: "I beg leave to return thanks for your having enabled me to pay all my savings (fifty pounds) into the Post Office Savings Bank."

At the beginning of the 1860s many of Gladstone's friends commented on how drawn and tired he looked and the degree to which he was overworking, but his mighty efforts in so many fields did not prevent his expending a fair amount of energy on his prostitute friends and their problems. Most of his personal comments for this period are at the moment unavailable and how regularly he was actually scouring the streets of London is unclear, but by this time he had established a network of correspondence with prostitutes, ex- or otherwise. The sort of correspondence he maintained can be gauged from letters written to him by the lady earlier mentioned who was then working as a housekeeper-companion in Leeds. Her name was C. E. Booth, or at least this was the name by which she chose to be known, and the first letter to Gladstone was dated December 1862, addressed to "My Dear Kind Friend," and thanked him most humbly for the kindness he had shown in her struggles. Throughout 1863 and 1864 she wrote to him fairly regularly, on one occasion thanking him for the picture of himself—"I think it is a good likeness and accept it as a proof of your faith in me"—and on another thanking him for the money he had sent (she had written to tell Gladstone about her sister's death, how much it had cost her and that she was down to her last £1). Mrs. Booth then moved to a job in Newport, Monmouthshire, where she became consumptive, and there was a gap until 1867 when she wrote from Regent's Park, London: "I promised to inform you of any important events in my life . . . I intend sailing for Melbourne on the 14th next with the intention of *never returning . . .* I should like to say Goodbye." She then wrote to ask Gladstone, "Can you meet me tonight at the Duke of York Column, say at ten to half?" There was some confusion about this meeting but one assumes that eventually Gladstone saw her at the favourite rendezvous of the Duke of York steps and she was able to hear "that soft kind voice again." Mrs. Booth duly emigrated to Melbourne, from where she wrote to tell Gladstone that she was hoping to get married, but by 1872 she was back in England thanking him for his kind little note and then for £10 he had sent her. Eventually she went to America, and the last letter he received from her was from Wisconsin in November 1882, by which time the correspondence had stretched over three continents and twenty years.

There is also further evidence at this period of the murky waters into which Gladstone's activities led him. At the end of May 1860 he received a letter from Mrs. Louisa Banks, who lived in Stratford, Essex, in which she requested "payment of an account for medicine etcetera for a Miss Houseley which I am informed you will pay." Mrs. Banks further informed him that the account came to £7.11.6 and said that as she was rather short of cash at the moment she would be grateful if Mr. Gladstone would settle it promptly. Gladstone instructed his secretary, "Please to say I have no information on this subject," which the secretary duly did. On 10 June Mrs. Banks wrote again at greater length. She said his secretary's reply had contradicted what Miss Housley (she spelled the name thus the second time) had told her and related the story thus: "now Miss Housley called on me on Saturday the 19th of May three weeks since & told me she had received a letter from *her Papa* who she represents to be you, requesting her to call on me, & say that you were about to send me a Post Office Order on the following Monday." When the money for the medicines did not arrive Mrs. Banks contacted Miss Housley, who said she could not understand why Mr. Gladstone had not sent the postal order but she would be going up to town shortly (implicitly to see him) and would return with the money. When the cash still failed to arrive Mrs. Banks said she visited Miss Housley's lodgings in Stratford only to be told that she had left them. She added that she was "puzzled to know why Miss Housley should have made such assertions as she must be well aware that I should communicate with you," and hoped that Mr. Gladstone would pay the account.

Gladstone replied personally to this letter (though his reply is not extant), presumably refusing to pay the money, because on 15 June the husband, Mr. A. J. H. Banks, entered the fray. He reiterated that Miss Housley had "stated she was connected with you in fact that she was your child" and that this statement had been corroborated by the gentleman who accompanied her and who occupied "a highly respectable position near Billiter St, City." He finished his letter with a threat, "If I have been misled I think it would be only justice to myself and the Public to make the whole matter as thoroughly known as possible by means of the local and London papers that it may act as a caution to others and prevent further deception." A reply was sent to this letter and another one on 1 August, in both of which presumably (they are not extant) Gladstone refused to pay the account, because on 20 August Mrs. Banks wrote again. She said that she and her husband had made every effort to trace the young lady in question but without success, they were therefore left £9.11.0 in debt (the amount had gone up) but should they hear any more of her they would again communicate with Mr. Gladstone. There the correspondence ends, with Gladstone presumably not paying the money.

It seems extremely unlikely that Gladstone was Miss Housley's "Papa," because while he may be called a hypocrite and the extent of his physical involvement with some of his prostitute friends may never be fully known, a liar he was not. If he said he had no knowledge of a Miss Housley he assuredly had not, and his refusal to be intimidated by Mr. Banks' covert blackmail threat would also suggest a clear conscience. Nonetheless the episode is peculiar and enveloped in question marks. It should be noted that the Bankses were, at least on the surface, a highly respectable couple; Arthur Joseph Humbley Banks is listed in the 1860s directories for the Stratford area as a surgeon. There is also some evidence in the Gladstone correspondence that he already knew Mr. Banks slightly—and in the rating returns for the Stratford area in 1860 one house is listed to a William Gladstone, though whether this was William Ewart and he actually owned a nearby house or whether it was sheer coincidence and the property of another Mr. Gladstone is not certain. As the Bankses and Gladstone appear to have had some connection, Miss Housley's arrival at the house of the local surgeon requesting expensive medicines on the strength of her relationship with the Chancellor of the Exchequer would not be a complete bolt from the blue. Why Miss Housley decided to go to the Bankses and con them for the medicines she required by using Gladstone's name is another matter. One can assume that she knew of the Chancellor's activities from other prostitute friends, she knew of the Bankses' connection and she decided to chance her luck; or one can assume a more regular trade of young ladies appearing at the Bankses' with the blessing of Mr. Gladstone—though the extant correspondence does not suggest an intimate association. Whether the Bankses' relationship was tenuous and whether in this instance Gladstone was completely innocent, the calmness with which Miss Housley apparently decided on her story and the alacrity with which the Bankses apparently accepted the information that Gladstone was the lady's Papa and would foot the bill would seem to suggest that already in various circles his association with prostitutes was not regarded as an entirely spiritual, highminded endeavour.

Another outstanding bill presented to the Chancellor of the Exchequer arose from his association with a higher class of prostitute, a lady by the name of Miss Throckmorton who would have preferred the title of courtesan. Miss Throckmorton was young and beautiful and when Gladstone made her acquaintance she was living in the fashionable Brompton area of London in a house paid for by her lover. At the end of July 1863 Gladstone wrote to tell Catherine that he had been occupied all day with the case of a woman who was at the very top of her tree but who fortunately was disposed to go to the Anglican refuge at Clewer. However, in her enthusiasm to be redeemed Miss Throckmorton left the Brompton area without paying her account at the livery stables, and on 5 August 1863 Gladstone received an application from the Inclosure Office for the balance of the debt. It was accompanied by a polite, slightly apologetic letter from the office which said that the owners of the livery stables who had taken out the application were a young married couple newly in business, and they could not therefore stand bad debts. When they had asked Miss Throckmorton for the money she had told them she was going into a convent with the assistance of Mr. Gladstone and they should apply to him for the balance of the debt. Gladstone duly paid it to the amount of £7, a gesture which suggests that had he been involved with Miss Housley he would have paid *that* bill.

While her husband was involved in his multifarious activities, Catherine was hardly less busy. Apart from the "sacred duty" of caring for the motherless Lyttletons and helping to ease the burdens of her "pretty bird" Lucy, Catherine's plunge into activity was probably a defence against the crushing loss of her beloved sister. Her older children were no longer in need of so much attention. Willie had gone up to Oxford in 1858, Stephy was settled at Eton where he was making progress, Agnes had had her first season, while Mary and Lena (Helen) were still under the care of governesses but were well into their teens. In selecting governesses for her daughters Catherine showed a conventional attitude, leaving the ladies in complete charge and failing to find out what her daughters thought about them. Mary later intimated that they crushed her inner confidence by telling her that she was no good at anything and suggesting that the area in which she had real talent, her music, was of minor importance. The two younger boys, Henry and Herbert, were packed off to boarding school at an earlier age than Willie or Stephy, and while this decision may have been reached because the Gladstones were into or approaching their fifties and had less energy to deal with young children, they were perhaps also sent away to give Catherine greater freedom of action. Again neither she nor her husband discovered what the boys thought about the main preparatory school to which they were sent. Henry wrote to his brother Willie, "I hope you will like Naples better than we like school," and, "I do not like Mr Church. I can't help telling you he gets into such a passion and is cross directly we arrive." Herbert later admitted that Mr. Church's was a dreadful school where the boys were beaten constantly and badly underfed, so that they spent much of their time in the kitchens trying to scrounge food. But to counterbalance the omissions in the educational field, there was the warmth and affection of the family background when the children were at home.

The outbreak of the American Civil War in April 1861 and the subsequent "cotton famine" in Lancashire gave Catherine good reason to accelerate the pace of her activities. There were many Relief Committees doling out charity to the destitute cotton operatives and their families but apart from the fact that the committees had what Lucy described as "a miserable mania for economising," neither she nor her aunt was inclined to sit in plush houses and discuss the situation. Catherine went into the whole business with the thoroughness she could display when her attention was caught, noting that forty-nine mills had stopped work completely, that the number of hands usually employed was 27,273, at the moment the number working full time was 3,967, that working short time was 5,575 and that totally out of work was 17,731. By October 1862 she had a scheme under way to employ some of the operatives and their families at Hawarden; early in November she had another scheme to set up soup kitchens in Blackburn (one of the worst-hit towns). Every available member of her own family was put to work writing letters for donations, and in mid-November she decided to visit the cotton belt herself. It was as Catherine prepared for her Lancashire onslaught that she took time off to visit Newcastle-on-Tyne with her husband, but while Gladstone's irresponsible speech about Jefferson Davis and the Confederacy dismayed all supporters of the Northern cause (most of whom lived in the north of England), it in no way diminished the warmth of Catherine's reception in Lancashire, nor the people's belief that Gladstone was their protector. On the third day of her visit to Blackburn, the Institute Band and a crowd of about four hundred and fifty people gathered outside the house where Catherine was staying, and she told Gladstone, "poor things it was *for me* . . . I ought to have mentioned the hearty cheer for me—& for my husband who had 'sent me' to them—it was heart stirring & very touching." Apart from Blackburn, Catherine visited Preston, Darwin, Ashton-under-Lyne and Stalybridge, and the appearance of the wife of the Chancellor of the Exchequer in these small, bleak towns was as great a novelty and innovation as her husband's forays into the provinces. A child summed up the general astonished reaction: "Mother, who do you think we have had in school today? The Government's wife."

From Blackburn Catherine penned a marathon letter to her husband describing the conditions of the people "so poor & ragged & bare of clothes," and the opening of her new soup kitchen: "I saw the 1st distribution of irish stew so hot & good . . . & 1000 people in one day & now 1200 are substantially fed." Catherine revealed her concern and the manner which enabled people to confide in her in an anecdote about a woman who came to see her in Blackburn: "I bid her sit by the fire, while I tried to comfort her. Her heart burst, 'Oh Maam this is like Heaven' & truly the poor pent up heart relieved itself & told its tale—a tale indeed of trial & suffering meekly borne." The patient dignity with which Lancashire endured its suffering struck Catherine forcibly; she communicated her opinons to her husband and they soon bore unexpected fruit. Initially the patient endurance was based on an acceptance of the inevitable and of one's lot in life, but later, under the influence of the pro-Northern, anti-slavery beliefs of the two great Lancastrian heroes Cobden and Bright, many of the operatives took a stand on principle and refused to work such Southern cotton as seeped through the Northern blockade. Abraham Lincoln wrote an open letter to the city of Manchester, as the heart of the cotton belt, thanking the inhabitants for their support of the Northern cause and saying they had shown "an instance of sublime heroism which has not been surpassed in any age or any country."

Catherine herself selected a dozen girls from the most destitute families in the cotton towns (she was besieged with applicants), and they were transported to Hawarden, where they lived in a large refurbished house in the yard and were trained as domestic servants, while a slightly larger number of unemployed men was found work laying roads through the Hawarden estate. The organisation, the day-to-day running and the cost of this private enterprise version of later governmental methods of relieving unemployment were borne by the Gladstones. The main burden fell on Catherine's shoulders but her husband was a willing participant (on one occasion she told him not to worry about bringing the toothbrushes with him from London as they had been intended for the factory girls and the matter had been dealt with). Once the roads had been laid most of the men returned to Lancashire but Catherine kept her domestic-training scheme in operation for several years, as the cotton towns continued to have their share of destitute families. She displayed her persistence of purpose in finding good posts for the girls, badgering her friends and acquaintances into accepting them into their households. The Duke of Argyll, who had become one of her husband's more enthusiastic patrician Whig supporters, wrote to say that he would be happy to place a Hawarden-trained factory girl in one of his houses, "where she will be in very good and kind care of an excellent housekeeper and a very comfortable rather old housemaid."

Apart from the disastrous effects of the American Civil War on Lancashire, there were two incidents which had major repercussions in England. One concerned the sloop *Alabama* and will be dealt with later as it encroached on Gladstone's first tenure of office as Prime Minister; the other also concerned a ship, the *Trent*. The Confederacy sent two envoys to Europe, Mr. Mason and Mr. Slidell, on a mission to persuade the British and French Governments to come out in support of the Southern states; when these two gentlemen were forcibly taken off a British mail boat, the *Trent*, by Yankees, the uproar in England was immense. Lord John Russell as Foreign Secretary drafted a fierce despatch demanding that the North pay reparations for the highhanded violation of British neutrality, that the envoys be returned to British custody and that an apology be tendered. The British Ambassador in Washington was instructed to withdraw if these demands were not met within seven days, instructions which if effected could lead to a declaration of war. Gladstone was in favour of a more moderate, temperate despatch being sent to Washington which would leave the Americans room for explanation and manoeuvre, and his view was supported by the Prince Consort, who was already ill and spent long hours when he should have been resting in making suggestions and alterations for a second draft. Eventually an amended version was submitted to President Lincoln and his Cabinet which enabled them to extricate themselves from a difficult situation without too much loss of prestige, the envoys were returned to British custody and the threat of war was averted.

On 14 December 1861, while the final British despatches were being considered and acted upon in Washington, the Prince Consort died and the light went out in Queen Victoria's life. Gladstone was among those who attended the memorial service, and Catherine wrote to him from Hawarden, ". . . it was soothing to feel that as *you* were in that Chapel at Windsor—we were praying and crying in Chester." While official court activity virtually ceased after Albert's death, guests were occasionally entertained at Windsor, with the Gladstones among the select few. In March 1862 Gladstone himself was summoned to Windsor to meet Her Majesty privately for the first time since her stunning, irreparable loss, a further indication of the esteem in which she then held him. Before the audience the Duchess of Sutherland instructed her dear friend how he should behave but as Gladstone waited the memories of his association with the dead Prince "joined with a vague uncertainty about the Queen and about my own behaviour to one at once my Sovereign and a widowed fellow-creature to give me a feeling of uneasiness very different from any feeling with which I had ever before anticipated her approach."

In fact the audience went off well, and afterwards Queen Victoria noted in her Journal, "Then I saw Mr G for a little while, who was very kind & feeling. We talked of the State of the country. He spoke with such un-bounded admiration & appreciation of my beloved Albert saying no one could ever replace him." After the audience, Gladstone the compulsive writer returned home and penned his thoughts on the occasion, which were a hundred times the length of Her Majesty's. The early conversation, apart from touching on the condition of the country and the distress in Lancashire, subjects which were of interest to the Queen, also ranged over Greece, the Greek Orthodox Church and the Roman Catholic Church, subjects which were less likely to attract Her Majesty, particularly in her mourning state. Then as Gladstone recorded, "The rest of the conversation turned almost entirely upon the Prince's character, & upon his last illness." He further noted that Her Majesty at one point seemed to him "the most womanly of all women in her dominions"; and she warned him that she was irascible, that she was not gifted with elasticity of temperament and that she was not disciplined as her beloved Albert had been. Gladstone would have done well to have taken these warnings to heart but he was overwhelmed by Her Majesty's humility, the firm texture of her mind, her marked dignity and strength of character—all of which traits she possessed, if the humility was not noticeably to the forefront.

In the late summer of 1863, when Gladstone was suggested as the Minister in attendance at Balmoral, the suggestion was accepted with pleas-ure by Her Majesty. He wrote long, quite enthusiastic letters to Catherine about the beauty of the place, the satisfactory state of the Queen's health and spirits and the household's being less formal and therefore less dull than at Windsor. (This last view was not shared by many of those who had to spend long periods at Balmoral.) But there were always two major hur-dles lying across the path of Gladstone's relationship with Queen Victoria. One of them was not so much that he did not understand women, as some people asserted—women in all walks of life seemed to think he understood them very well, and derived much satisfaction from his company—but his inability to separate "the most womanly of all women" from the reverence he had for his Sovereign and therefore to gauge when she wanted to be treated in which role. Catherine's suggestion that while her husband was at Balmoral he should have a good talk with the Queen, and her later well-known exhortation, "Do pet the Queen!" were sensible, because Gladstone was quite capable of petting ladies and getting them to accept his good advice. Another major handicap to a satisfactory relationship was that Gladstone had no small talk. "The incumbrance of pulp" which he rightly considered necessary in his reading matter and theatre-going was absent from his written or spoken words, and while many people found him a fascinating conversationalist, he needed an appreciative audience and he had to be accepted in his full flow. Even in the early amicable days Gladstone noted "the gaps" in his conversations with the Queen but in the early years his enthusiasm for examining *every* subject in depth did not matter so much because Prince Albert was alive.

Like Gladstone the Prince had an essentially serious mind and was absorbed by detail, and though Her Majesty later insisted that Mr. Gladstone's admiration for her husband had *not* been reciprocated, in reality the two men got on well. The death of the man whose mind had worked along similar lines to Gladstone's and who had appreciated his abilities (whatever Her Majesty later said) was a minor disaster for Gladstone. Queen Victoria remained in the rut of what her beloved Albert had done in the 1840s and 1850s rather than how he might have reacted to the changing situation of the 1860s, 1870s, 1880s and 1890s. On his first visit to Balmoral Gladstone himself noted, "Whenever she quotes an opinion of the Prince she looks upon the question as completely shut up by it, for herself and all the world." As Gladstone's mind moved towards subjects and attitudes which were anathema to Her Majesty, his uneasy reverence for his Sovereign and the overwhelming earnestness of his approach became barriers over which neither he nor she could leap—and there was no Prince Consort to act as the helpful stile.

CHAPTER 9

THE PEOPLE'S WILLIAM AND CATHERINE

BEFORE THE TITLE "the People's William" was bestowed on Gladstone, his wife can be said to have earned the title "the People's Catherine," though it was never officially given to her. The early 1860s saw the great expansion of the railways in the metropolis; thousands lost their homes and towards the end of 1863 stories were printed of homeless people dying from exposure and exhaustion on the streets of London. These produced an immediate response in Catherine and she formed a committee, mainly composed of the existing committee members of the St. Barnabas House of Charity, with the aim of providing a new type of refuge in which the homeless could find temporary overnight shelter and food. Obtaining a suitable building in the heart of the West End was not an easy matter, but eventually a disused slaughterhouse was discovered in the Newport Market which lay behind Leicester Square in the notorious Seven Dials area. The rent demanded was heavy; converting the building into a condition in which human beings could live, however temporarily and with the minimum trimmings, also cost money; and more was required to run the place. It was Catherine who personally raised the £1,200 which set the enterprise on its feet by writing dozens of letters to her friends requesting subscriptions, and in October 1864 the Newport Market Night Refuge was officially opened. The building remained bleak but it had been scrubbed and whitewashed, it had one hundred iron cots, with further strips of coconut matting on the floor for the overflow, and it provided coffee and bread when the inmates arrived in the evenings and left in the mornings. At first it had only a men's ward but a women's section was soon added and after *The Times* ran an article in December 1864 about the Refuge, Mrs. Gladstone's involvement and her urgent appeal for funds, donations to the sum of £3,473 flowed in and it became an established institution.

The rule of the Refuge was that people could stay for a maximum of seven nights, the principle being that it would provide them with a breathing space in which they could search for employment if they were jobless or for lodgings if they were employed. Catherine might have been uninterested in the reasons why so many thousands of people were homeless or destitute in the capital city of the world's richest country, but she was humanly aware that seven nights' respite was brief, that much of the flotsam was then thrown back into the same conditions from which it had emerged into the warmth and shelter of the Newport Market Refuge. She insisted that strenuous efforts were made to try to find work for the tide of lost humanity that floated through the establishment, and she became concerned about the plight of the children who landed on the Refuge's doorstep. She came up with the idea of starting an Industrial School for the boys in which the illiterate could be taught to read and write and all could acquire a trade. A generous donation from the Sassoon family (£1,000) enabled her to turn another part of the building into a school, and within a few years there were forty-nine children between the ages of eight and fourteen being made literate and taught trades such as tailoring or shoemaking. As the Gladstones were all enthusiastic musicians, those boys who showed a musical aptitude were trained by the bandmaster of the Scots Fusilier Guards and placed in regimental bands, and it was later said that nearly every regiment in the British army could boast a boy bandsman who had been rescued from the streets of London by Mrs. Gladstone.

By the beginning of 1863, when Catherine had only the Lancashire mill girls at Hawarden to deal with, she admitted to Lucy Lyttleton, "At times I feel exhausted & as it were pumped dry . . . William is a wonderful help though he is much shut up in that poor room looking at papers." William was the very model of a working wife's husband, and apart from being asked to bring toothbrushes or black velvet gowns or Catherine's diamond earrings with him to Hawarden, when he was in London he was frequently sent out to buy sponges or teapots or some other item his distracted wife had forgotten to order. During these years Catherine *was* a working wife, however much the description would have astounded or appalled her, and despite her general carelessness she was eminently professional in her charity work. Allied to her practical vision and compassion, she displayed an unremitting tenacity and persistence of purpose in collecting and appealing for subscriptions and donations, in finding suitable jobs for her various protégés and in keeping a personal eye on the running of her enterprises. Catherine was an early believer in the value of publicity; she made sure that her projects had the backing of the most eminent names in the land, and few years went by without some reference to, or appeal for, one of Mrs. Gladstone's charities in the newspapers. Her husband's was an eminently useful name which she could always draw on; the first annual general meeting of the Newport Market Night Refuge was attended by the Chancellor of the Exchequer (a fact duly noted in the newspapers) and Catherine later told Gladstone, "May I just throw in that when you can take up the things I do it makes my poor little work tell doubly?" As her "poor little work" continued to gain momentum and spread its net wider she became less apologetic, and by the second half of the decade

1. The Misses Glynne:
Catherine (left) aged 17,
and Mary (the future
Baroness Lyttleton).
Drawn by J. Slater.

. William Gladstone's
irthplace in Rodney
treet, Liverpool.

3. William Ewart Gladstone, M.P., at the time of his marriage.
A contemporary engraving.

4. William Ewart Gladstone, c. 1859.

5. Mr. and Mrs. Gladstone and their family, at Hawarden. Back row, left to right: Stephen and his wife; Mary and Harry Drew; Herbert; Helen. Front: Catherine and William with their grandchildren.

6. Mary Gladstone, aged 32. Drawn by Edward Burne-Jones.

Lady Frederick Cavendish (Lucy Lyttleton). From a portrait at Holker Hall.

8. William Gladstone in 1879. Painted by J. E. Millais.

9. Benjamin Disraeli, Earl of Beaconsfield. Painted by J. E. Millais.

10. "A Vacation
Exercise." Cartoon
by Phil May.

12. Torchlight procession
in Midlothian, 1880. A
contemporary engraving.

11. Gladstone reading the
lesson in Hawarden
Church. An idealised
drawing, 1880.

13. "William the
Conqueror and the Battle
of Hustings." Cartoon
from FUN, 14 April
1880.

14. 3rd Viscount Palmerston. Painted by John Partridge.

15. Lord Hartington: 8th Duke of Devonshire.

16. A cartoon of "Loulou" Harcourt, 1st Viscount Harcourt.

17. Lord Rosebery: 5th Earl of Rosebery.

18. Arthur Balfour, 1st Earl Balfour. Painted by Lawrence Alma-Tadema.

19. Gladstone in the "Temple of Peace" at Hawarden Castle

20. The Grand Old Man and the Grande Dame pose for the camera.

21. Felling trees at Hawarden: Gladstone's favourite hobby.

22. Gladstone in his retirement, with his granddaughter Dossie unintentionally caught in the background.

23. Gladstone acknowledging the cheers of the crowd at the Hawarden fete in 1896. Catherine stands to his left, slightly blurred.

24. The crowds filing past Gladstone's bier in Westminster Hall. A contemporary drawing.

25. Gladstone's austere funeral procession reaches Westminster Abbey.

26. The last photograph of Catherine Gladstone, taken shortly before her death.

she was telling her husband, gaily but firmly, that it was of "some consequence."

In 1864 Lucy listed the extent of her aunt's activities and implicitly the problems of being a working wife and mother: "Atie P. has undertaken to visit a hospital in St. Georges in the E. beside 3 other things. And how is she to do that, & all her own innumerable kind deeds, & her season & her societyums, & be deep in politics, & be everything to Uncle William—all at once? She looks terribly fagged already" (-ums on the end of a word was a Glynnese usage denoting deep involvement in a subject or conversation). Catherine managed to perform the difficult balancing act with slapdash efficiency and without collapsing again. Her interest in William's career never waned, she was always ready to accompany him on a provincial journey if required and she kept up her daily correspondence when she was away from him. When any of her children or the Lyttletons were ill or had a particular problem she would immediately devote her attention to it or them, and William and the family probably gained more than they lost by having a fulfilled wife and mother. The item on Catherine's agenda that claimed the least attention was London society, which was not particularly -ums as far as she was concerned, whatever Lucy might indicate, and to that extent William's career may be said to have suffered from his wife's work load.

However, when the society matter concerned her own children Catherine managed to throw herself into it with energy and enthusiasm, as for example Mary's coming out season in 1864. Mary was one of the most interesting of the Gladstone children, and given better governesses or the disciplined education that was lavished on her brothers (at Eton and Oxford if not at the younger ones' preparatory school), she might have been a renowned lady in her own right rather than as the daughter of Mr. Gladstone. Mary Ponsonby, the wife of Queen Victoria's private secretary Sir Henry Ponsonby, travelled to Germany with Mary Gladstone in the 1870s and described her thus: ". . . proved difficult to know; she was certainly not commonplace, a capital musician, & a kind of latent force about her reminding one of her father . . . but absent & dreamy like her mother." Miss Gladstone was not always vague and dreamy (but then neither was her mother); she had been a positive, determined child, and in the family circle her determination later earned her the nickname of "Von Moltke." Quite a few politicians considered her a formidable lady. But the latent force within Mary was never fully realised, the good brain inherited from her father never channelled itself but leapt from subject to subject and while her love for and appreciation of music was profound she did not receive the disciplined encouragement which might have turned her into a pianist of professional ability. Some of the blame must rest with Catherine because she was conventional in her attitude to her daughters. They received their full share of affection but she thought they should be content to fulfill their roles as daughters, wives and mothers in a manner which she herself did not exemplify. From the year of her coming out Mary started to keep a diary, and a highly entertaining, readable one it remains, with sharp observations and colourful Glynnese comments interspersed with those of an enthusiastic, child-like naïvety which was also typical of one side of her father.

The year 1864 witnessed another important family event in Lucy's marriage to Lord Frederick Cavendish (known to Lucy and the Gladstones as Fred). Lord Frederick was a son of the Duke of Devonshire, a younger brother of Lord Hartington, and his marriage to Gladstone's favourite niece forged a personal link between the risen hope of the Liberal party and one of the great patrician Whig families which in its turn effected a most useful political bond. The Cavendish family was more renowned on its female side than the male (though the 4th Duke of Devonshire was briefly Prime Minister in the eighteenth century). It was the formidable Bess of Hardwick who in Tudor times brought the Chatsworth estate into the family possession, and Georgiana the 5th Duchess of Devonshire had been famous for her wit and beauty. The men tended to be more plodding, cautious and charmless, and Lucy recorded, "None of the family seems to me quick or brilliant, but they have a most wonderful accuracy, thoroughness, & grasp of a subject." Few of the Cavendish family possessed oratorical ability either; Lord Frederick had a slight impediment and Lucy wrote of Lord Hartington making a major political speech and sounding less than usual as if his mouth was stuffed with potatoes. At times the ebullient, vivacious, informal Lucy found life in the staid, undemonstrative, formal Devonshire homes somewhat boring; at one dinner party she thought the conversation so portentously sleep-making that "I wonder I did not roll off my chair with a crash." But Lucy had her aunt's ability to take life in her stride and she was more than recompensed by her love for her darling Fred which shines through her diaries. Lucy's marital status did nothing to diminish the closeness of her relationship with Catherine, and the newlyweds soon bought a house in Carlton House Terrace so that the young Cavendishes and the Gladstones were virtually next-door neighbours.

Despite Catherine's heavy involvement in her charitable work, she was—as Lucy Cavendish, as one should now call her, intimated—everything, or nearly everything, to Gladstone. In the early 1860s he had need of his wife's loyalty, approval and encouragement because he was charting a new course and also because four of his oldest, closest friends died in this period. Lord Aberdeen was the first to go early in 1860, Sir James Graham and Sidney Herbert (latterly Lord Herbert of Lea) both died in 1861 and Lord Lincoln (by then the Duke of Newcastle) died in 1864. Typically, despite his many other commitments, Gladstone undertook the task of acting as executor of the will and trustee of the Newcastle estate, and it was a task which consumed a good deal of his time, as his friend had left his affairs in a state of chaos. The two Newcastle sons also presented their trustee with problems, as they had both inherited more of their mother's atti-

tude towards life than their father's and were addicted to gambling and unattached to hard work. Incidentally, both Gladstone and Catherine kept in
touch with "dearest Suzie." They saw her on her rare visits to London, and
when Gladstone finally gave up the position of trustee at the end of 1880,
he managed to obtain an allowance from the Newcastle Trust for the ageing ex-Lady Lincoln, who by then had been through various lovers and was
Lady Susan Opdebeck.

After the deaths of Sidney Herbert and Sir James Graham, Gladstone
had written to the Duchess of Sutherland, saying, "This is the gradual
withdrawal of props, preparing for what is to follow." But from the moment he introduced his first Budget as a member of a Liberal Government
in 1860, Gladstone was already on the road of what was to follow—his
emergence as the leader of a new brand of Liberalism and the champion of
the people. The Tory caterpillar nevertheless turned into the Liberal butterfly with apparently incredible speed because there were only three and a
half years between the post-Ionian spectacle of "half-dead, broken-down,
tempest-tossed Gladstone"—to quote from Greville's portrait of the gentleman in his famous diaries—and the fantastic reception accorded to him and
Catherine in Newcastle-on-Tyne; similar receptions occurred in Lancashire
in 1864 when he and Catherine went on another of their tours. While
Gladstone's political transformation had in reality been well prepared, the
pace at which he finally moved can be attributed to many complementary
reasons. On the wide political stage there was something of a vacuum. The
old territorial aristocracy retained great influence and theoretically was still
the strongest force in the political life of the country, but the will to govern
as a body had been sapped by events. The Tories had started to reorganise
and adapt themselves to the changing circumstances under Sir Robert Peel,
and Disraeli was taking the process further, but the Whigs, the traditional
upholders of the people's liberty, were out of harmony with the people's
requirements in an increasingly industrial, urban and demanding society.
The emergent force was the middle class, each year growing more homogeneous, attempting to define its values and standards and in search of a
leader to reflect its needs and aspirations; and while the working class
remained largely disorganised and inarticulate, it wanted somebody who
seemed aware of its existence and could give hope for the future. On Gladstone's side there was the fact that the party he had joined was strongly
Whig; it regarded him askance and could not provide the fuel of approval
that he needed, and he had to look for this in other directions.

Thus there existed a fluid situation in which the Whigs had not abandoned the idea of power but were becoming willing to accept a leader of a
newer breed who would not upset the applecart too vigorously and through
whom they could hope to continue to function, while large numbers of
"the people" were crying out for a new Messiah and Gladstone was looking
for those whom he could lead. His relationship with the people who became his bulwark as much as he became their lodestar was always and es-

sentially two-way. He was simultaneously public servant and mentor, as he considered every public man should be. Gladstone also had passion, and while the English are not supposed to be a passionate race, if their history is examined a strong undertow of passion becomes apparent (it was not deferential passivity that gained the English wider liberties at a faster rate than any other European nation). In Victorian times the passion partly evinced itself in a disproportionate sentimentality about little flower girls and lost dogs, but it also responded to the fire of Gladstone's oratory, which came from the tensions within him and again reflected the tensions within the new society, the yawning gap between the ideal and the reality.

At the end of his stump through Lancashire in the autumn of 1864 Gladstone recorded his own thoughts on the reception given him by the people (whom he did not separate into classes): "So ended in peace an exhausting, flattering, I hope not intoxicating circuit. God knows I have not courted them. I hope I do not rest on them. I pray I may turn them to account for good. It is, however, impossible not to love the people from whom such manifestations come, as meet me in every quarter . . . Somewhat haunted by dreams of halls, the lines of people, and great assemblies." Catherine's comments on "our Lancashire visits" were as typical as her husband's and show the enthusiasm with which she had accepted his new position: ". . . the speeches—oh Lucy it was almost too much to hear him & to see the marvellous feeling & to think all the time how good he is."

In the Cabinet Gladstone continued to be at loggerheads with Palmerston and many of his colleagues, and the gossip which was circulating about Lord Palmerston was not such as to make Gladstone admire him any more. For his lordship had become involved in a liaison with a Mrs. Cane, and Disraeli commented, "Good God, if the English learn that Palmerston, at the age of eighty, still has his affairs, they'll make him Dictator," while the favourite joke said she was certainly Cain, but was he Abel? A major source of Cabinet disagreement remained the defence budget, and Gladstone stood firm against the arguments that Britain had to keep up her defences because man was a quarrelsome animal. If that were true then it was England's duty to see that mankind became less so, and building gigantic armies and navies would not achieve the objective. He was regrettably unmoved by Palmerston's arguments that some of the money required was to improve the lot of the British soldier, which remained disgraceful (less per head per year was spent on a soldier than on a convict). But it was very difficult to quarrel with Lord Palmerston and Gladstone could again only threaten resignation which he did not effect because this time he decided he would serve his beliefs and his country best by remaining in the Cabinet. Gladstone's excitable, unpredictable side continued to worry his even-tempered leader and more phlegmatic, restrained or sleepy colleagues (it was said that half of Palmerston's Cabinet spent half of its time asleep).

In May 1864 Gladstone let loose a thunderbolt or, as he himself said, "I have unwarily, it seems, set the Thames on fire." The House of Commons was discussing in desultory fashion a resolution upon a subject which had erupted intermittently since 1832 and which John Bright had been pursuing with vigour, the extension of the franchise, when Gladstone rose to reply for the Government and delivered himself of these words: ". . . I venture to say that every man who is not presumably incapacitated by some consideration of personal unfitness or of political danger, is morally qualified to come within the pale of the constitution." He then qualified himself by saying he was not advocating sudden excessive or intoxicating change, but people were uninterested in his qualifications and the news rang round England that the Chancellor of the Exchequer had come out in strong support of manhood suffrage. On the one hand Gladstone was denounced as a democratic leveller; on the other he took a leap forward as the people's hero. Lord Palmerston and he had a brisk exchange of letters in which the former expressed the view that the vote was a *trust* not a *right* and could only be entrusted to those who had demonstrated that they had the experience, maturity and wisdom to use it properly. Gladstone answered this argument by drawing on Catherine's firsthand experience during the cotton famine; he told an audience in Lancashire that the qualities which in his opinion befitted a man for the franchise were self-command, self-control, respect for order, patience under suffering and regard for superiors; he then demanded, ". . . and when, I should like to ask, were all these great qualities exhibited in a manner more signal, even more illustrious, than in the conduct of Lancashire under the profound affliction of the winter of 1862?" In effect Gladstone was voicing beliefs which had been growing within him for some time, that the tide of democracy was as inevitable and "resistless" as the desire for religious freedom which he had once opposed and then vigorously upheld, but that it needed harnessing and guiding. He found the necessary moral corroboration in what Catherine had told him from Blackburn in 1862 and what he himself had later seen or heard.

Despite Gladstone's startling pronouncements, the question of the franchise lay dormant for a while, with John Bright preventing it from falling into a comatose state. In April 1865 Richard Cobden died, worn out by his many battles, and Gladstone was a pallbearer at his funeral in rural Sussex (though Cobden spent much of his adult life in the industrial North of England and was the special hero of Lancashire, he was in fact a Sussex man). Cobden's death was not a great personal loss for Gladstone, though he had grown to respect and admire the man, but it had an interesting side effect in that John Bright henceforward focused much of his energy and enthusiasm on Gladstone. Bright was a strong character, as famed an orator and conversationalist as Gladstone—Mary later wrote of her father and Bright fighting to control the conversation at Hawarden. He and Cobden had been a beautifully complementary partnership in which neither was dominant, but Bright had a melancholic strain: he flinched at the prospect of real personal power and he needed somebody with whom or for whom he could work to unleash his strength. After Cobden's death it was the furtherance of Gladstone's career for which he worked, and he was an invaluable if far from docile lieutenant.

In July 1865 Parliament was dissolved and Gladstone had to decide whether he should again contest Oxford University. Emotional loyalty told him that he should but reality warned him that this time he was likely to be beaten, as he was no longer a Tory and the Tories had found a strong candidate to oppose him. Many of his constituents at Oxford were as disturbed by Gladstone's religious stance as by his recent Liberal measures and utterances, because he had made a speech in the House of Commons in which he had intimated that he might favour the disestablishment of the Anglican Church in Ireland (in fact he had already moved towards this conclusion but the speech had been toned down by Lord Palmerston, to whom, for once, Gladstone had submitted a draft).

Gladstone was now in regular communication with Nonconformist ministers and had become a frequent guest at Nonconformist tea parties, and while there was a political link here, because the Nonconformists were part of the backbone of the new Liberal party, Gladstone's interest was also religious. He told one of his new Unitarian friends, "I am, as you know, one altogether attached to dogma, which I believe to be the skeleton that carries the flesh, the blood, and the life of the blessed thing we call the Christian religion"; but he went on to say that though he had been brought up to believe that salvation depended entirely on the acceptance of a narrow creed, though he still thought his creed was the best, he had long since cast the weeds of intolerance behind him and accepted that all Christians were partakers of God's mercy. However, Gladstone admitted that not all Christians shared his matured views; included among those were many of the Anglican electors of Oxford University, and he was duly defeated. He wrote to his friend Bishop Wilberforce (then Bishop of Oxford), "There have been two great deaths or transmigrations of spirit in my political existence. One very slow, the breaking of ties with my original party. The other, very short and sharp, the breaking of the tie with Oxford." He added enigmatically, "There will probably be a third, and no more"; if the Home Rule split of 1886 is accepted as a break instituted by Gladstone, it can be said to have been a prescient remark.

In a letter to her "dear Locket" Catherine described her husband's grief at his Oxford defeat and his emotional resilience: "I watched him anxiously as the workings of that dear pale face and the pacing of the room showed the deep emotion, but thank God he has been helped through all and though a few short hours afterwards he was on his legs facing thousands of people at Manchester and then Liverpool he seemed almost inspired." Gladstone's reason for travelling immediately to Lancashire was that he had another parliamentary seat on which to fall back, that of South

Lancashire.* It was appropriately in the Free Trade Hall in Manchester that he announced, "I am come among you, and I am come among you 'unmuzzled,'" a remark which indicated that he himself regarded the break with Oxford as inevitable and by now necessary. Gladstone did not emerge triumphantly at the head of the poll as might have been expected in a Lancashire constituency, though he was elected. But South Lancashire covered a largely rural, strongly Tory area and Gladstone's hints about disestablishing the Church of Ireland had aroused anti-Catholic, anti-Irish sentiment there, too. Catherine was as deeply involved in her son's electoral campaign as her husband's, because Willie was standing for Parliament for the first time, but he had little ambition and tended towards indolence (she asked her husband to "put a pin" in their eldest son, metaphorically speaking). However, with his mother's enthusiastic support, Willie was duly returned as the Liberal M.P. for Chester.

In the General Election Lord Palmerston and the Liberals retained power, but within three months his lordship was dead and it was almost the end of an era; almost but not quite, because Earl (ex-Lord John) Russell succeeded him as Prime Minister, the last of a long line of Whigs to hold that office. Thereafter the Whigs were no more than an element in the Liberal party and the term "Whig" became synonymous with an aristocratic liberalism that slowly withered away (whereas the term "Tory" remains in political usage and is either interchangeable with "Conservative" or used to denote an old-fashioned, dyed-in-the-wool Conservatism). Although Catherine had long detested "little Johnny" it was he who offered her husband the job she had coveted for him, that of Leader of the House of Commons. When Gladstone accepted (inevitably with some reservations and quibbles), many people, including his friends, were worried about how he would handle the important task. They feared that his rashness and vehemence might upset the Commons; they knew that he was already as greatly hated as he was loved and there were those only too anxious to provide the rope with which he could hang himself; and they thought he lacked tact in dealing with members of his own party. On the first scores Gladstone proved himself a model of firmness, authority and judicious caution, but the accusation about his want of tact in dealing with the lesser—and sometimes the greater—lights of the Liberal party remained true, and it was an area in which his wife was no help.

Neither Catherine nor Gladstone was a snob but she failed to appreciate that many political nonentities considered themselves to be important, and the occasional invitation to dine at Carlton House Terrace or 11 Downing Street would have smoothed ruffled fur. When she had time to spare from her charitable activities Catherine continued to invite people she liked to her functions, with visiting foreign celebrities thrown in. Her husband's failure to cultivate the rank and file of the Liberal party (who for most of

---

* Parliamentary candidates could then contest more than one seat, a practice made possible by the time span of General Elections.

his tenure of power remained socially more rank than file) stemmed from his basic lack of interest in people as individuals. Gladstone could be extremely kind and thoughtful to comparative nobodies; his attention to his prostitute friends has already been recounted and while they admittedly came into a special category, he sometimes extended his concern to men in distress, too. There is, for example, an anecdote about his missing the road-sweeper by the House of Commons, discovering that the man was ill and going to see him in his lodgings. But there had to be something specific about the person that caught his attention, and while Gladstone had an immense rappórt with a mass audience and understood many of the emotions and desires of people *en bloc*, he was too often alarmingly unaware that individuals suffered from lack of confidence and apprehension and yearned for personal attention. On the more intimate level there was the fact that Gladstone frequently failed to recognise even his friends because he was so shortsighted and refused to wear glasses; but it was not a factor likely to be appreciated by the normal-sighted or to soothe hurt feelings.

Whatever opinions Catherine may have held about Earl Russell, her husband's relationship with the new Prime Minister was considerably more harmonious than with Lord Palmerston, and the two men were in agreement on the topic which dominated the Ministry, namely the extension of the franchise. Russell had been the hero of the 1832 Reform Bill; for many years thereafter he considered it to be the ultimate in parliamentary reform (one of his nicknames was "Finality Jack"), but in his declining years—he was seventy-three and his always frail body was visibly weakening—he decided he wanted to be the hero of another Reform Bill. Early in March 1866 Gladstone introduced a Representation of the People Bill into the House of Commons that proposed to extend the franchise by some four hundred thousand voters by lowering the existing property qualifications. It was not exactly a sweeping measure of electoral reform (over eight hundred thousand voters had been enfranchised in 1832) but the storms of protest and opposition were almost as great as in that year. Part of the opposition said that there was no great demand for reform in the country, and despite the efforts of John Bright and the Reform League this was then a fairly true statement; but the majority of the opposition based its arguments on the unfitness of the lower orders to vote and the damaging effects to the fabric of society of the masses controlling the classes. The opposition was not confined to the Tories, indeed the most trenchant and damaging attacks on the Bill came from a member of the Liberal party, Robert Lowe, who was as startling a man physically as mentally, being an albino. Lowe's defence of an elite aristocratic system of government was brilliant, and he and his cabal of Liberal anti-democrats acquired lasting fame as "the Adullamites," a fame bestowed upon them by the vivid biblical phrasemaking of John Bright, who said that Lowe had "retired into what may be called his political Cave of Adullam—and he has called about him everyone that was in distress and everyone that was discontented." (Catherine with her equally vivid mis-phrasemaking referred to them as "the Dolomites.")

The debates in the House of Commons raged, and tempers in and out of Parliament rose. Among them was Gladstone's. In a speech at Liverpool he accused selfish aristocrats of conspiring to cheat the people of their just rights. In the Commons Disraeli taunted him with his speech in the Oxford Union in 1831 (when his position had been that of the Adullamites) but Gladstone was more than equal to such jibes and defended his change of heart and mind, and his entry into the Liberal party, in masterly fashion. In this same speech Gladstone himself coined some notable words when in the peroration he said, "You cannot fight against the future. Time is on our side." While this was true, temporarily it was against the Liberal Government, and on 18 June yet another amendment to the Bill was carried against them. Lucy Cavendish described "the fate of the poor Bill which is like a child dying of the chickenpox after it has got through measles, scarlet fever, & whooping cough." After the defeat Earl Russell wanted to continue the battle, John Bright urged the Government to dissolve Parliament and appeal to the country as Lord Grey had done in 1831, but though Gladstone had earlier supported Russell in his desire to fight, this time he voted with those members of the Cabinet who had little stomach for the Bill and favoured immediate resignation. His principal reason was that the Government should not be seen to be clinging to office, but later he considered that his decision had been wrong and that Bright had advocated the correct course of action. With the utmost reluctance Queen Victoria returned from Balmoral, where she had been throughout the mounting crisis—Lucy Cavendish noted, "The poor Queen's terrible fault in remaining (or indeed being) at Balmoral has given rise to universal complaint and much foul-mouthed gossip." (The brawny, handsome John Brown had recently been appointed Her Majesty's personal servant and was now in constant attendance upon her in London, Windsor or Osborne but principally at Balmoral; the foul-mouthed gossip was about what sort of relationship the Queen and her servant enjoyed.) Her Majesty begged Earl Russell to reconsider his decision but his Cabinet would not allow him to do so, and she had to accept the Liberal resignation; Lord Derby took office as the leader of a minority Conservative Ministry.

If there had been no strong feeling in the country about reform before the Bill was introduced, three months of debating the issue and in particular Robert Lowe's vitriolic language against the working classes had stimulated the feeling to fever pitch. After the Liberal resignation crowds roamed the streets of London shouting the praises of the man who had introduced the Bill and who had fought for it with such fervour in and out of Parliament, chanting "Gladstone for ever" and "Gladstone and Liberty." On 27 June what *The Times* described as "a mob" collected outside Carlton House Terrace, jamming the streets right down Pall Mall, calling for

Mr. Gladstone, the people's champion.† He was not at home but Catherine was, and on police advice that a brief appearance by *her* might disperse the crowds, she came to the balcony of the house, together with Mary, Agnes and Helen, and they all bowed and waved to the multitude, which indeed dispersed. Nevertheless, *The Times* accused the Gladstones of courting the mob in a disgraceful manner reminiscent of the worst type of demagogue.

As Gladstone was fighting the electoral reform battle which truly established him as the people's hero, a cholera epidemic struck the country and Catherine's activities during it made her a heroine, if in more restricted circles. The disease first appeared in Bristol in April 1866, and by July it had reached London. The worst-hit areas were in the East End; by the last week in July the death toll had leapt to 1,253 and panic gripped the population. The cholera bacillus had not then been identified, and it was not appreciated that water was a main carrier of the disease; therefore it thrived in areas where sanitation was minimal. It was also believed to be contagious. As the stricken people were bundled into the London Hospital in Whitechapel, many of the ancillary staff fled in fear of their lives and though the hospital offered enormous wages, few replacements could be found and it began to resemble a leper colony. The hospital secretary wrote, ". . . the state of the wards was frightful. Everywhere we had sawdust steeped in carbolic scattered about, and underneath every bed there was a large bag of sawdust. The beds themselves were made of sacks of straw . . . as soon as a patient died, or could be removed, we carried away the bed of straw and sack of sawdust, and took them to an open space at the back of the hospital, where every other night we had a bonfire." One regular visitor to the London Hospital was Catherine Gladstone, who, as the secretary again wrote, "faced all difficulties at a time when people outside seemed to be panic-stricken."

Catherine did not actually nurse the patients but she went fearlessly through the frightful wards, sitting by the bedside of the dying, giving them what comfort she could and assuring them that their children would be cared for. The child patients inside the hospital were one of her immediate concerns, and those who survived the ravages of the disease were taken into Catherine's care. Frequently she left the London Hospital carrying in her arms a child wrapped in a blanket and if she could not find immediate accommodation she would take it home with her. She asked her husband, "Should you mind three *clean* little children being taken to Carlton House Terrace?" (His answer was that of course he would not mind.) On 2 August Catherine wrote to *The Times* appealing for temporary homes for children orphaned by the cholera epidemic and on 15 August she again wrote to the newspaper, this time appealing for money for an orphanage. She had found a house at Clapton in northeast London and with the money collected, this was turned into a temporary orphanage and conva-

† The felicitous description "the People's William" was coined by the *Daily Telegraph* during the 1860s.

lescent home. Lucy Cavendish described how her aunt reacted to the influx of children: "She took over 150 poor tinies straight to her arms; all orphans & many weak after cholera themselves: all friendless & without even clothes on their poor little bodies. Of these not one has died at the Home, which she got in a hurry for them at Clapton: & she has provided for a great many in different ways: but 57 remain on our hands." Of the fifty-seven remaining Catherine later took a dozen boys north with her to Hawarden, where they were housed in an old coach house, with the Gladstones accepting full responsibility for their welfare, upkeep and education. (The Bishop of London's wife accepted responsibility for the orphaned girls who came into the Gladstone orbit.) Catherine's not very large staff at Hawarden was devoted to her, and they needed to be, because they had a clutch of Lancashire mill girls still living in the house in the yard and being trained as domestic servants, together with a dozen little urchins from the East End of London roaming round the coach house and grounds.

At the end of September 1866 Catherine temporarily abandoned her charitable duties and charges when she and her husband, together with their daughters, went on a continental holiday. Lucy Cavendish thought she was greatly in need of it, having strained her nerves and strength to their limits, and her husband too had been through a year of immense exertion. Gladstone's stated reasons for leaving England at that moment were that temporarily he thought he had said all he had to say, that he was being subjected to intolerable pressures from reforming quarters and that the breach in the Liberal party caused by the Adullamite revolt should be given time to heal. It may be thought that he should have stayed to make further comment on the subject of parliamentary reform which was tearing the country apart, but his absence in foreign climes was not noticeable, for John Bright toured the provinces, making rousing speeches at monster meetings in favour of "household suffrage." Gladstone thought Bright was going too far, outstripping the measure of reform the country wanted, but Bright knew what he was doing, and as in the popular estimation he and Gladstone were now associated, the speeches did the latter's reputation no harm.

While they were abroad the Gladstones did not trouble themselves over-much about such matters. In Rome they were granted an audience with Pope Pius IX and Mary recorded that His Holiness "trolled on very good-naturedly for about 20 minutes." From the Holy City—where their apartment was twice set on fire, which, as the fictitious Lady Bracknell might have observed, looked suspiciously like carelessness—Gladstone wrote to the real-life Duchess of Sutherland, "We go quietly about our work seeing Rome." Lord Clarendon gave a different version of the quietness of the Gladstones' life, writing to one of his friends, "Every morning at 8 he lectures his wife and daughters upon Dante, and requires them to parse and give the roots of every verb. He runs about all day to shops, galleries, and persons." (Lord Clarendon, who became one of Gladstone's Whig supporters, had as amusing a tongue as pen but he was notoriously flippant, tended to be indiscreet and earned Queen Victoria's undying displeasure by calling her "The Missus"). Towards the end of January 1867 Gladstone travelled to Paris, where his family soon joined him and Mary recorded, "Found Papa flourishing & tremendously sought after"; but by the end of the month they were back in England, where Gladstone discovered that in his absence the situation had changed dramatically and the cause of parliamentary reform had been espoused by Lord Derby and Mr. Disraeli.

Disraeli's Bill was given the name of the "Ten Minute Bill" because of the rush with which he presented it to his Cabinet colleagues, and Lord Derby said it was "a leap in the dark" intended to "dish the Whigs." But the Tory reaction to the mounting demand in the country was also sensible, practical and eminently realistic, while Disraeli's handling of the Reform Bill was brilliant and established him as a major political force and the undisputed if not then titular leader of the Conservative party. As with the Corn Law issue, Disraeli had no burning feeling for or against an extension of the franchise, but he wanted to give his party a broader base and appeal, and once he had accepted that reform was necessary and desirable he pursued the measure with enthusiasm. With consummate skill he soothed the fears of the Tory backwoodsmen, wooed his rank and file and handled a House of Commons which was as a whole in an uncertain, jaundiced frame of mind on the subject.

Gladstone, as the House of Commons leader of the Opposition which had introduced a Reform Bill a year before, was placed in a virtually impossible situation and one which he was badly equipped to handle. As Lucy Cavendish observed, he had "the profoundest *faithlessness* in Dizzy; almost the only man of whom he does not think better than he deserves." He therefore attributed the worst possible motives to Disraeli's every action in the House of Commons, and as the gentleman was playing the situation by ear but with enthusiastic conviction, Gladstone found himself for once completely outboxed. He attacked on high-minded principles—the vote was not there to be sold to the highest bidder in the Tory or Liberal party—and when he attacked the weaker parts of Disraeli's proposals he bogged himself down in tortuous hair-splitting detail. Lacking Disraeli's skill and tact as a party manager, he failed to carry many of the Liberals with him, and Richard Monckton-Milnes (by then Lord Houghton) noted, "I met Gladstone at breakfast; he seems quite awed by the diabolical cleverness of Dizzy." Gladstone was not exactly awed but he was becoming irritated and his temper was getting the better of him. The devoted Lucy recorded one speech which was "a more vehement, bitter onslaught than I have ever heard him make . . . he glared from one side to another, gesticulated with both arms; often spoke with a kind of bitter laugh, stumbled over the formal phraseology of the House, in his violent feeling"; but Lucy attributed the ill-controlled anger to "righteous indignation stirred up by moral conviction."

In the end the Bill was carried through the House of Commons in a shape that far outstripped the previous Liberal measure or even the Bill which Disraeli had introduced. When it became law in August 1867 it provided for male household suffrage in the towns, with the voting qualifications lowered in the counties; as a result one million voters were added to the electoral roll. It was the sort of ironic situation which Disraeli fully appreciated because it was part of the ridiculous, unpredictable quality of human life as it was lived (Palmerston would have appreciated it, too), but Gladstone could not understand it because it was not how life *should* be lived. The autumn of 1867 found him in a depressed frame of mind and with his reputation in the House of Commons, though not in the country at large, somewhat sunken because he had not proved a firm, tactful Opposition leader at a difficult moment but instead had been far too irritable, vehement and liable to be thrown off balance.

Catherine gave her husband the customary loyalty and approval during his fights against Disraeli and comforted him when he was "knocked down" by his adverse votes and receptions in the House of Commons, but she was also deeply involved in another scheme. Even before her days in the cholera wards it had struck her that those who survived the ravages of the various diseases that brought them into the London Hospital were then sent out in a weak state into appallingly bad housing conditions. She left others to deal with the housing conditions, but it occurred to her that a short free convalescence in a healthy atmosphere, with no strings attached, might work minor miracles for the patients in the East End. In March 1867 she again wrote to *The Times* appealing for donations for a free convalescent home which would be an adjunct to the London Hospital and part of the service it could offer its more seriously ill patients. A committee had already been set up whose members included herself, Gladstone, Lord and Lady Frederick Cavendish, Lord Lyttleton and Sir Stephen Glynne, though it was not entirely a family affair and had other members on its board. Apart from the appeal to *The Times'* readership Catherine again wrote dozens of personal letters; she told Lucy, "Fancy my courage—I have written to Lord Derby," but at her niece's behest she had *not* written to the Duke of Devonshire, though she was hopeful that Lucy might be able to persuade her father-in-law to make a contribution. Included among her letters was one to Queen Victoria, via a lady-in-waiting; she asked that the details of the convalescent home and its aims be laid before Her Majesty, as "It would be such a comfort to me to feel that the scheme had H.M's approval." She again told Lucy, "The Queen approved of the plan without giving money!" but what Catherine really wanted was royal patronage (with or without money). However, she was further informed that Her Majesty could not patronise a venture until it had established itself, as it would not do for the Queen's name to be associated with a failure.

Undaunted, Catherine pressed on and suddenly received the offer of a largish house at Snaresbrook in Essex which was already functioning as a convalescent home in a minor way. In establishing a convalescent home Catherine was not an original thinker, but she was a complete innovator in pursuing the idea that it should be *free,* and in the manner in which it should be run. The practice in the existing convalescent homes (and many charitable institutions) was that applicants frequently had to pay a proportion of the costs; therefore the most needy were ruled out. Catherine insisted that at Snaresbrook the convalescents should only be required to pay their return rail fare from London, that the subscribers should have no right to nominate candidates for admission and applicants should be selected by a specially appointed committee which would judge each case on its merits, without bias or favour. Her earlier experience of charitable committees had probably shown her the ills and abuses to which the subscribers' many privileges led, but the system she devised was a further example of her professionalism and her concern that charities should be freely open to as wide a section of the poor as possible. After prolonged opposition, Catherine won through and soon most charities had fallen into line with her scheme and were operating on a more professional, less biased basis. Catherine and Lucy spent hours shopping for the convalescent home at Snaresbrook—Lucy was delighted when she found "stone ware cup, *with* its saucer, price 2d!!"—and by November 1867 the home was well established, whereupon Catherine again wrote to Queen Victoria enquiring if she could now receive royal patronage. But it was again withheld on the grounds that Her Majesty had so many demands for her patronage that each application had to be carefully considered.

As Catherine's latest venture thrived, her husband emerged from his depression and once again demonstrated that he was terrible on the rebound. He himself considered that he showed his invaluable sense of right timing, which his opponents frequently called opportunism, by raising the standard of the Irish question. After their Reform Bill defeat the Liberals needed a standard around which they could rally—and Gladstone was not coy about admitting this fact—but it can be said that his timing *was* right. He had been considering the unhappy state of Ireland intermittently for the last few years, particularly the position ·of the established Protestant Church, which enjoyed vast wealth and privileges in a country that was largely Catholic. But 1867 was the year of Fenian violence‡ in Ireland, England and North America which focused attention on Irish affairs. While the reaction of much of the country was horror and an increased conviction that the Irish were at best untrustworthy children, at worst highly dangerous ones, it was not shared by Gladstone. For him the Fenian violence was evidence of the intensity of the Irish disaffection, because one did not (in his estimation) go around blowing up and killing people unless

‡ The word "Fenian" originated among Irish-American revolutionaries, coined by an exiled survivor of the 1848 rebellion, and it celebrated the folklore heroes who were a sort of Irish samurai. It was quickly adopted to cover the Irish Revolutionary (or Republican) Brotherhood in Ireland and England.

one had a profound sense of injustice. Gladstone perceived that his duty, as "the People's William," lay in persuading his flock that their duty was to promote reform in the religious and educational institutions of unhappy Ireland, and to adjust the long-festering sores of peasant rights and landlord wrongs.

In December 1867 Earl Russell intimated that he would not again seek office and though no official announcement was made—indeed Gladstone was never actually proclaimed leader of the Liberal party until Her Majesty invited him to form a Government—he was the only man who could take over the leadership. As Gladstone celebrated his fifty-eighth birthday on 29 December he faced the future assured that he would be Prime Minister—probably sooner rather than later, as a General Election could not be long delayed (the Conservatives being a minority Government)— and imbued with a sense of mission about Ireland that had the virtues of being morally right and politically useful.

CHAPTER 10

THE PRIME MINISTER AND HIS WIFE

IN FEBRUARY 1868 AN AILING Lord Derby retired from the titular leadership of the Conservative party. His successor had become as automatic as Earl Russell's and on the twenty-seventh of the month, at the age of sixty-three, Benjamin Disraeli formally kissed hands with Her Majesty as Prime Minister. His comment on assuming office is famous—"Yes! I have climbed to the top of the greasy pole"— and Lucy Cavendish made a similar comment, that the "Lord High Conjuror" had reached the top of the tree, adding, "I wonder how the Queen likes it." The answer was that Her Majesty liked it very much; within a week of Disraeli's appointment she noted that he was full of poetry, romance and chivalry. However, the relationship was not then given much time to develop. In March Gladstone fired the first shots of his political-cum-moral campaign by giving notice to the House of Commons of three resolutions whose intent was to disestablish the Church of Ireland (i.e. the Anglican Church would cease to be the State church and its privileges would be removed). Disraeli told Her Majesty that Mr. Gladstone had mistaken the spirit of the times and the temper of the country, but when the first resolution passed through the Commons with a majority of sixty-five, he realised that it was he who had been mistaken and that he could no longer continue to govern with a minority. He accordingly advised the Queen to dissolve Parliament (unless she wished the Conservatives to resign immediately, which she did not), but suggested that the dissolution be postponed until the new electoral registers necessitated by the Reform Act were ready.

It was in fact a practical suggestion—there would have been an uproar from "the people" if a General Election had been fought on the old limited register—but the manner in which Disraeli presented his case to the House of Commons implied that he was retaining office at the Queen's behest, and it was not an implication that pleased ardent constitutionalists or Liberals. Before Parliament was dissolved, in fact in the same month of March that his father launched upon the destruction of Disraeli's Ministry, Willie Gladstone made his maiden speech in the House and Mary told her cousin, "You may fancy the sort of state we were in, Mama rushing madly about the box [in the Ladies' Gallery], & now & then wildly clutching my arm." But Willie had none of his father's fire, and though he was a charming man personally he was never more than a dutiful member of the House of Commons.

By November the new electoral rolls were completed and Parliament was dissolved. Gladstone was already campaigning in South-west Lancashire (there had been some redistribution of boundaries in the Reform Act too, and South Lancashire had become South-west), and he stormed through the area making speeches. One of his perorations rang round the country when, in speaking of the Protestant ascendancy in Ireland, he compared it to "Some tall tree of noxious growth, lifting its head to Heaven and poisoning the atmosphere of the land so far as its shadow can extend." During the electoral campaign Gladstone also published *A Chapter of Autobiography*, a book which was far from autobiographical in the normal sense and was in fact a lengthy explanation how and why he had moved from the views expressed in *The State in Its Relations with the Church* to his present position of a politician who was proposing to disestablish the Church of Ireland.

In the book Gladstone reploughed the ground of his controversy with the now-dead Macaulay and said that while he did not accept the latter's assertions that the primary function of government was temporal and still believed that it must have a "moral dimension," he admitted that the principle of the marriage of a purified State and Church was no longer viable, indeed that as he was writing his book he had found himself "the last man on the sinking ship." He thought that to change one's opinion could be evil but it was always less evil than adhering to mistaken views, and he now considered that a Church divorced from its people, as the Anglican Church was in Ireland, became "the mere cemetery of a great idea." By much of the country *A Chapter of Autobiography* was well received; if not everybody grasped its more refined and tortuous defensive arguments, people liked a politician who took them into his confidence and was not frightened of admitting his mistakes. However, in the constituency of South-west Lancashire neither the splendour of Gladstone's oratory nor the explanation of his writing impressed the electorate; there, anti-Catholic, anti-Irish feeling proved too strong and he was defeated. But as at Oxford in 1865 he had half-expected defeat and had been nominated for another constituency, Greenwich, for which he was returned with a reasonable majority. Willie Gladstone was returned for the Yorkshire constituency of Whitby, so father and son were again in Parliament.

The result of the General Election was a startling victory for the Liberals with a majority of some one hundred and twelve seats, and despite his own initial defeat it was regarded as a personal triumph for Mr. Gladstone (it may be added that the establishment of an embryonic Liberal party machine also assisted the result). Generally, it was believed that the people had shown their gratitude to Mr. Gladstone for his efforts on their behalf and for having espoused the cause of parliamentary reform (no matter who had actually passed the Reform Act), and also that they accepted his explanations and approved of his new Irish policy. When the nature of the Conservative defeat became apparent, Disraeli accepted it calmly and offered his resignation to the Queen, a move which was then novel but thereafter became the normal practice (previously, ministries defeated in an election had returned to office to await defeat in the House of Commons, but in recent years few of them had been as massively rejected as Disraeli's and therefore had had more reason to hope to cling to power). Queen Victoria already had some reservations about Mr. Gladstone. She was personally opposed to the course he was pursuing over Ireland, as she considered it dangerous and reckless, and not a few of her advisers had recently been harping upon Mr. Gladstone's impulsive, impetuous nature which ill-befitted him to lead the country. But there was also much she admired about Mr. Gladstone and she immediately instructed her Private Secretary General Grey (the gentleman who had married Caroline Farquhar) to take a letter to Mr. Gladstone inviting him, as the acknowledged leader of the Liberal party, to form a Government.

On 1 December 1868 General Grey telegraphed to Hawarden asking Gladstone if he wished to receive the Queen's letter there or in London, and Gladstone replied at Hawarden as it would attract less attention. He was in the grounds of Hawarden Castle when the telegram arrived, and the story of its reception is renowned but worth repeating. Gladstone was indulging in his already well-known hobby of tree-felling, and on reading the telegram he merely said, "Very significant," handed it to his companion Evelyn Ashley and resumed his tree-felling. As Ashley later recorded, "After a few minutes the blows ceased, and Mr Gladstone resting on the handle of his axe, looked up with deep earnestness in his voice and with great intensity in his face, exclaimed, 'My mission is to pacify Ireland.' He then resumed his task, and never said another word until the tree was down." The next morning General Grey caught an early train from Windsor to Chester, where he was met by Catherine, and on the drive to Hawarden he was extremely surprised to learn "that Mrs G. knew every thing that had passed!" On arrival at Hawarden Castle Grey was only slightly less surprised to be taken into "an almost dark room—the only light by the fire, & the two candles by which Mr Gladstone was working." (Gladstone's frugality extended to illumination, to the detriment of his eyes, and when he was at the royal residences he commented on the number of candles the Queen burned and surreptitiously extinguished several in his room.)

The actual conversation between the two men proceeded amicably, Mr. Gladstone undertook to form a Government and the next day he travelled to Windsor, where he had his first audience with Her Majesty as Prime Minister. The only problem was Gladstone's wish to have Lord Clarendon as his Foreign Minister, an office he had already held in previous administrations. Privately Gladstone thought it would be inexcusable to exclude from office the most experienced foreign diplomat on the Liberal benches because of court gossip and Her Majesty's personal dislike, and he intimated as much to General Grey. (Gladstone displayed a touch of irony in saying that while court gossip seemed to him "absolutely irresponsible" it also appeared to be "uniformly admitted as infallible.") He agreed with Her Majesty that Lord Clarendon's tongue occasionally ran away with him and said that he would ensure that the gentleman had as little contact with the Queen as possible, and with this assurance she agreed to the appointment. By the end of 1868 Gladstone too had reached the summit, and his comment upon the assumption of the highest office in the land is as typical as Disraeli's: "This birthday opens my sixtieth year. I descend the hill of life. It would be truer to say I ascend a steepening path with a burden ever gathering weight. The Almighty seems to sustain and spare me for some purpose of His own, deeply unworthy as I know myself to be. Glory be to His name."

In Catherine's opinion God had manifestly sustained her husband for his supreme task, and though she did not concur with the unworthiness, in a letter written several months before he became Prime Minister but when it was obvious that he might soon hold that office, she showed that she was not blind to his faults, urging him to cultivate "great dignity, great patience but not too much humility & to guard against too much eagerness or violence one moment, & then too much civility & modesty another." However much Catherine's ambition had been realised, however thrilled, proud and assured she was that with a little restraint her husband would be the greatest Prime Minister England had ever known, it cannot be said that she immediately devoted the major part of her energies to playing the role of the Prime Minister's wife, at least not in an accepted sense of organising his social life and being the helpmate in constant attendance.

When Gladstone became Prime Minister at the end of 1868 the free convalescent home at Snaresbrook had run into serious difficulties, not because Catherine's system was not working well but because of strenuous opposition from local residents, who had no objections to the deserving poor being given a free holiday as long as it was not in their vicinity, lowering the tone of the neighbourhood and reducing property values. With the expiration of the lease on the Snaresbrook house, the landlord yielded to the pressure of the residents and refused to renew it, and Catherine had to evacuate the convalescents at a moment's notice. Several members of the committee considered abandoning the enterprise, but she would not hear of such defeatism and when a more spacious house, standing in its own grounds on the edge of Epping Forest, was offered to the committee, Catherine immediately launched another appeal for funds to buy the freehold for the sum of £3,000. By May 1869 Lucy Cavendish was so alarmed by the manner in which Aunt Pussy was overworking that she wrote a personal appeal to Gladstone urging him to make her rest. Gladstone himself was fairly busy at this moment but he replied saying that while some considerable restraint in his wife's labours was desirable, it was also true that her health and strength seemed to have borne up to a degree that excited his astonishment. He probably understood better than did Lucy his wife's need to have an independent life and the way in which she thrived under pressure. Occasionally, however, the pressure got the better of even Catherine's balanced temperament and in July she wrote a contrite little note to her husband saying, "Darling, I am sorry I spoke in haste, do forget it—my only excuse is that I was tired & hot & vexed at the time."

There was no relaxation in Catherine's labours. The response to her appeal for money to buy the freehold was good; this time Queen Victoria sent a donation for £100, and in November 1869 "Mrs Gladstone's Free Convalescent Home for the Poor, more especially of the East of London, Woodford Hall, Essex, E." officially opened its doors. (Catherine had no interest in her name being attached to the venture and only agreed reluctantly when it was pointed out that it was a name that carried weight and would be likely to attract the needed subscriptions.) As soon as she had seen the Woodford Convalescent Home launched she plunged into another scheme whereby the now empty Clapton house was turned into a temporary hospital for victims of the relapsing fever which had hit the East End. At the end of 1869 Gladstone told his wife that he had no doubt that her good works were useful and it was "only your knocking about or being knocked about that I am sorry for." If one detects a faint wish that Catherine was not knocking about quite so much, that was as close as Gladstone came to interfering with her free will and choice of action.

While Catherine was so deeply involved with her convalescents, Gladstone assumed his burden with the youthfulness that was part of his magic. Eight years earlier he had recorded in his birthday retrospect, "The strangest feeling of all in me is a rebellion (I know not what else to call it) against growing old . . . I will not be old." There was something of Peter Pan in Gladstone, in the determination not to grow old—rather than up—and in the sense that life—as much as death—was an awfully big adventure; it gave him the zest which attracted individuals as well as crowds and which his opponents found hard to counter. Gladstone's first administration was not only the best from the point of view of the results it achieved, it was also the best-balanced. Other of his ministries contained as talented a collection of men but they were unbalanced either by political views or personal animosities or both, and never achieved the initial harmony of that of 1868. Within the Cabinet the Whig guard was represented by the Duke of Argyll, Lord Granville, Lord Hartington and Lord Clarendon among others, but there was an infusion of the newer element with John Bright, Edward Cardwell and George Goschen, and a surprising appointment was Robert Lowe (Gladstone's Adullamite adversary) as Chancellor of the Exchequer. When Lord Clarendon died and John Bright resigned from the presidency of the Board of Trade due to ill-health in 1870, Lord Granville became Foreign Secretary, Lord Hartington was promoted, albeit reluctantly, to be Chief Secretary for Ireland (Lucy Cavendish wrote of his being "violently sat upon" by Uncle William to accept the post) and the staunchly middle-class figure of W. E. Forster was brought into the Cabinet.

Apart from John Bright, with whom Gladstone had now established a personal and political relationship—he wrote to Catherine asking if he might invite Bright to Hawarden—his closest colleagues in the Cabinet were Lord Clarendon and Lord Granville. It was the characters of the two Earls which made the friendships interesting, because each had a nice, irreverent sense of humour. However, Granville was more tactful than Clarendon and was renowned for his charm and ability to pour oil on troubled waters; he also had an aristocratic indolence, once remarking, "People think that I am a very idle man; I am sorry to say that is quite true." Yet both Clarendon and Granville, so dissimilar to Gladstone in temperament and approach to life, liked him as much as he liked them; "Puss" Granville became Gladstone's closest friend.*

Within the Cabinet, one colleague described Gladstone as having a curious mixture of deference and imperiousness, but he was not dictatorial; he encouraged wide-ranging arguments and seldom interfered with his Ministers' various departments. However, he believed absolutely in collective Cabinet responsibility and thus expected his colleagues not to tittle-tattle about disagreements and to support the majority decision once reached. To his staff Gladstone was a tough but kind and usually considerate taskmaster; he took it for granted that his private secretaries would be efficient and work nearly as hard as he did, and sometimes he forgot that they had private lives, but almost without exception they were devoted to him. Three of them, Arthur Godley (later Lord Kilbracken), Algernon West and Edward Hamilton (both later knighted), kept diaries and wrote books about Mr. Gladstone. Their devotion falls short of idolatry, but the praise coming from a diverse set of intelligent men is a further testament to his character.

At the end of 1869 Gladstone told his much-travelled, overworked wife that while Cabinet meetings were often *hard* they were usually *good* and he thought "my little family in general are doing well in their respective offices." Gladstone's Cabinet family were all much occupied from the moment they assumed office, including Granville, who was not always quite as idle as he made himself out to be, but none of them as intensely as the Prime Minister himself. The first major measure to be introduced to Parliament early in 1869 was the plank on which Gladstone had campaigned, the disestablishment of the Church of Ireland, and it was one in which he was in his element. It concerned the Church, about which he was as well-informed as any Bishop (and better than most); its sweep was dramatic,

---

* In an era when the use of Christian names was limited to very close relationships—and sometimes not even then—nicknames were common. Granville was known as "Puss" or "Pussy," while Lord Hartington rejoiced in the name of "Harty Tarty."

aiming as it did to remove the Anglican Church from its prime, privileged position in Ireland; yet its implementation required a hardheaded attention to detail. Gladstone worked on his Bill at Hawarden in typical fashion—"Wrote out a paper on the plan of the measure respecting the Irish Church . . . Worked on Homer. We felled a lime." The Bill went through the House of Commons with comparative ease, urged on by vocal Nonconformist groups who had no more love for the Established Anglican Church than had the Catholics, but it met with stiff opposition in the House of Lords, where strong Anglican beliefs held sway and many of the about-to-be-disestablished Irish Bishops sat. Temporarily it looked as if there might be a head-on collision between the Lords and Commons but moderate council prevailed, including that of Queen Victoria, who, while not approving of the disestablishment and partial disendowment of a section of her Church, accepted that the measure seemed inevitable and that a collision between the two Houses of Parliament would be infinitely more dangerous. Gladstone's only complaint about the Queen's role was that she could have assisted more effectively had she not been hundreds of miles from the scene of the crisis; for Her Majesty insisted on remaining at Balmoral. The Lords fought a last-ditch battle over amendments to the Bill but by the middle of 1869 they had capitulated and Gladstone had cut one branch from the noxious growth of the Protestant ascendancy. It *was* Gladstone who carried the measure, and during the battles a parliamentary journalist commented that "in the powers of embodying principles in legislative form and preserving unity of purpose through a multitude of confusing minutiae he has neither equal nor second among living statesmen."

Gladstone next turned his attention to the Irish land question, an area in which he rightly considered that reform was essential if he were to succeed in his mission of pacifying Ireland and making her citizens prosperous, happy members of the United Kingdom. In his 1870 Land Bill he attempted to provide some definition of tenant rights and some protection for the thousands of small tenant farmers, but in presenting the Bill he met with much stiffer opposition than over the Church question, both in his own Cabinet and in the Commons, because he was striking (however tentatively) at the established rights of property and land ownership. In one of their many oratorical duels Disraeli accused him of having, in his two Irish Bills, legalised confiscation, consecrated sacrilege and condoned high treason, assertions that gained loud cheers from many sectors of the House. By the early summer of 1870 Gladstone was described as looking worn and fagged, but he fought for his Bill tenaciously—and to some commentators it seemed almost singlehandedly—and eventually got it through both Houses. Long-term the 1870 Land Act was only a beginning to the·solution of Ireland's agrarian problems, but its omissions were not immediately apparent and it was one of Gladstone's major achievements, because the Act denied the inalienable rights of the landlords and established that the tenants had some also. With this novel principle enunciated in Ireland by Mr. Gladstone, when the next land war came to be fought against him, the Irish were better equipped to do battle than they had been previously.

It was during the 1870s that the great oratorical duels occurred between Gladstone and Disraeli. There is a nice description of how they appeared to the "common man," who in this instance was a member of the House of Commons staff. The gentleman told Wemyss Reid (the young journalist from Newcastle-on-Tyne who had progressed to parliamentary reporting) that it filled him with "an inexpressible amazement to listen to those two men, G and D, when they are conducting themselves as they 'ave been this evening. What I want to know, Sir, where do they get it from? You and me could never do such a thing—no, not for a moment. In my opinion they are more than mortal." While Gladstone was fighting for his immortal Irish Bills, other members of his Cabinet were introducing Bills whose terms were as strenuously opposed, if not necessarily from the same quarters. Edward Cardwell, the Minister of War, tackled the question of army reform, which had been overdue before the Crimean War. His proposals met with stiff opposition in most army circles, including the clutch of ducal officers, and they focused their hostility, their dislike of civilian interference and Liberal Governments on the right to buy a commission. By the summer of 1871 the Bill had finally passed through the Commons but the Lords dug their heels in over the question of the army commissions, whereupon Gladstone persuaded Queen Victoria to abolish their purchase by means of the Royal Warrant. His argument was that purchase had been endorsed by Royal Warrant (in the time of George III), therefore it could be ended the same way; but it brought down a storm of abuse on his head. Some critics said that he had browbeaten the Queen into signing the warrant, which was not true, for though she did not approve of the army reforms she quite enjoyed exercising an ancient but now rarely used royal prerogative. The more widespread criticism accused Gladstone, the great upholder of the constitution and the rights of Parliament, of bypassing parliamentary procedure. If he had wanted the Queen to act he should have gone for the Royal Warrant in the first place but *not after* he had introduced a Bill into Parliament. These latter criticisms had validity and provide an example of Gladstone's impetuousness getting the better of his good parliamentary sense.

Gladstone had comparatively little involvement in one of the great achievements of his first Ministry, the 1870 Education Act which provided elementary education for the children of England and Wales.† It was W. E. Forster who bore the burden of getting the Bill passed. Forster had been a vigorous, courageous campaigner for the North during the American Civil War and had undoubted ability, but he was noted for his tactlessness, had an even greater desire than Gladstone to be loved and was too eager to placate conflicting interests. In 1870 about half the children of

† Scotland had its own educational system and the question of education in Catholic Ireland was one over which many Governments had already stumbled and which was to trap Gladstone, too.

England and Wales were receiving some sort of elementary education in voluntary schools, mainly supported by religious bodies, and the proposal that all children should receive an elementary education to be administered by school boards roused passionate emotions. There were those who thought a little knowledge was a dangerous thing and the working classes were better left uneducated, with the brighter among them being absorbed into the existing voluntary system. There were many more who considered that education was a sacred *family* duty and therefore deeply resented the proposed interference by the State. Among those who fought for the Bill there were further passionate divisions; some thought the new elementary system should be free, compulsory and non-sectarian but a larger proportion, while agreeing on its being free and compulsory, insisted that England and Wales were Christian countries and that some religious teaching must be given. This led to further divisions: what manner of religious teaching? and what was to happen to the existing church schools that had carried the educational torch for the poor for so long?

Inevitably Forster compromised. Instead of the clean sweep of a free, compulsory elementary system to supercede the jumble of voluntary institutions, the new school boards were to come into existence only where no schooling was available, and the church schools were not to be touched. Unfortunately, some of the people most offended by these compromises were some of the staunchest Liberal supporters, the Nonconformists. Although Gladstone had been little involved in the struggles, indeed partly because of this fact, much of the Nonconformist bitterness turned on him, the man who possessed the legislative ability and tenacity to have steered a more satisfactory Bill through the House of Commons.

Other measures passed by the energetic gentlemen who formed Gladstone's first administration—and there are no stories of people falling asleep in his Cabinets—included the reform of the Civil Service, the repeal of religious tests for entrance to the universities, the legalisation of the status of trades unions, a Coal Mines Act which enforced some safety regulations in the pits for the first time and the Ballot Act whereby secret voting was introduced into Britain. The Ballot Bill—of which Gladstone himself had not initially approved—was thrown out by the House of Lords. But at Whitby, in September 1871, Gladstone told a mass audience that the people's Bill had been passed by the people's House and hinted that a dissolution and an appeal to the country might be necessary if the Lords again rejected it. Mary Gladstone said that Papa was received with "thrilling enthusiasm" in Whitby; the Lords duly took note of the enthusiasm and the threat, displayed the art of withdrawing from the precipice which had saved them innumerable times and early in 1872 passed the Ballot Bill as it stood.

During the early 1870s Catherine was scarcely less occupied than her husband. When she was in London, each Monday morning was spent at the London Hospital, where with Lucy Cavendish and other members of the committee she interviewed applicants for the Woodford Convalescent Home and then usually went round the wards chatting to the patients. Her visits were the highlight of the week, looked forward to by the patients with great excitement (one cannot think of another Prime Minister's wife who thus regularly cheered up the more deprived sectors of the community). At Hawarden she had the orphans to attend to but the major part of her energies went into her London ventures. As one of her devoted admirers recorded, money to run the Woodford Home never got past the convalescent stage itself so Catherine was constantly appealing for funds or arranging charity concerts. Apart from organising and financing the Woodford venture, the Newport Market Refuge and Industrial School also required attention and Mary Gladstone noted one of the problems her mother faced—the loss of interest: "To the Newport Refuge meeting. About 3 and a half for audience—absurd—had giggles." Early in 1871 Catherine ran into further opposition from local residents when she turned the Clapton house into a temporary convalescent home for sufferers from smallpox (one of the recurring minor epidemics had struck the East End). The matter had to go before a magistrate, with the local residents urging "the suppression or the removal of Mrs Gladstone's small-pox hospital" and telling lurid stories of half the neighbourhood being stricken with the disease; but their stories could not be supported by hard evidence and the Clapton house remained a convalescent home until the epidemic had waned.

In 1870 in particular Catherine was in almost perpetual motion. Early in the year Gladstone was unclear where she was—"I write to Hawarden, whither I had not the least idea you were going," and again, "I am rather uncertain about your address"—and towards the end of the year he told her, "I wish I could have an account of our travelling expenses this year. I think it would alarm you." Some of the travelling was caused by family pressures and commitments; in the spring Herbert, whose health had been poor for some time, was suddenly taken ill while living rough with his brothers in the North Welsh mountains and Catherine went dashing off to nurse him, and at the end of the year he had an attack of peritonitis and Catherine again rushed to him, this time at Eton. She also spent a fair amount of time at Hagley, where George Lyttleton had decided to remarry —with the Gladstones' blessing—and two of the Lyttleton girls had also become engaged. Catherine always remained involved in family affairs and it was in 1871 that she thwarted Agnes' bid for a life of her own. The beautiful, docile Agnes, who was by now twenty-nine years old, announced that she would like to train as a nurse and work full time in hospitals. Catherine, who had taken her eldest daughter round enough hospitals as a visitor and thus stimulated her interest, reacted with the refined sensibility of the most sheltered and reactionary of Victorian matriarchs. She wrote a long letter to Lucy Cavendish saying she had great sympathy for her daughter's "pretty thoughts" but the age of twenty-nine was in her opinion decidedly too young for Agnes to be thrust into the sordid side of nursing, particularly going round the wards with the doctors (male), and she trusted she would have Lucy's support in dissuading Agnes from any such course. Agnes, who had inherited neither her father's nor her mother's toughness of spirit, was alas dissuaded and dutifully stayed at home, accompanying her mother on the hospital visits rather than participating in the actual nursing of the patients, until her eventual engagement in August 1873, which her mother thought was "as it should be natural & comfortable."

Mary and Helen also stayed at home, their adventurous traits unconsciously dampened by their mother's surprisingly conventional, imperiously protective attitude, but they both had more spirit than Agnes. Mary had her music and built a very interesting circle of friends, and Catherine appreciated that Helen had a good brain and wrote to her husband saying, "Will you allow Helen to study the cypher that she may be the more ready when any unearthly telegram arrives? I think it very wholesome for her to feel herself useful and to master a thing." It was typical of Catherine that having thwarted one daughter's desire for a wholesome career and fenced the others in, the *thing* she should consider Helen might master should be the Government cypher and state secrets. Catherine's four sons—"the happy woodcutters" as she called them—were expected to make careers for themselves and therefore received the maximum encouragement from their mother. Willie was already settled, if not exactly thriving, in Parliament, while Stephen had adhered to his childish pronouncement and, to his father's intense pleasure, had been ordained as an Anglican minister. By 1870 he was working as a curate in South London and was a proponent of the popular muscular Christianity—he was a great mountaineer, progressing from ascents of the Snowdon range to the Swiss Alps; when his uncle, the unlucky Henry Glynne, died in 1872 Stephen became the rector of Hawarden. Henry had not gone up to Oxford after leaving Eton but had instead attended King's College in London and was beginning to show an aptitude for business affairs. Herbert, the youngest child, was still at Eton in the early 1870s, and though his father thought he was not working hard enough, Catherine defended him vigorously, pointing out that he had suffered much ill-health, therefore his scholastic work must also have suffered. Indeed Catherine became slightly heated in her defence of Herbert, telling her husband, "I don't say he has *your* energy or *your* ability but I do say he has done his best, and worked up to his powers" and furthermore that his (Gladstone's) "incessant and *never*-ending hard work" prevented him from thinking of his home interests and pleasures as much as she was sure he would like to.

There were those who thought that Catherine's incessant and never-ending charitable work prevented her from fulfilling her political and social duties as well as she might have done. From the early days of Gladstone's first premiership there were innumerable stories about his wife's offhand, disordered attitude. The family did not move into 10 Downing Street as they had moved into number 11, but continued to live at Carlton House Terrace, so there were two houses in which Catherine could be casually disorganised. There were stories of people wandering round the official residence trying to find somebody to attend to them, of the German Ambassador left sitting forlornly in the hall at Carlton House Terrace, and of Gladstone eating a frugal lunch of a peach and a slice of bread, that being all the food he could discover. Mary Gladstone recorded a return to the Terrace with her mother from the London Hospital in deepest midwinter and the scene that met them, ". . . all the fires out, the drawing [room] in a despairing state of disorder, & a heap of flowers to arrange with nought to put them in, & a dinner party impending in half-an-hour." Catherine's want of social attention and concentration was not confined to London, and there is one of those amusing stories which was not in the least funny while it was happening about Gladstone's later secretary, Arthur Godley, and his bride being invited to Hawarden early in 1871. On arrival at Queensferry in a snowstorm, the young Godleys found no transport to meet them, as had been promised by Catherine, and after waiting a considerable time, eventually all they could discover in the deserted station was a hawker's cart, onto which Godley piled his luggage, his wife and her maid and leading the horse himself trudged the two miles to the castle in pitch darkness and driving snow. When the little caravan finally reached Hawarden Castle, freezing cold, soaking wet and furiously angry, Catherine was naturally filled with horrified contrition at her forgetfulness and in this instance all was soon forgiven in front of a blazing fire and the equal warmth of the Gladstones' belated welcome.

Despite her social shortcomings and to some eyes her overinvolvement in her own affairs, Gladstone remained the lynchpin of Catherine's life; the depth of her feeling for him was never more touchingly expressed than in a letter written to Lucy Cavendish in February 1871. Lucy was again worried about the extent to which her aunt was overworking and this time she wrote directly to Catherine, suggesting that one task she might forgo was her constant attendance at the House of Commons to hear her husband speak, after a long hard day at the London Hospital or the Woodford Home or Clapton or the Newport Market Refuge. Catherine replied, "I can never take amiss anything you say & I know love prompts it but I must just observe that the H of C is really about the only real relaxation after all, you can hardly judge—I don't mean that just the exciting bits may not tire but on the whole it comforts me. I can look at him & be in peace." To be able to write such words after thirty-two years of marriage, at the age of nearly sixty, is a testament to Catherine's love, and its depth and solidity were such that the minor irritations were smothered. One particular irritation at this period was Gladstone's parsimony and financial rectitude. In August 1871 Catherine asked her husband *please* could he send her £18 as she was desperately short of money, and in October of the same year she was again stung into a slightly heated reply to an admonishing letter of his: "I will attend to your wishes with regard to not sending letters to you on private means through the official bag. I have never telegraphed through the Foreign Office at all & I paid 1/- for a wretched government telegram from Downing Street . . . it does seem funny that when writing to you from Downing Street I must put stamps on my letters. However your wish is law though I don't see it."

As much as Gladstone remained the focal point of Catherine's life, she was his anchor and provided the warmth, devotion and stability that he needed during the years of his first Ministry. Occasionally he might have wanted her to be more constantly by his side and more organised in her life, though her lack of concern for social niceties was not an area which worried him, but he relied on her being there, whether in spirit or corporally, and was for example perturbed when one day he failed to receive a letter from her (it was a postal error and two turned up the next day so all was well). The balance of their relationship was as excellent as that of his first Cabinet: there was the mutual respect and trust; he could unburden three quarters of his heart and mind to Catherine, she all of hers to him. Each was interested in the other's work, their family brought them great joy, yet they had their own spheres of activity.

In the field of foreign affairs Gladstone's commitment never equalled that to home affairs, but no British Prime Minister of the nineteenth century and few in the twentieth were less chauvinistic or more European in outlook. He adhered to the views he had expressed so passionately over the years: that England should not lightly intervene in the affairs of foreign nations, that she should use her fund of power and credit "thriftily," and above all that she should "seek to develop and mature the action of a common, or public, or European opinion, as the best bulwark against wrong." In 1870, with the outbreak of the Franco-Prussian War Gladstone was dealing with Otto von Bismarck, who had little belief in European opinion and a great deal in the necessity and effectiveness of force at certain times. Bismarck had a large contempt for "Professor" Gladstone and his theories, but the latter was not a pacifist and in no sector of his public life was he the starry-eyed idealist sometimes depicted. There was a strain of blood and iron in Gladstone too which made him such an effective practical politician, though it was more usually in evidence in home than in foreign affairs.

The matter which can be regarded as one of the greatest achievements of any of Gladstone's Ministries—though it was not one which earned him widespread plaudits in the country at the time—came in the field of foreign affairs, being the protracted *Alabama* negotiations which were finally settled by arbitration in Geneva in 1872. The *Alabama* affair went back to the American Civil War and concerned the sloop which had been built at Birkenhead and launched in the summer of 1862. Long before the ship sailed down the river Mersey and out of Britain's territorial waters, strong representations were made to Lord Palmerston's Government by the American Minister in London, Charles Adams, to the effect that she was being built as a war vessel for the Confederate States and should therefore be prevented from leaving. For a variety of reasons the representations were ignored until it was too late; the *Alabama* duly cleared territorial waters, thereafter hoisted the Confederate flag and preyed on Northern shipping to devastating effect. The Americans claimed reparations based on Britain's negligence in allowing the *Alabama* to sail, which Lord Palmerston and then Earl Russell stoutly denied. Russell eventually accepted a degree of British culpability but refused to submit the case to arbitration, saying that England's honour and her law would become a mockery if foreigners were allowed to decide whether her Ministers had been negligent or not. By 1868 Lord Derby had reluctantly agreed to a conference at which American and British commissioners would arbitrate upon the *Alabama* claims, but he continued to hedge and it was Lord Clarendon, as Gladstone's Foreign Secretary, who ratified the agreement. The actual step of setting up a conference was not helped from the British point of view by the statement of American Senator Charles Sumner that the British must pay the indirect as well as the direct damage caused by the *Alabama,* particularly as he considered that Britain's indirect culpability included the prolongation of the Civil War by the recognition of the Confederacy as a belligerent. Eventually a conference took place in Washington in 1871; the treaty signed there between Britain and America enunciated the principles of retroactive guilt, attempted to define the rules of maritime neutrality and accepted that the *Alabama* claims be judged by an international tribunal, with Geneva finally being agreed upon as its setting.

With the tribunal arranged, the Americans nearly jammed the delicate new mechanism by insisting on reintroducing their claims for indirect damages. Gladstone was furious, his Cabinet threatened to split down the middle but he held tenaciously to his view that negotiations should continue and eventually carried the Cabinet with him. At the eleventh hour it was Charles Adams, the American representative at Geneva, who saved the day and mutual honour by stating that on a point of international law the indirect claims could not be admitted. In September 1872 the five arbitrators—drawn from Britain, America, Spain, Switzerland and Brazil—found Britain liable for three and a quarter million pounds sterling damages, including interest. Gladstone thought the award rather high but he instructed Robert Lowe, the Chancellor of the Exchequer, to pay up and added an unusual note of humour to the proceedings by suggesting that an immediate cash payment might warrant a discount. Thus ended one of the greatest triumphs of the Gladstonian Liberal belief in reason, and one which established the principle of international arbitration. Both sides deserve credit —Gladstone was loud in his praise of Charles Adams' tact, patience and diplomacy—but the greater credit in this instance should go to Mr. Gladstone and Lord Granville because England was the world's most powerful nation. It was suggested that the British Government needed to settle with the Americans because of renewed Russian activities in the Black Sea and a threat of war there, but in effect there was no rush of practical help for the Americans and if England had wanted to thumb her nose at the only recently reunited States there was not then a great deal America could have done.

By the end of 1872 the steam was beginning to run out of Gladstone's Ministry and the initial harmony was becoming discordant. Disraeli had already made one of his most famous speeches, brilliant in its use of imagery, when at Manchester on 3 April 1872 he said, "As I sit opposite the treasury bench, the ministers remind me of one of those marine landscapes not very unusual on the coasts of South America. You behold a range of exhausted volcanoes. Not a flame flickers upon a pallid crest." Gladstone himself did not think much of the speech as a whole, though he considered the volcanic metaphor was rather good, and Disraeli wisely added a rider by saying, "But the situation is still dangerous. There are occasional earthquakes, and ever and anon the dark rumblings of the sea."

CHAPTER 11

THE EXHAUSTED VOLCANOES

THE MATTER WHICH rumbled most ominously and continuously throughout Gladstone's first Ministry was the one he himself designated "the royalty question." Since the death of her beloved Albert, Queen Victoria had managed to convince herself that she was a weak feeble woman suffering from poor health, and that if she did her duty in attending to the ministerial boxes and governmental crises no more should or could be expected of her. She had let her very genuine grief overwhelm her so that at times she wallowed in self-pity like a baby hippopotamus—in the 1860s when she was leading such an inactive secluded life she came to resemble one physically. From Balmoral Gladstone told Catherine that he would let her into a secret, namely that Her Majesty weighed 11 stone 8 lbs. which, as he commented, was "rather much for her height!" By 1869 popular feeling had mounted against an invisible monarch who was drawing large sums of money for failing to do her duty, not to mention the sums she was demanding from Parliament for her innumerable offspring as they came of age. At a serious level the disenchantment manifested itself in the Republican Clubs which by 1870 were springing up all over the country—encouraged by the example of the French Commune—with the dynamic young Radical-Liberals, Joseph Chamberlain and Sir Charles Dilke, at the spearhead of the movement. At another level the discontent displayed itself in "To Let" notices pinned to the railings of Buckingham Palace and in the malicious jingles and gossip that circulated about the Queen and John Brown—for example "Mrs. Brown is out of town, Riding on her pony" was sung to the tune of "Yankee Doodle" and the verses varied in lewdness according to the company.

Before Gladstone became Prime Minister a great many people were worried about "the royalty question," which was a twofold problem, as it concerned the Prince of Wales as much as the Queen herself. The priority was to get Her Majesty back into circulation, but it was also deemed essential to find suitable employment for the Prince of Wales, who would be thirty years old in 1871 and who, in the absence of any responsibility or official purpose to his life, had already acquired a raffish reputation which was not in accord with the new middle-class morality. The great questions were how was the Queen to be persuaded to reassume some of her official duties and share others with the heir apparent? and who had the guts and diplomacy to undertake the task? Gladstone had the guts but not unfortunately the diplomacy, though just before he assumed the supreme office he was offered the best possible advice by Dean Wellesley of Windsor, an old Etonian friend who knew the Queen well by virtue of his royal deanery. Wellesley wrote: "Everything depends on your manner of approaching the Queen. Her nervous susceptibility has much increased since you had to do with her before, and you cannot show too much regard, gentleness, I might even say tenderness towards her. Where you differ, it will be best not to try and reason her over to your side, but to pass the matter lightly over, with expressions of respectful regret . . . Put off, until she is accustomed to see you, all discussions which are not absolutely necessary for the day . . ."

Gladstone's inability to be relaxed with his Sovereign made it impossible for him to be tender or gentle, and passing matters off lightly or postponing them until another day were approaches unknown to his temperament. In writing, he continued to submit long, densely argued memoranda or blank impersonal letters to Her Majesty, and though she had not had Mr. Disraeli long as her Prime Minister she had grown accustomed to *his* letters, such letters as she had never received in her life. It must be admitted that if the choice had to be made between Gladstone or Disraeli as a correspondent, ninety-nine people out of a hundred would almost certainly choose the latter. For Disraeli was not only a master of the art of political précis, with all the boring details omitted, he had style and wit, he was personal and gossipy—Lord So-and-So was hardly up to standard in the House today, or Mr. Blank had behaved in a most odd way in the Cabinet. Gladstone, apart from having such a monochromatic, unwitty style, was uninterested in gossip and would have been appalled at the idea of informing Her Majesty what anybody had done or said in the Cabinet—the collective decision was all she was entitled to know.

Had Disraeli been returned to office in 1868 he might have succeeded in coaxing the reluctant Queen back into the limelight because he, without the advantage of Dean Wellesley's advice, managed to put it into practice, with the addition of his well-known use of flattery. Disraeli told Matthew Arnold, "You have heard me called a flatterer and it is true. Everyone likes flattery: and when you come to royalty you should lay it on with a trowel." But for all his wiles, knowledge of the female heart and outrageous flattery, Disraeli genuinely liked Her Majesty (as did Gladstone), and it is difficult to read her letters and Journals for any length of time without growing fond of Queen Victoria as a person. She was maddening, capricious, imperious, frequently selfish and wrapped in self-pity; she thought in blacks and whites and she had a startling ability to live for the emotional moment and erase previous beliefs or convictions, unless they were connected with the Prince Consort. Sir Robert Peel, Lord Palmerston and Lord Clarendon, all of whom she had often disliked while they were alive, assumed saintly mantles once they were dead and it was a question of balancing their actions against those of Mr. Gladstone; while *The Times* was an "excellent" newspaper when it disapproved of Mr. Gladstone's actions in the early 1870s and a "mere tool" when it supported him over the Bulgarian crisis in 1876, and the *Daily Telegraph* vice versa. But on the sympathetic side, Queen Victoria was incredibly bereft and lonely after Albert's death and she had real burdens which even at her most perverse moments she took seriously. The ministerial boxes arrived relentlessly and had to be read, digested and if necessary acted upon because, though she was the only constitutional monarch in Europe, the constitution still allowed her power; and the problems of her many children were those of a *royal* family in an era when monarchy flourished and their marriages were therefore affairs of state. She tried as hard as Mr. Gladstone to be good, she had a fund of common sense, like Catherine Gladstone she could sometimes go to the heart of a problem and extricate it for immediate airing, and she could also be loyal and was genuinely concerned about the welfare of her subjects.

However, in 1869 and 1870 the Queen's less attractive characteristics were to the forefront, and the more she was attacked publicly the more defensively stubborn and autocratic she became in her determination not to be pushed in directions in which she had no wish to travel. Whether even Disraeli's tact, guile, flattery and ability to recognise a brick wall when he saw one would then have triumphed over Her Majesty's nervous susceptibilities and iron will is a matter of conjecture. Disraeli was perhaps fortunate in not having to deal with Queen Victoria at this particular juncture, and while Gladstone was the person least likely to succeed in the delicate task of negotiating Her Majesty back onto the path of public duty, he was also extremely unfortunate in becoming Prime Minister at the moment when republicanism was in the air, when the Queen's popularity was at its nadir and her temper consequently at its most erratic, and yet when some action had to be taken.

Apart from Gladstone's personal deficiencies in the Queen's eyes, and Disraeli's unbounded attractiveness, there was one major area in which Her Majesty and Mr. Gladstone clashed dangerously and into which Mr. Disraeli never entered, namely "the people" and their affection. In their earlier days Disraeli, the coiner of the famous phrase "the two nations," had been considerably more aware of the gulf that existed between the rich and the poor and the horrors of poverty than had Gladstone; but unlike his rival he had no need of the people's affection and there was no mutual love affair between them and him. But Gladstone's hold on the people was already considerable, and early in 1869 Lucy Cavendish recorded that she screwed up her courage to have a talk with Princess Helena—the Queen's fifth child and third daughter—on the subject of Her Majesty's semi-retirement and the necessity to prise her out of it. Princess Helena quite agreed and thought that Mr. Gladstone should talk to the Queen personally, but she told Lucy that he should "not use the 'people say' argument, which, she said, 'exasperates Mama.'" In fact, the "people say" argument and the sort of reception Gladstone had received in Newcastle-on-Tyne and Lancashire more than exasperated Queen Victoria—they infuriated her. For the people were *her* people, not *his*, it was to the Queen that they owed their loyalty and devotion, not to one of her Ministers, and a very fundamental jealousy of Gladstone as "the People's William" was a root cause of Her Majesty's increasing dislike and distrust of him. It did not occur to her that Gladstone had emerged as "the People's William" during the period when she was the remote, unseen figure at Balmoral or Osborne, when her subjects had an extra need for somebody to whom they could give their affectionate loyalty.

Gladstone brooded over the royalty question from the moment he assumed office, and he had the strong if not particularly useful support of General Grey, who considered that there was nothing wrong with the Queen's health or strength and that it was "simply the long, unchecked habit of self-indulgence that now makes it impossible for her, without some degree of nervous agitation to give up, even for ten minutes, the gratification of a single inclination, or even *whim.*" Grey's support was not overhelpful because he was temporarily out of favour, because he himself had not succeeded with the firm peremptory tone he urged Gladstone to adopt and because he was already in poor health. In March 1870 Grey had a severe stroke which left him paralysed. He died shortly afterwards, and Colonel (later Sir) Henry Ponsonby became Her Majesty's new Private Secretary. Henry Ponsonby, a member of the illustrious Whig family, was an attractive character of good intelligence, a fair sense of humour and a nicely balanced observant eye. He left an invaluable record of personal, political and social life at Queen Victoria's court from 1870 to the early 1890s in the shape of letters to his wife Mary, a correspondence even more voluminous than the Gladstones' because the Ponsonbys were separated even more frequently. Mary Ponsonby was a lady of defined decided views on most subjects (she later became a Socialist of highly idiosyncratic ilk); she hated court life, particularly Balmoral, and was rarely by her husband's side, leading her own life to a greater degree than Catherine Gladstone. The Ponsonby correspondence is bathed in affection in much the same manner as the Gladstones', but one feels that the success and endurance of both marriages was based on the fact that the partners had such nice long separations.

Ponsonby liked "Gladdy," as he called him, and usually found him an entertaining companion, though he noted "even Gladstone's friends wish him sometimes to be quiet." He was wryly amused by his first meeting with the Liberal leader on the Isle of Wight in 1869, telling his wife, "He has evidently been lately accustomed to popular receptions for he looked round to see if there was anyone to bow to." But Ponsonby had his limitations as an ally: he was slightly younger than the Queen and could not therefore enact the role of wise father figure; he was a gentleman bred in the tradition of public service and would not have dreamed of being peremptory to Her Majesty (even if it had been a good idea); despite her many maddening faults he liked "Eliza," as he (privately) called Her Majesty; for several years he felt somewhat insecure; and he enjoyed his job and had no desire to lose it in a head-on collision. The major stumbling block facing everyone who was trying to lure the Queen from her burrow was her personal physician, Dr. (later Sir William) Jenner. He saw his duty as protecting the Queen's health; if she said she was ill then she was, and Jenner did *not* regard it as his duty to enquire why she developed headaches when it was a question of opening Parliament or spending a night at Buckingham Palace and yet was able to indulge in hearty walks up Scottish mountains or dance half the night at gillies' balls. Jenner was also an extremely conservative gentleman who considered the public attacks on the Queen to be monstrous, and as they mounted he tended to redouble his efforts to protect her tender susceptibilities.

Gladstone's proposals to draw the Queen back into public life and give the Prince of Wales a task befitting his status as the heir apparent were mainly connected with Ireland. As soon as he became Prime Minister he suggested to Her Majesty that she spend some part of each year in Dublin —he had already had the offer of a sumptuous residence in the Irish capital from a loyalist Anglo-Irishman—as she did at Balmoral in Scotland. Thereafter he was himself much involved with his two Irish Bills, and it was not until December 1870 that he wrote a long, detailed memorandum of his further plan, and not until June 1871 that he actually presented it to the Queen. This plan proposed that the post of Lord Lieutenant of Ireland be abolished, that the Prince of Wales be installed in Dublin as the permanent Viceroy and spend several months of each year in the Irish capital. Gladstone had privately and publicly announced that the mission of his Ministry was to pacify Ireland, so the proposals had political overtones, but they were practical and they might have succeeded in easing the Anglo-Irish tensions, with a royal personage actually living in Dublin, visible to the populace and showing an interest in its welfare.

The first suggestion, that the Queen spend a short period each year in Dublin (for which Gladstone himself had not much hope), was politely rejected on the grounds that Balmoral was good for the Queen's health whereas damp Erin would not be, a view heavily endorsed by Dr. Jenner. Gladstone was well aware that the Queen had little love for Ireland or her Irish subjects, her dislike having stemmed from a visit paid only a few months before the Prince Consort's death, when he had been subjected to hostile demonstrations because of an intemperate remark about the Irish. Her Majesty's reaction to the second proposal was even less enthusiastic; basically she had no desire for a job to be found for "Bertie." However much she protested about the onerous nature of her royal burdens, she was no more willing to part with them than she was to share the people's affection with Gladstone. Moveover she had a lack of faith in her eldest son's ability and discretion that was shared by many people. Even the easygoing Lord Granville was somewhat shaken when, having in 1871 agreed to allow His Royal Highness access to Foreign Office papers, he found that the Prince of Wales had been discussing them at a dinner party. Gladstone himself served on several committees with the Prince and considered him an excellent chairman in short sharp bursts but admitted that he tended to lose interest and then become indiscreet if the matter were prolonged. However, those who like Gladstone were campaigning for a job for the unemployed Prince argued that once given a task which would attract his whole attention, the bored, restless Bertie would show his true mettle.

While the subject of the Prince of Wales' employment in Dublin was being coldly viewed by the Queen, another matter rose which froze the temperature further. In February 1871 Her Majesty actually opened Parliament, though her critics said that she had only appeared because she wanted money from Parliament for her daughter Louise's wedding dowry and her son Arthur's coming-of-age annuity. The 1871 session was a stormy one, with the debates on the army reforms and the Ballot Bill; it was consequently extended and Gladstone asked Her Majesty to delay her departure for Balmoral until Parliament had been prorogued. This simple request blew into a major crisis which provoked Queen Victoria's often-quoted letter, "What killed her beloved Husband? Overwork & worry—what killed Lord Clarendon? The same . . . & the Queen, a woman, no longer young is supposed to be proof against all & to be driven & abused till her nerves & health give way with this worry & agitation & interference in her private life . . . etcetera." Gladstone wrote to Catherine on 10 August 1871, saying, "The conduct of the Queen however has been my great trouble. It weighs on me like a nightmare . . . She has been in a state of great excitement, complaining of everybody and saying things you would not believe, & this . . . but simply to postpone for 3 days the journey to Scotland." On 13 August he again wrote to Catherine, "Today I have from her a piteous detail of how she has suffered and how she has been overset and I have no doubt it is true; but to think of the cause! It is the strangest and subtlest working of the selfish principle in a fine character that I have ever seen." He told Henry Ponsonby, "Upon the whole I think it has been the most sickening experience which I have had during near forty years of public life. Worse things may easily be imagined: but smaller and meaner cause for the decay of Thrones cannot be conceived."

Catherine wrote back to her husband sympathising with him about the Queen's "wayward ways" and saying how sad they were, but as his relationship with Her Majesty deteriorated she was, for a variety of reasons, of little assistance. Both her and the Queen's children were now grown up so the royal tea parties had ceased; a major link with the Crown had been through the Lyttletons, as the Dowager Lady Lyttleton had been in charge of the royal nursery and Lucy had been a lady-in-waiting for a period, but the Dowager had recently died and Lucy was no longer at court. Catherine was so involved in her own activities that she had little thought to spare for seemingly peripheral matters. But at root she simply could not believe that Her Majesty could really dislike her "dear old man." In her opinion the Queen was suffering from a temporary aberration from which she would soon recover, so there was no need for her intervention.

After the row about the prorogation of Parliament, the Queen was taken ill, genuinely this time, and it was not until the end of September that she was sufficiently well to receive Gladstone at Balmoral. Once there he saw very little of her; he was instructed by Dr. Jenner to avoid any topic that might excite or upset Her Majesty—which virtually put a stop to conversation—and spent most of his time with Henry Ponsonby. They went on long walks together, "at a rattling pace" as Ponsonby recorded, and on one occasion they discussed Disraeli's recent speech, the future of the Queen and the monarchy in general. In this speech, made at a harvest festival at his Hughenden home, Disraeli had defended the Queen by saying that she was "morally and physically incapacitated" from participating in the round of pageantry demanded of her. On their eleven-mile hike Gladstone told Ponsonby that he thought the speech had been most unfortunate—the interpretation had been made that the insanity lurking in the Queen's Hanoverian ancestry had finally overtaken her—and said he could not think why Disraeli had made it, unless prompted by Dr. Jenner. However, as Ponsonby told his wife, "Gladdy says it has set the ball rolling if asking what the Queen intends to do . . . He says she has laid up in early years an immense *fund of loyalty but she is now living on her capital* . . . he like me does not think Republics thrive in old states . . . But he was very gloomy as to the prospects of the monarchy here."

Gladstone became even more gloomy when he finally had an audience with the Queen and she used what he termed "her repellent power" on him, and he wrote to tell Catherine how grieved he was at the Queen's behaviour. She immediately wrote back saying, "Oh I can hardly think H.M. could be changed really after such a thirty years. She must see it right what you did *now* or *later*. Now she is weak we must I suppose wait." For Catherine it remained a question of time before the Queen again loved and respected the greatest man in the kingdom, her own dear husband, but for Gladstone himself it seemed as if time were running out for the monarchy. When the Prince of Wales was stricken with typhoid fever at the end of 1871 and the illness produced an upsurge of royalist sentiment, Gladstone suggested that a thanksgiving service for the recovery be held in St. Paul's Cathedral. He saw this as a means by which the Queen could show herself to the people and demonstrate her appreciation of their loyalty during the illness; Her Majesty agreed, and the procession to and from the service in St. Paul's was a notably successful display of pomp and emotion. Encouraged by this success Gladstone again raised the matter of the Prince of Wales' employment in Ireland. Again he met with an icy royal reaction, and he was told that the Prince himself had no desire to go to Dublin, though he was also informed that His Royal Highness would be interested in being attached to various departments in England in which he could learn how Government worked. This suggestion did not appeal to Gladstone, nor to the various Ministers to whom the Prince would have been attached, so the Prime Minister turned his attention to formulating yet another plan.

In this one, presented to Her Majesty in July 1872, Gladstone proposed that the Prince of Wales spend roughly four months of each year as the Viceroy in Dublin, with another three months in residence at Buckingham Palace deputising for the Queen (and thereby proving to the inhabitants of the English capital that they possessed a royal family). The proposals were again sensible and practical, but implicit in them were the criticisms of Her Majesty's seclusion and refusal to allow the heir apparent to be suitably employed. Queen Victoria was outraged by her Prime Minister's impertinence and interference; she told him that she always fulfilled her duties as far as her health permitted and that she considered the whole matter a private one which properly concerned the members of her family. Lord Granville begged Gladstone to drop the matter, as it had now been pressed as hard as was possible. But Gladstone considered that the monarchy was still in danger of collapse and that it was his duty to make Her Majesty see reason. In a further long memorandum he told the Queen that there were two questions involved, "the first that which relates to the Prince of Wales personally and for his own sake; the second that which embraces the general interest of the Monarchy, and the importance of increasing and husbanding its strength"; he added that a nation "ceases fully to believe in what it does not see," which was stronger language than Her Majesty was accustomed to.

The matter dragged on until September 1872, by which time even Gladstone had accepted that he could do nothing further with the Queen, and relations were so strained that he did not go to Balmoral in the autumn for his usual visit. But the Prince of Wales and his advisers had not abandoned hope, nor had Henry Ponsonby; in December 1872 the Gladstones were invited to Sandringham and Francis Knollys, the Prince's Private Secretary, was convinced that Gladstone would raise the subject of his Royal Highness' employment and that the Irish scheme would be rehatched or another one laid. But after the visit Knollys wrote to Ponsonby, "He did not even mention the subject to the Prince . . . G will never again have so good an opportunity & the whole thing is too disheartening." Knollys added, "Mrs G was gushing & ridiculous to the last degree," which shows that not everybody appreciated Catherine's inconsequential, bubbling manner.

The friendship between the Prince of Wales and Gladstone was surprisingly warm and close. Surprisingly, because as Lucy Cavendish noted, "Of the said Prince I have little to say. He does not get on with me, nor indeed with any but chaffy, fast people . . . and the melancholy thing is that neither he nor the darling prss. ever care to open a book." Yet the Prince got on famously with the distinctly un-chaffy, un-fast Mr. Gladstone, who could not have lived without books, and what the mutual attraction was is difficult to assess. On Gladstone's side there was the factor that the Prince was not his Sovereign, so he could be relaxed with him. On the Prince's side there was perhaps the replacement father figure, the admiration for the superior intellect without the heavy hand and perhaps some instinct for the sexually passionate wellspring within Gladstone. There was little problem about the Prince of Wales' own sexual promiscuity, as neither of the Gladstones was morally censorious in practice, though they both possessed high-minded Christian principles in theory (an unusual reversal, particularly in Victorian times). Catherine and "darling Princess Alix" got on as famously as the two husbands, though their friendship was less surprising, as both were warmhearted ladies and Catherine's informality was welcomed by the often lonely Princess Alexandra (she would drop into tea unannounced at Carlton House Terrace).

As Gladstone's relationship with Her Majesty deteriorated, friendship with the Prince of Wales (and other members of the royal family) provided some compensation. An obvious reason for the deterioration of what had been a friendly if never close relationship was Gladstone's persistence over "the royalty question," but there were other reasons. One of these was his role as a Liberal reformer. Queen Victoria was not a hidebound reactionary; she was not opposed to *progress,* but she was opposed to *change.* Her ideal of life was for things to get better, for injustices to be rectified, for poverty and suffering to be ameliorated, but for attitudes and beliefs to remain basically unaltered. In her opinion Gladstone was not making judicious improvements, he was rushing around changing everything—the Irish Church and land system, the educational structure, the position of the trades unions, not to mention his attempts to change her and her eldest son —and his piercing eyes were fixed on further alterations to the fabric of society. If Her Majesty herself was not unsympathetic towards gentle progress, she was mainly surrounded by people who were absolutely opposed to anything that smacked of reform; Henry Ponsonby noted that the court was "enveloped in Tory density." Thus Her Majesty was subjected to a constant dripping process of people telling her what a bad Prime Minister Mr. Gladstone was, how much they disliked him and how little they trusted him, with only a few exceptions such as Henry Ponsonby putting forth any contrary views.

By the end of 1872 there was the slowing-down of the activity of Gladstone's Ministry. Part of his personal exhaustion and depression was caused by his prolonged and unsuccessful battles against Her Majesty. Why he had failed so dismally in what he saw as his eminently necessary task of trying to refurbish the monarchy's image and find employment for the Prince of Wales was something Gladstone never understood, and the failure ate into his soul. Despite his frustration, bewilderment and anguish over these matters, the other compartments of Mr. Gladstone continued to function, and one mighty reforming effort had yet to come. It was on 13 February 1873 that he introduced to the House of Commons the third Bill aimed at limiting the Protestant ascendancy in Ireland. This was the Irish University Bill, on which Gladstone had been working with immense concentration for three months. The basic aim was to give Catholics the benefit of a first-class university education comparable to that of the famed Protestant Trinity College. But Gladstone also tried to take some of the heat out of the fiery religious tension in Ireland: he proposed that Catholics should share the new university on equal terms with the Protestants, that the controversial subjects of theology, moral philosophy and modern history should not be taught and that professors could be dismissed if they offended the religious beliefs of their students. By his attempt to provide Ireland with a reasonably fair, non-sectarian higher education Gladstone managed to offend nearly everybody's beliefs. The Protestants had no wish to share Trinity College or any offshoots with the Catholics; the Catholics had less desire to share and demanded their own university in which they could teach their own faith; less jealously religious critics pointed out that it would be a somewhat castrated institution if it could not discuss theology, philosophy or modern history; while the idea of students dismissing their tutors was regarded as ridiculous. Archbishop Manning, with whom Gladstone was once again on friendly if not intimate terms, did his best to persuade the Irish Catholic hierarchy to accept the Bill and see how it worked in practice, but they preferred nothing rather than the spread of "godless colleges," issued a pastoral letter which bitterly condemned Mr. Gladstone's proposals and therefore denied him the Catholic vote.

The second reading of the Bill occurred on 11 March 1873 and was in fact defeated by only three votes. The ladies of the Gladstone family packed the Ladies' Gallery to hear Gladstone's closing speech: Lucy Cavendish recorded, "Up sprang Uncle W & made the finest speech of his life," Mary Gladstone reiterated the sentiment—"the most perfect speech *as whole* he has ever made in his life . . . Everybody said it was the finest speech ever heard"—and there was general agreement that it was one of Gladstone's greatest oratorical efforts. It contained the beautiful, stirring words, "There is a voice which is not heard in the crackling of the fire or in the roaring of the whirlwind or the storm, but which will and must be heard when they have passed away—the still small voice of justice." Nonetheless the Ministry had been defeated, Gladstone himself was tired and discouraged and regarded it as personal defeat of his Irish mission, his colleagues agreed that it was a serious matter, and the only question was whether they should resign immediately or ask for a dissolution of Parliament. After a Cabinet meeting, the last of more than one hundred and fifty, at which Gladstone broke down and tears came into the eyes of most of his colleagues, it was decided to tender the Ministry's resignation without asking for a dissolution.

The only difficulty to this touching scenario, to the Liberals sweeping out of office with the narrowest of defeats on the crest of Gladstone's golden oratory and with four years of major reforms and triumphs behind them, was that Mr. Disraeli had to agree to form a new Ministry. This Mr. Disraeli refused to do, for why should he allow the Liberals to resign on a successful peak? harry his minority Government? regather their strength and probably be returned at the next election? There was considerable to-ing and fro-ing between Mr. Gladstone, Henry Ponsonby, Mr. Disraeli and the Queen—who for once, fortunately, was actually at Buckingham Palace—with Gladstone insisting that constitutionally the Opposition leader must form a Ministry on the previous Government's defeat, and Disraeli saying that he would of course form one if Her Majesty were left without a Government, but there had been no necessity for Mr. Gladstone to resign and there was therefore no constitutional chain around him. The upshot was that the Liberals had to crawl back into office.

From this moment in 1873 nothing went right for Gladstone's Ministers and they indeed became the extinct volcanoes of Disraeli's imagery. In the summer the tactlessness of Mr. Ayrton, the Commissioner of Works, reached a peak and Gladstone reluctantly agreed to remove him from a post which brought him into direct contact with Her Majesty, his office being responsible for the upkeep of the royal residences. At the same time irregularities in the administration of the Post Office funds came to light—there had been no actual malpractice but large sums of money had been used without Parliamentary sanction—and the Ministers involved, the Postmaster General (Mr. Monsell) and Robert Lowe, the Chancellor of the Exchequer, had to be removed. In fact, Lowe had been a conspicuous failure as the Chancellor, being one of those men who thrived when he was attacking but, as Gladstone nicely told Lucy Cavendish years later, "was so helpless under attack that he was like nothing but a beetle on its back."

Gladstone took over the job of Chancellor of the Exchequer, combining it with his role as Premier. The assumption of his old office raised a legal difficulty, the question of a Member of Parliament having to stand for re-election when he accepted paid office under the Crown. But Gladstone was already in a paid office, the highest in the land, and the best legal brains in the country went to work on the problem of whether in the circumstances he need submit himself for re-election at Greenwich. The problem was complicated by the fact that the Greenwich seat was marginal; if Gladstone were forced to present himself for re-election he might be defeated and there would be the ridiculous, unparalleled situation of a Government in office but its leader out.

It was the sort of difficulty that weighed heavily on Gladstone's constitutional conscience and caused him a great deal of *Angst*. However, according to Henry Ponsonby, it was in fact resolved at Balmoral on 30 August 1873, when the Attorney General decided that "Gladstone must resign everything & then be appointed by one Commissioner, First Lord & Chancellor of the Exchequer. Then he will not need re-election." In her Journal Queen Victoria confirmed that on 30 August, "in consequence of some doubts raised by the lawyers," Mr. Gladstone was reappointed. But the information was not given to Parliament, so the matter dragged on, with some legal luminaries insisting that Gladstone need not seek re-election, others that he should, with the Opposition naturally seizing hold of the issue and threatening a debate upon it, and Gladstone apparently still perturbed about it when he finally resigned several months later. As the Balmoral information was never made public one can only assume that the Attorney General had second thoughts about the solution of reappointing Gladstone by a single Commissioner.

The 1873 visit to Balmoral was a success, for curiously the Queen's outrage against Mr. Gladstone tended to mount not when she met him personally, as might be supposed, but in his absence, fanned by reports of his actions or by court antipathy. On many occasions when they were officially on bad terms the Queen noted in her Journal that Mr. Gladstone had been pleasant or considerate during an audience, and in May 1872, when their relationship was at a low ebb, the Queen proposed "to present him with a residence at Blackheath for the remaining time of his life." Quite why Her Majesty made the offer is unclear from the correspondence, and Gladstone, after consulting Catherine and thanking Her Majesty for her kindness and graciousness, declined "for reasons purely domestic and personal to himself." But it was not the sort of offer one would expect from somebody who was already supposed to detest Mr. Gladstone; it is an indication of the ambivalent nature of the relationship and perhaps of the Queen's inability to dislike him in practice as much as she did in theory.

At Balmoral Queen Victoria even chaffed Mr. Gladstone when he received from Catherine the surprising news that their daughter Agnes had become engaged. In fact Catherine had been throwing out heavy hints for some time to the effect that one of their pretty birds might be flying from the nest (at the age of nearly thirty-one), but the hints had apparently not been taken. Henry Ponsonby said he did not seem pleased at the news of the engagement anyway, and Gladstone's letter to Catherine on the subject was more concerned with the financial settlement than with thoughts of Agnes' happiness. He told his wife that *her* family had not been worldly-minded but even Sir Stephen Glynne had immediately spoken to him about *his* pecuniary affairs when *their* engagement had been announced. While he had not been too surprised that her first letter should not mention "any sublunary particular," he was astonished that the letter received that day should arrive "with all about the charms of the orphanage, but not a syllable on beef and mutton, bread and butter, which after all cannot be altogether dispensed with." As soon as he returned to Hawarden Gladstone rectified this oversight and drew up a satisfactory marriage settlement with Agnes' suitor, Edward Wickham, the headmaster of Wellington College. On 27 December 1873, Agnes was married in a simple ceremony in the mediaeval church at Hawarden that had witnessed her parents' wedding nearly thirty-five years previously.

Twelve days later Gladstone wrote one of his lengthy memorandum-cum-letters to his confidant Lord Granville, expressing his reasons for thinking the Liberals should now dissolve Parliament. He then consulted his Cabinet colleagues. There was general agreement to the dissolution, for the Ministry had run out of steam, there had been a series of losses at by-elections, there was no great issue unifying them and Gladstone was at loggerheads with Edward Cardwell (at the War Office) and George Goschen (at the Admiralty) on his old hobbyhorse of defence cuts. At a General Election the Liberals might be returned to power and the Government could be reorganised for a further period of triumphant reforming office. Gladstone thought he had the issue which could assure a Liberal victory, apart from the record in office, namely the abolition of income tax, and his colleagues agreed to his proposals and electoral platform. Nevertheless, the announcement of the dissolution on 23 January 1874 came as a surprise to most people, including the two faithful Gladstonian diarists. Lucy Cavendish recorded, "An extraordinary thunderclap exploded this evening . . . Parliament is to be dissolved!" while more tersely Mary Gladstone recorded, "Thunderbolt. Dissolution of Parliament."

CHAPTER 12

THE RETREAT TO ELBA

CATHERINE HAD BEEN kept informed of events, and Gladstone wrote to her on the day of the dissolution, "You are admitted among the first of those outside the absolutely sacred circle to a knowledge of the great news." She had also been informed that her husband's intention was not only to dissolve Parliament but once the General Election was over to retire from the leadership of the Liberal party. This desire had been growing on Gladstone steadily for the last twelve months. He had managed to convince himself that he was now an old man, that it was essential that he retire in order to concentrate his mind on the greater battle for the Christian faith and to compose his own soul for the day, not far distant, when he would meet his Maker. Many people remarked upon his loss of interest in politics and the lack of his usual buoyancy, and Queen Victoria made several comments in her Journal about how tired and ill Mr. Gladstone was looking. However, she had a fixation about the apparent ill-health of Ministers she did not like and her eye frequently told her what her mind hoped might be true, that the disliked gentlemen were in poor health and might therefore shortly resign.

Catherine was stunned and appalled by her husband's declared intention because she knew him better than anybody and was therefore well aware that physically he was in excellent health and that mentally he was merely in a period of temporary exhaustion and depression. She could not accept that Gladstone had nothing further to offer or do in the political arena, nor could she believe that he could retire permanently. For the first time in nearly thirty-five years of marriage she was certain that her husband had come to the wrong decision, and to discover that William's sense and judgement might not after all be infallible was a nasty shock. On the day of the dissolution she wrote an anguished letter to Lucy in which she said, "I have indeed used arguments the other way to my husband . . . & gone through a kind of agony in seeming to be just otherwise than 'A Star whose light is never dim, A Pillar to uphold & guide.'" Catherine ended by telling her niece that she now felt calm and proud of her husband and consoled herself with the thought that should his Queen or country need him he would be the first to fly to their help.

The calmness was illusory; the consolation to which Catherine was clinging was that Gladstone and the Liberals would win the General Election
with a handsome majority, that her husband would be persuaded that his
Queen and country needed him *now*. It is an interesting but unanswerable
question what Gladstone's reaction would have been had the Liberals won
the election, but one suspects that he might have allowed himself to be convinced that he should remain at the helm. As the results started to come in
at the beginning of February 1874, it was obvious that the Liberals were
unlikely to gain a victory; by 14 February the Conservatives had a majority
of nearly fifty seats, and the only question was whether Gladstone would
follow Mr. Disraeli's precedent in 1868 and resign without submitting to a
defeat in the House of Commons. Showing a peculiar attitude for a man
who was desirous of quitting the temporal stage, Gladstone did not favour
immediate resignation but said that it was the ancient prerogative of the
House of Commons to dismiss the Government. However on 17 February
he decided to accede to the general wish for immediate resignation, and he
travelled to Windsor with copies of Thomas à Kempis and *The Merchant
of Venice*—"each how admirable in its way!"—to sustain him in his hour of
defeat. On the fourteenth Gladstone had received from Her Majesty a letter which he considered to be of scant kindness and it had kept him awake
for three hours at night, which was a rare occurrence for him. He noted in
his diary, "But such hours are not wasted, or need not be. In them we are
alone with God; & no medicine can at this time be better." He said that
during his final audience with Her Majesty on 20 February she had been
very kind, and Queen Victoria's own record of the interview was calm and
showed little feeling that she was then absolutely delighted to have Disraeli
back in office, though she did finish her account by saying, "It was a relief
to feel that this rather trying interview was over."

The electorate had rejected "the People's William" and his party after
their four years of strenuous reforming effort, and all sorts of reasons were
advanced to explain why the rejection had been so complete. Her Majesty
thought the people had rightly shown their lack of confidence in Mr. Gladstone's leadership and rejected his proposal to abolish the income tax for
what in her opinion it was, electoral bait. Mr. Forster attributed the disaster
to Gladstone's indisposition during the vital period of the election campaign and therefore his inability to drum up support by stirring speeches;
Gladstone himself said that the party had been "borne down in a torrent of
gin and beer." The "gin and beer" comment referred to the unpopular Li-
censing Act which the Liberals had introduced in an attempt to minimise
the problem of widespread drunkenness. It *was* a cause of the defeat, if not
as torrential as Gladstone indicated. The Catholic displeasure over the Irish
University Bill had also played a part, and a larger one was attributable to
the Nonconformists' sense of betrayal over the Education Act, though the
latter registered their displeasure more by abstention than by voting for the
Tories. Another sector of the populace that Gladstone had managed to dis-

please was the trades unionists, for though he had legalised their status, in his legislation he had omitted to provide for the right to picket peacefully (and this omission was speedily rectified by Mr. Disraeli). Then there was Gladstone's foreign policy, which might be wise and noble but indubitably lacked glamour and excitement; Disraeli had already begun to tap a renewed desire for prestigious glory. Overall Gladstone and the Liberals paid the penalty for being a reforming government and the country at large registered its wish for a less turbulent period at home and a more adventurous approach overseas.

Gladstone's intention to retire from the leadership of the Liberal party was strengthened by the Liberal defeat, and it contained an element of hurt pride and bruised vanity. When Her Majesty offered him a peerage as a reward for his services he declined with the comment that he could not possibly accept "in the face of such condemnation from the country," and when he was returned a poor second in the Greenwich constituency he told a colleague, "In some points of view it is better to be defeated outright, than to be pitched in like me at Greenwich." Gladstone's feeling that if the country did not want him it could do without him was allied to a disenchantment with the party he had welded into shape in the last four years. The Liberal party was made up of many varied streams at whose confluence stood Gladstone, but in mid-1873 he had told Henry Ponsonby, "To attempt to govern a party who pretended to support him & in reality thwarted him was impossible." At his final audience with Her Majesty he told her "that the greatest intelligence, upon the whole, he believed was to be found in the Liberal party . . . but . . . there was far greater cohesion in the Cons Party than in the Liberal," and that the Liberals must learn "how through their divisions & self-seeking they had brought the present disruption about." Gladstone was not one of nature's autocrats, but he had a spring of vanity as well as humility; he thought he was entitled to support, and if the various sectors of his unruly party chose to oppose him at nearly every turn, then they too could see how they would fare without him.

Immediately after the Liberal defeat Gladstone had conversations with various colleagues on the subject of his resignation as leader but although his stated intention was to resign, his actions were to say the least ambivalent. The news of his resignation was not made public; for the best part of the year the Liberals were left in limbo, with Gladstone still officially their leader, still appearing in the House of Commons from time to time when his interest was aroused by a religious matter but generally showing little concern for the future of the party. At no point in the proceedings did he suggest resigning his parliamentary seat, which, had he truly wanted to recede into the shades, he should have done. However, he had convinced himself that he would shortly retire from the wranglings of the political arena and he managed to convince Catherine that such was his intention. She remained extremely "wretched," as Lucy Cavendish noted, and in

March 1874 she wrote to her niece saying that her many blessings "ought to prevent much of the wrench & perhaps the conflicting feelings the kind of struggle within causes—shall I call it a kind of war." The belief that she should be grateful for her general good fortune did not in reality override Catherine's depression, which was as much caused by the shock that her husband could take such a wrongheaded decision as by the withdrawal from the centre of the storm.

Catherine's depression was not lifted by two events which occurred shortly after her husband stated his intentions (even if he did not immediately act upon them). The first event had been maturing for some considerable time, but it reached a crisis point in April 1874 when Gladstone heard that his brother Robertson's mismanagement of the Seaforth property had been such that Gladstone would lose £6,000 (since the death of his wife whom he had loved dearly and who had been the lynchpin of the household, Robertson had gone to pieces). The loss of his Seaforth investment worried Gladstone deeply—he noted in his diary, "I am ashamed to have been wakened between 4 & 5 by the Seaforth trouble"—and the reasons were partly emotional and partly practical. Seaforth was the house in which he had spent so many happy childhood days and he told Catherine, "But how utterly trumpery is money when it in any moment comes into competition with love . . . What I am really sorry for is the house of my childhood, if it is, as I fear, hopelessly defaced." But while money might be trumpery, Gladstone *had* sustained a £6,000 loss; he always believed in living strictly within his income and at the end of May 1874, having reckoned up the state of his affairs, he decided that they could no longer afford their London house in Carlton House Terrace and that it must therefore be sold.

Once Gladstone had weighed matters and taken a concrete temporal decision, that was it as far as he was concerned, for he had the fortunate, slightly ruthless ability to put such decisions from his mind. The London house was immediately shut and put up for sale, and though Gladstone also noted that the process was "like a little death," because he had "grown to the house having lived more time in it than any other since I was born," he omitted to offer such consoling inner thoughts to Catherine. The proposed sale of the house which for her too contained so many memories was not only a severe wrench but it underlined the apparent firmness of her husband's decision to retire, because one of his arguments for sale was that they no longer needed a permanent London home. Catherine tried gallantly to accept Gladstone's actions at this time, she assured him that whatever came in the way of trial and disappointment she would do her best to share them and to follow his beautiful example of resignation (literally and metaphorically), but her buoyancy was badly deflated, and it was not assisted by the nagging feeling that her husband was being somewhat wilful.

The second event which threw Catherine even more off-balance was the sudden death of Sir Stephen Glynne, who on 17 June 1874 dropped dead from a heart attack in the unlikely setting of Shoreditch High Street in the East End of London. Stephen had not been Catherine's favourite sibling, she had not loved him with the same fervour as she had Mary or even Henry, but she had been fond of him and she had also seen a great deal of him because for many years he had occupied the peculiar position of host and guest at Hawarden Castle. Apart from the loss of a familiar friendly face, Stephen's death left Catherine as the last surviving member of the Glynne family; in her already unsettled state the memories came flooding in with extra poignancy and she was more affected than she might otherwise have been. Stephen's death also raised practical issues, which were dealt with by Gladstone with his customary efficiency, sense of honour and financial probity. He commented on his personal relief that the Hawarden inheritance had passed neither to Catherine, as many people erroneously believed it had, nor to himself as he had always had "a strong repugnance to becoming either the actual or virtual master." In fact Gladstone was briefly the master of Hawarden but it was always in the capacity of care-taker and on 24 September 1875 he took the greatest pleasure in signing the deed which made his eldest son Willie "absolute owner in law of the Hawarden Estate."

Despite, or perhaps because of, their differences over the question of re-tirement and the sale of the London house, the Gladstone correspondence in 1874 and 1875 was filled with a renewed rush of affection and need for each other. Early in the year Gladstone begged his wife to "come as soon as you can, stay as long as you can." She kept telling him how large a gap his departures made, how much she clung to him and how greatly his letters refreshed her, and at the beginning of 1875 he noted in his diary, "Dearest C's birthday. It is wonderful to me her power: what a blessing she is & to how many!" As his letter indicates, the mutual desire for affectionate reas-surance did not extend to a more constant being together. On the contrary, once she had started to recover her equilibrium Catherine's reaction to the stresses of the past few months was similar to that after her sister Mary's death—she again plunged into activity. She threw herself even more fe-verishly into her charitable concerns and in one letter she told her husband, "Tomorrow will be crammed Hospital" and that energetic and useful meas-ures were being taken "regarding the Naughty House," this latter being a reference to a new House of Charity which had been opened specifically for the redemption of prostitutes. For much of 1874 Catherine was on the move and it was at this time that Gladstone told her, "I have some fear lest you should go into perpetual motion. I am afraid our tastes move in oppo-site directions for I feel an increasing aversion to journeys."

Gladstone adjusted to his semi-retired position with ease and the first subject to which he devoted his attention was his beloved Homer. In a series of articles in the *Contemporary Review* which were published in the summer of 1874, he enlarged his thesis about the links between the ancient

Greek and early Christian civilisations and defended Homer from the charge that he had been a warmonger, arguing that the Trojan War had been a defensive war (entered into for reasons curiously similar to those by which he had justified the British entry into the Crimean War). Next, despite his aversion to journeys, he went to Germany to visit his sister Helen, on whom he had not set eyes for six years. Since her miraculous cure in 1848 Helen had led an erratic life, for a period in the 1850s living in Rome, then finding her way back to England in the 1860s. Wisely she had kept out of her brother's way because he still ached to redeem her, but by the early 1870s Helen was so badly in debt that she again disappeared to the Continent, for, less wisely, she had dissipated her inheritance on Catholic charities and by general mismanagement (as her brother had predicted she would). By 1874 Helen was settled in Germany, with sufficient money obtained from somewhere to have a comfortable flat and to employ a maid, though "settled" is perhaps the wrong verb as Miss Gladstone was constantly on the move or threatening to move, with her maid endlessly packing and unpacking her belongings.

Gladstone visited his sister with her acquiescence, and encouraged by a reasonably friendly reception he immediately tried to persuade Helen to return to England, where he hoped she would rejoin the bosom of the family and re-enter the Anglican fold. He received no support from his wife, who recognised that her sister-in-law was far too old to start leading a well-ordered life, that she had no intention of reverting to the Anglican faith, that she had come to some sort of terms with life, however disorganised and lonely they might appear to her brother, and that she wanted to be left alone. In characteristically polite but clear terms Catherine told her husband that he was wasting his time with Helen and suggested that he return to Hawarden, where his family would be delighted to see him.

Gladstone had another reason for visiting Germany at this moment, one which was less personal but as deeply felt as his mission to redeem Helen. In 1870 the doctrine of Papal Infallibility had been promulgated and by 1874 the refusal of those who could not accept the new Vatican decrees, those who became known as the Old Catholics, had reached the point at which many of them were excommunicated. Included among the number was Gladstone's old friend, the famed German theologian Dr. Döllinger, and he told Catherine "it makes my blood run cold to think of *his* being excommunicated in his venerable but, thank God, hale and strong old age." Gladstone's blood had in fact been running hot rather than cold since the Vatican decrees had been made known in 1870, for in his opinion the doctrine of Papal Infallibility struck a blow at individual liberty by its absolutist and centralised spirit; it jeopardised the peace of Europe by raising the spectre of renewed papal temporal power, it placed Catholics in an intolerable position with regard to their allegiance to their own country and it denied the ancient principle that the Pope was answerable to the Christian world for his judgements and actions. Gladstone's many long conversations with Dr. Döllinger in Munich in the early autumn of 1874 convinced him that the time had come for him to speak out; now that he was no longer Prime Minister and was unofficially retired he felt free to do so, and he accordingly returned to Hawarden and dashed off a pamphlet.

The pamphlet, entitled *The Vatican Decrees in Their Bearing on Civil Allegiance: a Political Expostulation,* was published at the beginning of November. Its reception was startling, because the subject of papal arrogance was still of interest in Protestant England, because Gladstone focused his argument on the position of English Catholics and the nature of their allegiance, because it was written in trenchant terms. Lucy Cavendish commented, "The whole pamphlet is in better & clearer style than anything of his I ever read." Sales were given a boost when the Pope launched a vitriolic personal attack on the pamphlet which, as Gladstone told Catherine, was the best possible advertisement. By 27 November, 52,000 copies had been sold, by 5 December the number had leapt to 104,000 and it was still selling between 4,000 and 5,000 copies per day.* Gladstone told his friends that the tremendous success of the pamphlet should strengthen and hearten the Liberal party, but he was now firm in his determination to resign from the leadership and to sell his London house (which was still on the market). The ambivalent nature of his stated wish is again apparent, for what help to the Liberal party could a pamphlet about Vaticanism be, unless the man who had created the storm and onto whom the attention was focused continued to lead it?

On 7 January 1875 Gladstone noted in his diary that he had had a long conversation with Catherine on the subject of his decision to retire forthwith. He then left Hawarden for London to discuss his resignation letter with his colleagues, and Catherine, who was not well and was building up to another attack of the erysipelas from which she now suffered, wrote to him from the confines of her bed in "the grubous and solitary House!" It was for her a carefully composed and tidily written letter, two factors which emphasise the deep emotion and the convictions she held. She told her husband, "I know full well your soul is bent on doing right. You would go to death in a righteous cause. Who could hold you when the battle-cry sounded? . . . I expressed myself so badly in the hurry of parting—alas, it seemed to you I was going against you, & that my judgement was formed! . . . remember there are those who can speak more frankly to me than to you, & who desire your honourable course of action . . . Great Church questions may arise when your power & influence would be valuable. Would you have the same power by a sudden rush to fight after putting *the rein upon others?* Is there no medium course? . . . could you not take it quite easily? . . . If you had any organic illness which made it wrong to expose your precious life it would be different." She finished her letter by saying, "I hope I have not troubled you with my twaddle. At all

---

* Eventually Gladstone made £2,300 from his pamphlets on the Vatican decrees (another one followed, though it was not as successful as the first).

events you may feel that I write with the one object that you may be guided aright to the Glory of God & the good of your fellow creatures."

Catherine's arguments against resignation were far from twaddle, but her husband wrote back saying he must stand by his decision, as he was acting on convictions long entertained and arrived at after deep probing within himself, and the only concession he would allow was that after being examined by Sir Andrew Clark (his personal physician) he could not plead ill-health as a reason for resignation. Even in this field he thought the attacks of diarrhoea from which he suffered intermittently were more debilitating than Catherine (or Clark) allowed. By return of post his wife said she still felt she had a duty to lay before him her and other people's feelings on his resignation, and she became martial in her arguments: "Perhaps I am too sensitive in the feelings of anything like running away when the road is dark & hopeless . . . I have looked upon your career very much as that of a general in a dangerous battle, whether winning or losing." She finished by saying that she wished to act "as a kind of drag on so important a step." Gladstone was not in the mood for "drags" of any sort; he had made up his mind and the middle course of continuing as the Liberal leader but temporarily taking things more easily did not appeal to his dramatic side. On Catherine's simile of the general he pounced with an Aristotelian enthusiasm for precision, saying, "A general is working for a victory or a peace. I am not asked to work for either but to carry on for years longer a work which is in its nature perpetual and which must when I disappear be taken up by another."

Gladstone's colleagues were no more willing than was Catherine for him to resign the leadership, and Lord Granville told him that his departure would sorely grieve the whole Liberal party, with the possible exception of Sir William Harcourt. Harcourt was then in his mid-forties, a lawyer by training, a gargantuan figure physically and a man of equally big, uncomplicated mental characteristics. He was large-hearted, rumbustious and he adored a good fight, but while he had the happy knack of forgetting and forgiving, he overlooked the fact that not all those who had been subjected to his bulldozing attacks possessed the same faculty. In the early 1870s, as Harcourt rose to prominence during the *Alabama* negotiations—he specialised in international law—one of his major subjects of attack was Mr. Gladstone, whom he then regarded both as a tiresome sophist and as a man whose flighty nature could lead the Liberal party in any will-o'-the-wisp direction. When Gladstone spoke of elements within the party which constantly thwarted him, he had no one more clearly in mind than Harcourt, whose own opinion of the situation at the end of 1874 was: "G. still sulks and says he will not lead . . . they have been so long like babies in leading strings that they can't walk alone. There is no whip, no office, no *nothing*. The thing is ridiculous and disgraceful." This criticism had considerable validity but it was not widely held in the party and most members wanted

Gladstone to remain as leader and give them a renewed sense of purpose and direction.

The majority arguments were to no avail and on 14 January 1875 Gladstone's resignation letter was made public. In it he said he could see no public advantage in his continuing to act as the Liberal leader, that at the age of sixty-five after forty-two years in public life he considered himself entitled to retire, but he would remain in Parliament and support any measures which were to the advantage of the Liberal party and the principles on which he had heretofore acted. The letter had the merit of being short and to the point, particularly for Gladstone, but it could hardly be termed a graceful missive of resignation. His sense of betrayal and rejection by the people and of the lack of support within his own party was apparent in its curt contents. These emotions again surfaced in comments Gladstone made in his diary at the end of March 1875: "I endeavoured to lay out before C. my views about the future & remaining section of my life. In outline they are undefined but in substance definite. The main point is this: that, setting aside exceptional circumstances which would have to provide for themselves, my prospective work is not Parliamentary. My tie will be slight to an assembly with whose tendencies I am little in harmony at the present time: nor can I flatter myself that what is called the public, out of doors, is more sympathetic." Even in his private comments Gladstone left an option open by referring to "exceptional circumstances," and in an earlier letter to Catherine he had covered himself by saying he would remain in Parliament as an independent member so as to be "ready to come out again upon the arrival of any worthy occasion."

As far as the country was concerned, from January 1875 Mr. Gladstone had largely retired from the political fray. After considerable internal fighting, the leadership of the Liberal party was split, with Lord Granville directing it in the House of Lords and Lord Hartington in the Commons, though Gladstone himself considered that Granville was the leader. It was not a satisfactory solution; it always had the air of a stopgap measure, and there was a widespread belief that Granville and Hartington had accepted their respective roles with the utmost reluctance. Exactly how reluctant they were is open to doubt. Arthur Godley, who became Lord Granville's Private Secretary in 1875 when Gladstone had no further apparent need of his services, was emphatic that Granville saw himself as the Liberal leader. Lord Hartington, the future Duke of Devonshire, one of the greatest dukedoms in the kingdom, played the role of the English aristocrat *par excellence*, always calm and unenthusiastic, apparently indifferent to the lure of office—what did being Prime Minister mean when one was already a Cavendish?—seemingly more interested in racing than in politics and merely doing his duty as a high servant of the State. But *his* Private Secretary Reginald Brett (later Viscount Esher) commented that Hartington was more ambitious than was imagined and politics were his life. It is a view that any perusal of Lord Hartington's private papers endorses, for his letters are almost entirely political, and even those to his mistress the Duchess of Manchester are untinged by personal anecdote and devoted to political matters. (Hartington had a long-standing and well-known liaison with the beautiful German-born Duchess, to whom he remained steadfastly if undemonstratively faithful until her husband finally died in the 1890s, whereupon he married her.)

With the actual resignation, and Granville and Hartington's assumption of the leadership, Liberal views about Gladstone's action diverged. There were those who, while mourning his departure, thought he was entitled to his rest and continued to admire his shining integrity; but there were others who now supported Harcourt's opinion that Gladstone was sulking and that "the retreat to Elba" was just that, a tactical move. There was general agreement within the parliamentary party, if not at grass-roots level, that ex-Prime Ministers roaming at large, aged only sixty-five and in full possession of their outstanding physical and mental faculties, were, to use Gladstone's own metaphor about Sir Robert Peel, as dangerous and unpredictable as great rafts floating unmoored in a harbour. The unsatisfactory situation was accepted as it existed, as one that could only be played by ear, and its cause retired to Hawarden assured at least in the upper reaches of his mind that he had quit the temporal arena.

In the weeks following the official resignation Catherine herself, battling against an attack of erysipelas, was engaged in another sad task at Hagley, that of nursing her niece May Lyttleton through what proved to be a fatal illness. Gladstone was left to cope by himself with the completion of the sale of 11 Carlton House Terrace and with the removal of their furniture, a task which he did not enjoy, as normally Catherine undertook such chores; but he made no complaint. When May Lyttleton died in her aunt's arms on 21 March Gladstone wrote his wife two touching, consoling letters in which he said that May had gone to her mother's arms "but by what a road of pain and bewildering darkness." He asked how and why this should be, and said he could find no answer and could only reacknowledge how infinitely good and loving God had been to him. The rest of the year was brighter—Mary Gladstone called 1875 an April year of shadows and sunshine. In May Agnes bore her first child, a daughter who was also the Gladstones' first grandchild and therefore an occasion for rejoicing, though Gladstone commented that the baby did not seem to like his old face. Then in July Willie announced his engagement to Gertrude Stuart, a daughter of Lord Blantyre. Both his parents were delighted, as Willie had shown something of a roving eye towards the female sex, and they were therefore pleased that he was settling down. The wedding had in fact to be postponed because on 23 September Robertson Gladstone died; but his demise was neither a great shock nor a great loss, because the Robertson whom both Gladstone and Catherine had in earlier days loved had died many years before.

The real shock was to find that the company John Gladstone had founded had dwindled almost to nothing through Robertson's lack of inter-est, and that what was viable had been appropriated by Sir John's ex-employee and later partner, a man called Wyllie. Wyllie's first action on as-suming control of the shattered company was to dismiss young Henry, who at the end of 1874 had gone out to India to work in the offices of Gladstone & Company. Gladstone's outrage at the manner in which his revered fa-ther's business had been allowed to disintegrate and then fall into the hands of the unscrupulous Wyllie did not allow his pleasure at his eldest son's wedding to be diminished, and on 19 October 1875 William Henry Gladstone and Gertrude Stuart were married in Hawarden Church. In his 1875 birthday retrospect Gladstone noted, "In the great business of un-winding the coil of life & establishing my freedom I have made some prog-ress by resigning the leadership, selling my house (needful for pecuniary reasons) and declining public occasions. But more has yet to be done. To minimise my presence in London is alike needful, for my work, for the great duty & business of solemn recollection & preparation. I hope my polemical episode is over."

It was not of course over, and the controversial years that lay ahead were at times to make the first sixty years of Gladstone's life seem like a vicarage tea party. But 1876 started quietly and the Gladstones were together at Ha-warden or at their temporary London abode for most of the early months. Throughout 1875 Catherine had continued to rush around, but in 1876 there was some lessening of her activity and she entered a temporarily calmer phase; though her husband noted, "At 64 she has the vigour & freshness of 34." In March, the sacked Henry returned from India and his sister Mary recorded, "The whole family flew to the door & received him with yells," but in April another shadow darkened the scene when Lord Lyttleton committed suicide at Hagley. The Gladstones mourned him deeply, but they accepted this cardinal sin of the Christian faith with re-markable tolerance, and Catherine comforted his second wife and rendered every assistance she could to her three small children, as nineteen years be-fore on her sister Mary's death she had comforted George Lyttleton and cared for his motherless children. In June the news was more cheering: the family heard that Herbert, of whom his father had entertained such low expectations a few years previously, had gained a First Class honours de-gree in history at Oxford. Catherine wrote to her youngest son to congrat-ulate him and told him, "I know the pleasure you have given your father is one of your chief delights—you should have seen his countenance all lighted up!" The pleasure their children gave the Gladstones was equally savoured, and in August 1876, on the occasion of the flower show at Ha-warden, Mary was so overwhelmed by the family spectacle that she wrote, ". . . everything was so lovely & so bright & happy I quite cried from the pure pleasure of mere existence. It rushed over me in a moment what bless-ings we had, and as I looked round all seemed so unbroken & beautiful,

Agnes and E[dward Wickham] with their baby, Stephy, Herbert, Willy and Gerty, Mama & Papa—such moments are rare and so precious."

The family continued to visit the great houses of Britain, and they had established friendships with the Balfours and the Cecils. The Balfours' London home was in Carlton House Terrace and the Gladstone and Balfour children therefore grew up together, with long holidays spent at the latter's house at Whittingehame in East Lothian. Arthur Balfour and Mary Gladstone were especial friends, with a bond in a love of music, and at one time her parents hoped they would marry; Gladstone told Catherine that he "really delighted" in the company of the young man. The fact that the Balfours were staunch Conservatives in no way interfered with the friendship, nor did the position of their uncle, the Marquis of Salisbury, as a leading figure in the Conservative party impair the harmony of the personal relationship with the Gladstones. Lord Salisbury was twenty years younger than Gladstone but the two men had much in common; they were both serious-minded, both had tough intelligences and both were deeply religious Anglicans, though Salisbury was a more self-contained character than Gladstone and was without his passion, vehemence and unpredictability. The Gladstones and Balfours frequently descended on Hatfield House, and Mary recorded evenings spent in the splendid rooms there when everyone told "thrilling" ghost stories in front of the log fires.

The Gladstones also continued to entertain and be entertained by other of their select group of friends. During 1876 Catherine told Lucy Cavendish of a dinner party at Lord Acton's: "Uncle W & I dined with the Actons meeting only his 3 French women! all unable to speak English excepting Lady Acton who hardly speaks at all." Lord Acton was also several years younger than Gladstone but a friend of long standing and he is probably best remembered by his dictum, "Power tends to corrupt, and absolute power corrupts absolutely. Great men are almost always bad men." It is doubtful that he had Gladstone in mind when he penned those lines, for though his admiration for the Liberal leader was not uncritical it was profound. He became a close friend of Mary Gladstone's too, and in the 1870s she commented that nearly all her male friends seemed to be about fifty; but she said it was a pleasant footing because it was delightfully safe. In November 1876 Lord Tennyson and his son Hallam were guests at Hawarden and Mary recorded, "Tennyson read us *Harold* not yet published . . . It lasted 2 hours and ½—Papa seemed sleepy and not forthcoming, Willy rather giggling, Helen fierce . . . myself rather on pins & needles for Papa . . . We were forced to take no heed of such earthly things as luncheon." On a visit to Tennyson's home on the Isle of Wight the next year, Mary discovered that the age of fifty (or upwards) did not necessarily provide safety, and she was somewhat alarmed by the Poet Laureate's far from avuncular comments and gestures.

In May 1876 the Gladstones took a lease on another London house at 73 Harley Street. They did not buy it and it was not nearly so grand as Carlton House Terrace but Gladstone had decided that in reality he still needed a London base. The decision was interpreted by the political gossips as an indication that he was, consciously or unconsciously, more ready to enter the full-time political arena. If his association with prostitutes is accepted as a symptom of his being restless or under inner stress, it may be noted that the familiar "Saw one" (i.e. a prostitute) began to reappear in his diaries more often in the early summer of 1876 than for some time, though with nothing like the frequency of the crisis years of the 1850s. In fact by May 1876, the exceptional circumstances and the worthy cause which Gladstone had always allowed might drive him back to the temporal stage were already in being.

The worthy cause was again connected with the always rumbling "Eastern Question." Under the terms of the Crimean War peace treaty the Russians had forfeited their previous guardianship of the Christian subjects of the Ottoman empire, and in the intervening years Turkish despotism and repression had become more rampant, particularly in their Slav provinces in the Balkans. Sporadic revolts against Turkish misrule erupted in Bosnia and Herzegovina during 1875, and the League of the Three Emperors (of Germany, Russia and Austria) met and proposed that the Turks be forced to treat the Christians better. But Disraeli declined to support the other European powers; he saw the pan-Slav movement in Russia as further evidence of Russia's territorial ambitions: should the Russians gain control of the Balkans they would be in an excellent position to seize both Constantinople and the new British naval base in Alexandria and thus pose a dual threat to India. Moreover Disraeli had little sympathy with the sufferings of Christians in remote territories, he had no appreciation of the *nationalist* impulse which was at work in the Balkans and above all he was determined that nothing should happen in that sensitive area of Europe without Britain being clearly and firmly involved to the furtherance of her prestige and interests.

The action which raised the temperature in England to a fever pitch was the Turkish suppression of a revolt in Bulgaria which began in April 1876 and in May resulted in the massacre of some twelve thousand men, women and children, mainly by Circassian troops, the notorious Bashi-Bazouks. As news of the massacre and the attendant stories of torture, rape and bestialities filtered through to England there was a spontaneous reaction, largely Liberal and middle-class, inspired in equal measures by guilt at England's support of the Turks, by sympathy for the fellow Christians thus slaughtered, by a certain prurient outrage at the horror stories and by a genuine feeling that this was not what civilisation should mean in nineteenth-century Europe. Mr. Forster first raised the subject of the Bulgarian massacres and how they should affect British foreign policy, in the House of Commons at the end of June 1876. It was a question that had considerable relevance, as Disraeli had ordered a British fleet to the Dardanelles as a warning to Russia not to intervene in the Balkans, an action which negated hopes of concerted European measures against the Turks and gave them the extra confidence to be intransigent. Early in July Disraeli replied somewhat flippantly to Forster's persistent questions by saying he doubted the extent of the horror stories because the Ottoman peoples seldom, he believed, resorted to torture but generally terminated their connection with culprits "in a more expeditious manner." When at the end of July he had to admit that the reports of the Bulgarian massacres were well-founded, he added that they had been grossly embroidered by "coffee house babble," and that he saw no reason for Britain to alter her policy towards the Balkans or the Eastern Question in general.

Disraeli's views were held in most upper-class circles. Indeed Disraeli was so little impressed by the anti-Turkish lobby or by thoughts that it might grow to such proportions as to precipitate Mr. Gladstone's return from Elba and to threaten his Government, that he accepted Her Majesty's offer of a peerage. In August 1876, as the parliamentary session came to an end, he bade a totally undramatic farewell to the House of Commons. Virtually nobody was aware that he had made his final speech in the Commons, that henceforth he would be the Earl of Beaconsfield, take his seat in the Lords and therefore be unable to fight Mr. Gladstone on level terms. As Mr. Disraeli departed from the Commons, the agitation for a reversal of Britain's Eastern policy and for a strong line to be taken against the Turks spread like wildfire, particularly in the North of England where it was fanned by the young William Thomas Stead, who was then the editor of the *Northern Echo* based in Darlington. Stead was not only a first-class, extremely enterprising journalist, but he had as great a passion for moral causes as had Gladstone, particularly if they had sexual undertones or overtones. It was at a mass meeting in Darlington that the first public call was heard for Mr. Gladstone to intervene and lend his moral weight and authority to the campaign, though privately quite a few people had been urging Gladstone to take a stand.

Gladstone has been criticised for appearing so late on the Bulgarian platform, as a further example of his never being an original thinker or innovator, but it should also be admitted that once he had appeared the campaign assumed a formidable aspect. He himself ascribed his tardiness to a natural reluctance to interfere because he was supposed to be retired and was no longer the leader of the Liberal party; but he said that once he had realised that Mr. Disraeli's Government intended to pursue its reckless Eastern policy he felt it his duty, notably as the last surviving Member of the House of Commons who could be held responsible for the disastrous Crimean War and its unsatisfactory pro-Turkish solution, to uphold England's honour, oppose despotism and support the justified national aspirations of the Christians in the Balkans. At the end of August, from Hawarden where he was laid up with a severe attack of lumbago, Gladstone started to write a pamphlet; he recorded in his diary, "Made a tolerable play in writing on the Bulgarian Horrors: the back is less strained in bed, where I write against the legs." By 3 September Gladstone had more or less completed the pamphlet and was on his way to London. As he prepared to leave Catherine wrote to Lord Frederick Cavendish a letter more than usually devoid of punctuation, grammar or syntax, underlining the extent of her emotion: "Uncle W is off for London tonight sleeping at Lord Granvilles I leave it to your imagination his state of *righteous indignation* & his energy & pluck a pamphlet nearly written he has been boiling over at the horrors & at the conduct of Government very proud that England's voice is speaking its gt heart throbbing & in this pumped out moment with no backing it speaks . . . He has just been saying 'this is the most extraordinary moment in all my recollection I have ever known' . . . What a blessing if it might prove fatal to d'Izzy . . . William goes to the British Museum to look up facts." One has to laugh at the idea of Gladstone, even in a moment of righteous indignation, using the language his wife ascribed to him, but he was certainly by now boiling over, and the fruits of his passion appeared on 7 September as *The Bulgarian Horrors and the Question of the East*. Its sale was as phenomenal as the earlier pamphlet against the Vatican decrees (and Gladstone made nearly £3,000 from it); its language was quite as trenchant and considerably more vehement. The passage which rang round Europe was, "Let the Turks now carry away their abuses in the only possible manner, namely by carrying off themselves. Their Zaptiehs and their Mudirs, their Bimbashis and their Yuzbashis, their Kaimakans and their Pashas, one and all, bag and baggage, shall I hope clear out from the provinces they have desolated and profaned."

From this moment Gladstone was again at the centre of the stage. Early in September he attended a monster protest meeting on Blackheath, held in pouring rain and howling winds; Mary described how "Papa gave vent to his boiling feelings in one of his most glorious speeches." At the end of September he and Catherine went on one of their tours of the great houses, in this instance to Yorkshire and Northumberland, staying at Castle Howard, Raby Castle and Alnwick, but the private tour developed into a triumphal public procession. At Castle Howard their carriage was taken over by hundreds of cheering people and they were manually pulled up the long drive to the great house which Sir John Vanbrugh had designed. At every halt Gladstone felt obliged to say a few words to the patiently waiting crowds. Apart from attacking the iniquities of Turkish misrule he also focused on the theme of the selfishness of the upper classes: "When did the Upper Ten Thousand ever lead the attack in the cause of humanity? Their leads are always full of class interest and the main chance." The climax of the first phase of the Bulgarian agitation came on 8 December 1876, at a mass meeting in St. James's Hall in London. Among the speakers were Anthony Trollope, the Bishop of Oxford and Lord Shaftesbury, but the star was William Ewart Gladstone, who noted in his diary, "Spoke (I fear) 1½ hours, with some exertion, far from wholly to my satisfaction. The meetings were great, notable, almost historical." As her husband's involvement in the Bulgarian campaign mounted Catherine wrote to him, "This is indeed a moment in our lives for your life feels mine. God help & strengthen you in the noble work. I consider that this work of yours may be one of the most interesting chapters of your life." Her feeling was correct.

CHAPTER 13

THE EASTERN QUESTION

In January 1877 a conference which had been held in Constantinople to try and sort out the problems of the Ottoman empire and its Christian subjects broke down, and towards the end of April Russia finally lost patience and declared war on Turkey. Opinion and allegiance in England were further split by this action, as among many of the anti-Turkish battalions there was a deep-rooted suspicion of Russia and her intentions; but Lord Beaconsfield's Cabinet was also divided and not all of its members were ardent pro-Turks, so for the time being the attitude of the British Government was one of watchful neutrality. For Gladstone this attitude was not good enough; before the Russian declaration of war he had decided that he must speak out if no one else would, and he noted in his diary, "Psalm XXIII 5," whose verses are "Thou preparest a table before me in the presence of mine enemies: thou anointest my head with oil; my cup runneth over." By the end of April his cup had run over and Gladstone decided to face his enemies by introducing into the House of Commons five resolutions which censured the Turks and recommended self-government for their Balkan territories.

Since the previous September, Gladstone's emergence as the leader of the Bulgarian campaign had placed the official leadership of the Liberal party and many of its members in an extremely difficult position. In March 1877 Mr. Forster wrote to the Duchess of Manchester, "Mr Gladstone seems to be a sort of political torpedo on the Eastern Question," which was a particularly apt simile as torpedoes were then notoriously unpredictable in their movements. His decision to introduce five trenchant resolutions into the House of Commons put an even greater strain on the party because the mass of Liberals in the country were now hanging on the words and actions of the man who had of his own volition retired from the leadership. Lord Hartington expressed the difficulty in a letter to Lord Granville: "I think we have some right to ask Mr G. to look at the facts, as they exist . . . He does not cease to be the leader of the Party merely by saying that he will not be the leader. If, as he has done since the autumn, he takes the lead, he *is* the leader, and all that he can do is to disclaim (for I do not think he can really divest himself of it) the responsibility which naturally attends upon leadership!" Gladstone continued to shut his eyes to the facts as they existed and it was only Granville's tact and Hartington's loyalty that saved the situation.

It was on 7 May 1877 that Gladstone rose to introduce his resolutions into a House of Commons which was extremely hostile, as much on the Liberal as Conservative benches, and as an initial expression of displeasure many Members pointedly walked out of the chamber. But within a short while they were back because, though Gladstone had lost his glasses and was therefore unable to refer to his notes, the words were pouring out of him in a golden cascade, and whatever their feelings few Members of Parliament were willing to miss Mr. Gladstone at the peak of his oratorical form. In growing silence they listened as Gladstone told them, "There were other days when England was the hope of freedom. Wherever in the world a high aspiration was entertained, or a noble blow struck, it was to England that the eyes of the oppressed were always turned . . . You talk to me of the established tradition and policy in regard to Turkey. I appeal to an established tradition older, wider, nobler far—a tradition not which disregards British interests, but which teaches you to seek the promotion of these interests in obeying the dictates of honour and justice." Mr. Forster commented that during the peroration Gladstone seemed like a man inspired, and years later Arthur Balfour said, "I shall never forget the impression that speech left on my mind. As a mere feat of physical endurance it was almost unsurpassed; as a feat of parliamentary courage, parliamentary skill, parliamentary endurance, and parliamentary eloquence, I believe it will always be unequalled."

Gladstone had scored another triumph and his renewed appeal to the honour and justice that transcended national interest thrilled the hearts of his supporters throughout the land; but the resolutions were defeated, the Government did not change its policy and the Liberal party was left in an even greater crisis. The devoted Lucy Cavendish was soon driven to comment, "I am come round to the conviction that he should either have continued to lead the Party, or withdrawn from Parliament altogether, or taken a Peerage," but as Lord Hartington's sister-in-law Lucy too was subjected to great stress and divided loyalties.

If the official leadership and many members of the parliamentary party were dismayed by the anomalous situation, one sector which rallied to Gladstone's side after his forthright resolutions was the Radicals led by Joseph Chamberlain and Sir Charles Dilke. The latter was a staunch republican who had been in Parliament since 1868, but the former had only been elected in 1876. Chamberlain was then approaching his fortieth birthday and was a shining example of the new breed of able, thrusting, ambitious middle-class men, one who had already made his mark in the 1870 educational battles and then as the reforming Mayor of Birmingham. Both Dilke and Chamberlain made the mistake of thinking they could use and control Gladstone, and Chamberlain told his friend, "If he were to come back for a few years (he can't continue in public life for very much longer) he would probably do much for us, and pave the way for more."

At the end of May 1877, in furtherance of the new accord between the younger radical element in the Liberal party, Gladstone accepted an invitation to speak in Birmingham at a meeting of the National Liberal Federation, which Chamberlain, who was also an exponent of organised professionalism in politics, had recently helped found. Lucy Cavendish recorded that Uncle William's reception was "more like a Royal progress than anything," that it was a "great break" for Aunt Pussy and that a man had told her it was not curiosity that drove people to stand for hours waiting for Gladstone but sheer love of him. Whatever views his more sophisticated supporters held, it was during this period of leading non-leadership that Gladstone's bond with the masses was re-established and that for millions he became the true prophet. For the millions, his was the not-so-still, not-so-small voice of justice reverberating in the wilderness; he alone among major politicians was following the high moral course of denouncing the bestial Turks, protecting European peace and salvaging England's honour.

In August 1877 Gladstone was almost submerged by the evidence of the people's affection when Catherine put into operation a personal scheme she had long cherished, the opening of the grounds of Hawarden Castle to the public. While Sir Stephen Glynne was alive he had refused to open the park, in this instance showing a rare determination, exerting his authority as the titular owner of the estate and clinging to his privacy. Catherine had said, "To me it is quite horrid, the entire solitude and the feeling that scarcely anybody may enjoy the innocent pleasure of the lovely park"; once her son became the owner she started to share the pleasure by throwing open the grounds to the local inhabitants, and in 1877 the hordes descended. It was an appallingly wet, cold summer but thousands of people made the long journey from the Lancashire cotton towns, as much to pay homage to Mr. Gladstone as to enjoy the rare pleasure of rambling through acres of private parkland. Gladstone noted, "A party of 1400 came from Bolton! We were nearly killed with kindness," and "Confronted the Salford & Darwin parties. They were nearly 3000," and "Addressed the 2000 who came today from Bacup"; while Mary recorded, "1400 people came to see the place and Papa, and watched & cheered him cutting down an ash: curious & pretty sight, evening sun, lovely spot (near Niagara), intense enthusiasm." She came to the conclusion that a rule would have to be made that the crowds could not roam in the vicinity of the house while the family was at home, or at least not while Papa was. The organised excursions were limited, except on specific days such as the annual bazaar or flower show when Catherine wanted the crowds to spend their money for one of her charities, but the right to enter the grounds of Hawarden Castle was never withdrawn.

The speeches which Gladstone felt obliged to make to the patient excursionists and those he made in other parts of the country continued to focus on the selfishness of "the Upper Ten Thousand," but he directed his passion and outrage towards the figure of the newly elevated Earl of Beaconsfield, who was *the* man tarnishing England's honour and leading her on a disaster course. Lord Beaconsfield's initial reaction to the Gladstonian onslaughts was flippant. When the Bulgarian pamphlet appeared he told the new Lord Derby (his old colleague and leader was now dead) that it was "Vindictive and ill-written—that of course. Indeed in that respect of all the Bulgarian horrors perhaps the greatest," and pleased with his gibe he repeated it in public. Such flippancy only goaded Gladstone into a greater fury of righteous indignation because it epitomised everything he was fighting against in Beaconsfield's leadership and the attitude of the upper classes. But at the same time as he thundered about the failure of responsibility and narrow self-interest of the Upper Ten Thousand, he retained his reverence for the continuity of English life and tradition, and for the principle of *noblesse oblige* at its highest level of public service, as exemplified by Lord Granville or Lord Hartington or Lord Salisbury.

It was while Gladstone was storming the class ramparts that John Ruskin paid his first visit to Hawarden (in January 1878), albeit armed with a telegram of recall in case he could not endure the righteous morality of the Gladstone family circle. In fact, Ruskin found the Gladstones delightful company, even though Catherine was away from home, and while he considered that Mr. Gladstone's intense simplicity and earnestness of character laid him open to every sort of misinterpretation, he also thought that he was absolutely sincere and unwarped by ambition. In one of their many long, spirited conversations Ruskin accused Gladstone of being a leveller, producing the often-quoted reply, "Oh dear no! I am nothing of the sort. I am a firm believer in the aristocratic principle—the rule of the best. I am an out-and-out *inequalitarian*." Ruskin chuckled with delight at the word, and Gladstone was particularly pleased with it as he thought it expressed his meaning more precisely than "inegalitarian."

In his role as the people's prophet and the conscience of the nation, Gladstone was assiduously supported by Catherine. From the beginning of 1877 there was a subtle, at times not altogether attractive change in her attitude towards her husband and his career. For she too had found a mission: it was to ensure that now her husband had returned to his rightful position at the centre of the stage, he stayed there. Gladstone had shown that he was capable of error by his retirement in 1875 and Catherine was determined that he should not make another mistake. In furtherance of her aim, which was entwined with her personal if unconscious desire to be part of the mainspring of history, Catherine's always partial assessment of her husband's genius became decidedly biased. Gone were the days when she queried his vehemence or excitability, and some of her utterances about that "horrid Jew," the Earl of Beaconsfield, were to say the least childish and un-Christian. (Catherine was not particularly anti-Semitic; rather her comments were a pale reflection of the widespread and deep-rooted prejudice.) Fortunately her general sense of the ridiculous and her ability to deflate a pompous situation did not desert her, nor did the rushing enthusiasm for causes other than her husband, but as Gladstone's guiding star and pillar she assumed a new unblinking light and a rigidity which was not always admirable or helpful.

Catherine was not the only notable female in the United Kingdom of Great Britain and Ireland whose always partial, emotional, subjective opinions and judgements assumed a fiercer aspect during the period of the Bulgarian campaign. It was in these years that Queen Victoria's prejudices and bias also hardened and her wary dislike and distrust of Mr. Gladstone turned at times into an almost pathological hatred. In mid-September 1876, as Gladstone re-emerged into the limelight, Her Majesty merely considered him to be "that incomprehensible Mr G—that most mischievous tho' I believe unintentionally so of men"; but by the end of the month her attitude had already changed and she was writing of "the disgraceful conduct of that mischief maker & firebrand Mr G," and by 1877 he had become "that madman Gladstone."

There were many reasons for the crystallisation of Her Majesty's emotions. To an extent Gladstone was again unfortunate in his royal timing, because now he was out of office he rarely saw the Queen, and *in absentia* Her Majesty was able to give full rein to her imagined portrait of the gentleman. Whereas in 1868 she had been firmly ensconced in her far-flung residences with the drawbridge metaphorically up, by 1876 she had finally recharged her batteries and was ready to assume her royal duties. Her great rapport with Lord Beaconsfield assisted the process but having herself emerged from the shades Her Majesty considered that she, who had been on the throne for nearly forty years and had blood or marriage connections with all the crowned heads of Europe, possessed an unparalleled knowledge of foreign affairs. She tended to regard the power struggle in Europe as a personal struggle; the Turkish Sultan posed no threat to her authority as the doyenne of European royalty, nor to the power and prestige of her beloved country, but the Czar of Russia did. Anybody who could not see that the Czar—and his subjects—needed a severe lesson was at best misguided and misled, at worst a traitor.

As she re-entered the political stage Queen Victoria failed absolutely to comprehend the change that was occurring, and the nature of the new two-party political system was something she never understood. She harked back to the days when Prince Albert had been alive, when because of the political instability the monarchy had exercised considerable power, particularly in foreign affairs, but when above all Members of Parliament had supported the Government of the day and their Sovereign (her memory was faulty, however—even in the days of faction rather than party, the support had never been wholehearted or uncritical). Her Majesty was both baffled and outraged by the behaviour of the Liberal Opposition. She told her daughter Vicky, the Crown Princess of Prussia, ". . . when the (so-called but not real) Liberals are in opposition, they always behave in the most factious way possible," and further, "The Opposition have again behaved most shamefully . . . no wish to maintain the honour of the country or to be a help to their widowed & lonely Queen."

The failure of political comprehension and the ever-present tinge of self-pity were given extra fuel by the similarly ever-present jealousy of Mr. Gladstone. For his campaign was directed at "the people," and while *he* regarded it as one to save the soul of the country and *she* as an iniquitous attempt to poison the nation's mind, a root cause of the animosity was *his* effort to influence *her* people. Gladstone's fierce attacks on the aristocracy obviously did not appeal to Her Majesty, and they appealed even less to the Upper Ten Thousand. To them it was clear that Mr. Gladstone was consumed by personal ambition, that his espousal of the Eastern Question and his vindictive outbursts against Lord Beaconsfield and themselves were the desperate clutchings of an unprincipled demagogue at the straws of renewed popularity. It was by members of the Upper Ten Thousand that Her Majesty was surrounded, and the drip-drip process of her being told what a bad dangerous man Mr. Gladstone was developed into a torrent from 1877 onwards. Temporarily, Gladstone lost the support of the Prince of Wales because he was as outraged by the Liberal stance as was the Queen. Virtually the sole ally Gladstone had at court was Henry Ponsonby, whose own position was seriously undermined by the tenacity with which he tried to put the moderate Liberal, albeit Gladstonian, point of view.

Then there was the Earl of Beaconsfield, with a direct line to Her Majesty. In Henry Ponsonby's opinion he helped warp her mind against Mr. Gladstone, the Liberal party and himself. It has been argued that Queen Victoria's mind did not need warping, that it had already come to its own startling conclusions, and that Beaconsfield was playing both ends against the middle by using Her Majesty's anti-Russian frenzy to stiffen the sinews of his less warlike colleagues, while painting sombre pictures of the Cabinet doubts to restrain the Queen. Undoubtedly Lord Beaconsfield had his royal problems at this period too—he told one of his sympathetic lady friends, "The Faery writes every day and telegraphs every hour"—and he also had to deal with her newest weapon—the threat of abdication if her wishes were not met. While Lord Beaconsfield might not have inspired Her Majesty's hatred of Mr. Gladstone and all those so-called but not real Liberals—Queen Victoria always saw herself as the genuine article—it seems unreasonable to suppose that he did not encourage it. His own utterances about Mr. Gladstone were not free from rancour and vitriol; he told the young Lord Derby, "Posterity will do justice to that unprincipled maniac, Gladstone—extraordinary mixture of envy, vindictiveness, hypocrisy, and superstition; and with one commanding characteristic—whether preaching, praying, speechifying, or scribbling—never a gentleman!" In 1878 he produced his famous parody of Gladstonian rhetoric (or at least one assumes it was a parody and he was not carried away by *his* verbosity) when he described his opponent as "a sophistical rhetorician inebriated with the exuberance of his own verbosity, and gifted with an egotistical imagination that can at all times command an interminable and inconsistent series of arguments to malign an opponent and glorify himself."

It was also in this period that the first overt gossip about Gladstone's associations with prostitutes was bandied about in upper-class circles, including the court, though Lord Beaconsfield was not a major culprit. It would have been beneath his dignity as a gentleman to have discredited his rival by such means, though he probably took a cynical pleasure in the gossip which reached his ears. Other members of the upper classes were less scrupulous in spreading stories which only confirmed their views about Gladstone's hypocrisy. For what could a man approaching his seventieth year possibly be doing scouring the streets of the West End at night and visiting prostitutes in their homes, except gratifying coarse sexual instincts? Apart from the gossip about Gladstone's association with low common street women, his friendship with Olga Novikoff was also the subject of much speculation, in this case publicly as well as privately.

Olga Novikoff, or "OK" as she was popularly known, was a Russian lady of high birth who had been in England for several years—the Gladstones first met her in 1873. She was an ardent Anglophile and a pan-Slav who worked assiduously, pulling every political string she knew, to effect a closer co-operation between England and Russia and to promote the cause of Balkan nationalism. To her opponents she was the arch-intriguer, the archetypal femme fatale-cum-spy; to her friends she was "the MP for Russia"; certainly she was a formidable lady who exerted some influence on the Anglo-Russian scene in the late 1870s. In January 1877 Gladstone's relationship with the lady made the columns of *The Times*, which remarked upon "many letters which do greater honour to the heart than to the head of our emotional statesman." The relationship continued to fill a fair amount of column space in various newspapers and magazines for several years but the innuendoes were in this case off-target, because though Gladstone indubitably saw a good deal of Madame Novikoff and their correspondence was large, the main interest was political. He frequently asked Catherine to deal with "OK" for him, his secretary Edward Hamilton commented that he did not think Mr. Gladstone appreciated her overmuch, and it was W. T. Stead whose friendship with her was more than platonic.

Nevertheless, the gossips had fertile ground on which to work. Gladstone was again engaged in his night work on a fairly regular basis when he was in London, and though by this time he seems to have accepted it as a necessary part of his existence, the theme that his whole personal life was so little worthy of anybody's love and praise, particularly in contrast with his public life, was a recurrent one in his diaries. For example, at the end of 1876 he wrote, ". . . oh that I could live my personal life as I live my public life which however speckled with infirmity is upright in intention"; in a very long birthday retrospect in 1878 he commented, "I am still under the painful sense that my public life is & has the best of me: that it draws off my personal life almost all moral resolution, all capacity for Christian discipline in the personal & private sphere."

Gladstone invited the probings into the infirm, speckled side of his private life by the violence of his attacks on the upper classes, who retaliated with the most obvious means at their command. The scandalous rumours about Mr. Gladstone's nocturnal habits were then confined to a smallish circle. No particular plots were hatched to use them to destroy him publicly, but some anonymous letters were sent to Catherine, who treated them with the disdain that in one way they deserved. However, in another way it might have been wiser if she had regarded them in a more serious light, because her husband's night work was definitely open to misinterpretation and was a potential source of grave danger to his career. But Catherine was in no mood to hear ill of her husband; any fleeting doubts she might have had about his motives had evaporated, or she had grown so accustomed to his activities that she had forgotten them. The imperviousness and ingenuousness with which both she and Gladstone faced his sexual detractors heartened those who believed in him and partially spiked the guns of those who did not.

Although Gladstone was convinced that in espousing the Eastern Question he was fighting a spiritual battle which was infinitely greater than party politics, and although many people's passions were stirred at this period, some of the bitterness which henceforward corroded the political scene was directly attributable to him, because when Gladstone's passions were aroused their fervent strength produced vibrations that shook the country. The year 1878 was a particularly tumultuous one. In January the Turks, who had put up a more spirited defence than had been expected, finally capitulated to the Russians, and the collapse produced an upsurge of anti-Russian feeling in the country: it was one matter to support the Russians when they were doing nothing in particular and quite another when they were within sight of the domes of Constantinople. Lord Beaconsfield again ordered the fleet to the Dardanelles; Gladstone rushed from Hawarden to London to rally the Liberal Opposition and was astonished to find "Ld Hartington bolted" and that only with great difficulty could he be "brought up to the mark again." Having persuaded an official Liberal leader to support his fresh anti-Government resolutions, Gladstone then rushed to Oxford, where he denounced Lord Beaconsfield's action as a breach of international law and said he would continue to counterwork what he believed to be his lordship's purpose with every means at his command. On 4 February he was back in London, where he spoke against the Government's provocative, martial measures for "1 hr 50 at my best," but on 8 February the resolutions were defeated and Gladstone spent the next day in bed "boiling myself down." Opinion in the south of England was boiling itself up and jingoism was erupting like the bubonic plague:

> We don't want to fight but by Jingo if we do,
> We've got the ships, we've got the men,
> we've got the money too.

A Liberal version of the obnoxious rhyme was similarly obnoxious:

> We don't want to fight,
> By Jingo if we do,
> The head I'd like to punch
> Is Beaconsfield the Jew.

On 24 February it was Gladstone's head that was in danger of being punched when a crowd descended on Harley Street and windows in his house were smashed. Gladstone can never be accused of lacking courage, nor can he be accused of solely courting mass popularity, and the evidence of the people's displeasure in no way dissuaded him from his pursuit of peace and international justice. (Gladstone's supporters in the North of England remained faithful, though even there peace meetings were broken up by jingoist mobs.)

In March 1878 Russia imposed on Turkey the treaty of San Stefano by which she obtained access to the Mediterranean and some territory in Asia Minor, and it was agreed to create a large autonomous Bulgaria which would include most of the Christian subjects of the Ottoman empire and would be under Russian guardianship. News of the treaty inspired a further war fever in England because it seemed that Russia had got everything she wanted and Britain's prestige was threatened because she had supported the Turks. The reserves were called up, an action which delighted Queen Victoria, who had earlier said that if she were a man she would give those horrid Russians "such a beating," but it proved too much for two members of Lord Beaconsfield's Cabinet, Lord Derby and Lord Carnarvon, who resigned in protest. Restrained by its new Foreign Secretary Lord Salisbury, the Government withdrew from the brink of war and agreed to attend a conference of the involved European powers in Berlin, at which the treaty of San Stefano would be ratified, rejected or amended but with Britain having a large finger in the pie. At the Congress of Berlin which began in June 1878, those two elderly, ailing, pragmatic realists the Earl of Beaconsfield and Prince Bismarck got on like the proverbial house on fire, and a compromise treaty was agreed which held until 1914. Russia retained her outlet to the Mediterranean and her gains in Asia Minor but the big Bulgaria of San Stefano was split into three. In a secret deal with the Turks Britain acquired Cyprus, ostensibly as a base from which she could guarantee Turkey's future territorial integrity against Russian encroachment and neutralise her gains in Asia Minor; but in this deal Britain also undertook to act as the guarantor of reform within the Ottoman empire.

Much of the donkeywork at the Congress was performed by Lord Salisbury, who exhibited a command of the facts, an energy and a mastery of detail which was not inferior to Gladstone's; but it was the Earl of Beaconsfield who reaped the rewards. In the middle of July 1878 he landed in Dover, with Bismarck's praise *Der alte Jude, das ist der Mann* ringing in his ears, to announce, "Gentlemen, we bring you peace, and I think I may say, peace with honour." The phrase "peace with honour" was repeated several times by Lord Beaconsfield and rang round the country (though it was first used by an ancestor of Lord Salisbury's, Lord Robert Cecil, in the time of James I). Lord Beaconsfield and to a lesser extent Lord Salisbury became the heroes of the hour and Queen Victoria recorded, "High and low are delighted, except Mr Gladstone who is frantic."

Gladstone was not so much frantic as placed in a difficult position because his rival had displayed his pragmatic realism to the full, done an almost complete *volte-face* and implemented most of the demands for which Gladstone had been campaigning for nearly two years. Another war had been avoided, eleven million Balkan Christians had been removed from the yoke of Turkish oppression and Britain's policy of supporting Turkey at all costs had been reversed. Gladstone could only accept the achievements of the Congress of Berlin and focus his continuing deep distrust of Lord Beaconsfield's foreign policy on the annexation of Cyprus. Unfortunately he became overvehement in his attacks, calling the deal "an insane convention . . . an act of duplicity not surpassed and rarely equalled in the history of nations." For the majority of his countrymen the acquisition of Cyprus was another small but splendid jewel in the imperial crown and the majority temporarily disagreed with Mr. Gladstone.

During these tumultuous years, the private life of the supposedly retired Mr. Gladstone was as energetic as his public life. In October 1877 he paid his first visit to Ireland, accompanied by Mary and Catherine, who was now rarely away from his side. It was not an auspicious moment for an ex-Liberal leader to visit the country, because the Catholic hierarchy had little love for its Russian Orthodox brethren and was resolutely pro-Turkish. But the Gladstones confined their visit to Dublin, were mainly entertained by members of the Anglo-Irish Protestant ascendancy, and he had only one day of public speaking. On the way home the boat ran into a fearful storm and stopped to help another ship in distress and Mary noted the distaff side of being loved by the people when they finally staggered into Holyhead hours late: ". . . we were forced to perk up and . . . struggle thro' enthusiastic crowds to the Town Hall, where we smiled & bowed as if we weren't dead."

Mary was now the only Gladstone child permanently at home in an unmarried state. In 1877 Helen, at the age of twenty-eight, achieved her heart's desire and enrolled as a student at Newnham Hall, Cambridge, which had been established as a college for women six years previously. In achieving her ambition Helen was considerably assisted by Mary's help in persuading their mother that it was not too daring a proposition (Gladstone had no particular objections), and also by the fact that Arthur Balfour's sister was the Principal of Newnham Hall. Helen read history and literature, then political economy and logic for the Cambridge University High Local Examinations—as a woman she was of course unable to read for an actual degree—and distinguished herself in political economy. She was a rather large, self-contained lady, imbued with deep religious beliefs and a sense of duty, but she had inherited her mother's grace of movement and possessed an unexpected warmth of manner. In the cloistered but determined pioneering world of female higher education Helen found her niche; she remained at Newnham Hall for the next twenty years and became its Vice-Principal.

By 1877 Mary herself was thirty but though she was unmarried there was nothing "spinsterish" about her and she had a capacity for enjoying life. Her music, as performer and audience, gave her great pleasure; she had entrée to rehearsals at the Albert Hall, noting one occasion when Wagner "flew into an awful rage" and another when she managed to smuggle in the Princess of Wales without anybody's realising who she was. Catherine said her daughter was always wonderfully thoughtful and Gladstone wrote, "Mary is all sufficing in point of society." She had already begun to take over some of the day-to-day running of her parents' lives—she had inherited her mother's erratic organisational ability together with the desire to manage other people's lives—and it was at this time that Mary acquired the nickname of "Von Moltke." It was also in 1877 that she acquired a lady's maid named Auguste Schluter. Fräulein Schluter was Hanoverian by birth and was officially engaged as a maid for both Helen and Mary, but as the former was now away from home during term-time it was the latter who became her particular lady. Auguste Schluter and the Gladstones were made for each other, because she was a deeply religious young lady who examined the state of her soul and believed in the will of God as fervently as did Mr. Gladstone. Like him she kept a diary and copies of her letters, and if their content is considerably less intellectual and their spelling of an original Anglo-German variety, they are interesting documents, providing a downstairs view of life at the top and showing what benevolent employers the Gladstones were.

Willie Gladstone and his wife Gertrude also stayed at home for some years after their marriage but the arrangement whereby the owner of Hawarden Castle shared the house with his mother and father was not entirely satisfactory because Catherine continued to be what she had been for over forty years, in fact since her mother had suffered the slight stroke in 1834: the mistress of Hawarden. Neither Willie nor Gertrude was a forceful character, neither had the courage to suggest that they did not wish their entire lives to be managed by Catherine and it was left to Gertrude's father Lord Blantyre to intimate that the couple should have their own house. The idea that the Gladstones should move was unthinkable, and indeed part of Sir Stephen's testamentary arrangements had been that his sister and her husband should live at Hawarden for the term of their natural lives. Lord Blantyre's suggestion was very coldly received by the Gladstones; neither Catherine nor her husband could see any reason why their eldest son and daughter-in-law should want to move and upset such a cosy arrangement, but after some minor storms the young Gladstones departed. They did not go far, however; they soon built the Red House at the end of Hawarden village. Thus the amity of the family circle was preserved, and Catherine's feelings (in particular) were assuaged without Gertrude's having to suffer too persistently from what her father described as "Mrs Gladstone's zeal and habits of management."

Just as Catherine's feelings about her husband's career became more defined in these years, she herself was becoming more the *grande dame*. It was again an unconscious process, partly attributable to the fact that her manners and speech belonged to an earlier age; the idea of actually acquiring a title, which was mooted at this time, did not appeal to her. After Sir Stephen Glynne's death, the College of Heralds intimated that Catherine, as the last surviving member of the Glynne family, was entitled to claim the extinct Baronies of Percy and Poynings. Gladstone himself was quite enthusiastic about the suggestion and at the end of 1877 he wrote to Catherine, "What I feel is that the revival of this title would serve as a memorial to your family . . . if you had it, it would pass to Willy and would not be likely to be superceded by any higher title." But Catherine was not interested in becoming a Baroness; for her the title Mrs. Gladstone was the most illustrious she could possess. If she became more of a *grande dame* she remained one with the common touch; she would drop into houses in the village for a cup of tea without being patronising, she would rush to help villagers in distress and she was always ready to lend her musical talent and play the piano at a village concert. Catherine also frequently played the piano at sing-songs at the Hawarden Orphanage, which continued to demand a fair amount of attention and which now had thirty boys permanently in residence, with a long queue of applicants. Soon she turned her attention to a problem concerning those at the other end of the age scale, elderly women who were widowed or had fallen on hard times and had nowhere to go but the workhouse. A collection of cottages lying near the yard, some of which had housed the departed Lancashire factory girls, was refurbished and became "Mrs Gladstone's Home of Rest," where groups of elderly women spent their last years in peace and security.

Catherine's major preoccupation was to ensure that her husband had the maximum amount of security in the love and protection of his family, and enjoyed as much peace as was possible by the removal of minor irritations and responsibilities. She was not always successful in her aim—Mary recorded a return to Harley Street in 1879: "Everything was beastly, had to tramp about in the rain, & there was every sort of bother about our baggage. Papa looked rigid & Mama hot & excited." In reality, despite her renewed focus on her husband's career, Catherine had far too many other irons still in the fire and was too much of a personality in her own right ever to fulfill the role of dutiful, efficient "little wifie," even if she occasionally saw herself in it. But at Hawarden she organised the household so that her husband could spend days arranging his books or, as he noted, "6½ hours on Homeric Primer. What a treat!" followed by snug evenings in the Temple of Peace, in which Gladstone would hold forth on an infinite variety of subjects. One of his favourite themes was the nature of the English people, which he considered to be "full of stuff" but "disgustingly lazy," a theme which might surprise those who believe that once upon a time, notably in the nineteenth century, the English worked hard as a matter of course and not when they felt like it. In the mornings Mary assisted with the correspondence, which, as Gladstone noted, had almost doubled since his supposed retirement.

Away from Hawarden theatre-going remained a major treat; Gladstone's taste was still catholic: he would drop into a music hall which was "certainly not Athenian" in his view, but an increasing number of visits were made to the Lyceum, where Henry Irving was now installed with his company. By 1876 Irving was already lending the Gladstones his private box and in 1878 Gladstone wrote to the actor/manager to say how much he had enjoyed his performance in *The Lyons Mail*. Irving, who also had a mission in life, immediately wrote back asking Gladstone if he would give his public support to that mission, which was to raise the status of the actor from rogue and vagabond to professional respectability and that of acting from the lowest of the art forms to one that demanded the highest critical attention. Gladstone replied saying that Irving's mission was "a rich and worthy subject," but it was not one which he had considered in depth and for the time being he withheld his support. However, invitations to visit Mr. Irving in his dressing room followed, Gladstone was taken on a conducted tour backstage which he loved and the friendship ripened.

Gladstone's vanity, or his sense of history, had led him to have his portrait painted at fairly regular intervals throughout his adult life, and during these stormy years he sat for two of the leading artists of the day, George Frederick Watts and John Everett Millais. The family hated the Watts protrait; Mary said it made her feel quite wretched because it was the face of a weak, peevish old man which bore no resemblance to her beloved Papa, and Catherine was just as miserable. But the Millais portrait was greeted with the reverse amount of enthusiasm; the family considered it an admirable representation of Gladstone in his seventieth year. In March 1878, accompanied by Mary, he found time to visit the exhibition which demonstrated the powers of two new machines, the telephone and the phonograph. Gladstone noted that they were very interesting but Mary recorded much livelier impressions: "Off to see the telephone & the phonograph. The former is nothing to compare with the latter for wonderfulness, tho' likely to be much more practically useful. The pho. keeps your words & voice shut up for any length of time & then repeats them back word for word." (By the end of 1880 Gladstone had been persuaded to have a telephone installed at Hawarden Castle, one of the first in private use in the country, but though his family were enthusiastic callers he, according to Lucy Cavendish, would have nothing to do with it.)

At the end of 1878, conscious that he was approaching the biblical lifespan of threescore years and ten, Gladstone penned longer birthday and yearly retrospects than for some while. He admitted that the last three years, instead of unbinding and detaching him from the cares of life, had immersed him more deeply in them; but he thought, "This retroactive motion has appeared & yet appears to me to carry the mark of the will of God. For when have I seen so strongly the relation between my public duties & the primary purposes for wh God made & Christ redeemed the world?" He stressed that his return to the fray had been most reluctant and that he had only undertaken the Bulgarian campaign because he felt he was serving God's purpose. However, he showed his awareness of false prophets by writing, "And language such as I have used is often prompted by fanaticism. But not always. It is to be tried by tests. I have striven to apply them with all the sobriety I can." He returned to the theme that his public life drew off all resolution from his private one and in the yearly retrospect he added, "I see scarcely a glimmering of improvement in the kinds of self-command that I most need, & I have still to fear lest in a darkened conscience I tamper with the law & judgment of my God." The final words of his birthday thoughts were, "If I am to be spared for another birthday God grant that by that time there may have been a great shifting of events & parts, & that I may have entered into that period of recollection & penitence which my life much needs before its close."

Despite the running theme of his wish to retire and compose his soul for the day of reckoning, there was in 1878 a buoyancy and a return of the vigorous mental youthfulness which had been absent in 1875. Although he wrote of the hope that events would have returned him to the shades by the end of the following year, Gladstone was hardly being realistic, because he had committed himself to an undertaking which would require every ounce of his campaigning skill and which, if successful, must place him in an even more dominant position. It was to contest the constituency of Midlothian at the next General Election.

CHAPTER 14

SETTING THE HEATHER ON FIRE

SINCE HE HAD SCRAPED home a poor second at Greenwich in the 1874 election Gladstone had made it known that he had no wish to stand for that ungrateful inglorious constituency again, but though several were offered to him he was in no hurry to commit himself to another. However, by early 1878 the Liberal party needed a major pre-election campaign which would redefine Liberal principles, refocus attention on itself and reactivate its supporters. Who could perform this task more admirably than the erstwhile leader, the redoubtable, the unique Mr. Gladstone? In June 1878 Gladstone noted in his diary, "Saw Adam cum Ld. Rosebery on the Midlothian scene," Adam being the Liberal Chief Whip entrusted with the task of reorganising the party after its electoral defeat, Lord Rosebery one of the brightest, most aristocratic young Liberals. Early in December 1878 Gladstone privately indicated that he was prepared to contest the Scottish constituency of Midlothian and enter into the major campaign which would be required to win it. It was on the basis of rejuvenating and inspiring the party and ridding the country of "Beaconsfieldism" that Gladstone said he was undertaking the formidable task; he continued to insist that Lord Granville was the Liberal leader and, as he later told Lord Acton, that he was working for "a decisive ascension of the Liberal party to power, without me." But as John Bright, who was staying at Hawarden as Gladstone composed the official letter accepting the invitation to stand for Midlothian, told *him*, the entire Liberal party would require *him* to come forward in a crisis.

There was no immediate likelihood of Lord Beaconsfield calling a General Election, the Midlothian campaign had to be organised and in the meanwhile the Gladstones passed some of the quietest months of their lives. The New Year was spent at Hawarden and on 6 January 1879 Auguste Schluter noted, "Our dear Mrs Gladstone's birthday and in the early morning we sung Home Sweet Home near her bedroom door." It was a bitterly cold winter—Auguste again noted "splendit skating" on the ponds in the park—and early in March both the Gladstones were ill in bed, but Catherine was up in time to attend a concert at Grosvenor House in aid of the Hawarden Orphanage. In April Gladstone was at Clumber in his capacity as the executor of the Duke of Newcastle's estate, trying to salvage precious documents from the fire which had gutted the house; in July there were visits to the theatre to see Sarah Bernhardt—Mary went three times in the week; in August there was the annual bazaar at Hawarden and a troop of guests; and in mid-September a family party, including Mary and Herbert, departed on a continental holiday. They travelled first to Germany, visiting Gladstone's sister Helen, who was, according to Mary, "beyond words contrary at first, and I shall never forget our reception, nor will Herbert"; they then stayed with Lord Acton at Tegernsee. At the end of September they saw Robert Browning in Venice; by mid-October they were in Paris, where Olga Novikoff was among their visitors; and by the end of the month they were home, refreshed in mind and body and ready for the coming fray. Catherine immediately dashed off to Wellington College, where her daughter Agnes was expecting another baby, but she was back at Hawarden in time for the grand departure for Midlothian on 24 November 1879.

The chief organiser of the campaign was the young Lord Rosebery, who had become the president of the newly inaugurated Midlothian Liberal Association the previous year; it was he who had invited Gladstone to contest the seat. Rosebery was a man on whom fortune had scattered innumerable blessings—wealth, estates, intelligence—but there had been a wicked fairy at his birth too, and she had given him a morbid sensitivity. If Rosebery was always something of a Hamlet figure, in his younger days the bouts of activity were more frequent and he threw himself into his role as entrepreneur of Gladstone's Scottish campaign with considerable enthusiasm.

Rosebery had recently visited the United States and had been greatly impressed by the organisation and showmanship that went into the making of the Democratic Convention in New York, and the receptions that greeted Mr. and Mrs. Gladstone and Mary as they travelled round Scotland were by no means entirely spontaneous. (Edward Hamilton, Gladstone's secretary, was also a close friend of Lord Rosebery's, and he later said that the 1879–80 Midlothian campaigns cost his lordship £50,000 one way and another.) It was Rosebery who decided that the Gladstones should travel by the Midland Railway as that company had recently introduced the Pullman car with its platform at the back, from which Mr. Gladstone could easily make a speech at the various stations and halts. As the train steamed north from Chester through Lancashire the receptions were warm enough but it was at Carlisle that "the real hubbub" began, as Mary recorded, and at Edinburgh it was "perfectly overwhelming" with the station packed with "roaring crowds." Lord Rosebery had not dragooned the roaring crowds—though he had made certain that the arrival was well-publicised—but he was responsible for some of the hundreds of people who raced alongside the Gladstones' open carriage as it drove from Edinburgh to his ancestral home at Dalmeny, where they were staying as his guests. Lord Rosebery was also responsible for the waving torches, the fireworks and the bonfires which greeted the Gladstones as they neared Dalmeny in the darkness and which, inspired by his example, became such a feature of the tour —towns and villages vying to outdo each other in the brilliance of their nighttime welcomes, with bonfires on the hillsides, lamps burning in cottage windows and torchlight processions winding through the streets.

On 25 November the Gladstones had a stupendous reception in Edinburgh, with Princes Street jammed with thousands of people and the police having to erect barricades to restrain their enthusiasm; on 26 November they were in Dalkeith; on 27 November they visited West Calder, travelling under triumphal arches which had been erected all the way from Dalmeny to the town; by 1 December they had reached Perth, where Gladstone was given the freedom of the city; and by 4 December they were in Glasgow. There, the next day, Gladstone gave his address as Lord Rector of the University of Glasgow—and was escorted by two thousand students holding aloft flaming torches—and also delivered a speech in St. Andrew's Hall. It was said that 70,000 people applied for tickets for this later meeting of whom only 6,500 were fortunate to gain admittance; Gladstone himself estimated that he addressed audiences totalling 87,000 and nobody tried to estimate how many people turned out to see him. Not only him but Catherine, for everywhere he went, she went. She was showered with plaids and rugs, shawls and tablecloths. Their daughter wrote of the horrors they experienced "from the reckless crowding of the people, pressing on to the carriage, hanging on to the wheels, such pinched, haggard, eager faces," while Lord Rosebery described Gladstone "calmly perorating about Bulgaria while the fainting people were lifted over pale and motionless into the reporters' enclosure."

The fantastic fortnight, then unprecedented in the annals of British political history and never since surpassed, with an ex-Prime Minister storming through the countryside accompanied by his wife, raising and responding to an enthusiasm which was at times terrifying and verging on mass hysteria, at times thrilling and touching in its demonstration of affection and belief, was undertaken by a man who was nearly seventy and a woman who was nearly sixty-eight, in the rigours of early Scottish winter weather. Lucy Cavendish was at Chester to meet her uncle and aunt as they returned home on 8 December, and she recorded the further frantic enthusiasm which greeted them there. She also noted that Uncle William was "fresh as paint" and that for the first time he seemed "a little *personally* elated" by his triumphant Scottish tour, but she said that poor Aunt Pussy was affected by the fortnight's exertions in the bitter cold and had to be put straight to bed on arrival at Hawarden.

Gladstone had relit the torch of Liberalism as brilliantly as the torches which had greeted him on the banks and braes and in the back streets of Bonnie Scotland; or, as Lord Rosebery said, he set fire to the Scottish heather. In speech after speech, collected into special editions by enterprising Scottish newspapers to be sold like the proverbial hot cakes, he indicted

"Beaconsfieldism" and enunciated the Liberal ideal. He denounced the Conservative Government's profligate spending at home and abroad, saying, "I do not hold forth that good finance is the beginning and the ending of good government, but I hold this, that it is an essential of good government—it is a condition of good government. Without it you cannot have good government—and with it you almost always get good government." Lord Beaconsfield's foreign policy he attacked in its spirit and its detail. In one speech in Edinburgh he compared Great Britain before the Beaconsfield Government took office to Gulliver, mighty in its sense of duty and honour as much as its strength and wealth, and said that in the last six years the country had gone to sleep like Gulliver in Lilliput and been tied down by Lord Beaconsfield's foreign ventures so that it could barely lift an honourable arm.

Lord Beaconsfield himself spoke with contempt of "the drenching rhetoric" in Midlothian, but Gladstone's speeches were designed to impress and persuade and they did. He was at the peak of his oratorical power during this fortnight: his similes and analogies were easy to grasp, his language was direct and it was not without playful humour before it swept into another passionate denunciation of Lord Beaconsfield's frantic chase after false phantoms of glory, his encouragement of the baleful spirit of domination and his rejection of the principle of the sisterhood and equality of nations. The wide Liberal message that Gladstone delivered was the slogan John Bright had coined, "Peace, retrenchment and reform"—the very antithesis of "Beaconsfieldism" (though the Tories had managed to enact quite a few reforms). The notable omission from his speeches was reference to Ireland, the country whose problems were to press hardest on his next administration. Gladstone later admitted that he did not know (an accurate statement), that no one knew (a less accurate statement) the severity of the Irish crisis "that was already on the horizon, and that shortly after rushed upon us like a flood."

Gladstone's success in Midlothian also refocused attention on the dilemma of the party leadership. John Bright had said that the entire party would demand Mr. Gladstone's resumption of office. Mr. Forster admitted that the Liberal masses had "gone Gladstone mad." But by no means every Liberal saw him as the automatic leader, even after Midlothian. Sir William Harcourt stormed around (privately) saying nothing would induce him to accept office in a Cabinet of which Gladstone was the chief, while Mr. Forster conducted a private poll which assured him that the Liberal M.P.s would serve only under Lord Hartington. But if Hartington and the other titular leader Lord Granville had more ambition than was commonly supposed, both of them realised that a Liberal Government without Gladstone would now be an impossibility and the only position he could accept in that Government would be the top one. After the first Midlothian campaign Lord Hartington wanted to resign his leadership of the Commons and make Gladstone face the facts, but Lord Granville told him, "Your resignation would throw much cold water upon the party . . . What form could you adopt which would avoid the appearance of hostility to Gladstone and of some pique and jealousy?"

His secretary Reginald Brett told Lord Hartington, "The next election ought to be fought under the leadership of whomsoever is to form the Liberal Cabinet. That seems so self-evident a proposition," but he also admitted, "Mr Gladstone having restated his determination not to take office, you cannot—whatever you may think of the likelihood of his remaining steadfast to that declaration—answer that he means otherwise than what he says." Gladstone continued to insist that he had undertaken the Midlothian campaign for the sake of his party and his country and not himself, that he did not want the leadership and that the party would be better served without him in the forefront because of the hostility he personally excited. This latter was a valid point because inasmuch as the Liberal masses and many of the "floating voters" had been stirred by Gladstone's Midlothian speeches, the emotions of those who already detested him had been equally roused. Thus the leadership dilemma was left, with the popular pressure for Gladstone's return mounting.

In January 1880 Gladstone rushed to Germany, accompanied by his morose brother Tom and his equally morose wife, at the news that their sister Helen was dying. Catherine longed to go with her husband but the exertions in Midlothian had brought on another attack of erysipelas and she was still far from well, so she had to content herself with his letters. These were particularly lengthy ones, written in the minute handwriting that Gladstone used when under stress, as his mind was engrossed by a matter which he considered of infinitely greater importance than his position in the Liberal party, namely the question of Helen's religious faith and the nature of her burial. As his sister lay dying Gladstone was impressed by the fervour with which she responded to his recitation of the Psalms and echoed "Amen" to the Lord's Prayer, and this helped convince him that she had "undoubtedly contemplated burial at Fasque." Tom needed no convincing; to him it was evident that their sister must be buried in the family chapel; but burial at Fasque meant by the rites of the Church of England, and Gladstone's conscience was less easily salved. Helen's contemplation of an Anglican burial was one matter, finding actual proof that such had been her wish was another, and Gladstone spent hours "in a most curious and interesting examination of her books of devotion, and have also learned much from her library." He confessed to Catherine that he could not be absolutely sure that Helen would have wished to be buried in the Anglican faith, but he drew up a list of the circumstantial evidence which pointed towards the Anglican sympathies. Helen's body was accordingly brought from Germany, the country in which she had found some peace, to Scotland, a country she had not visited for years, to be buried by the rites of the Church of England rather than by the rites of the Catholic Church which she had followed for the last thirty years. It can be said that Gladstone won the last battle for his errant sister's earthly soul, if not without some pangs of conscience.

Gladstone's attention was soon refocused on temporal matters, when at the beginning of March 1880 Lord Beaconsfield decided to dissolve Parliament. The summer of 1878 and the Congress of Berlin had proved to be the peak of Lord Beaconsfield's career; since that time he had run into an increasing number of difficulties, not only on the home front which was not his forte, but in the foreign affairs of which he considered himself master. In South Africa the Conservatives had decided upon a policy of the federation of the existing Boer and British states under British domination, and while it was not a policy which appealed to the Boers, in 1877 the Transvaal was annexed without a war. However, the annexation brought Britain into conflict with the Zulus, with whom she had previously been on quite good terms, because the Zulus were constantly fighting the Boers, and now that Britain was responsible for the Transvaal it was felt she must subdue the tribesmen. The first attempt at subjugation ended in a disastrous defeat of a British force in January 1879, and though the Zulus were decisively beaten the following July and Zululand was duly annexed, the venture did not enhance Lord Beaconsfield's reputation.

Lord Beaconsfield also met trouble in Afghanistan. This buffer state between British India and Russia had long been a sensitive area, with Britain and Russia watching each other's activities like hawks, but until the Conservatives came into power in 1874 the British policy had been one of "masterly inactivity." Beaconsfield decided to reverse this policy into a "forward" one but in September 1879 the British mission which had established itself in Afghanistan was massacred (by the local inhabitants, not the Russians). Both the South African and Afghan imbroglios obviously provided Gladstone with the specific ammunition with which he attacked Beaconsfield's foreign policy; it was into such disastrous, bloody episodes that the spirit of aggrandisement and glory and the disregard for the rights of other nations led. In addition to the unfortunate foreign ventures, the Conservatives also hit stormy weather at home over their proposals for a Metropolitan Water Board. When two by-elections occurred early in 1880 in seats previously held by the Liberals, and Conservatives were returned for both, Lord Beaconsfield and his party organisers misread the signals and decided that Gladstone's Midlothian rhetoric had failed to drench the nation. They therefore thought the best method of extricating themselves from their present difficulties was by dissolving Parliament and being returned to power with *their* batteries recharged.

It was a fortunate decision for the Liberals because Reginald Brett among others had wondered how the Midlothian "pot of enthusiasm" was to be kept boiling if Lord Beaconsfield decided to let his Ministry run its full allotted course. With the dissolution of Parliament only three months after the Midlothian campaign, Gladstone was able to embark upon another tour while the memories of the first fantastic success were fresh.

However, this time there was a family contretemps which centred on the question of whether Catherine should accompany him. Her mission was now to be by her husband's side as much as possible; she rightly saw herself as part of the strength and appeal of his public appearances because the crowds reacted to her almost as much as to him, and even if she sometimes ended up exhausted she also enjoyed the campaigning (though this was not such a conscious factor). But Gladstone preferred the previous balance of their relationship, when Catherine was always there in spirit but was involved in her own activities which took her off to various parts of England, and he made an effort to restore that earlier balance. He was not successful, as Mary recorded: "Mama lets out to Papa she intends going to Scotland with him—scene, Papa imagining himself *en garçon* in lodgings, expostulates, says it's absurd." In fact, Catherine started to quail before her husband's expostulations but Mary kept her mother up to scratch; in the face of the combined weight of his wife and daughter the great man capitulated and Catherine duly accompanied him on his second Midlothian campaign. It was an even more whirlwind tour than the first and as great a success, with Lord Rosebery again stage-managing the scene with an expertise that any theatrical impressario would envy, and Gladstone not only thundering against the Conservative Government's profligacy and disastrous foreign policy but returning to his earlier theme of the classes and the masses. In soaring, effectively repetitious sentences he said he was afraid that the aristocracy could not be reckoned upon to save the country, neither could the landed gentry nor could the Established Church, for they were narrow sectional interests; but, he said, "Above all these, and behind all these, there is something greater than these—there is the nation itself. The nation is a power hard to rouse, but when roused, harder still and more hopeless to resist."

Gladstone's election campaigning was not entirely devoted to Midlothian and a visitor to one of his meetings in Marylebone in London described how he was "Gladstonized": "We were fairly launched on a sea of passion . . . In that torrent of emotion . . . the opinions of the people became as the edicts of eternity . . . we became persuaded that the Government were the most incompetent set of reprobates that an angry heaven had ever sent to be the curse of the country . . . Why we had lived under such diabolical ineptitude astounded us with a sense of shame . . . all through a speech of long tortuous sentences he endowed us with a faculty of apprehension we did not know we possessed . . . with a swing of the arm clear round his neck, and a superb uplifting of the whole frame, he sent his trumpet voice into every cranny of the hall . . . and a frantic mass of humanity roared itself hoarse for a full two minutes." As the gentleman emerged in a dazed condition from the Marylebone hall he decided, "clearly I had been Gladstonized; and I voted for him that election."

It can be said that Gladstone helped rouse or "Gladstonize" the nation during March 1880, and the call to which it responded was the Liberal cry

of "Peace, retrenchment and reform," with a dash of Gladstonian class war-
fare thrown in. As the election results began to be counted early in April, it
was soon apparent that the Liberals had won a great victory. Modern historians have tended to discount the personal effect of Gladstone's intervention and oratory. They have proved that the Liberals polled more votes
than the Conservatives in both the 1874 and 1880 elections, and it was the
areas in which the votes were cast that shifted, to give the party more or
fewer seats. Therefore the Liberals were the majority party at that time. In
1880, unaided by modern psephology, the Liberals were unaware that they
were the natural majority party, and most people—including Gladstone's
many enemies—thought he was responsible for the Liberal victory. Lucy
Cavendish was in Yorkshire as the election results started to come in, campaigning with her dear Fred who was standing for Bradford. She was actually at a meeting in Halifax when, as she recorded, "I became aware of an
ecstatic whisper going round the platform—'Gladstone's in! Gladstone's
in!' By some magic, the multitude found out in a minute, & there uprose
an immense cheer like the roar of waters." The ecstasy was repeated in
many parts of the country and was not untinged with relief, because it had
been by no means certain that he would be returned for Midlothian.

Since 1841 the Whigs or Liberals had held Midlothian only once; the
sitting Member had been the Earl of Dalkeith, eldest son of the Duke of
Buccleuch, and if Lord Rosebery was a rich and influential Scottish aristocrat and landlord, the Duke of Buccleuch was quite as rich, quite as
influential and his peerage was considerably more ancient. Because one
knows how successful the Midlothian campaign was, it is easy to underestimate the difficulties Gladstone faced, the formidable nature of the task he
undertook in that particular constituency. If he had failed he would indeed
have been placed "out of the range of practical politics"—the phrase he
coined in the first Midlothian campaign, though not in connection with
himself. In fact, Gladstone was not returned by a large majority—he polled
1,579 votes, the Earl of Dalkeith 1,368—but to have unseated such a sprig
of the Scottish aristocracy on his own back doorstep was victory enough,
and nobody much bothered about the margin.

The Liberals had been returned to power with a handsome over-all majority of some fifty seats, the country had spoken and the loudest cries to
be heard were demanding the return of Mr. Gladstone to the leadership. It
was a demand personally and privately reinforced by Catherine and Mary,
who had become a formidable duet in Gladstone's life. In April 1880
Catherine sent Lucy Cavendish a letter which began with a modified enthusiasm: "I do miss you *so much* dearest child. You see this is a very peculiar time. I dread lest anything I say to Father may be wrong. I am burst-
ing all the time." The letter then gathered strength and conviction: "Can
Father, having brought up his soldiers run away? Now however excellent
Hartington and Granville are would it not be cowardly to think of self
when the giant's hand is needed? Were there ordinary simple work the an-

swer would be simple; Father might rest. But look! See the rocks—Finance, Foreign Matters." It ended on a mystical overblown note: "I have never looked upon Father but that he was the nation's. I have seen him go forth ill I have seen him nearly exhausted going forth night after night, leaving home wife children. Shall he fail now in his country's cause? The mighty the brave spirit, if he is wanted shall he shrink now? NO!" Mary scribbled a postscript to her mother's letter, begging Lucy to burn it after she had read it, but a letter she herself wrote to her cousin on the subject of the leadership was as buoyantly emphatic, and she finished by saying, "I think it would be glorious, Papa forced by England to become Prime Minister, & bringing the ship once more into smooth waters & then retiring in prosperity & leaving it to Lord Hartington."

Lucy herself, while convinced that Uncle William's motives were noble and true and that he would only come forward again if the country demanded it, was considerably more appreciative of the position in which Lord Granville and Lord Hartington were placed. Lucy realised that the "splendid humbleness" which Mary urged Lord Hartington to adopt by retiring gracefully—after which he could in due course one day or eventually become Prime Minister—was more easily said than done: she, alas unlike the Gladstones, appreciated that the reticent unenthusiastic Hartington was possessed of feelings and ambitions. Lucy also knew that there were those who saw no reason why Lord Hartington should retire, who thought he would make an excellent Prime Minister, one who might now be able to handle the dissenting Liberal groups more ably than Gladstone and would certainly quench the opposition hatred. However, Hartington himself followed the female Gladstone belief that he could not escape the mighty shadow of "Father," and *before* Queen Victoria sent for him to ask him to form a Government he had written a memorandum enumerating the reasons why he could not accept. His basic reason was that no Liberal Government could function without Mr. Gladstone, and the only position in which he could function was that of Prime Minister.

Queen Victoria herself was a very different proposition from Lord Hartington; she became as overwrought and overblown in her determination not to have Gladstone in the leadership as Catherine was to ensure that he reassumed that office. While the General Election ensued Her Majesty had happily departed for Germany, certain that her beloved Lord Beaconsfield would be returned to power. She had been extremely annoyed with Gladstone, dashing around the country at his age like an American stump orator, but it had not occurred to her that his Midlothian stumping might have an effect nor that the country might wish to be rid of the "Beaconsfieldism" which she held in such high esteem. When the first results reached Her Majesty in Baden-Baden on 2 April 1880 she noted, "The Queen is vy disgusted at the news of the election"; the next day she wrote, "This is worse & worse. It is incredible." When the idea that Gladstone might again be the leader was conveyed to her she wrote her often-quoted lines, "She will sooner *abdicate* than send for or have any *communication* with *that half-mad firebrand* who wd soon ruin everything & be Dictator." But Her Majesty also assured Henry Ponsonby that however disgusting the news, however personally upset she was at the thought of Lord Beaconsfield's departure as Prime Minister, she would carry out her constitutional duty and send for the Liberal leader.

The question remained *which* leader and Ponsonby told his wife that he foresaw much trouble because "She dont care for Hartington and positively dislikes Granville." The latter had previously been a favourite of Queen Victoria's but she now considered him weak as eau-de-rose, mainly because he had supported Gladstone so wholeheartedly over the last few years. Her lack of enthusiasm for Hartington centred on his not being a hard worker, his relationship with the Duchess of Manchester and the undue influence she exerted over him, and his being too friendly with the Prince of Wales. Ponsonby thought Her Majesty might possibly come round to the idea of Gladstone as Prime Minister, as long as other influences did not prey on her. But the other, anti-Liberal, anti-Gladstonian influences were all around her or bombarding her with letters, none more forcibly than her son Leopold, on whom she now greatly relied. Prince Leopold wrote to her about "This dreadful news . . . It shows what wretched, ignorant, misled idiots most of the electors must be . . . I really cannot conceive what has come over the people . . . it is simply incomprehensible." Queen Victoria could not accept that her people were idiots, but they had obviously been misled by Gladstone's cunning brand of madness. She also thought the secret ballot might have had something to do with the disastrous result, forgetting that Mr. Disraeli had been returned on a secret ballot in 1874.

Some letters expressing the people's views were sent to Queen Victoria. A Mr. Copley wrote saying, "May I be permitted to point out how desirous the people are that Mr Gladstone should return to power. It is only from those like myself who mix and belong to the middle and lower orders that Your Majesty can have their real opinions. To them, they only know Granville as an Earl—Hartington as the son of a Duke—neither likely to have the people's welfare at heart." And a Frank Hoare wrote from Clapham saying, "The public ear is tickled with rumours of a *strange* dislike entertained by Your Majesty towards the most illustrious of all living Englishmen—Mr Gladstone to wit. The people of these realms have elected him into the post of supreme administrative power—surely it will not be for your most gracious majesty to forfeit in no small part the love and veneration of your people by turning a deaf ear to the universal acclamation of 'Gladstone for Premier?' There can be no *second* place in the Government for Gladstone; other names are those of relative insignificance besides his. He alone commands the universal love and affection of the toiling millions in whose ranks I count myself." Mr. Hoare's letter, while it would have reassured Gladstone, was not calculated to improve Her Majesty's love for "the most illustrious of all living Englishmen." She preferred to listen to those who told her that should Mr. Gladstone be returned to power, England's enemies would rejoice and the country would be reduced to the status of cotton spinners (this was one of Her Majesty's favourite terms of denigration).

By 18 April 1880 the Queen had reluctantly returned to Windsor, still uttering threats of abdication if Mr. Gladstone were forced upon her. She immediately consulted her beloved Lord Beaconsfield. He was well aware that the demand was for Gladstone but he saw no reason why he should smooth his rival's return to power. He advised Her Majesty to send for Lord Hartington rather than Lord Granville, probably because he knew the latter would never fight Gladstone for the leadership but half-hoped the former might. Her Majesty complied with Lord Beaconsfield's advice with comparative enthusiasm—the indolent, adulterous Hartington was better than the madman Gladstone—but his lordship had already made up his mind and outlined the reasons why he could not accept the commission. The Queen informed Hartington that she could not give Mr. Gladstone her confidence, but while his lordship eventually agreed to return to London and, at the Queen's further request, to ask Mr. Gladstone if he would be willing to serve under himself, he refrained from transmitting the message about the Queen's lack of confidence. The next day Hartington and Lord Granville were back at Windsor, and, Henry Ponsonby said, "Granville kissed hands with a smile like a ballet girl receiving applause, and Hartington threw himself into a chair with a Ha! Ha!" Their embarrassment was understandable, as they had to inform Her Majesty that Mr. Gladstone had declined to form any part of a Government led by Lord Hartington and they could therefore only advise her to send for the gentleman. Faced with the crunch—abdication or Gladstone—Her Majesty chose the latter and at a quarter to seven the same evening, 22 April 1880, he arrived in Her Majesty's presence. She still clutched at the hope that he might not be able to form an administration, that the *real* Liberals would refuse to serve under him, but Gladstone disabused her of any such idea and in a cloud of royal disapproval that matched the popular approbation he became Prime Minister for the second time.

Nothing shows the duality of Gladstone's nature, his Janus face, more than his return to power in 1880. From one view he can be seen as the temperamental prima donna, lusting for the applause which he had helped create but with consummate skill waiting until it had reached fever pitch so that he was forced to return to the centre of the stage, with God at his elbow telling when to move. Yet the desire to retire was consciously genuine, he had not ceased to examine his motives, the causes in which he believed were not false, he was not deluding himself in thinking he had special (God-given) talents, the clamour for his return was real, the people trusted him and wanted him, and beside his titanic figure Hartington and Granville were comparative pygmies. One result of Gladstone's resumption of the supreme office was that he became more convinced of the divinity of his mission. It was God's will, revealed through the medium of the people, that had forced him to take up the burden again and while he insisted that he would only carry the load temporarily, until such time as he had set the country on the right path, the likelihood of his doing so was not increased by the renewed sense of divine mission. His belief was obviously endorsed by Catherine but one is pleased to report that she was not as fanatically stirred by the actual event of her husband's second tenure of leadership as she was by the prior thought. Lucy Cavendish recorded that while her aunt was proud and happy she was by no means "tête montée; on the contrary, grave & rather awe-struck." Auguste Schluter said that in the hours leading up to Gladstone's resumption of office the tension in Harley Street was such that she could not bear it, and she consequently went out for a walk. When she returned, "I heard already outside that our dear gentleman had been sent for by the Queen. My heart felt so ful [sic] that big tears stole down my face . . . he returnt [sic] amongst loud cheers at night, will he satisfy the people let us hope so."

It was a good question. Gladstone's utterances over the last few years of semi-retirement had led many people to think that he was now a convinced Radical but though he believed in change and progress, he retained his reverence for the aristocratic principle, for individual effort and free will, and his radicalism was based on a touching, one could say naïve, belief in the natural goodness of "the people." He had a profound disbelief in what he called "construction," that is, State interference in matters that were best left to the individual, but "construction" under various guises more or less extreme was in the air. Gladstone was also faced with the composition of his own party. The Liberals had never been homogeneous—nobody had complained more bitterly than he about their lack of unity—and by 1880 they were less united than ever in their beliefs and aims. In one way the diversity of opinion gave the party great strength because there was the constant pull which negated apathy and kept the cauldron of ideas boiling; but it presented the man whose hands were on the reins with an almighty task in driving the Liberal coach.

Another problem which faced Gladstone from the start of his second Ministry was, of course, Queen Victoria. She agreed with Lord Beaconsfield that Gladstone was the A. V. (Arch Villain), and as he now loomed larger in infamy than the Czar of Russia, she saw it as her sacred duty to prevent him from dismembering the empire and plunging the country into ruin. In person Her Majesty did not even now always find Gladstone as horrendous as she imagined but once he had departed the image took over and she returned to her task of trying to thwart his reckless actions. The Queen's effect on Gladstone's reforming activities, or any of his activities, has been dismissed as negligible but she certainly expressed her disapproval of most of them and remained a power which could not be totally ignored. In any case Gladstone had no wish to ignore his monarch but he became aware, only too quickly, that he did not possess her confidence. Stories were soon circulating about a Miss Lambert dancing before the Queen and on being asked what favour she would like for the pleasure given, replying, "Mr Gladstone's head on a charger." It was not a story which amused Queen Victoria, and she was equally indignant when somebody told her that somebody else had told Mr. Gladstone that she hated him. She informed Henry Ponsonby that she did *not* hate him, though she was not overflowing with love for him, but as Ponsonby wrote to his wife, "Everyone tells me that he is sore at his treatment by H.M. But no wonder he gets angry if these things are said to him." In confidence Gladstone told his secretary that his relationship with Her Majesty was worse than he could possibly have imagined; he himself described it as one of armed neutrality and in a moment of anguish he admitted to Lord Rosebery that the Queen was enough to kill any man.

Catherine's reaction to the "armed neutrality" was peculiar. She obviously heard some of the stories, and her husband confided in her—though most of the time, even in private, his reverence for the monarchy made him circumspect. On one or two occasions Catherine herself was upset when the Queen failed to invite the Gladstones to an important function or to extend many invitations to visit Windsor or Osborne, particularly when the wives of leading Conservative Ministers were frequent royal guests. (And Queen Victoria's explanation for her conspicuous failure to invite the Gladstones to the Duke of Connaught's wedding in 1878 had been that for political reasons she did not include Opposition leaders.) Catherine said she did so much enjoy meeting, dining or staying with the Queen, who was always so pleasant to her. She therefore believed that the Queen's relationship with Gladstone had been temporarily poisoned by *phantods*—a Glynnese word for an imbecilic person incapable of rational behaviour—and that improvement must be just around the corner. Another reason was of course she could not accept that any nice person could really dislike her husband.

The problem of the Queen's antagonism to Gladstonian reforming Liberalism, in conjunction with the wide spectrum of views within the party and Gladstone's own temperament, played their part in the composition of the 1880 Cabinet. Mary described it admirably: "The Cabinet is highly respectable, rather aristocratic, with a democratic dash in the shape of Mr. Chamberlain." Included in it were members of the old Whig guard such as the Duke of Argyll, Lord Granville and Lord Hartington (both of them loyally agreed to serve under their new/old master) and Sir William Harcourt, who had sworn that he would never sit in a Cabinet of which Gladstone was chief. The loyalty of the noisy, ebullient Sir William—known to the females of the Gladstone family as "Sir Bow-Wow"—was shifting, and he became one of Gladstone's more devoted, if always trying lieutenants. The two immediate problems which faced the new Government were described by Henry Ponsonby as concisely as Mary Gladstone described the composition of the Cabinet: "Between Atheists and Papists the Govt. are having a lively start of life."

The atheist problem focused on Charles Bradlaugh, who was returned as an M.P. for Northampton for the first time in 1880. His return was an immense stroke of ill-luck for Gladstone, because the question whether Bradlaugh could affirm his loyalty or swear the oath which as an atheist he did not believe bedevilled the entire life of his second Ministry. In 1883, when Gladstone tried to introduce an amendment to the Parliamentary Oaths Act which would have allowed Bradlaugh to affirm, he made another of those speeches which many people considered to be his greatest. He informed the House of Commons, "I shall make a very dull, unexciting, and uninteresting speech," but in fact he was at his most lucid, cogent, eloquent and liberal. He showed how far along the road of toleration he had travelled since *The State in Its Relations with the Church* by saying, "I am convinced that upon every religious, as well as upon every political ground, the true and wise course is not to deal out religious liberty by halves, by quarters, and by fractions, but to deal it out entire." But though the Commons was impressed by Gladstone's oratory, it failed to respond to his dual plea for toleration and an understanding of the constitutional position, the Bill was narrowly defeated and the Bradlaugh affair lumbered on.

The Papists who caused Gladstone's second Ministry so much trouble were of course the Irish, even if they were now led by the Protestant figure of Charles Stewart Parnell. Gladstone's focus for the last few years had been on the Eastern Question and he had failed to notice what was happening in Ireland. Initially, he also failed to realise that in Charles Stewart Parnell the Irish had found a leader of stature. Parnell was thirty-four in 1880, a proud, aloof, aristocratic figure who appealed to the people, who was apparently emotionless and fearless and could fight the English on level terms. He had reached an agreement with the Fenians; partly by virtue of his American ancestry he had gained the confidence of the Irish-Americans, and was gaining that of the Catholic hierarchy.

After the 1880 election Gladstone could not fail to be aware that the previously ramshackle Home Rule movement now had some sixty Members at Westminster, and he soon appreciated that in the hands of Parnell it could become a genuine and formidable party. Once returned to office Gladstone also quickly recognised some of the loopholes in his 1870 Land Act, notably the question of eviction without compensation. As a stopgap measure to stem the rising tide of evictions and the consequent increased militancy of the Irish Land League, in June 1880 he and Mr. Forster introduced a Compensation for Disturbance Bill (the latter had reluctantly undertaken the task of Irish Chief Secretary). The terms were extremely moderate but the Bill met with furious opposition; it was raising the masses against the classes, it was interfering with the rights of the landlords. After a series of bitter and exhausting debates the Bill managed to scrape through the Commons, but in August 1880 it was thrown out by the Lords by an overwhelming majority.

Gladstone meanwhile was suffering from a severe attack of congestion of the lungs and Mary recorded the effect this illness created. On 2 August 1880 she noted, ". . . an astonishing day. About 2000 people called and all thro' the day the crowds hung about Downing Street eager for news"; on 4 August she said that ten thousand cards, telegrams and letters had been received from home and abroad enquiring after Mr. Gladstone's state and wishing him a speedy recovery. Lucy Cavendish recorded the incident that started to effect the recovery, namely the information that the Compensation for Disturbance Bill had been rejected: "Instead of being worse, he went to sleep afterwards & began improving from that moment." After a cruise on one of his friend's yachts accompanied by Catherine, their three sons and Helen, which included a very brief visit to Ireland, Gladstone returned in buoyant spirits to face the second session of his second tenure of leadership.

CHAPTER 15

THE GRAND OLD MAN

IT WAS IN THE early 1880s that Gladstone became known as the Grand Old Man. The title was coined by Henry Labouchere and though the Tories tried to turn it into one of derision, it, or simply the initials G.O.M., was used affectionately by millions of people. (Labouchere was a Liberal M.P. and magazine owner, known to everybody as "Labby.") In functioning as the Grand Old Man under many and varied pressures, Gladstone was heavily cushioned by Catherine and other members of his family. The gentleman who attended the Marylebone election meeting noted that as Gladstone struggled towards the platform he was followed "by a simply clothed woman who busies herself in warding off the hands of enthusiasts eager to touch him . . . that is Mrs. Gladstone, with the soft face, high-coloured like a girl's and tremulous mouth; intent on only one thing in this life—her husband." During the Midlothian campaign Lord Rosebery wryly observed that Catherine's protectiveness extended to tipping out of the window a particularly noxious cup of tea and returning cup to saucer without either her husband or their hostess having noticed. When the Gladstones were invited to Sandringham early in 1883, Princess May of Teck (who later became Queen Mary) told her brother, "Mrs Gladstone is awfully fidgety and is always rushing after Mr Gladstone." To ease his burdens Mary was acting as her father's unofficial secretary, with special responsibility for the ecclesiastical appointments in which he took such an interest, and it was at this time that quite a few political figures began to regard her as a formidable member of the Gladstone entourage. When Sir William Harcourt and his son Lewis—known as "Loulou" or "Lulu"—visited Hawarden towards the end of 1881, Loulou noted in his diary, "Mrs G and 'Mary' are willing to keep you company at any hour. The latter is (to me) particularly disagreeable and she seems to have a finger in every pie and can be very rude when she likes (which she does often)." Of Catherine he recorded, "Mrs G is very good natured, very untidy, very careless and very kind," but he thought Lady Freddy (i.e. Lucy Cavendish) was "a bit of a prig and a good deal of a prude."

Mary Gladstone was now mainly in charge of the social and domestic arrangements at 10 Downing Street. For this tenure of office the Gladstones lived at the official residence because they no longer owned a London house; on 16 May 1880, Auguste Schluter noted, "We have moved into our Government House, 10 Downing Street it is a jolly old place." The Gladstone women's attitude towards the renewal of high office was almost as ambivalent as Gladstone's own, if for different reasons. Mary recorded: "The house all day like a rabbit warren, people in the hall, people in the drawing-room, dining room, messengers, ministers-to-be, touts, friends . . . Isn't it dreadful to think of beginning all over again, cards & parties & things, it makes me sick to think of." After 1880 Gladstone had two sons in the House of Commons, as Herbert and Willie had been returned to Parliament. By this time his father had accepted that Willie was lacking in fire, drive and ambition but Herbert showed political promise. Gladstone's new principal Private Secretary, Edward Hamilton, observed that the other sons had not proved themselves up to the mark of such a father (though Henry was prospering in business and managed to become quite rich), but Herbert was soon installed as a Commissioner of the Treasury. Catherine was a little upset that her beloved first-born son Willie should have been passed over for office, however minor and officially unpaid, but Herbert was also a favourite and she rejoiced that he could be of assistance to his father.

In addition Gladstone had the loyalty and co-operation of his nephew-by-marriage Lord Frederick Cavendish, whom he loved and admired as much as he did Lucy. Finally he had the inestimable, invaluable services of the man whom several newspapers later designated the perfect Private Secretary, Edward Hamilton, known to the Gladstones and all his friends as Eddy. Hamilton was extremely hard-working, reliable, affable and tactful —and he was another indefatigable diarist whose Gladstone-oriented but shrewd observations provide a further inside record of the public and private life of the family in their later years. Eddy Hamilton was the devoted but not uncritical secretary, and soon after his appointment in 1880 he noted, "I have been offered and have undertaken the post of Chief Wine Butler to Mr G, which I hope will secure something rather less nasty in his cellars." Supported by such personal love, care, concern and talent Gladstone was able to shoulder his burdens with comparative lightness, even if occasionally he sagged beneath them.

From 1880 to 1882 the home front was dominated by Irish affairs, and Gladstone found himself squeezed into the position of every English Minister dealing with Ireland. On the one hand he had considerable sympathy with the land grievances and a renewed sense that his mission was to heal the festering sores of Anglo-Irish relations. On the other hand he was the Prime Minister of the United Kingdom of Great Britain and Ireland; he believed in the supremacy of the law and that it should be changed when necessary by legal means, not by the sort of lawless militancy that Parnell and the Land League were adopting. Gladstone was subjected to immense pressure from the Opposition which almost to a man disbelieved in the

Irish discontent and thought that Ireland should be freed from the clutches of a few agitators and brought to her senses by coercive means. The Liberal party and the Cabinet were not without people who held such views, and among them by the end of 1880 was the Chief Secretary for Ireland, Mr. Forster.

Faced with such opposition, divided in his own mind, Gladstone produced the stick and the carrot. The stick came in the shape of comparatively minor charges against Parnell and the Land League leaders (which were thrown out by a Dublin jury) and in the more serious form of a stringent Coercion Bill. The carrot was the promise of a radically new Land Bill. Parnell and his followers fought the Coercion Bill in Parliament by the use of the obstruction tactics which Gladstone himself had been accused of having initiated during his battle against the Divorce Bill in 1857. Eventually the Parnellites overreached themselves by forcing a continuous forty-one-hour sitting, and a closure measure was introduced which effectively ended unlimited debate in the House of Commons (and for which some British Members never forgave Parnell). With their most valuable weapon gone, the Parnellites were unable to stop the Coercion Bill from becoming law, though some stormy scenes and threats of unilateral declarations of Irish independence ensued before they succumbed. The rest of the session was devoted to the Land Bill, which was an immensely complicated measure—it was said that only Gladstone himself and the Irish M.P. Tim Healy really understood its terms—and many people remarked upon the phenomenal energy, skill and courage with which Gladstone piloted the Bill through the Commons. Lord Hartington declared that the parliamentary history of the year was the history of a single measure carried by a single man, but perhaps Mary Gladstone's words sum up the situation most vividly, "Papa in a childish state of glee over the end of the Land Bill Committee. 2000 amendments tackled in 34 nights, & all the world open-mouthed & open-eyed with his power of work & will." The Lords did not throw out this Bill, though Gladstone lost his old friend and colleague the Duke of Argyll, who could not accept its terms or its implications and resigned, and by the summer of 1881 Ireland had a new Land Act.

However, coercion remained in force in Ireland and the country was in a continuing state of unrest. By the beginning of October 1881 Gladstone had had enough; Eddy Hamilton recorded that he had "really reached boiling point with Parnell." Gladstone had strained every fibre of his being to pass the Land Act that Ireland had demanded, and yet here was the Irish leader trying not only to obstruct its implementation but continuing to preach a doctrine of Irish lawlessness. (In reality Parnell was dealing with a team even more disharmonious and disunited in its methods and ultimate aims than was Gladstone. But his efforts to keep a tight grip on his reins, by being alternatively conciliatory and militant and thus placating the moderates and the extremists, were not apparent to outsiders, particularly if they were English.) At the beginning of October 1881 Gladstone was in

Leeds for a three-day visit which had been planned for some time, its main purpose being to extend belated thanks to the Liberals there for having returned him to Parliament in 1880. (Gladstone had had the staunchly Liberal Leeds seat to fall back upon in case he failed in Midlothian and when he succeeded in Scotland his son Herbert took it over in a by-election.) The visit became another of those demonstrations of the people's love for the Gladstones, with monster torchlight processions and an estimated twenty-five thousand people attending an open-air meeting, but it was also seized by him as an opportunity to make a major speech.

On 7 October 1881, in a specially erected hall in the yard of the famous Leeds Cloth Hall, with constructional chaos reigning until the last minute and nails being banged in almost as the Gladstones entered to attend the banquet, he spoke to the listening world. The speech was devoted to Ireland and towards the end Gladstone warned Parnell and his followers, "If it shall appear that there is still to be fought a final conflict in Ireland between law on one side and sheer lawlessness upon the other . . . then I say, gentlemen, without hesitation, the resources of civilisation against its enemies are not yet exhausted." In these words Gladstone not only warned Parnell but enunciated his faith in the power of what he believed civilisation to mean. Before the banquet, Wemyss Reid, who was now the editor of the *Leeds Mercury,* saw Gladstone with his head in his hands; Catherine later told Reid, "He was praying, you know, he always prays before he makes an important speech, and he felt that speech very much."

Parnell ignored the warning contained in Gladstone's deeply felt Leeds speech and in return at Wexford delivered one of his more famous speeches in which he accused the Liberal leader of being "this masquerading knight-errant, this pretended champion of the rights of every nation except those of the Irish." On 13 October, less than a week after the Leeds speech and Parnell's reply, Gladstone acted by implementing one of the resources of civilisation at his command and imprisoning the Irish leader in Kilmainham Gaol, Dublin. It was not a position to which Parnell objected politically, though personally he was distressed because the married lady whom he had met in the summer of 1880 and who had quickly become his mistress, Katharine O'Shea, was expecting his child. But politically Parnell realised that the Land League was being strangled by its own success and Gladstone's Land Act and he had no desire to be present during the death rattles. He could hope to emerge from prison crowned with the Irish martyr's halo and as the one man who could control Ireland, and from a position of increased authority concentrate his attention on what he regarded as the main issue—Home Rule. In effect that was what happened, though the resolution was not as speedy as Parnell would have wished.

Apart from Ireland, foreign affairs obtruded more in this second Ministry than they had in the first, and unfortunately Lord Granville was growing old and tired. Gladstone had earlier noted in his diary, "I do not think his water drinking has been favourable to his general mental force & especially to his initiative"—Granville frequently took the waters at various spas—but this opinion did not deter him from reappointing his lordship as Foreign Secretary. The old team acted promptly over the Afghan imbroglio bequeathed to them by Lord Beaconsfield and decided to withdraw the British force which had established itself in Kandahar. Queen Victoria was appalled, particularly as Lord Hartington (who was the Secretary of State for India) had hoped to avoid trouble by omitting to inform Her Majesty that the decision was included in the Queen's Speech for the opening of the 1881 parliamentary session. When her Ministers made the long journey to Osborne to obtain the Queen's endorsement to the speech—she had of course no intention of opening a Gladstonian Parliament and reading it in person—a stormy scene ensued. Her Majesty declared that she had never been so badly treated by her Ministers since she came to the throne—Gladstone commented, "Poor woman!"—and refused to sanction the paragraph containing the announcement of the withdrawal from Kandahar, whereupon her Ministers threatened to resign. Eventually, with the greatest reluctance and protest the Queen approved the paragraph. In this instance the Liberals were able to withdraw on a peak of success, for Lord Roberts had taken Kandahar after a spectacular forced march which had captured the popular imagination. The foreign rebels had been taught a lesson, British honour had been salved and few people were overinterested in Afghanistan anyway.

Gladstone and Granville had a similar success over one of the clauses of the Congress of Berlin which had stated that the Turks must cede territory to Greece and Montenegro and about which, since 1878, the Sultan had done nothing. Both men believed that treaties were made to be observed and they decided to force the Sultan's hand. The week of October 1880 during which they waited to see if the Sultan would respond to what was in effect British bluff was extremely tense, and Gladstone used Catherine (who was at Hawarden) as a safety valve. On 4 October he wrote to tell her that the Turkish delay was killing his chance of travelling to Hawarden and said, "God prosper the good, the true, the right! and *mum* till I open your lips!" In a further letter on the same day he informed his wife that there was still no definite answer from Constantinople and that the ubiquitous Olga Novikoff had turned up in London again. By 10 October Gladstone was able to send Catherine "A large sheet for a good day, and good news," the latter being his belief that the European concert was working "for the purposes of justice, peace and liberty, with efficiency and success, which is the great matter at issue." In effect, Britain was largely going it alone but Catherine replied saying, "It is almost too much to think of this consummation, the 'ideal of your life' in foreign policy. God grant it may be all right and no more bolting." Until 12 October it seemed possible that the Turks might still "bolt" but on that day the news was received that the Sultan had agreed to cede the treaty territories forthwith. Lord Granville brought the vital telegram to Downing Street, executing a triumphal dance round Gladstone's study as he arrived, and Eddy Hamilton recorded the Prime Minister's own reaction: "God Almighty be praised; I shall go to Hawarden by the 2.45 train."

Gladstone's handling of the other foreign dilemma bequeathed to him by Lord Beaconsfield—the Transvaal and the Boers—was not nearly so decisive, and far from successful in the popular estimation. Having read Gladstone's Midlothian speeches the Boers expected that he would, immediately upon resumption of office, reverse the Beaconsfield policy of confederation and return their independence. When he did not do so they felt that Parnell should have added to his Wexford speech the rider that Gladstone was the pretended champion of the rights of every other nation except the Irish —and the Boers. Retrospectively, Gladstone's failure to recall forthwith Sir Bartle Frere, who was then the chief exponent of a South African federation under British suzerainty, was a bad mistake. But one of the reasons for Gladstone's reluctance to relinquish the British annexation of the Transvaal was connected with the rights of the indigenous inhabitants, because the Boers had already acquired a foul reputation in their dealings with the African tribesmen. (Queen Victoria, fervently imperialist as her attitude might be, was genuinely horrified by the stories of Boer brutality and thought Britain should protect the natives.) Lucy Cavendish outlined another reason why Gladstone failed to recall "Sir B.F.": ". . . there was the united strong pressure of all the best authorities on the spot . . . who all wd. have it that the country wd. be perfectly happy under English rule but for a few 'agitators' (well known fatal talk that is in other matters besides S. Africa)." There was also the more politically sensitive factor noted by Sir Charles Dilke: "as we were retiring from Kandahar we had better not also retire from Pretoria."

When the Boers broke into open rebellion towards the end of 1880, Gladstone (deeply involved in the Irish quagmire) acted with considerable firmness and decision. Sir Bartle Frere was recalled, the widespread, deep-rooted nature of the Boer resentment was recognised and negotiations were entered into to restore the Transvaal to virtual independence, with Britain retaining only minimal rights of guardianship. In this instance the Liberal withdrawal was not assisted by a Kandahar-like victory; on the contrary the men on the spot in South Africa decided to teach the upstart Boers a lesson which culminated in the defeat of a British force (albeit a small one) at Majuba Hill. In the face of the outcry to avenge British honour, headed of course by Queen Victoria but not confined to the ultra-Tory ranks, Gladstone adhered to his conclusion that the Boers detested British rule, and manoeuvred with great skill to ratify the Pretoria Convention in August 1881 which recognised the *de facto* independence of the Transvaal.

Lucy Cavendish regarded the Pretoria Convention as one of her uncle's noblest acts, and in the context of the period it was a piece of wise, skilful statesmanship in which Gladstone implemented his belief in the principle of nationality. Whether, bearing in mind the later nineteenth- and twentieth-century history of South Africa, it might have been better if he had implemented his other beliefs in the rights of the native inhabitants and England's role as an advanced, guiding nation is a debatable point. In the 1880s his failure to recall Sir Bartle Frere immediately gave his actions the appearance of indecision, and as the public was unaware that negotiations were in hand *before* the defeat at Majuba Hill, the Pretoria treaty also seemed to be a capitulation to force and a surrender of British honour.

In the spring of the year Gladstone faced another unpleasant task, though of an entirely different nature from the South African and Irish problems (which had a great deal in common). On 19 April 1881 Lord Beaconsfield died, wheezing, full of rheumatics and gout but retaining his wit to the end (when he was asked if he would like the immense honour of a personal visit to his sickbed by his beloved Sovereign he replied, "No it is better not. She would only ask me to take a message to Albert"). Lord Beaconsfield's death presented his rival with a Gordian knot which Gladstone could not see how best to cut. He had disliked the deceased gentleman personally and had detested and denounced everything he had stood for, yet his conscience told him that "Dizzy" had been a remarkable man, and as the Prime Minister he felt it was his duty to make comment upon the Conservative leader's death. Gladstone did not attend the funeral at Hughenden, an omission which drew censure upon him, but he managed to compose a letter of condolence to Queen Victoria which actually pleased the bereft lady. After a severe attack of diarrhoea brought on by worry, he decided to utter a form of funeral oration when he asked the House of Commons to vote in favour of a public monument to the dead leader. On 9 May 1881 Gladstone performed his difficult task, praising Lord Beaconsfield for his strength of will, consistency of purpose, devotion to his wife and parliamentary courage, but not uttering panegyrics about the world's great loss or Lord Beaconsfield's being an irreplaceable shining light. However, Lord Acton considered that even this qualified praise was an act of moral hypocrisy and sophism, and in a long letter to Mary he said that her father should not have allowed himself to execute popular wishes when they contradicted his own feelings, emotions and beliefs. This stern, pure attitude was not generally reflected and Gladstone earned praise for the balance he achieved in his obsequies.

Towards the end of 1881 there were strong rumours circulating that Mr. Gladstone intended to retire; throughout the year his health and spirits had whirred up and down like a yo-yo. In February he had a bad accident when he slipped in the snow and cut his head open on his return from a visit to the Prince of Wales at Marlborough House, and Downing Street was again inundated with callers, telegrams and letters, particularly with those from Italy and "the oppressed nationalities." Gladstone recovered from the accident with remarkable speed and in March Hamilton recorded him as being in tremendous force; but in May he was "seedy," in July he was "like a sucked-out orange," in October he was enumerating his reasons for retiring—his age, the party strife, the bad relationship with Her Majesty, the claims of Lords Granville and Hartington and the personal disinclination to continue. But by the middle of November he was again in good spirits. At this moment in November Mary had a long talk with her father "on the great vexed question of retirement," during which he elaborated the theme that he had only returned conditionally and that the cohesion of the Liberal party could not and did not depend on one man. However, there was the qualification that he could not retire until the Irish question was settled, though at the moment Gladstone hoped that it soon would be.

Catherine was, temporarily, veering towards the idea of her husband's retirement, mainly one suspects because she had been in poor health with an attendant lowness of spirit for much of the year, only rallying her reserves for such occasions as the visit to Leeds. When the Harcourts, father and son, paid their visit to Hawarden early in November 1881 Loulou recorded, "Mrs G herself was rather in favour of his abdication, her reason being that she wishes him to retire before he makes a failure." The notion that her husband might fail does not sound like Catherine but she presumably made some such remark, and it is an indication of the seriousness with which the question was being considered in the Gladstone family. The continued wish to retire was an usettling factor for the Liberal party but Gladstone's colleagues mainly accepted it with a remarkable lack of irritation, partly because they knew it had a genuine base, partly because some of them appreciated that it was the thought of retirement that kept him going, and because they needed him. For what party would willingly overthrow a man of such stature, whose intellectual powers were unrivalled in Parliament, who could hold in thrall audiences of twenty-five thousand people, command thousands of enquiries from home and abroad when he was ill, still get a Land Act onto the statute book and manoeuvre with extraordinary political skill?

By the beginning of 1882 it was apparent that in Ireland the pacification process had begun, not ended, with the Land Act. Without difficulty Gladstone accepted that coercion, which he detested personally, was not working; with slightly more reluctance he recognised that Parnell was the man who might control the country, and that his release from Kilmainham prison was therefore necessary. Several months of secret negotiations ensued, because Gladstone had no intention of giving everything for nothing in the face of what he regarded as Parnell's unnecessary lawlessness. Joseph Chamberlain acted for the Cabinet and Captain O'Shea, the husband of Parnell's mistress, for the Irish leader. Eventually, "the Kilmainham treaty" was agreed upon. In return for the release of all the major Irish Nationalists from prison and Gladstone's promise to relax coercion and introduce amendments to the Land Act, Parnell pledged himself to try to lessen the level of violence in Ireland and to co-operate with the Liberal party in forwarding Liberal principles and measures of reform. Gladstone considered this latter offer was "an *hors d'oeuvre* which we had no right to expect, and I rather think have no right at present to accept," but nevertheless on 2 May 1882 Parnell was released from prison.

Gladstone's belief that the Irish question might soon be settled seemed to have validity because cordial co-operation between the Liberals and the Nationalists was on the horizon, if not immediately capable of being reached. However, the release of the Irish Nationalists proved too much for Mr. Forster to accept, as he continued to believe that Parnell was the leader of a few agitators and that the "Kilmainham treaty" had been a capitulation to force. He therefore resigned, which meant that a new Chief Secretary for Ireland had to be appointed. It was now a position of crucial importance; one man who thought he could fill it was Joseph Chamberlain, and it would have been an interesting appointment, as Chamberlain was then known for his nationalist sympathies and his ambitious ability was straining for a role in which he could stretch himself. But Gladstone had another idea—to appoint Lord Frederick Cavendish to the onerous position. It was not nepotism which led him to the decision because he always leaned over backwards not to promote members of his family unless and until they had proved themselves. (That was the reason Herbert was initially paid from Gladstone's own pocket, and later when Agnes' husband Edward Wickham was in line for an ecclesiastical appointment, Gladstone wryly commented that the only drawback he could see was that the gentleman was his son-in-law.) Lord Frederick himself was not too enthusiastic but after several family conclaves he allowed himself to be persuaded that he was up to the task and that working in harmony with his uncle-in-law, he might be able to effect the final peaceful settlement of centuries of Anglo-Irish bitterness.

Lucy Cavendish said goodbye to her dear Fred as he left London on the boat-train for Holyhead for a brief preliminary visit to Dublin. It was the last time she saw him alive. Lord Frederick arrived safely in the Irish capital, but then decided to take a stroll in the early summer evening sun, in the pleasant surroundings of Phoenix Park. His companion on the stroll was the Permanent Under-Secretary, Thomas Burke, and it was Burke who was the target of the assassins who lay in wait in the park. But Lord Frederick tried to help Burke as he was attacked and suffered the same fate: both men were brutally stabbed to death. The murders took place about 7:30 P.M. but the news took some time to be confirmed to London and it was later in the evening before the first of Lord Frederick's relatives were told. They were his brother Lord Hartington and his sister, Lady Louisa Egerton, who were both attending a grand ball at the Admiralty. The Gladstones had been to a dinner at the Austrian Embassy but while Catherine felt that she should put in a brief appearance at the Admiralty ball, to which she and her husband had also been invited, Gladstone decided to go home, walking of course from the Embassy to Downing Street. Mary Gladstone was at the opera to hear *Die Walküre* and Lucy Cavendish herself was at home in Carlton House Terrace. She had been invited to the Admiralty ball too, but with a social absent-mindedness which was also typical of her aunt she had forgotten the engagement and had spent the evening reading one of her Uncle William's *Gleanings* (these were collections of his past writings on various subjects which Gladstone revised and edited into book form). Lucy was in the act of writing a note to her uncle about his book when Lord Hartington and Lady Louisa Egerton arrived and broke the news to her that her beloved, adored Fred, the joy of her childless life, had been murdered.

Catherine was stopped as she was about to enter the Admiralty and told the frightful news. Loulou Harcourt said she collapsed into a chair in a fainting condition, but she soon pulled herself together and decided she must go at once to Downing Street where her husband would shortly be arriving, unaware of what had happened. In fact Gladstone took some time to return to Downing Street and it was Eddy Hamilton who broke the news to him; he recorded both the Gladstones then sinking to their knees in the entrance hall and praying to God to give them, Lucy and all those who had loved Lord Frederick strength in their hour of anguish.

When they had finished praying the elderly couple immediately set off for Carlton House Terrace to comfort Lucy. She said that her uncle "came up & almost took me in his arms, & his first words were 'Father forgive them, for they know not what they do.' Then he said, 'Be assured it will not be in vain'. . . I saw in a vision Ireland at peace, & my darling's life blood accepted as a sacrifice for Christ's sake, to help bring this thing to pass." Catherine stayed with her niece that night and the next night, and their deep Christian faith helped Lucy and the Gladstones survive what was for all of them a shattering blow. It was one from which Lucy never really recovered, but her behaviour and bearing after the murder were in the noblest tradition of the Christianity which was fundamental to her life. Lucy wrote a letter to her brother which with her permission was made public, in which she begged that bitterness and recrimination should not surround her husband's assassination and said that she could accept his death if it worked for the good of his fellow men in Britain and Ireland.

Catherine and Gladstone suffered deeply too; several people commented that the shock of Lord Frederick's murder aged both of them, and when Gladstone entered the House of Commons after the death, his normally sallow complexion was ashen. Loulou Harcourt said that he looked like a living ghost. Lord Frederick's assassination was probably the worst blow Gladstone had endured since Jessy's death, but in this instance his iron self-control did not desert him, nor did his power of concentration and capacity for work. He allowed himself no time away from office—apart from attending the funeral—and the day after the murder he found or made the time to compose a poem for Lucy in her dead husband's honour. It is not one of the masterpieces of English literature—the first verse starts:

> Another star of purest ray
> Is added to the starry fires
> Another spirit soars today
> And worships with the angel choirs

but it contains nineteen verses and they are all fluent and easy. An element of the iron in Gladstone's control and character, the element which counteracted his passion and enabled him to function in his separate compartments, was apparent in Lucy Cavendish's account of the dreadful evening and early morning of 6 and 7 May 1882. As Gladstone was leaving Carlton House Terrace she called out to him, "Uncle William, you must never blame yourself for sending him," to which Gladstone replied, "O no, there can be no question of that."

The funeral took place at Chatsworth, Lord Frederick's ancestral home, and when Mary Gladstone viewed his body the previous day she was immensely relieved to see that "one slight cut on his face was the only sign of his cruel death." Among Mary's talents was that of floral arrangement and decoration, and it was she who made the wreath that lay on the coffin, a seven-foot-long cross of white flowers and ferns with "deep red roses in the middle the only colour." Catherine and Gladstone travelled north to Derbyshire on the day of the funeral, 11 May, in a special train which carried the mourners, including two hundred of Lord Frederick's parliamentary colleagues, from London. It was a perfect early summer day as Lord Frederick's body was laid to its rest in the little church on the Chatsworth estate surrounded by its bowl of hills, watched by a crowd of fifty thousand people. Gladstone summed up the family feeling when he wrote to Willie that the loss of Lord Frederick "will ever be to us all as an unhealed wound."

There was a great wave of public sympathy for the Gladstones as much as for the Cavendish family but it did nothing to still the mounting tide of rumour and innuendo that was circulating among the ranks of the Upper Ten Thousand about Gladstone's association with prostitutes. On the contrary, the juxtaposition of his noble bearing in the public eye and what was believed by some to be the truth of his night-walking activities only exacerbated the situation.

From the start of his second Ministry Gladstone was under great pressure, and some of his tension was relieved by frequent visits to the theatre. He now had a special chair on the prompt side of the Lyceum stage into which he could slip to watch a part of the show and enjoy the backstage atmosphere whenever he wished. There is the story, given as authentic in Laurence Irving's biography of Sir Henry Irving, that during a performance of The Corsican Brothers in 1880 Gladstone happened to be backstage and asked if he could be one of the "supers" in the Opera House scene so that he could obtain an actor's view of the proceedings. Gladstone was apparently installed behind one of the flats which represented the opera boxes and warned to keep well out of sight, but he peered too far forward at one moment and was recognised by the audience, whereupon a round of applause echoed through the Lyceum Theatre and he took a bow to cries of "Bravo Gladstone."

Unfortunately the theatrical stimulus and excitement did not completely allay his tensions and when Gladstone was in London he was out fairly regularly at nights consorting with prostitutes. Allied to his nocturnal ramblings there was his friendship with the notorious Laura Thistlethwayte, at whose house and in whose company he was frequently known to be. She was born Laura Bell in Ireland on an uncertain date—some sources said 1829, others 1832—but there was no uncertainty about her being one of the most famous courtesans of the nineteenth century, with Napoleon III included among her lovers. In 1852 she had married Captain Augustus Frederick Thistlethwayte, a wealthy gentleman who had a London house in Grosvenor Square and leased estates in Ross-shire; he was also said to have a foul temper. During the 1860s Laura Thistlethwayte underwent a religious experience, and with the passion of the convert became a noted evangelical preacher (though it was intimated that her conversion did not necessarily interfere with her former occupation). Gladstone had made her acquaintance by 1870; in September of that year a colleague wrote to him from Scotland, "Mrs T. preached or 'spoke' & did a bit of praying on Tuesday last at Ballachulish to the quarrymen, their wives & children. I am past being moved by such things, but there is no doubt of her great power, & if a man & in the House she would warm us all up." Another observer (Lady St. Helier) wrote of Mrs. Thistlethwayte arranging herself in a bleak Scottish chapel, "so that all the light which entered through the small windows was thrown on her . . . and the large black mantilla which covered her masses of golden hair, the magnificent jewels she wore round her neck, and the flashing rings on her hands with which she gesticulated, added to the soft tones of a very beautiful voice."

Laura Thistlethwayte was tailor-made for Mr. Gladstone, a beautiful, emotional, intelligent lady, with high oratorical powers and a strong sense of the dramatic who had ostensibly abandoned her former ways, was engrossed in spreading the gospel and loved discussing the finer points of theology. They became very good friends indeed. On 7 July 1881 Henry Ponsonby wrote to his wife, "The Duchess of Somerset was in full abuse of Gladstone—personal abuse. She was very bitter on his devotion to low women—which she said was simply an improper devotion. That was at the bottom of his devotion to Mrs Thistlethwayte—and she said she could name others. Lady Salisbury still more bitter & violent."

By the end of 1881 Gladstone's many friends had become extremely worried about the mounting virulence of the gossip and the fear of what would happen if somebody made the rumours public. On 9 February 1882 Eddy Hamilton noted in his diary, "Rosebery came to see me today much exercised in his mind as to further proof of Mr G's walking in the streets at night. It is a terribly unfortunate craze of his, and the only wonder is that his enemies have not made more capital of it. It is a quite unpardonable indiscretion for a man in his position. Rosebery is prepared to say a word about it, and as he is almost the only man who has ever dared broach the subject of Mrs T. [i.e. Laura Thistlethwayte] with Mr G., probably he would be the best spokesman in this instance." In fact, Hamilton and Rosebery tossed a coin to see which of them should have the disagreeable task of talking to Gladstone and Rosebery lost; on 10 February Hamilton noted, "Mr G took it in good grace, and was apparently impressed with Rosebery's words which will (I am in hopes) have good effect."

"Mr G" had merely listened to what Lord Rosebery had to say and had not given any promises that he would refrain from his contentious activities. Hamilton's hopes were not only quickly dashed but his fears were increased when Gladstone formed a friendship with another notorious lady, Lillie Langtry. It has been suggested that Gladstone took Mrs. Langtry under his wing at the direct request of the Prince of Wales, who hoped that the Liberal leader's patronage would help effect her entry into good society, but Hamilton's diary entries suggest that it was the ice-cold ambitious brain of Mrs. Langtry which thought Mr. Gladstone's friendship would assist her. On 3 March 1882 Hamilton wrote, "Last week Mr G. received an invitation to a Sunday 'at home' for Mrs Langtry. He did not avail himself of it, but he went and called at her house. He did not even see her, but all kinds of rumours are already abroad about his intimacy with 'the professional beauty.'" Lillie Langtry's letter to Gladstone after his call is extant among the Hawarden Papers. It reads:

Feb 25/82
18 Albert Mansions

Dear Mr. Gladstone,

I was so dreadfully disappointed to find I had missed you yesterday. How most unusual for me to be out at that hour—& had I had an idea that there was a chance of my seeing you I should have been in.

I hardly dare hope you will honor me by coming tomorrow. There are a few artistic people coming & knowing how interested you are in Art I ventured to ask you. Sunday is the only spare one that we professional people have & therefore I was obliged to chose it.

Yrs. very sincerely,
LILLIE LANGTRY.

Mr. Gladstone later honoured Mrs. Langtry with quite a few calls; their correspondence blossomed and on 1 April 1882 Eddy Hamilton noted, "I have been concerned again about the Langtry affair. Mr G presented her with a copy of his pet book, *Sister Dora*.* She is evidently trying to make social capital out of the acquaintance she has scraped with him. Most disagreeable things with all kinds of exaggeration are being said, I took the occasion of putting in a word and cautioning him against the wiles of the

---

* This best-selling biography of Dora Pattison was read by everybody from Queen Victoria and Mr. Gladstone downwards. She was a well-born lady who had worked as an Anglican nursing sister in lowly surroundings in the Midlands before dying comparatively young. The biography had a theme of will power, triumph over adversity and strong Christian faith which was particularly attractive to Gladstone.

woman, whose reputation is in such bad odour that, despite all the endeavours of H.R.H., nobody will receive her in their house." Hamilton's words had no more effect than Lord Rosebery's earlier ones, and on 16 April 1882 he wrote, ". . . the intimacy on paper with Mrs Langtry is increasing. She has evidently been told to resort to the double-envelope system which secures respect from our rude hands, and she is now making pretty constant use of this privilege." In his diary Loulou Harcourt recorded, "G does the most extraordinary things and has indeed been accused of being at Mrs Langtry's house when he ought to have been moving 'previous questions' in a Bradlaugh debate."

Gladstone's delight in the company of Mesdames Thistlethwayte and Langtry made many members of society believe he was having an affair with each of them, but it was his night-walking which presented the greater danger and was his Achilles' heel. The proclivity reached a crisis point on the night of Lord Frederick Cavendish's murder, when both a member of the public who idolised Mr. Gladstone and a Conservative M.P. who did not saw him with a young prostitute near the Duke of York steps at 11:30 P.M. The M.P. was Colonel Tottenham, who said he was about to cross the road to offer Mr. Gladstone his deepest condolences on the news of Lord Frederick's murder when he witnessed the Prime Minister accost, get into conversation with and move off in the direction of Piccadilly Circus in the company of "an abandoned woman." The member of the public was the Bermondsey Workhouse master and he finished his corroborative account of what he had seen with the words, "For years that statesman has been my idol—so much for human frailty and credulity . . . I almost disbelieve my own eyes and knowledge." Colonel Tottenham told the story everywhere he could, including a dinner party attended by a Mrs. Louisa Pepys, who wrote to Eddy Hamilton asking if he could not flatly and openly contradict what she believed to be a foul calumny against Mr. Gladstone.

Unfortunately Hamilton could not; but what he could, and did, do was to write to the workhouse master and Mrs. Pepys telling them that if they had been within earshot of the scene it would have acquired a different complexion from the obvious interpretation which had been put upon it. Hamilton told Mrs. Pepys, ". . . he has at different times been the means of retrieving unfortunate women from a fallen position. The prudence of such conduct in a man of his position may be questionable, but of the high, unselfish and kind motives which guide his conduct there can be no doubt." After consultation with Lord Rosebery and Lord Granville, Hamilton decided to show the letter to Mr. Gladstone (as he told Mrs. Pepys he had). He noted that Gladstone was "perfectly frank about the affair, as I knew he would be, and promptly related everything he remembered of the incident." The devoted secretary also begged Gladstone to stop "the practice of parleying with people in the streets," and temporarily he did. On 13 June 1882 Hamilton was happy to note in his diary that he had spoken to

Howard Vincent, who was the head of the recently created Criminal Investigation Department, and "that since the 6th ult . . . no further reports of any incidents concerning the night walks." (Owing to Fenian threats on Gladstone's life he had been placed under police protection, which meant that quite a few ill-paid London policemen were in possession of evidence that Mr. Gladstone frequently consorted with prostitutes at night, a further circumstance that worried his colleagues.)

Catherine's attitude towards the stories which were circulating about her husband in such menacing, potentially dangerous fashion is something of an unknown quantity in that no mention of it occurs in her letters (nor in her daughter's or niece's diaries). Catherine had lived with the night-walking on and off for years, she accepted its Christian values and presumably she could see no reason why her husband should stop it now that he was in his seventies. What she felt about the friendships with the professional beauties is again not known from any reference she made, but in September 1884 Henry Ponsonby told his wife that "Mrs G" had been having "a roughish time of it there with 'William.'" "There" was a Scottish house they were visiting and "the roughish time" was on account of Gladstone's attraction to Lady Lonsdale, another well-known beauty. (On the subject of Lady Lonsdale, who was known to the Prince of Wales, Catherine managed to have a row with her darling Princess Alix, an indication perhaps that William's proclivities were causing some stress at this period.) But Catherine had also lived through and accepted her husband's deep friendship with the Duchess of Sutherland (who was long dead), and if she could not attribute the same political usefulness to Mrs. Thistlethwayte or Mrs. Langtry or Lady Lonsdale as she had to the Duchess, she knew that Gladstone's liking for other women in no way diminished his love and need for her. She was his guiding star, and as the least introspective of women she had no need to analyse or rationalise her position. In some ways it is a pity that she had not, as a word from Catherine might have helped. But then it might not. Gladstone did not heed the warnings of either Lord Rosebery or Eddy Hamilton, both of whom he liked and respected, and in the one battle in which Catherine had felt deeply and strongly enough to oppose her husband, namely the question of his resignation in 1875, she had not emerged as the victor.

CHAPTER 16

THE SERBONIAN BOG

ONE QUESTION WHICH Lord Frederick Cavendish's murder had temporarily solved was that of Gladstone's retirement, for in the circumstances it was unthinkable that he should desert the front line. In the aftermath of the brutal murders and the wave of anti-Irish feeling in Britain, it was equally unthinkable that large steps could be taken towards Liberal/Nationalist co-operation, but Gladstone did his best to implement his side of the secret Kilmainham treaty (which became public property when Mr. Forster revealed it in the House of Commons, thus causing further difficulties for his erstwhile colleagues who were trying to implement it). To the widespread demands for a renewal of the Co-ercion Act Gladstone acceded, but on the question of amendments to the Land Act he fought tenaciously. He managed to get an Arrears Bill through the House of Commons and when the Lords threatened to throw it out, Gladstone threatened resignation. This time it was not simply his own resignation but that of the Liberal Government, for with consummate skill he had managed to carry a majority of his Cabinet and his party with him on an issue which deeply divided them.

Gladstone's resentment against the House of Lords had been growing over the years and had no initial connection with Ireland; it went back to 1860, when their lordships had thrown out his Paper Bill. During his first Ministry there had been a steady drift to the Tory benches of Whig peers who were unable to accept his reforming Liberalism, and this had created a permanent Tory majority in the Upper House. As their lordships tried to thwart most of his major measures, Gladstone became more convinced that they had lost touch with the people, that their power had become destructive and should therefore be curtailed. The House of Lords and its opposition to any Liberal Government was a running theme in Gladstone's correspondence and memoranda from the 1860s onwards, and it was one which led to acrimonious correspondence with Queen Victoria. (She believed that the House of Lords was an essential ingredient in the protection of the people's rights because their lordships, unlike the Commons, were not swayed by the need to pander to the electorate, nor were they swayed by horrid party considerations; they could therefore exercise their judgements without bias or favour.)

Unfortunately Gladstone failed to make public his deep-rooted feelings about the Lords and his correct belief that sooner or later their power would have to be challenged—his public attacks were confined to the general blasts against the Upper Ten Thousand. Would that Gladstone had committed himself to the task of curtailing the power of the House of Lords, for it was one which he was superbly equipped to have fought and brought to a triumphant conclusion, even against Queen Victoria's absolute opposition. (It might have enabled an Irish Home Rule Bill to have been concluded during Gladstone's lifetime.) But his reverence for the aristocratic tradition overrode his political acumen and personal feelings, and though there were skirmishes, the battle to reform the House of Lords was one which Gladstone did not seriously contemplate until it was too late.

Over Ireland Gladstone persevered, even though the Irish question receded from its dominant position for a period after 1882. His perseverance was tangential and in part initiated by a letter from Katie O'Shea in which she suggested that in the difficult circumstances an indirect link between the Liberals and the Nationalists—i.e. herself, who had Mr. Parnell's political confidence—might be a good idea. Mr. Gladstone agreed, though neither Lord Spencer (the new Lord Lieutenant of Ireland) nor Eddy Hamilton was happy because both of them were fearful that further revelations of secret Liberal/Nationalist negotiations would cause further harm, particularly if the intermediary were also revealed as the lady known in certain circles to be Parnell's mistress. Katie O'Shea has been added to the list of Gladstone's female friends; she indeed later wrote of Mr. Gladstone's charm, courtesy and wonderful eagle eyes, and of his habit of taking her by the arm and walking her up and down his study in Downing Street while they discussed Irish affairs. But Katie's interest was Parnell, and in this instance Gladstone's liking for women enabled him to keep open a channel to the Irish leader which was politically useful.

By 1882 Catherine had recovered much of her health and spirits, and in January an event occurred which gave her and her husband great pleasure—the birth of a daughter to Gertrude and Willie Gladstone. It was the first child to be born safely since the marriage in 1875, but it was a harrowing experience for "our dear Gertie," and Catherine wrote to Lucy Cavendish, "Poor Willie had indeed a *terrible* experience & seems to have been nearly 31 *hours* by her side, helpless as he said to assuage the agony . . . the confinement was exceptional, so suffering & so long . . . dear Lucy how I long to fly to her . . . Uncle W. wrote to him yesterday telling him of his experience when he *Willy* was born!! & the horror of seeing the suffering." Gladstone's horror of suffering, whether at first or second hand, and the considerate side of his nature had been demonstrated six months earlier when he wrote a letter to President Garfield's wife. He began his letter, "You will, I am sure, excuse me, though a personal stranger, for addressing you by letter, to convey to you the assurance of my own feelings and those of my countrymen on the occasion of the late horrible attempt to murder the President of the United States, in a form more palpable at least than that of messages conveyed by telegraph." The letter was written as the news of the assassination attempt reached England and while President Garfield was still fighting for his life, and it shows the genuine humility Gladstone had—he was about the best-known "stranger" in the world—and the struggle the emotional part of him always had to break through the formal precision, certainly in print.

Catherine was again dashing to the London Hospital or the Woodford Convalescent Home, dealing with "bothers" about the Hawarden Orphanage and raising funds for another convalescent home for the victims of scarlet fever. Eddy Hamilton described her skipping around like a two-year-old, and in August 1882 her husband told her, "In ardour, spirits, readiness and locomotion, you are not 2 but 20 years before me." Lord Frederick's murder had, if possible, increased Catherine's bond with her niece; like Lucy she believed that the murder would and must, through Christ's mercy, bring peace to Ireland. It was a belief which reinforced Catherine's conviction that it was her husband, as God's instrument on earth, who would and must effect the settlement of the Irish problem. After the Phoenix Park murders she was adamant that he should stay in office, at least until the Irish question was resolved.

By November 1882 Gladstone was again harping on about retirement, but he was also engaged in the reconstruction of his Cabinet and as Hamilton noted, "Here is a slight inconsistency." The reconstruction involved Gladstone's giving up the Chancellorship of the Exchequer—the dual role of Prime Minister and Chancellor had proved too much even for him in the pressures of his second Ministry—but among those who were *not* promoted was Lord Rosebery. The failure led to Rosebery's resignation in the middle of 1883 and was an example of Gladstone's lack of tact and understanding in dealing with his younger colleagues. His loyalty to older colleagues and his dislike of firing people played some part in his reactions but the root was the basic lack of interest in people as individuals, in their emotions and ambitions. Though he himself was soon dubbed "an old man in a hurry," he also thought young people these days were far too impatient and he regarded Rosebery's justified disappointment—for he had much ability and was particularly concerned about long-neglected Scottish affairs—as "a tempest in a tea-kettle."

Catherine was also involved in the Rosebery contretemps and her contribution to the proceedings was as tactless as her husband's. Rosebery's wife Hannah had been born Hannah Rothschild—and quite a few eyebrows had been raised at the marriage of the Scottish aristocrat to a Jewess, however rich. But the marriage was an extremely happy if unfortunately short-lived one, and Hannah Rosebery was as devoted to her husband and the furtherance of his career as Catherine was to hers. Sir Charles Dilke had earlier commented that Lady Rosebery could be silly and Mrs. G. was even sillier so there were bound to be rows between the ladies. When the matter of Lord Rosebery's non-promotion and his threats of resignation came to a head, Catherine and Hannah indulged in a spikey correspondence in which the former said that Rosebery was too young for high office and incidentally too interested in horse racing, and the latter retorted that he was not young in wisdom or intelligence (she might also have pointed out that Mr. Gladstone had been a Cabinet Minister in his early thirties). The incident culminated in a stormy personal interview between the two ladies at the end of which Catherine swept out and Hannah Rosebery commented that the dramatic exit had saved her from having to kiss Mrs. Gladstone, thank God.

December 1882 presented Gladstone with the best possible opportunity for retirement, one which could have appealed to his dramatic instinct, because he celebrated the fiftieth anniversary of his return to Parliament. But by December he had abandoned the idea of resignation *pro tem*. However, in January 1883 Gladstone suddenly started to suffer from bad nights, and as he normally slept like a top he went into a deep depression. Hamilton thought the sleeplessness was induced by worry over the Rosebery affair and the question of the appointment of a new Archbishop of Canterbury (over which he was in conflict with Queen Victoria), for as his secretary said, Gladstone was immensely calm in a crisis but tended to fret over the smaller matters. At this juncture nobody in the Liberal party wanted their leader to retire so Gladstone was persuaded to depart on an open-ended holiday, to recuperate his health and spirits. In the middle of January 1883, accompanied by Catherine, Mary and other members of his family, he set off for Cannes to stay at a friend's house. Within a few days he was, as Catherine recorded, "a different creature, good appetites & spirits, *elastic walk*" but she unfortunately was not. Auguste Schluter, who had gone on the trip as Mary's personal maid, wrote that while Mr. Gladstone was much improved, "Mrs. Gladstone is not at all well. She has the shingles." Throughout February Gladstone remained in Cannes, his spirits and energy increasing every day, while his colleagues in England wondered when, if ever, he intended to return (even though they had urged him to depart, with a *carte blanche*). Mary Gladstone said that a little girl asked the pertinent question "how P.M. can govern England while drinking tea at Cannes?" and in a letter to her cousin she wrote, "It is too funny the way people imagine he is panting to return & that it is we who are restraining him. It is exactly the contrary. Mama and Spencer (Lyttleton) are simply dying to get home. They are both bored to death." Eventually, at the end of February Gladstone decided he too had had enough of the delights of the South of France and on 2 March the family landed in Folkestone to a triumphal reception.

The year 1883 was a comparatively calm one, with no major battles fought either literally or metaphorically. Gladstone remained interested in Ireland; his thoughts had turned to a thoroughgoing reform of its local government structure which would give the country a measure of autonomy (the idea was adopted and worked out in detail by Joseph Chamberlain).

He was reluctantly persuaded that 1883 was not the year in which he could force through a serious measure of Irish reform because it was the one in which "The Invincibles" who had been responsible for the Phoenix Park murders were brought to trial, and a considerable amount of murky information—from the British and some Irish Nationalist viewpoints—was made known about Irish and Irish-American societies plotting to murder British politicians and overthrow the British Government. It was also the year of dynamite explosions in London which caused some loss of life and damage to property in the Fenian efforts to further their cause and intimidate the British people and Government. Sir William Harcourt's Municipal Bill, which aimed to reform the local government structure in London, was abandoned, and the major legislative measure carried was the Corrupt Practices Act, considerably tightening the procedures during parliamentary elections. (Eddy Hamilton noted that Parnell wanted Ireland omitted from the Corrupt Practices Bill because Ireland was pure and unbribed, which, as he commented, was "a tolerably cool proposal.")

It was in 1883 that Gladstone first floated the idea of a knighthood for Henry Irving but Irving himself then rejected the suggestion on the grounds that it would be invidious to single him out before the acting profession as a whole had gained an advance in its status. But Gladstone spent a fair amount of time trying to persuade Queen Victoria and other uninterested colleagues that the arts in general, and the stage in particular, had been sadly and in his opinion unwarrantably neglected with regard to honours for services rendered to the nation. It was not Gladstone who eventually obtained the knighthood for Irving but Lord Rosebery (in 1895); nevertheless the first official recognition of an actor's contribution to the national heritage came from Gladstone.

One matter which caused Gladstone considerable anxiety in 1883 was a series of highly radical speeches made by Joseph Chamberlain in the early summer, including one in which he coined a memorable phrase by attacking Lord Salisbury as a member of a class "who toil not neither do they spin," and another in which he advocated universal manhood suffrage, one man-one vote, payment of M.P.s and equal electoral districts. Queen Victoria was furious, and letters streamed from her demanding that Mr. Gladstone control the speeches of members of his Cabinet. Gladstone was of the opinion that controlling the utterances of any member of the Liberal party would be a full-time job, and he did not believe that it was his brief to do so—England was supposed to have freedom of speech—but he was angry with Chamberlain for enunciating policies that had not been agreed by the Cabinet, and for the personal attack on Lord Salisbury.

In August 1883 he was only too pleased to depart for a cruise on a friend's yacht, in the company of Catherine, Mary, Henry, Herbert, Willie and his wife Gertrude, Lord Tennyson and the Harcourts. Unfortunately, this pleasure trip caused a further breach in the relations with Queen Victoria. After a sail round the Scottish coast, as the weather was so beautiful and the sea so calm, the assembled company decided to steam across to Norway and then pay a visit to Copenhagen (it was a motorised yacht). In the Danish capital there happened to be a gathering of European royalty and Mary Gladstone recorded, "The whole thing was rather amusing & interesting, loads of crowned heads," while Auguste Schluter commented on the departure from Copenhagen: "3.30 p.m. we are off again . . . loud cheers arrive and all from the warships. God save our Queen is played oh it was grand to see all the Kings, Emperors, Empresses, Queens here." However amused Mary was and impressed Fräulein Schluter was, neither emotion was shared by Her Majesty, who was again furious that her Prime Minister should go charging abroad without her permission and seem to function as a head of state. Gladstone penned a contrite letter to the Queen in which he said that neither intention had been in his mind and the visit to Copenhagen had been an impromptu one, but Her Majesty was not mollified. Privately Gladstone agreed with Eddy Hamilton that the Queen's communication had been disagreeable in tone and ill-mannered and that to put the matter bluntly—which Hamilton did but Gladstone did not—her reactions could be attributed to jealousy.

By the end of 1883 Gladstone's political attention was focusing on the question of further electoral reform; he proposed that the franchise be extended to the counties in England and that it be widened in Ireland. Over the latter proposal he met immediate opposition within his Cabinet, notably from Lord Hartington; Catherine was of the opinion that Hartington had become biased against the Irish since his brother's murder in Phoenix Park (an understandable reaction) but his lordship's stated objections were that an extension of the franchise in Ireland without a redistribution of seats would return to Parliament an even more solid group of Home Rulers and threaten the Protestant minority. Gladstone argued that to refuse the franchise extension to Ireland would be to place the existing Home Rulers in the Tory camp and kill his proposed Bill altogether, and that if Hartington resigned the Radical element in the Liberal party would be strengthened. Once again, with consummate skill, he managed to keep his diverse Liberal cohorts behind him, and Hartington did not resign. But it was the matter of an extension of the franchise without any redistribution of the electoral boundaries which created a mounting crisis, because the Conservatives feared that apart from the Protestant minority in Ireland, they as a party could suffer badly in Britain. When Parliament broke for the summer recess in 1884 the Franchise Bill had passed through the Commons but had twice been stopped by the Lords for redistribution amendments. What had begun as an electoral reform measure was threatening to develop into a major battle between the two Houses on a constitutional issue, particularly the right of the Lords to force a dissolution on the Government by again rejecting the Bill as it stood.

The Radicals were spoiling for a showdown with the Lords, and Hartington was one peer who then considered that their (his) days were numbered. In a long conversation with Henry Ponsonby at Balmoral in September 1884 he predicted that the Lords would soon be abolished, and when Ponsonby asked how one of the pillars of the State could be despatched against its will without a violent revolution, Hartington replied that there were several ways, the simplest one being that as the Lords were summoned to attend by writ, no writs should be issued! Gladstone himself was not in favour of a collision with the Lords on this subject, and on a tour through Scotland at the end of August and into September his speeches were markedly moderate. The tour included another mini-Midlothian campaign, with the Gladstones staying at Dalmeny; they were again on cordial terms with the Roseberys and there was now no question of Catherine not accompanying her husband. Mary Gladstone said, "the entry into Waverley Market is still overwhelming to think of; it looked like millions of faces & millions of voices," and that in the evening, "Princes St. was one rushing mass of human beings."

Catherine and Gladstone went on to Balmoral, where he showed his wife the Minister's room to prove to her that it was not such a hole as Sir William Harcourt had described! The Balmoral visit was a reasonable success, but Gladstone then proceeded to make speeches at every station between Balmoral and Aberdeen. Queen Victoria did not disapprove of their moderate content but she was, as Ponsonby noted, "very sore" that he should stump "under her very nose" and by what she called his "Court Circular," i.e. the reports of his every word printed by the phalanx of journalists which followed him. In the ensuing months, as the constitutional crisis mounted, Queen Victoria acted with considerable moderation herself, for once not aligning herself absolutely on the Tory side but playing a valuable role in averting the head-on collision between Commons and Lords and persuading the opposing factions to discuss the question rationally. Towards the end of November Mary Gladstone recorded endless meetings at Downing Street between Lord Salisbury, Sir Stafford Northcote, Sir Charles Dilke, Lord Hartington and Gladstone (Dilke was much engaged in the negotiations, and at one point Mary said she seemed to live and die in his company). Eventually, towards the end of the year, a compromise was reached in which it was agreed that the Lords would pass the Franchise Bill as it stood in return for the Liberal guarantee that they would introduce a Redistribution Bill into the next session.

Gladstone's spirits, energy and political acumen remained high throughout the prolonged Franchise Bill wrangles, and he was supported by Catherine's love and care. Eddy Hamilton remarked upon the mutual devotion of a couple who were so unalike in temperament; in February 1884 Mary Gladstone wrote, "I was in my room at 9.30 & heard him and Mama coming up the stairs singing 'A ragamuffin husband and a rantipolling wife' at the top of their voices." (This was one of the Gladstones' favourite jingles, and Herbert Gladstone also told the story of his parents waltzing in front of the fire singing the song.) But even with a return to full power and when

events were mostly going his way, Gladstone now had need of his coun-
terexcitements. At the end of January 1884 Henry Ponsonby told his wife
that some mutual friends ". . . talked about their dinner & Gladstone . . .
Mrs. T. brought him there in the carriage & took him away again," and
how furious another friend had been "at G's. devotion to this lady." In February 1884 Eddy Hamilton wrote a long letter to his chief on the related
subject of the night-walking and a further ramification which had developed, the entry into brothels.

Hamilton said that he had been prompted to write by a sense of duty; he
told Gladstone that however much he might resent being guarded by the
police while he was in London, the surveillance was considered vital for his
safety and as a result, "reports are made on your daily movements, and it
appears from those reports that you have recently visited places, as to which
the bare statement of facts (and nothing but a bare statement is likely to
become public) would be ruinously prejudicial to yourself and those connected with you." Hamilton observed that these facts were in the hands of
"men paid a pound or two a week who may or may not be corrupt," that
the information exposed the ill-paid policemen to enormous, unfair temptation because there were unscrupulous, malicious persons who would give
large sums of money for a simple affidavit. He ventured to suggest that in
his philanthropic desire to do good Mr. Gladstone did not adequately appreciate the terrible dangers to which his actions exposed not only himself
but everybody connected with him, and begged him "most earnestly to
desist from entering houses which may give rise to the slightest suspicion or
to imputations however unfounded." Hamilton also begged Mr. Gladstone's forgiveness for his presumption, reiterated that nothing but the
strongest sense of duty would have induced him to write the letter and
finished by saying that even if the police surveillance were dropped, the
gravity of the risk Gladstone took each time he patrolled the streets and certainly when he entered brothels (though Hamilton did not actually mention the word) was immense. As a postscript he begged Gladstone to destroy the letter, saying he had only committed himself to paper because he
had thought he would express himself more precisely by writing than by
word of mouth.* Temporarily Gladstone heeded the eminently sensible
warnings and advice, though not, alas, permanently.

At the beginning of 1884, as Gladstone started to wrestle with the exten-
sion of the franchise, the problem of Egypt and the Soudan came to a head.
Britain and France had become involved in the mess and corruption of
Egyptian affairs in the 1870s and by the early 1880s an internal, nationalist
Egyptian movement led by Arabi Pasha was in open revolt, though as
much against the Khedive as against the European intruders. For once
Gladstone underestimated the nationalist impulse, viewing Arabi Pasha as
an unjustified, unlawful rebel, and he and Lord Granville tried to get the

---

* This letter is in Hamilton's papers in his handwriting, so either Gladstone failed to destroy it and Hamilton retrieved it after his death, or Hamilton kept a copy.

European powers and Turkey (who had suzerainty over Egypt) to act in concert to suppress the rebellion. But when, in the summer of 1882, some fifty Europeans were murdered in Alexandria, it was Britain who acted alone, with Gladstone ordering a section of the fleet to bombard the fortifications which Arabi's troops were erecting in Alexandria. By this action he lost the support of one of his oldest and closest colleagues, John Bright, who thought it was an abominable decision for a Liberal Government to have taken unilaterally and resigned. Nevertheless Gladstone was pleased with his decision and a few days later he agreed to further decisive action, despatching an expedition to Egypt under the command of Sir Garnet Wolseley to restore order in the country. Wolseley duly achieved a victory at Tel-el-Kebir, heavily defeating Arabi's forces; there Gladstone's bout of imperialism and touch of jingoism ended. Having shown that Britain could act promptly in the defence of law and order, that her army was now efficient (thanks to the reforms enacted by Gladstone's two Ministries), he wished to return the Egyptian imbroglio to the attention of the Concert of Europe. But the European powers were interested in their sectional policies, and the British were established in Egypt as the only bulwark between the Khedive's legal if rotten government and the revolutionary nationalist impulse.

To complicate an already complicated matter, Egypt had control over the Soudan and already by 1881 the figure of the Mahdi had appeared in its deserts, proclaiming a *jhad* or holy war in which all Moslems would unite to throw off the yoke of Turkish and Egyptian oppression (the fact that the Turks and Egyptians were Moslems was ignored). Soon much of the Soudan was under the Mahdi's control and the tribesmen were flocking to his banner, and in the autumn of 1883 the Egyptians decided that they must mount a campaign to destroy him and re-establish their authority. At the beginning of November a ten-thousand-strong Egyptian force, led by an Englishman who was a general in the Egyptian army, was decimated by the Mahdi's force at El Obeid. Gladstone was now convinced in his own mind that the British must withdraw from Egypt, but his Cabinet and the country were divided, Queen Victoria headed those who believed that Britain must again exert her authority and aid the Egyptians, and the fact that the decimated force had been led by an Englishman considerably assisted the jingoists. Still, there was a strong body of opinion which supported Gladstone, particularly (at this moment) in the country as opposed to fashionable society, and had he stood firm he could have effected a British withdrawal.

Unfortunately, Gladstone allowed himself to be persuaded that Britain had a moral obligation at least to supervise the evacuation of the Egyptian garrisons which were scattered throughout the Soudan, notably in Khartoum, and were in danger of extermination by the Mahdi's forces. Even more unfortunately he acquiesced in the decision to send General Charles Gordon as the British representative to supervise the evacuation. It was

Lords Granville, Hartington and Northbrook, together with Sir Charles Dilke, who took the fatal decision. Even if Gordon was not given the clearest of clear-cut directives he was told by the Liberal Ministers that his mission was to superintend the evacuation of the Soudan as quickly as possible. But Eddy Hamilton gloomily noted in his diary on 23 January 1884, five days after the appointment had been made and when Gordon was already on his way to Egypt, "He seems to be a half-cracked fatalist; and what can one expect from such a man?"

Gordon was more than a little mad, and his fatalism extended to a death wish; he was notoriously depressive, erratic and unsusceptible to orders, and he believed in the divinity of *his* mission as much as Gladstone did in *his*. But Gordon was also a Christian soldier who loved the thrill of battle, and he was already a hero to large sections of the British public, the loner who defied authority and achieved spectacular military coups when lesser men had failed. To send such a man on a mission of withdrawal was an act of almost criminal folly and one can only feel that the far-from-stupid Liberal Ministers who did so succumbed to temporary panic, to the pressure of the newspaper campaign for Gordon's appointment and to the lack of unity in their ranks. They were not assisted by the detachment of their leader on this issue, literally in his being over two hundred miles away at Hawarden, politically in that Egypt and the Soudan attracted so little of his interest. During 1884 Mary Gladstone described her father's reactions to the matter: "Everything peaceful save Egypt, and even that does not seem to disturb the even flow of Downing Street much . . . the most serene evening. The P.M. in dressing gown asleep . . . Alfred [Lyttleton] snoozing on the sofa. Mama and I reading."

When Gordon arrived in Cairo on 24 January 1884 he was met by the British civil and military authorities on the spot, Sir Evelyn Baring and Sir Evelyn Wood (the brother of Katie O'Shea). Neither Baring nor Wood was much in sympathy with the Liberal Government's policies but it was re-emphasised to Gordon that his mission was to report on the situation and supervise an evacuation and that on no account should it be changed. However, once Gordon reached Khartoum it quickly became apparent that he had no intention of withdrawing and thought that he personally could settle the problem. Despite all the evidence to the contrary the Liberal Cabinet continued to believe that sooner or later he would implement his original mission, and it was not until July 1884, as Gordon's life lines to Egypt were cut by the Mahdi and only the Nile remained open to him, that the Cabinet began to be worried. On 5 August, with the greatest reluctance, Gladstone asked the House of Commons for the money to mount a relief expedition to Khartoum, but though it was immediately granted, the Liberals then ran into further misfortune which was not entirely of their making. There were arguments in Cairo about the size of the relief expedition, which route it should take and the question of supplies; then as the expedition finally neared Khartoum its commanding officer was killed in a skirmish with the Mahdi's troops, an event which caused further delay. The result is well-known: the relief expedition reached Khartoum two days after the Mahdi's forces had stormed and sacked the city, spearing General Gordon to death on the steps of the residency and killing most of the inhabitants whom he had been sent to protect.

Before the news of Khartoum's fall reached England on 5 February 1885, Gladstone had relapsed into one of his depressions and was again talking about retirement. On 1 January 1885 Lucy Cavendish noted in her diary (which she had begun to keep again for the first time since her husband's murder), "Each of these 3 sad Xmases I have spent at Hawarden. All wonderfully well here this time, except that poor Uncle W has had bad nights again . . . His powers are undiminished, but he works with increasing reluctance & distaste . . . Today he had to go to London for a Cabinet on anxious Egyptian crisis, after only sleeping one hour." Having attended the Cabinet, Gladstone was immediately examined by his personal physician, Andrew Clark; Eddy Hamilton recorded that Clark "found him in a very excited condition—pulse very quick, heart thumping—and under great stress . . . Mr. G. is depressed about himself: but he always is. He 'runs down' directly. Sleeplessness is a special trial to him . . . I don't think, however, we need apprehend a break-down such as occurred two years ago." However, Clark recommended that the Prime Minister have a complete rest, possibly including another visit to Cannes; but Gladstone decided to return to Hawarden. After several more flying visits to London for anxious Egyptian Cabinets, at the end of January he was in Liverpool for the personally happy event of his son Stephen's marriage to Annie Wilson, the daughter of a Liverpool doctor. Hamilton commented that it was not much of a marriage for the son of the Prime Minister (even if Stephen was unprepossessing in appearance), but he also said, "Mr. & Mrs. G have not an ounce of false pride between them . . . and are just as pleased with the arrangement as if their son were marrying a lady of high rank or fortune."

From Liverpool, Catherine and Gladstone travelled north to Holker Hall, one of the Duke of Devonshire's country houses, beautifully if remotely situated in the detached part of Lancashire, with the sweep of the sea below it and the hills of the Lake District behind. Gladstone's health was now better—the sleepless nights were past—but his spirits had not improved and there is the theory that he went to Holker to discuss the question of his immediate retirement with Lord Hartington, to whom he would finally hand over the reins of government. It is a theory unsubstantiated by concrete evidence; the only account of what happened at Holker Hall in February 1885 is Lucy Cavendish's, and it concentrates on how the news of the fall of Khartoum was received:

"The message came to Cavsh [i.e. Lord Hartington, who had become the War Minister in the 1882 Cabinet reshuffle], & as it was a long one in cypher & he had no secretary . . . he was a long time making it out. We were full of good hopes, for the last telegram that had been heard of from

General Gordon was 'All right—could hold out for years' & the English troops were within 3 days of the place . . .

"I was in my sitting room about 11 when I heard Cavsh stalk into Uncle W's room (next door). But as he visited him every day, I thought nothing of it. Going down soon after to go out, I found a telegram to me, from Eddy Hamilton in Downing St. to this effect, 'Make him come up: his colleagues wish it & the country expects it.' I was much astonished at his not telegraphing straight to Uncle W & rather affronted at the tone; but found out aftds. that there had been unaccountable delays in the telegraph. The news ought to have come early enough for us to have got him off by the 10.35 train. I took the message up & found them both in great distress; Cavsh had just told them. Atie P said, 'Have you heard? Khartoum has fallen.' I said, 'What! have we taken it?' for I cd. not believe it cd. be the other way . . . They got away, Cavsh with them, by the next train."

When the Gladstones reached Cartmel station to catch the next train to London, Queen Victoria's famous, *unciphered* telegram was handed to the Prime Minister by an embarrassed stationmaster. The telegram read, "These news from Khartoum are frightful, and to think that all this might have been prevented and many precious lives saved by earlier action is frightful." Her Majesty's action in sending such a telegram *en clair* was frightful (Granville and Hartington were sent one, too), but she mirrored the horrified, emotional feelings of the majority of her countrymen and -women, including many of the Liberal masses. In the eyes of the people the initials G.O.M. temporarily stood for "Gordon's Old Murderer" or were reversed to M.O.G., "Murderer of Gordon." When Gladstone attended the theatre a few nights after the news had been received, at a moment when, as Eddy Hamilton commented, he should have been in sackcloth and ashes, the howls of protest and the reaction against him mounted. Mary Gladstone returned to London on 19 February; she wrote, ". . . drove through the mob in Downing St., finding parents at tea as usual, the P.M. deep in George Eliot's *Life*." When later the same day she attended the House of Commons to hear her father speak on the subject of the Soudan, a speech in which his only comment on his countrymen's dead hero was the phrase "the lamented Gordon," even Mary was driven to admit, ". . . the P.M.'s speech utterly failed to cheer or strengthen or comfort any human being."

Gladstone's behaviour stemmed from the self-centred quality which enabled him to survive, but it was also based on a firm conviction that he was not responsible for Gordon's death. He had been pursuing the correct policy in wishing to withdraw the British from Egypt; Gordon had failed to implement his instructions and could have extricated himself and those whose lives he had been directed to save until virtually the last minute. But it was Gladstone's Liberal Government which had sent Gordon to Khartoum and had then compounded its initial disastrous error of judgement by refusing to accept that he would not evacuate of his own volition. Gladstone's convictions also ignored the tide of grief and outrage and sense of national humiliation which was sweeping through the country. Swimming against the tide can be an admirable trait in a politician, and it was one which Gladstone had used to good effect, but in this instance he might have taken more note of the popular pulse, because he was not blameless over Khartoum. His attitude was endorsed by Catherine, if not by Mary or Hamilton, and his wife's explanation for not dissuading him from attending the theatre at a moment when the country was deep in mourning for Gordon was that he hated to have his arrangements upset and the seats had been booked. In letters to her family and relations Catherine showed her single-minded concern for her husband by concentrating on her relief that the news had not caused him any further sleepless nights.

The relief expedition, if it had failed in its objective, had established a British presence in the Soudan, and Gladstone's *political* sensitivity made him aware that he could not immediately pursue his policy of withdrawal from the area. Almost immediately after the Khartoum disaster the threat of another war in Afghanistan materialised when the Russians, thinking that Britain had her hands full in the Soudan, advanced on a village called Penjdeh. Over the Penjdeh incident Gladstone acted promptly, asking the House of Commons to vote the money to meet the Russian threat and saying that the resources of the British Empire would be brought to bear if the Russians continued their advance. Alarmed, the Russians promptly withdrew, and with this triumph behind him Gladstone was able to tell the House of Commons that there could now be no question of conquering the Soudan, as the British forces were needed for the more important task of guarding British India and its exposed flank in Afghanistan.

The news that Gordon's death was not to be avenged and that the Soudan was to be left to the mercies of the Mahdi produced a flurry of furious letters from Queen Victoria. Among their recipients was Lord Wolseley, who was in Egypt poised to conquer the Soudan; he was urged to resist and oppose all ideas of retreat and if necessary to threaten resignation. In reply Wolseley told Her Majesty that not even Prince Bismarck had as great a contempt for Mr. Gladstone as had educated Englishmen in Egypt, though he believed that the great uneducated mass still clung to him. At the end of April 1885 he wrote again to thank Her Majesty for a copy of "Her high-spirited, Queenly minute of the 17th instant addressed to the first Minister of the Crown. I feel proud to think there was at least one person in England . . . who had a fine appreciation of the national honour, of what is and is not worthy of this nation, and who also has the courage of Her opinions . . . my blood boils at the fact that there should still be millions of people who still believe in the Minister who has brought us down to our present humiliating condition . . . I should like to hide away and never draw sword again as long as Mr. G. remained in office." Her Majesty's beliefs and position had long been clear—though she had no business writing to Wolseley as she did. But Wolseley's attacks—and he had even less business than Her Majesty to indulge in such a correspondence—tend to stick in the gullet because he owed a good deal to Gladstone, including his peerage.

Gladstone was not aware that the country's Sovereign and one of its generals were in correspondence behind its elected Prime Minister's back, but it is doubtful that he would have been too surprised had he known. He would have attributed the correspondence to "the fiend of Jingoism" and particularly to its new form which he saw as "a general grabbing of land by this country." But the last great grab for colonies by the European powers was under way, the desire for the false phantoms of imperial glory was reviving throughout Europe, and in Britain the fall of Khartoum marked a watershed in the public's attitude. A section of the population remained faithful to Gladstone's views, to his passionate (if not *always* implemented) conviction that sweet reason and negotiation were the weapons of civilisation, that while less advanced nations might need a guiding hand it was the duty of countries such as England to encourage them towards self-government. But a larger section of the population now believed that "the single red line" of which Lord Rosebery had spoken during a tour of Australia in 1883 should be splashed across the map of the world, and that "the Commonwealth of Nations" of which Rosebery had also spoken during his Australian tour should be forever dominated by the English. After Khartoum there was a feeling that Gladstone had let the side down on foreign affairs and that he failed to understand the realities of world power politics.

As with Lord Frederick Cavendish's murder, one matter Gordon's death had settled temporarily was the question of Gladstone's retirement. He had no intention of surrendering office over Gordon's dead body. In the crisis nearly everybody in the Liberal party became reconvinced that he was the one man who could hold them together; his Cabinet rallied round him and Lord Rosebery offered to rejoin the Government as a gesture of solidarity, a noble offer which was accepted. But the ministerial rallying round did not last long, and it was again on the question of Ireland that the Cabinet divided. Joseph Chamberlain had worked out a detailed scheme for the devolution of local government in Ireland which became known as the Central Board Scheme. He had been in negotiation with the Nationalists (alas through the untrustworthy medium of Captain O'Shea) and he believed that his modified version of Home Rule would satisfy the Irish. While Gladstone viewed the Central Board Scheme with a favourable eye, other members of the Cabinet were opposed to it and insisted that some sections of the Coercion Act must be renewed in Ireland. In May 1885, somewhat impulsively, Chamberlain and Sir Charles Dilke resigned on the Irish issue, but Gladstone was back in full command of his powers and was not deterred by their resignation. He was about to reconstruct his Cabinet when on 8 June the Government was defeated on the Budget proposals by a combination of Tory and Parnellite votes. The combination was not too surprising because the Tories had been flirting with Parnell, who might, as a result of the Franchise Act, hold the balance of power after the next General Election.

On 11 June 1885 Catherine wrote to Lucy Cavendish to tell her how Gladstone had accepted his final defeat: "Herbert appeared at my bedside about 2 his father was walking just *outside* up & down *alone*—my 1st exclamation of concern was 'Where is Papa. How is he?' & then came quite well 'one of his finest speeches.' Oh dear I pass over the conflicting feelings. Then in came the dear form all grand though I who know him so well could see the struggle for the fact of that speech of his was to win & the parliamentary division lost was like a clap of thunder." But Catherine reassured herself and her niece by finishing her letter, "Before he fell asleep came the lovely calm words from his lips 'All praise to God for his mercies.'" Lucy herself noted in her diary, "an outcry was got up that the Govt had 'ridden for a fall' & that the Whips had not brought up numbers properly. This was not true . . . at first he was a good deal mortified at the defeat." Mortified he might be—and Eddy Hamilton confirmed that Gladstone was not as relieved at the prospect of escaping from office as he thought he would be—but it was unanimously agreed that the Liberals should resign.

However, the same sort of problem appeared as had arisen when Disraeli's Government had been defeated after the 1867 Reform Act—the new electoral registers necessitated by the 1884 Act were not ready, therefore a General Election could not be called. As Disraeli had been when Gladstone wanted to resign in 1873, Lord Salisbury was reluctant to form a minority Government unless he could obtain specific guarantees of support from Gladstone and the Liberals. The matter dragged on for nearly a fortnight, unassisted by Queen Victoria's being at Balmoral (though she eventually returned to Windsor), and by the stringent guarantees Lord Salisbury was demanding. Eventually on 22 June, after what Mary Gladstone described as an extraordinary day with Henry Ponsonby "trotting backwards and forwards" between the Tory and Liberal leaders, Lord Salisbury agreed to form a Government until such time as the new electoral registers were ready. Most people were convinced that the end of Gladstone's political life was at hand, including Mary and Lucy, if not Catherine, and on balance his friends and relations thought he would depart on a note of success. The second Ministry had not lived up to its high expectations but it had been plagued by unforeseen misfortunes such as Bradlaugh. If in most people's opinion it had fallen badly over Gordon and the Soudan, it *had* effected peace in the Transvaal, it *had* stopped a further Afghan war and at home two notable pieces of legislation had been passed in the Irish Land Act and the Franchise Act, their safe passage directly attributable to the parliamentary skill and courage of Mr. Gladstone. He would leave behind him a Liberal party devoted to the concept of international justice, to the rights of individual countries and peoples, to negotiation by reason and to balanced reform, which was largely his creation.

On 13 June, as the negotiations between the Liberals and the Tories were in full flood, Queen Victoria wrote what she considered to be a very civil letter to Mr. Gladstone offering him a peerage. Gladstone also considered it a most civil, indeed generous letter, but though he said he prized every word of it and it would ever be "a precious possession to him, and to his children after him," he regretted that he could not accept Her Majesty's offer. For, "Any service that he can render, if small, will, however be greater in the House of Commons than in the House of Lords; and it has never formed part of his views to enter that historic chamber." Queen Victoria was disappointed that her offer had been refused as she held the House of Lords in high esteem, but when Gladstone attended the final audience on 24 June she noted, "Saw Mr. G who appeared very much excited but was very amiable." Her Majesty's burst of enthusiasm for Gladstone and her lack of serious worry whether he accepted the Earldom or stayed in the Commons was based on the conviction that he must, in his seventy-sixth year, relinquish the leadership of the Liberal party and retire from the political scene in any major capacity. She would therefore never again have to endure the half-mad, dangerous firebrand as her Prime Minister.

CHAPTER 17

THE IRISH CORNFIELD

GLADSTONE HIMSELF MADE little reference to his retirement, or at least little in comparison to the wishes he had expressed over the last decade. A reason for his change in attitude was Gordon and Khartoum because while many people regarded the episode as one of the major blunders of his career which destroyed his second Ministry, the effect on him was of rejuvenation. Yet again he proved himself terrible on the rebound. Another reason for his changed attitude was the growing belief that the crisis of the Irish question was approaching. He was one of the few English politicians to appreciate that Parnell had a touch of genius, that he was a masterly tactician who might prove to be a masterly statesman (Eddy Hamilton noted that Gladstone had a sneaking regard for the Irish leader). Everybody was aware that after the General Election Parnell would almost certainly have a party of considerable strength at Westminster, and Gladstone believed that he would use that strength to demand Home Rule for Ireland and nothing less. Equally importantly, Gladstone had come round to the idea that Home Rule was morally justified, that the English had badly misgoverned Ireland over the centuries and that the Irish were a separate race and were entitled to have an autonomous government in Dublin, working within the larger framework of the United Kingdom. In the summer of 1885 he reopened the private link with Parnell via Katie O'Shea which had lapsed in the last year, and through the medium of his mistress, Parnell, who was at this juncture enjoying a honeymoon with the Tories, responded to the Liberal leader. But these approaches were tentative and publicly Gladstone made no pronouncement on Ireland.

In July 1885 there was an interlude of much personal happiness when on the fourteenth Willie Gladstone's wife Gertrude finally managed to bear the son who would be the heir to Hawarden.* In August 1885 the

---

* Young Will grew into a charming, attractive boy of considerable ability who gladdened the declining years of his grandparents. After their death he exhibited more promise as a politician than any member of the Gladstone family since his illustrious grandfather, but though he inherited Hawarden he did not live long to enjoy it, for he was among the millions of men who died in the mud of Flanders. In honour of Mr. Gladstone's memory, King George V requested that Will Gladstone's body be brought home to England, and he was buried in the Hawarden church that his grandparents had loved so dearly.

Gladstones went on a cruise to Norway on a friend's yacht. Among the majesty and serenity of the fiords, in contemplating the success that a small nation such as Norway had made of its autonomy (the Norwegians had not then managed to sever the final links with Swedish overlordship), Gladstone became even more certain in his mind that Irish Home Rule was both God's will and politically viable.

However, his certainty had not yet reached boiling point and the shoals round which he would have to manoeuvre if and when he came to his final conclusion were innumerable. After a brief visit to Fasque to attend the somewhat gloomy celebrations of his brother Tom's golden wedding anniversary, the Gladstones returned to Hawarden; there he had to decide whether or not to lead the Liberal party into the General Election which was now pending. Gladstone had already decided to recontest the Midlothian seat, which was a pointer in the direction of his not resigning the reins to Lord Hartington (Granville was now out of the running). Mary said the *real* crisis of the leadership occurred during the first fortnight of September, but whatever conscious doubts her father may have had, however many letters he may have written to his colleagues, the result was a foregone conclusion.

The Liberal party appeared to be splitting apart at the seams, with the Radicals and Whigs pulling in opposite directions on the stitching, and the only man who could still hold them together was Gladstone. Now more or less constantly at his side, his wife reinforced his belief that God had given him a mission to guide the people, help enact His will on earth and complete the healing of the Irish wounds. For much of 1885 Catherine was writing to Lucy about Ireland and the need for her husband to stay in, or return to, office: "Oh Lucy I am often longing to be together as the gigantic question unfolds more and more, the tremendous interest and the tremendous difficulties, you and I and Uncle William who all have the same feeling as to Ireland." Quite a few people commented on Catherine's increased influence on her husband; there was a joke going around that Gladstone should be made a Duke and Mrs. Gladstone should become Prime Minister, and Henry Ponsonby related a story to his wife of how Mrs. G. was supposed to keep her husband up to the mark by tying knots in his nightshirt "to remind him and her of things to speak about next morning . . . and he finds himself sometimes on rising entirely tied up."

On the question of the leadership Lucy Cavendish was *not* in agreement with her aunt—she thought the time had come for Uncle William to hand over to Lord Hartington—but many Liberals shared Catherine's view, notably Sir William Harcourt. When he told Catherine, "Nobody is caring about Ireland now—everybody is sick of it—why should he go for anything of the sort?" she replied tartly, "If you wish to keep him as the head to fight the election, *that* is not the line to take with him." By the middle of September Gladstone had decided that he would lead the party, at least into the election, and he put the finishing touches to his electoral manifesto with, as Mary noted, "uncommon care and thought," though his daughter also admitted that the manifesto did not exactly give the party "any wild cry with which to go to the country."

With uncommon care and thought Gladstone refrained from making any clear statement on Ireland, for he believed he could not commit himself or his divided party on the issue, at least not until he was certain what Parnell wanted, what the Conservatives might do and how far he could keep his own cohorts intact. But he proceeded to sound the ground, if in tangential fashion, and in September Lord Hartington told the Duchess of Manchester that he had received an alarming communication from Gladstone on the subject of Ireland which had prompted him to offer to visit Hawarden. In October 1885 there was a fairly steady stream of political visitors to Hawarden, including Joseph Chamberlain, whom Gladstone invited at his wife's suggestion. Chamberlain had been treated extremely tactlessly by Parnell over his Central Board Scheme for Irish devolution (and he was a bad enemy); he had also now enunciated his "Unauthorised Programme" which proposed sweeping social reforms in Britain and on which he thought the Liberal party should concentrate, so his interest in Irish Home Rule was, both politically and personally, at a low level. Catherine regarded Chamberlain with suspicion and not a little jealousy—she thought he was after her husband's job (which he was) and presented some threat because of his hold on the masses, at least in the Birmingham area. But in this instance she had the sense to realise that her husband in private conversation and on his home ground could be extraordinarily persuasive. One can only wish that she had intervened more in the relationship between Gladstone and his prickly ambitious lieutenant. But Gladstone did not take Chamberlain into his confidence—he felt, rightly as events matured, that Chamberlain was a fairly unscrupulous careerist and that his radicalism might prove to be skin-deep. Nevertheless there was a part of Chamberlain that could care about people and causes, and more encouragement and careful handling by Gladstone might have tipped the balance. As it was, the visit to Hawarden solved few of the political differences between the two men.

In November the Gladstones departed for the Midlothian election campaign, and Mary asked her cousin to imagine doing the thing for the *fourth* time, the same carriages, the same routes, the same people. Fortunately, there was the same enthusiasm and Gladstone was returned for Midlothian with a majority of 4,600 votes (the electorate had been considerably widened by the 1884 Franchise Act). The Gladstones were at Lord Rosebery's home at Dalmeny when the election results started to come in towards the end of November. Hannah Rosebery told Loulou Harcourt that "the depression and abject misery of Mrs. and Mary Gladstone at the returns of the borough elections as they arrived by telegram was past description." Lady Rosebery also told Loulou that Gladstone's Midlothian speeches were "wretchedly feeble" in 1885 and that his voice was "weak."

One suspects that this was sour grapes, as he made a markedly unfeeble speech in Edinburgh on the subject of Ireland, in which he emphasised the need for Home Rule (though without committing his party to it). When the Gladstones returned to Hawarden after their campaign, the love and affection they inspired among their employees and the villagers were demonstrated. The lights in the castle and the various outbuildings were lit (Gladstone might not have approved of that extravagance), the orphanage children were lined up in the yard and Auguste Schluter described how "the moon rose majestically to brighten the way of our dear veteran champion . . . Auld Lang Syne was sung when Mr and Mrs Gladstone and Miss Mary drove into the courtyard, they lookt [sic] so noble . . . then everybody sang Home Sweet Home."

The results of the election were that the Liberals had a majority of eighty-six over the Conservatives. But eighty-six Parnellites had also been returned to Westminster, so the Irish held an exact balance of power. The failure of the Liberals to win a decisive or landslide victory was attributed by many people to Parnell, not because of what had happened in Ireland—that had been expected after the Franchise Act—but because he had instructed the many Irish voters in Britain itself to vote against the Liberals (though modern historians have doubted how crucial Parnell's instructions were). The Irish leader's reason for issuing the "Vote Tory" orders was that he had been unable to obtain from Gladstone any clear commitment on Home Rule. Correctly gauging that the Liberals would win the election he decided that he must try to obtain a balance between the British parties with which he could force *one* of their hands.

With no over-all majority for either British party, Lord Salisbury's Government stayed in office. But Parnell again felt that it was a Liberal Ministry under Mr. Gladstone which was likely to introduce a Home Rule Bill, and the letters once more flowed between Mrs. O'Shea and the Grand Old Man (whom Parnell preferred to call the Grand Old Spider). Gladstone continued to emphasise to Mrs. O'Shea the difficulties he faced with a large heterogeneous party, unlike Mr. Parnell who had a small compact group with, at the moment, one clear aim. Gladstone was not in office and therefore was unable to introduce any legislation; and there was the problem of the Tory majority in the House of Lords, which would indubitably throw out a Home Rule Bill. With regard to the permanent Tory majority in the Lords, towards the end of December Gladstone had a fairly extraordinary conversation with Arthur Balfour, who happened to be staying near Hawarden at the Duke of Westminster's stately home, Eaton Hall, and who apart from having been one of Gladstone's favourite young men was also becoming the right-hand man of his uncle, Lord Salisbury. In the conversation Gladstone told Balfour that if Lord Salisbury would introduce a Home Rule Bill which he as the leader of the Conservative party could get through the Lords, Gladstone would pledge Liberal support. Balfour duly transmitted this astonishing offer of bipartisanship, but it was rejected because Lord Salisbury had no intention of granting Home Rule to Ireland.

On 17 December, when everything was in a state of flux and nobody was sure what anybody might do, least of all Mr. Gladstone, Herbert Gladstone released what became known as "the Hawarden Kite," a statement to the effect that his father now favoured Home Rule. What Herbert had been trying to do was to stop Joseph Chamberlain and his supporters from plotting against and ousting his father, for the Chamberlain group had been insisting that the Liberals must not adopt the Irish cause and drop social reform, nor must they accept office on the strength of Mr. Parnell's votes. They felt the best policy was to keep the Tories in office temporarily. But keeping the Tories in by implication meant keeping Mr. Gladstone out, and apart from being an ardent Home Ruler, Herbert was as keen as his mother to see the G.O.M. back in power. Accordingly he rushed down to London and had conversations with various people, including Wemyss Reid of the *Leeds Mercury* and the indefatigable Henry Labouchere.

"The Hawarden Kite" was first flown in the *Leeds Mercury,* as Reid too was intent on thwarting Chamberlain, keeping Mr. Gladstone in the lead and, to a lesser degree, furthering the cause of Home Rule. Herbert Gladstone plaintively and naïvely insisted that he had indulged in private conversations and his confidence had been betrayed (Eddy Hamilton had earlier noted that Herbert was "unfortunately very pig-headed and won't see the danger of being indiscreet. He won't submit to the penalties attaching to being a son of Mr G"). The general reaction was that Gladstone himself was behind "the Kite," but in fact he had not known in advance and would not have sanctioned it because it was a maladroit move which cast a large stone into a situation which he was trying to keep as placid as possible. After a qualified repudiation of the statement, Gladstone decided the best policy to be followed until Parliament reassembled in January 1886 was silence, and he stayed resolutely shut away at Hawarden.

At Hawarden, on Christmas Day, an event occurred which took Catherine and Gladstone—and Auguste Schluter—by surprise: Mary became engaged to a young curate named Henry Drew who had arrived at the Hawarden rectory two years previously. Everybody seems to have been curiously blind to the burgeoning romance, probably because Mary was by now thirty-eight years old and thus regarded as a confirmed if spirited spinster. Auguste Schluter wrote that Mary "tried all day to make me believe it . . . when I saw Mr. Drew (at the dance) I felt like a tigress wishing to throw herself upon the enemy . . . a burst of bitter tears was my answer." The reaction of Mary's parents was fortunately not so wild, and Catherine and Gladstone accepted the loss of the daughter who had for both of them become a prop with good grace and their blessings. The reaction to the engagement among their friends was mixed, partly because Harry Drew was eight years younger than Mary, partly because he was a comparative nobody and Mary was attractive, intelligent and the daughter of the Liberal leader. Eddy Hamilton said that it was a very *small* marriage for her; somewhat bitchily Loulou Harcourt noted, "Harry Drew . . . looks very ascetic. I wonder if he is so in his conduct! If he is I do not think he will satisfy Mary"; while more tactfully Lord Granville wrote to Catherine, "So remarkable a woman as Miss Gladstone is not likely to make a mistake on this point." Lord Granville was right. The marriage was an extremely happy one. Harry Drew had a strength of character and a sense of humour to match Mary's and they enabled him to emerge triumphantly from a position which could have submerged lesser men, that of husband to Mary Gladstone and son-in-law of the Grand Old Man and the Grande Dame—as Catherine had now been dubbed—and that of spending the first ten years of his married life at Hawarden Castle.

During the respite there was a steady stream of visitors to Hawarden, including Sir Henry Ponsonby's wife, Mary. She was another person who was able to resist the charm of Catherine's conversation and she told her husband, "We found Mrs G (of course) all gush." She also described how "We went into what they call the Temple of Peace, i.e. the library, on one side his political table, on the other his literary, which he said he greatly preferred. And, rather a touching sight, that terrible picture of the Queen with the bust of Pr Cons [i.e. Albert] in the middle of the room . . . The rule is, the first time you go into the room you may speak, but afterwards dead silence is enforced." Despite the slight acerbity which was part of the sophisticated Mary Ponsonby, she enjoyed her visit to Hawarden, as did virtually everybody who went there. Quite a few people went to Hawarden prepared to mock, or, like John Ruskin, dreading that they would be submerged in a sea of reverential piety. They emerged pleasantly surprised or even sometimes amazed by the informality, the absence of blanketing Christian piety and the lack of reverence which attended Gladstone within the family circle.

With the Liberal plots thickening, the tumultuous year of 1886 started. The Conservatives made it clear that their honeymoon with the Irish Nationalists was ended, announcing in the Queen's Speech that they thought a renewal of the Coercion Act in Ireland would be necessary, and five days later on 26 January making this a definite proposal. Gladstone immediately replied, saying that in the light of the Government's statement he was prepared to give the signal to go forward on Ireland; Loulou Harcourt commented that while the first half of this speech dragged, "the last half was one of the most brilliant displays of rhetoric I have ever heard. He seemed exhausted and needed the accustomed egg flip which Mrs G. always provides in a pomatum pot." Parnell then got in touch with Gladstone, via Katie O'Shea, to say he was willing to defeat the Tories, providing that Mr. Gladstone would form the next Liberal administration and that it would not be headed by the Hartington/Chamberlain joint front which seemed to be coalescing in opposition to Home Rule. Parnell suggested that it would be better to turn the Tories out on a general issue rather than on a specifically Irish one, and privately Gladstone agreed. At 1 A.M. in the morning of 27 January the Government was duly defeated on the issue of "three acres and a cow," the cry on which Chamberlain and his friend Jesse Collings had campaigned to improve the lot of the agricultural worker and which had not been mentioned in the Queen's Speech. As the count was taken in the division lobbies in the early hours of 27 January Loulou Harcourt recorded, "Never were victors less triumphant or vanquished less depressed."

One person who was fairly triumphant was Gladstone because he had finally made up his mind that the Liberal party under his leadership would charge into battle flying the banner of Home Rule for Ireland. There were many people who thought, or hoped, that he would not be able to form a Government behind such a banner; chief among them was obviously Queen Victoria. She had been deeply dismayed when Gladstone embarked upon yet another Midlothian campaign, and astounded when "the Hawarden Kite" was flown, but she was not seriously alarmed because her dear Lord Salisbury remained in office, and the likelihood of Gladstone's returning to power seemed to her remote. She told Henry Ponsonby that nobody believed in Home Rule, therefore Gladstone could not possibly fight on that issue; Ponsonby replied that the Parnellites did, to which Her Majesty responded that they did not represent the true feelings of the Irish (admittedly they did not represent the views of any Irishman Her Majesty knew, as her circle was restricted to Tory members of the Anglo-Irish Protestant ascendancy). Apart from her profound disbelief in Home Rule, Queen Victoria had recently been engaged in trying to further a pet scheme of hers, the formation of a coalition Government of the moderate men in both parties, either under the leadership of Lord Salisbury or Lord Hartington, but with the two men acting in close harmony. She had had many conversations on the subject with one of the few Liberals she liked, George Goschen, and he encouraged Her Majesty to believe that the party was tired of Gladstone, that should he go for Home Rule all but the faithful few would desert him and flock to Lord Hartington's side.

There is little doubt that if the leadership had then been offered to Hartington he would have accepted it gladly, and if he had taken a clear stand in opposition to Gladstone it is possible that a good number of Liberals would then have supported him. But Hartington lacked the will or drive to fight for the leadership, and as his hour struck more forcibly than in the 1870s he exhibited a curious lethargy and, for such an aristocratic figure, want of confidence. He told the Duchess of Manchester, "I don't think there would be the slightest chance of my being able to form a Government," and that Mr. G. should be given his chance over Home Rule, though if he failed—as he almost certainly would—*then* Lord Hartington might finally come into his own. However, Hartington decided he must take one stand, particularly as he had been known to have been at loggerheads with Gladstone and on the point of resignation so many times in the past, and so he declined to join an administration whose intention was to examine the possibility of Home Rule for Ireland. Gladstone tried to persuade Hartington to remain within the ranks, using Catherine as an intermediary as she had always got on well with his aloof, languid lordship. (She once prompted him into exclaiming that her eyes were as blue as her dress and on another occasion he actually kissed her on the cheek.) She told Lucy Cavendish, "I was sent to Devonshire House and had *armed* myself with a short note I had written to Lord Hartington. We waited at the door, out he came in a *genial* way not in one of his ——! . . . Oh may it please God that Uncle W might keep Lord H." But it was to no avail; Hartington adhered to his decision and Lucy herself lamented that her beloved husband was dead because she had "the feeling that Freddy would have drawn Uncle W and Hartington together as he had done before."

Gladstone's instinct that he could carry the majority of the leading members of the party with him was correct. Among those who agreed to examine the question of Home Rule was Sir William Harcourt, who was an important acquisition as he had a good deal of influence and had a previous reputation for being anti-Irish; Lord Spencer, the Liberal Irish Lord-Lieutenant who was henceforward known as "the Red Earl"—Queen Victoria was horrified to learn that "Lord Spencer of all people is a convert (*pervert* I think I ought to say) to Home Rule!"; Lord Rosebery; and, to most people's surprise, Joseph Chamberlain. A newcomer to the ministerial ranks who was offered and accepted the vital position of Irish Chief Secretary was John Morley, the man who became one of Gladstone's most devoted lieutenants, the close friend of his declining years and the author of the first major biography. In 1886 Morley was in his early forties, had already established a reputation as biographer, critic, essayist and exponent of philosophic radicalism and was regarded as a close associate of Joseph Chamberlain's, though in fact the friendship had begun to wear at the edges. In some ways it was a good appointment, as Morley was intelligent and favoured Home Rule, but in other ways it was not because he had no parliamentary experience (he had only recently been returned as an M.P.), he had a depressive strain and while he admired men of action, he was a man of ideas, happier and more able with the pen than the sword.

On 28 January, as Lord Salisbury tendered his resignation, Queen Victoria composed a memorandum in which she wailed, "What a dreadful thing to lose such a man as Lord Salisbury for the country—the World—and me!" But the next day she sent Sir Henry Ponsonby to invite Gladstone to form a Government. He arrived at Lucy Cavendish's house in Carlton House Terrace just as Gladstone was going to bed. However, the G.O.M. came downstairs and assured Ponsonby that he was willing to accept the Queen's invitation. Her Majesty accepted the inevitable with less anguish than usual, mainly because she was sure that Home Rule would be Gladstone's speedy and final undoing, partly because there was a crumb of comfort in Lord Rosebery's appointment as Foreign Secretary. On 1 February Gladstone travelled to Osborne to kiss hands with Her Majesty for the third time as her Prime Minister, and she noted, "Saw Mr G. before luncheon. He looked very pale when he first came in, & there was a momentary pause, & he sighed deeply . . . I remarked that he had undertaken a great deal."

He had *indeed,* but he went into battle with his formidable power and energy, and Reginald Brett commented that Mr. G. was positively revelling in the Home Rule problem, "plunging about in it, like a child in a tub." Alas, Gladstone's handling of Joseph Chamberlain *was* childish because he refused Chamberlain the office he wanted and then proceeded to cut the salary of his friend, Jesse Collings (who was more in need of that salary than most). There is the theory that Gladstone was leading up to the *coup de grâce,* that he recognised Chamberlain was an ambitious disruptive force and that the only question was—who went? he or Chamberlain? But Gladstone could have been more generous and tactful in his handling of Chamberlain and made a greater effort to retain and control him as he had in the past. Helen Gladstone expressed the family feeling in a letter to her brother Henry: "It's a marvellously exciting time . . . the anxiety at one moment as to forming a Government was rather terrific—right in the middle of the wedding time too—he is a splendid man and no mistake."

Mary's wedding was on 2 February 1886, on a lovely Candlemas Day at St. Margaret's Westminster. The service was conducted by Stephen Gladstone and it was on the whole a quiet family affair, though the Prince and Princess of Wales were among the guests and a large crowd gathered outside to cheer the new Prime Minister and his daughter (Gladstone had travelled overnight from his interview with the Queen at Osborne). Mary was determined that as a curate's wife she would live within her husband's income of £300 per annum; she started out as she meant to continue by having herself and her bridesmaids dressed in simple white muslin dresses (with material bought from the local Co-operative stores), carrying nosegays of snowdrops which she had arranged.

As Mary departed on her country honeymoon, her father faced his mammoth task, and the atmosphere was already extraordinarily bitter. Some of the bitterness was Gladstone's own fault because though he had sounded the ground to an extent among his high-ranking colleagues, he had lamentably failed to prepare the country at large for Home Rule. His conversion appeared to be the most dramatic since Saul was overcome by his vision on the road to Damascus, and there was a feeling of resentment and betrayal among many Liberal supporters. In all ranks of society, families split down the middle on the issue, and contemporaries who wrote of the period said it was virtually impossible for those not then alive to appreciate the tension, the bitterness and the passion which the question of Irish Home Rule aroused in Britain. Catherine had developed a high degree of imperviousness to attacks on her husband, a faculty for ignoring the hostility and fastening onto the acclamation, but even she was shattered when later in 1886 the Duke of Westminster took down from its position of honour at

Eaton Hall and flung into the cellar a Millais portrait of Gladstone which his family loved, as a mark of ducal anger over Home Rule and Mr. Gladstone's conduct. In 1887 Catherine wrote, "Oh can you believe it? We hear that the Duke of Westminster has sold father's beautiful picture . . . really I felt it so much it came like a shot!"

It was on 8 April 1886 that Gladstone actually introduced his Bill, which proposed a separate Parliament for the Irish in Dublin to deal with (nearly) all their internal affairs.† The ladies of the Gladstone family packed the Ladies' Gallery—Catherine, Mary, Helen, Agnes and Lucy Cavendish, who paid her first visit to the House of Commons since her husband's murder on this occasion which might lead to its vindication. Mary described how they drove through the torrential rain and cheering crowds and then listened to Gladstone: "For 3 and a half hours he spoke— the most quiet earnest pleading, explaining, analysing, showing a mastery of detail and a grip and grasp such as he had never surpassed. Not a sound was heard, not a cough even . . . a tremendous feat at his age." For the next two months the fate of the Bill hung in the balance, though Gladstone himself had from the earliest moment told Queen Victoria that it was 49 to 1 that he might fail. Lord Hartington had "bolted"; so had a group of M.P.s who followed him and became known as the Liberal Unionists; but though Joseph Chamberlain had resigned from the Cabinet when Gladstone had declared what everybody had known to be his intention—i.e. to introduce rather than to examine Home Rule—the former was still keeping his options open. If Chamberlain and his supporters could be persuaded to abstain rather than to vote against the Bill it could still pass its vital second reading. But on 13 May Sir William Harcourt, who was busily acting as an intermediary, warned Gladstone that he would be deluded if he thought Chamberlain had any ideas but "war to the knife." At the end of May hopes were further dashed when Chamberlain held a meeting of his supporters in Committee Room 15 of the House of Commons. At the meeting Chamberlain read out a letter from John Bright in which the latter said that he intended to vote against the Bill. This information was crucial, because if Bright, the veteran Radical, a long-time supporter of the Irish cause, was so unhappy about the Bill, and particularly the rights of the Protestant minority, that he could not abstain, then neither could Chamberlain's waverers. Bright was upset that his letter had been read out and said he had no intention of influencing anybody's vote, but the damage had been done.

The second reading occurred on 7 June. Gladstone still hoped he could win by a small majority but when the count was taken at 1 A.M. on the morning of 8 June, despite great oratorical efforts by both Parnell and Gladstone in which the latter urged the Commons, "Think, I beseech you, think well, think wisely, think, not for the moment, but for the years that

† The superstitious noted that on 8 April Big Ben suddenly stopped and the already famous, slightly cracked chimes failed to boom across Westminster.

are to come, before you reject this Bill," the result was defeat by thirty votes, with ninety-three Liberals voting against their party's measure. When the Cabinet met they agreed to an immediate dissolution and appeal to the country, for resignation would have implied a repudiation of the measure and Gladstone had now nailed the Liberal party colours to the mast of Home Rule. The ensuing General Election was fought in an at-mosphere quite as bitter and venomous as that which had enveloped the battle for the Bill; it was during its course that Lord Randolph Churchill launched a vitriolic but brilliant attack on Gladstone in which he called him "an old man in a hurry," a phrase which did much damage. Gladstone himself was unopposed at Midlothian so he rushed round other parts of Scotland and Lancashire, but while Catherine accompanied him to Lan-cashire she also indulged in a little campaigning in London on behalf of her young friend G. W. E. Russell. (Russell was a cadet member of the ducal Bedford family, a sometime parliamentary reporter, journalist and M.P. who was devoted to Catherine.)

Early in July both she and her husband were back at Hawarden but as the results started to come in, indicating that the Gladstonian Liberals were suffering a bad defeat, she was no assistance when her husband temporarily lost control of himself and fired a volley of ill-judged letters and telegrams from Hawarden. For once Queen Victoria had some justification for writ-ing to her daughter Vicky that he was "no longer the G.O.M. but really the wicked old man . . . For long I stood up for his motives, but now they are clearly actuated by vanity, ambition, malice & show signs of madness." On 17 July *The Times* launched an unprecedented attack on Gladstone in which it similarly accused him of being half mad, motivated by nothing but selfish ambition and lust for power, and of betraying the masses who had placed their faith in him. Even Mary (Gladstone) Drew was forced to admit in a letter to her cousin, "All those letters and telegrams from Ha-warden I think gave the whole world (and no wonder) a mistaken impres-sion as to his condition of mind. Nobody thinks more strongly than he does that it was a mistake writing those letters, but you see he had no Secre-taries, each was dashed off without reflection in the rush of the moment." By the time Gladstone returned to London he had calmed down and ac-cepted that the country was not, at the moment anyway, in favour of Home Rule, for 316 Tories and 74 Liberal Unionists had been returned, to overwhelm 83 Parnellites and 196 Gladstonian Liberals. When he had his final audience with Queen Victoria on 30 July—and this must be *the* final one, she thought—Gladstone was composed though looking pale and nerv-ous, according to Her Majesty, and they talked amicably on a variety of subjects. It may be noted that when Lord Salisbury arrived to kiss hands with the Queen and accept his second tenure of office as Prime Minister, he was looking "remarkably well."

Inevitably but too late in the day, Gladstone went into print to explain his reasons for espousing Home Rule; he likened Ireland to a ripened cornfield which if harvested would bring happiness and prosperity, but which if left unattended would lead to blight and disaster. It was a pretty, apt analogy, and it underlined Gladstone's own belief that he had shown his invaluable sense of right timing over Home Rule, but the pamphlet as a whole did little to explain his motives for the conversion, which had seemed so sudden. Was he the half madman lusting after power at any price who seized the Irish issue as one which could re-establish his supremacy over his party? Was he the brilliant political animal who realised that the party was breaking apart and needed an issue around which it could rally? Was he the "old man in a hurry" who wanted to depart from political life in a blaze of glory? Or was he prepared to sacrifice himself and his party for an issue which he accepted as morally right and politically in urgent need of resolution? The answers probably lie a little in each question but the offer to Lord Salisbury, via Arthur Balfour, of the bipartisan approach emphasises that Gladstone was too complicated a man and too devout a Christian to be solely lusting after power or manoeuvring against the internal opposition in the Liberal party; though his failure to draw up contingency plans to deal with the House of Lords should his Bill pass through the Commons—for everybody knew that the Lords would throw it out—indicates an element of unusual Gladstonian haste.

The whole Home Rule issue in 1886 consists of "on the one hand" and "on the other hand"—Catherine told Loulou Harcourt "that sooner than split the party he will make his bow and return to Hawarden," only a few weeks before her husband split the party. Apart from the damaging split, other results had emerged from Gladstone's abortive attempt to settle the Irish question in 1886. Home Rule had come to stay; there was no hope of a bipartisan approach, and Parnell had therefore lost his position as "the third party" and was committed to the Liberals. But it had also proved that at the age of seventy-six Gladstone could still work out a highly intricate piece of legislation at breakneck speed, still nearly get such an explosive measure through the Commons and command the support of the majority of the Liberal party. With such consolations he departed on a well-earned holiday in Germany.

Catherine did not accompany her husband, much as she wanted to, because her daughter Mary's health was already giving rise to some alarm. However, she did not tell her husband the real reason for concern, and much as Gladstone loved his children, Mary in particular, with old age he was becoming increasingly oblivious to their emotions or ailments until they were thrust under his nose. Thus he set off for Germany in a contented frame of mind to indulge in the intellectual delight of the companionship of Lord Acton and Dr. Döllinger. Mary's problem was both a joy and a worry: she had quickly become pregnant, but bearing her first child when she was in her thirty-ninth year was proving difficult. In mid-August Auguste Schluter wrote, "Mrs Drew expects the stork in due time but she is not very well and keeps to her bed," and a month later, on 24 September

1886, she recorded, "We have nearly lost my beloved lady . . . she gave birth to a wee boy 5½ months old." Whether this very premature child was stillborn or survived a few hours is unclear but after the birth Mary's condition weakened, Andrew Clark was summoned from London and on 7 October an emergency operation was performed at Hawarden Castle. For several days Mary's life hung in the balance but by 17 October the crisis had passed, though it was not until the New Year that she was sufficiently recovered to circulate again.

Before Gladstone went on his German visit and then returned home to face his daughter's illness, indeed as the election results were coming in and his political behaviour was at its most erratic, the final flare-up about his night-walking occurred. On 13 July 1886 Eddy Hamilton was again constrained to write a "most private" letter in which he warned Gladstone that certain people were setting spies on him and that there was "a conspiracy on foot to blacken your private character." Hamilton continued, "These calumnies, believe me, are not to be lightly disregarded. They have already been worked with baneful effect by canvassers in the metropolitan constituencies who have been traducing your private character. Some of your most devoted followers are greatly exercised in their minds." He finished by saying, "I will only add that I am told that your traducers have in their pay a certain woman prepared to support their calumnies." On 16 July Gladstone replied, "As I fear there does exist in the world the baseness you describe, I believe on the whole that what you say is true and wise, and I give you my promise accordingly. There are two cases, which I should have liked not to drop altogether, one of them particularly, where the person concerned had desired to get away and join friends in Australia. But it may be possible to do something in this, concomitantly with what I have written." One presumes that having given his *promise*, something Gladstone had never done before, he thereafter ceased accosting prostitutes on the streets, entering brothels or visiting their lodgings, though it is doubtful that he stopped writing to his many prostitute friends.‡

There is no further reference in Hamilton's diaries to the night-walking and the last time he became exercised on the subject was as Gladstone lay dying. At that moment Canon Malcolm McColl, who was a friend and admirer of Gladstone's and a popular Anglican figure, wanted to write an article about Mr. Gladstone and fallen women, and he consulted Eddy Hamilton. The reason he gave for wishing to write his article was that "the mind of many is still poisoned on the subject. Even his present illness has been attributed to his supposed irregularities . . . ," and McColl's aim was to clear Gladstone's name. But Hamilton was opposed to the idea perhaps be-

‡ Not all Gladstone's correspondence was with "fallen" women. In 1878 he received a sweet letter from a youngish woman which said, "I want to be rich, or rather I mean I am tired of being poor and unable to help myself or others," and that the lady had decided to write to Mr. Gladstone to beg his advice on how she could become rich because "there is nobody in the world I have such confidence in and such respectful love for as I have in and for you."

cause much as he respected and loved Mr. Gladstone he may have suspected that there was a more sexual side to the proclivity and he thought
that dragging up the issue, certainly in 1898 as Gladstone died, would not
change the minds of his traducers and might put unwelcome thoughts into
other minds. (One or two articles *were* written about Mr. Gladstone's work
with prostitutes but they stressed his high-mindedness.)

Thus one comes to the question why Gladstone's many enemies did not
use the information to destroy his political career. At the eleventh hour,
with presumably a sworn statement by a prostitute in their possession, the
enemies probably desisted because the 1886 election results produced such
a defeat for the Gladstonian Liberals. At the age of seventy-six, with his
party split, he could not possibly become Prime Minister again and must
soon slip into comparative oblivion, so *requiescat in pace*. But this does not
answer the question why the enemies failed to use the information between
1880 and 1886, when Gladstone was in power; when many of those enemies sincerely believed that he was leading the country on the road to ruin
and it was only he who held a reforming Liberal party together; when his
night-walking was so persistent and there must have been prostitutes and
ill-paid London policemen who would have been willing to swear what was
the truth—that Mr. Gladstone consorted frequently with "low women"
and actually entered brothels.

The reasons for the surprising lack of action seem to be varied and various. There were the respective characters of Lord Beaconsfield and Lord
Salisbury, for though they were unalike in temperament, any ambitious
politician or overzestful Tory who had dared to blacken Mr. Gladstone's
reputation by such unsavoury means would have received short shrift from
both of them. There was the general Victorian ambience, and while the
mood was beginning to change to a more vigorous appreciation of the realities of life, the idea of human perfectibility—notably in sexual mores—still
predominated. A great many Victorians were in fact aware that the flesh
was weak, and in an effort to protect the image of marital bliss and sexual
constancy, a conspiracy of silence arose. Anybody who breached the wall of
silence had to be unscrupulous, morally courageous or subjected to the
final straw that broke the camel's back. Then again, there could have been
an element of doubt in the enemy minds. They had concrete evidence, yet
Gladstone was so open about his activities, and the mutual love, trust and
confidence of him and his wife was known to all. If the enemy had moved
was there not the faint possibility that the great orator—imagine Gladstone
in open court defending his reputation—and great Christian might explain
everything away and emerge victorious?

On balance it was fortunate for Gladstone and, as Queen Victoria would
not have added, for the country and the world that the information was
not made public. Some mud would surely have stuck, too many people
would have queried the root of his motives, and though Gladstone's solution to the dilemma of his strong sexuality had worked, the association with

prostitutes was a peculiar activity. In particular the entry into brothels was odd and suspect, and if Gladstone convinced himself that he was Daniel entering the lions' den or that in following his friends into their place of work he was attempting to save them from rapacious brothel owners, he probably also obtained some voyeur's satisfaction. Two of the nicknames by which he was known in the 1880s perhaps sum up the ambivalence of his motives, while reinforcing the belief that his Christian conscience overcame his vigorous desires, for they were "Daddy-do-nothing" and "Old Glad-eyes."

His association with prostitutes was only a part of the many-compartmented Mr. Gladstone; but more important were the love and affection he inspired in so many people. These were shown in a letter Catherine wrote to him two days before their wedding anniversary in 1886: "We are away from each other but not in spirit . . . Thank you for all you have done, for all you are and for the lovely example you have been to me in sorrow or in joy! And Almighty God strengthen and help you more and more and lift you up *continually* . . . Darling old thing, I long to give you such a kiss. We are just going to church and the best thing of all will be to pray for you and to thank God for the extraordinary mercies which for 47 years have been given to us, Till tomorrow, Your loving Wifie."

CHAPTER 18

AN INDIAN SUMMER

IN THE YEARS FOLLOWING Gladstone's brief third Ministry he and Catherine lived through an Indian summer of unexpected warmth and vitality. For both of them the question of retirement was settled; Gladstone could not relinquish the leadership after the Home Rule declaration, he must continue the fight until there was once again, as there had been until the Act of Union in 1801, an Irish Parliament on College Green, Dublin. Much of Catherine's time was as usual devoted to her charitable concerns and to raising funds for them. Once anybody made a contribution to one of Mrs. Gladstone's charities, unless he or she was very strong or measly-minded, there was no escape, as Sir Henry James wryly noted to Lord Hartington: "Mrs G has £100 out of me for some charity—claiming to maintain such friendly relations." The reason for his wryness was that "Mrs G" got the £100 out of him after the Home Rule split in which Sir Henry joined the Liberal Unionists. Political affiliations had no relevance for Catherine as far as her charities were concerned.

In 1887 Catherine rushed into another activity, and "rushed" is the correct verb as she originally went in the wrong direction without pausing to confirm her facts. By 1887 a Women's Liberal Federation was being inaugurated to weld into a potent body the various Women's Liberal associations which had formed in the last few years. Its aim was to promote Liberal principles among women of all classes, and while it was an indication of the growing political interest and activity of women as women, as opposed to women as men's helpmates, it did not include female suffrage among its objectives. Gladstone had opposed the various attempts to introduce Bills or amendments for female suffrage, including one to his 1884 Franchise Act (for which he received Queen Victoria's congratulations). Mary Gladstone was an advocate of votes for women and she tried hard to convert her father, but while he agreed that he now had little objection in principle, in practice he thought the measure might be difficult to implement and harmful to women. Catherine had no clear ideas about women's suffrage, though she tended towards her husband's view and thought women could exert their influence without directly soiling their hands. But she believed in activity as well as influence, and when she was invited to become the first president of the new Women's Liberal Federation she agreed.

Everything was set for the grand inaugural meeting to be attended by the famous Mrs. Gladstone, when the ladies who had been organising the Federation suddenly to their horror read in the newspaper that Mrs. Gladstone had graciously consented to become the president of the Liberal League of Great Britain, which was an entirely different organisation. The explanation was simple; Catherine *had* agreed to become president of the small one-man band (and the Liberal League was led by a man), but under the erroneous impression that she was confirming the first invitation from the Federation. Her casual muddling led to a great deal of embarrassment all round and eventually a notice had to be issued to the effect not that Mrs. Gladstone had accepted the wrong presidency and joined the wrong society, but that there had been an inadvertent clerical error somewhere along the line by someone unnamed.

At the age of seventy-five Catherine embarked upon her political career as the president of the Women's Liberal Federation, attending the correct inaugural meeting in February 1887. Her presidency added immense prestige to the organisation, and one of the male sympathisers said at a meeting in 1889, "Mrs Gladstone was no ornamental president" (he then hastily corrected himself, "Of course I meant to say, not merely an ornamental president"). But in truth, though Catherine worked diligently for the cause and in her seventies went round addressing Federation meetings and opening functions, she was not very good at the job. She was accustomed to mass meetings and monster demonstrations of enthusiasm, she was brilliant at smiling and bowing and chatting to people individually and, as her daughter Mary would have said, standing on her hind legs all day during her husband's campaign. But she herself was no orator—nobody beyond the first few rows of her audience could hear a word she said—and she had no idea how to control a meeting if somebody raised points of order or it threatened to become rowdy. Nevertheless everybody admired her pluck and her stamina; she was still a joy to behold, erect, silver-haired and incredibly youthful-looking for her years. Despite her deficiencies, as president of the Women's Liberal Federation Catherine was considerably more of an asset than a liability.

While Catherine laid her oratorical emphasis, for those who could hear it, upon the need to settle the Irish question, her husband continued to do the same in speeches up and down the country. The majority of people in Britain were, as Sir William Harcourt reiterated, heartily sick of Ireland, and there was the suggestion that Ireland be cut loose from its moorings and left to float across the Atlantic where the Irish-Americans and American sympathisers who had all the answers could take the problem to their bosoms. The joke underlined the general British weariness or anger on the subject after the burst of passion in 1886, but Home Rule was now the core of the Gladstonian Liberal policy. Some Liberals protested that it was diverting attention from the growing number of problems in Britain but the majority accepted Gladstone's argument that no real progress could be made in any area until Home Rule had been settled. In support of this argument the manner in which the Irish problem had interfered with Gladstone's 1880–85 Ministry was cited.

The Gladstonian thesis was given further weight by the way in which Irish affairs intruded on Lord Salisbury's second Ministry. During the General Election Lord Salisbury had announced that he would subject Ireland to twenty years of resolute government which would settle the problem; but his plans were long-term and the immediate pressing problems were the unresolved questions of evictions and rent arrears. When the Conservatives rejected a proposal of Parnell's at the end of 1886, the Irish embarked upon the Plan of Campaign, which was an amalgam of the principles of "boycotting" (first introduced during the 1880 Irish Land War) and trades union collective bargaining and solidarity. In some areas the concerted Plan against the landlords worked well, but in many others, as the Irish peasants were not noted for their disciplined solidarity, it led to violent disorder. The reaction of Lord Salisbury's Cabinet was to appoint a new Irish Chief Secretary and then to introduce a particularly fierce Coercion Bill which had the novel feature of being open-ended (all previous Coercion Acts had had a strict time limit, until the temporary troubles were over).

The new Chief Secretary was the Gladstones' friend from happier days, Arthur Balfour, who was then known as "Clara" or "pretty boy Balfour." But "pretty boy Balfour" proved to be virtually the only English politician to emerge from the Irish bog with his reputation enhanced, at least in England—in Ireland he was soon known as "Bloody Balfour." As the new Chief Secretary introduced the Coercion Bill to Parliament in March 1887, *The Times* launched its attack on Parnell and Parnellism. Under the editorship of G. E. Buckle *The Times* had abandoned its policy of supporting the Government of the day and had become fiercely Tory and even more fiercely anti-Gladstone. The aim of Buckle's attack was to convince the country and the world outside that the Conservative policy was right and justified, by blasting Parnell's reputation and thereby that of Gladstone, who had recently supported him and Home Rule. Lurid article followed lurid article accusing Parnell and his followers of being vicious revolutionaries backed by American Fenian money, bullets and dynamite. The *pièce de résistance* appeared in April 1887 when *The Times* printed the facsimile of a letter supposedly written by Parnell in which he said that publicly he had to condemn the Phoenix Park murders but privately he thought that Mr. Burke had received no more than he deserved (though he regretted the murder of Lord Frederick Cavendish). Parnell made a brief statement in the House of Commons saying the content of the letter was ridiculous and the whole thing a forgery, but otherwise he took no action and the revelations in conjunction with his silence caused a slump in the British support for Home Rule and thereby in the Liberal stock. The temperature changed in September 1877 when the Irish police fired on a crowd in Mitchelstown and killed three demonstrators. In a speech at Nottingham Gladstone showed that he had lost none of his oratorical ability when he urged his audience to "Remember Mitchelstown" as they considered the respective merits of prolonged bloody coercion or granting Home Rule. British public opinion tended to go up and down like a yo-yo as stories of Irish and British violence were printed. In the intervals there was a distinct lack of interest, and even the magic of Gladstone's oratory failed to endow the issue with the fervour which had characterised the Bulgarian campaign.

In 1887 there was also a major attempt to heal the split in the Liberal ranks but nothing came of the negotiations and the result was to place Joseph Chamberlain and Lord Hartington more firmly in the Liberal Unionist party, which then drifted further towards the Conservatives. Gladstone was not unduly perturbed, for as Lord Rosebery wrote in August 1887, "The defects of his strength grow on him. All black is very black, all white is very white." Politically Catherine had always tended to think in blacks and whites, and more people were commenting upon her increased influence on her husband. In addition the Gladstones were now living not a secluded life—they both still travelled a good deal and had their multifarious activities—but an enclosed one, surrounded by devoted children and friends. Mary and Harry Drew lived at Hawarden Castle, Stephen and his family at the rectory, Willie and his family at the other end of the village, while both Herbert and Henry spent a fair amount of time at Hawarden. All the children loved and admired their parents, and together with their mother they regarded part of their affectionate duty as protecting Gladstone from the minor irritations of life which others saw as the realities. Few of Gladstone's colleagues ventured to contradict him to his face; by now they were mostly years younger than he, and the contemporaries who had been able to argue with him were spent forces (John Bright died in 1889, Lord Granville in 1891).

If his everyday life was partially enclosed, Gladstone's mind was as wide-ranging as ever; he read voraciously, the *Iliad* for "the twenty-fifth or thirtieth time, and every time richer and more glorious than before," but he also kept up-to-date with contemporary literature and held forth in person and in print on a diversity of subjects. One subject which was particularly exercising his mind at this time was the question of "unbelief," and he argued passionately that the rationalists' attempt to separate Christian morality from Christian dogma was fatal and would lead to despair—"It is still required of us to fly, and to fly as high as ever; but it is to fly without wings."

When they were in London the Gladstones now spent most of their time at a villa in Dollis Hill loaned to them by Lord and Lady Aberdeen. Dollis Hill was then in the country north of London and was highly inaccessible, but the Gladstones loved the place and gave little thought to the problems created for their colleagues and friends by the remoteness, mainly because it caused them no difficulty. Eddy Hamilton related the story of the Gladstones' carriage surrendering to a pea-soup London fog late one night in Hyde Park, whereupon the elderly couple had to walk to a temporary lodging, but his comment was that nobody else but they would have dreamed of attempting the five-mile drive to Dollis Hill late at night in an open carriage in midwinter in a thick fog. During 1887 the Gladstones were invited briefly to Osborne and to attend some of the celebrations for Queen Victoria's Golden Jubilee year, though they owed their invitations largely to Lord Salisbury, who wrote to Her Majesty thus: "Lord Salisbury still thinks it would be a gracious act, and tending to allay the bitterness of feeling which exists, if Your Majesty were to include Mr Gladstone in Your Majesty's invitations. He is so famous a man that many people would be shocked by any neglect of him, even where they differ from him."

August 1887 witnessed a scandal which briefly rocked London society when Laura Thistlethwayte's husband shot himself—or at least, he was found dead at his home in Grosvenor Square with a revolver by his side. This event caused some ripples to flow from the gossips in Gladstone's direction because though he had promised Eddy Hamilton that he would cease his night-walking, he had not been asked for and had given no such promise with regard to the professional beauties. His friendship with Laura Thistlethwayte continued unabated and on 15 August 1887 Gladstone received a longish letter from a Mrs. Helen Agar on the subject of "the fatal accident." In the letter, on behalf of "dearest Laura," Mrs. Agar begged Gladstone "to be careful what news you receive about the matter from people who know nothing," and informed him that Laura was "bearing up through the nightly grace of God in revealing to her that her husband is at rest with his saviour whom he loved."

Gladstone also maintained his links with Lillie Langtry, though they were growing more tenuous; in April 1890 she wrote to tell him that she had just opened in *Antony and Cleopatra* at the Princess Theatre, Oxford, ". . . and I cannot tell you how grateful I should feel if Mrs G and yourself would honour me by coming one evening. It is so difficult to get Shakespeare a hearing these days and I feel that with your kind heart and for old acquaintance sake you will help me. *Please do* and let me know which evening I may have the honour of sending you a box. Yours very truly, Lillie Langtry." There is no available record showing whether Gladstone and/or "Mrs G" accepted this invitation but Mrs. Langtry, who was not the world's greatest actress and received some extremely adverse reviews for her performance in one of the most demanding female roles in the English drama, managed to get a reasonable hearing for Shakespeare on the strength of her reputation. As a postscript to 1887, which was for both Gladstones one of the more contented and happy years of their lives, there is a nice story told by one of Mary (Gladstone) Drew's many correspondents, Sir Arthur Gordon. In 1887 Gordon was in Burma, and he was being conducted round a

Buddhist monastery when he was asked if he would like to examine one of the Buddha's bones. He replied "Yes" and the bone was being stripped of its wrapping when, as Sir Arthur recounted, "Behold we came suddenly on a whole layer of red cotton Manchester handkerchiefs, each adorned with a well-known portrait of the G.O.M.!"

By the middle of 1888 Ireland was back at the centre of the stage, though the matter began calmly and obliquely when Frank Hugh O'Donnell, a veteran of the pre-Parnell days of Home Rule, sued *The Times* for libel against himself contained in its "Parnellism and Crime" articles. The action came to court in July 1888 and *The Times* seized the opportunity to produce more damaging letters allegedly written by Parnell, in one of which in particular he appeared not only to have condoned the Phoenix Park murders but to have been implicated in them. This time Parnell responded to the serious allegations, demanding that a Select Committee be set up to enquire into the matter of the letters and the libels against his reputation. As a Member of Parliament he was entitled to a Select Committee but many Conservatives, including Lord Salisbury, had prejudged the issue, refusing to believe that so august and reputable a paper as *The Times* would have produced and published such letters without first checking their absolute authenticity. The Government thought the occasion presented them with a justified and splendid opportunity to examine publicly the whole range of matters raised by *The Times* in its original articles and in court. Thereby, it was believed, Parnell and Home Rule would be finally discredited and the Conservatives would be able to pursue their Irish policy without interruption. A Bill was introduced which empowered the Government to set up a Special Commission to enquire into the charges laid against Parnell and other Irish leaders, or as was said, to put the Irish nation on trial. Although Gladstone made one of his impassioned speeches against the Bill, it duly became law.

The proceedings of the Special Commission opened in the Number One Court of the Royal Courts of Justice in September 1888 and after an adjournment it soon became apparent that *The Times* and the Government were intent on the most thorough examination of Irish "crimes," and that the Irish were fighting back with equal thoroughness. Repetitive and frequently boring witnesses followed day by day, and interest in the Special Commission became dependent on who was on the stand. Captain William Henry O'Shea, for example, was an early witness who attracted attention because he was known in limited circles to be the husband of Parnell's mistress and in wider ones as an erstwhile friend and colleague of the Irish leader's. When O'Shea swore that the signature on *The Times*-produced letters appeared to be genuine, there was considerable satisfaction in Government circles. However, O'Shea's and other damaging evidence did not produce too much apprehension in some Irish Nationalist and Liberal circles because they knew for an almost 100 per cent certainty that the letters were forgeries and who had forged them. The indefatigable Henry Labou-

chere, among others, was on the trail and in October 1888 he wrote to tell
Mr. Gladstone that one Richard Pigott, an ex-Irish Nationalist, sponger
and pornographer, had privately confessed that he had forged the letters.
"Labby" said he did not think they would get anything more concrete from
Pigott at the moment so the proceedings would have to take their course.

It continued to be a very slow course, though Catherine was among
those who were fascinated by the proceedings; she had her special seat just
below the jury box, into which she slipped for some part of the day whenever she was in London. When Mary came to London on one of her now
infrequent visits, she too was an enthralled audience to the Special Commission hearings, and she was in court when the matter of the actual letters
was finally reached in February 1889. How they had come into *The Times'*
possession was discussed in detail—it may be noted that Reginald Brett and
W. T. Stead recorded being offered the letters as early as 1886—and it
proved a very shaky chain. A well-known Irish Loyalist journalist had
purchased them on behalf of *The Times* in a series of cloak-and-dagger
meetings with Richard Pigott in Paris but neither the Irish Loyalist nor the
Times management had bothered to ascertain how they reached Mr. Pigott's hands. When Richard Pigott himself took the stand, his cross-examination by Sir Charles Russell (an eminent Anglo-Irish Nationalist barrister) was, as Mary recorded, "a marvel of smashing." The bait which
trapped Pigott was the spelling of the word "hesitancy" which he spelled
"hesitency" as in the 1882 Kilmainham letter allegedly written by Parnell.
Pigott's cross-examination was unfinished when the court adjourned for the
weekend, but on the following Monday morning he was not in the witness
box to resume his evidence, and Sir Charles Russell was able to tell the
court and the listening world that Pigott had fled the country, leaving
behind him a confession that he had forged the letters. A week later, at the
beginning of March, the news arrived that utterly demolished *The Times*
and the Government case, as Mary again recorded graphically, "Pigott is
dead, shot himself on his arrest in Madrid. What a drama!"

The proceedings in fact continued for several more months and the final
official verdict was not delivered until February 1890; it was that while the
evidence exonerated Parnell completely from the charges that he had been
involved in or had condoned the Phoenix Park murders, it did not entirely
absolve either him or his followers from some of the charges of incitement
to violence and illegality that had been laid against them. But as far as the
public was concerned Parnell had been exonerated in March 1889, and
few people cared about the other charges. As a result of Pigott's confession
and suicide, Parnell had been shown to be the victim of a vile plot, and
though nobody openly accused *The Times* or the Government of having
been parties to the plot, or having known that the letters were forgeries, it
was felt that both the newspaper and the Conservative leaders had descended to a low and ineptly handled level in their efforts to discredit Parnell and Home Rule.

Overnight the Irish leader became the great British hero—a position he regarded with considerable scepticism—given a standing ovation in the House of Commons, offered the freedoms of cities, showered with invitations to functions and dinner parties. Most of the invitations were refused, but one Parnell accepted was to attend a *soirée* held by the Women's Liberal Federation on 25 May 1889. Gladstone, as well as his wife the president, was present at this annual jamboree and it was recorded that "a flutter of excitement" ran through the hall of the Grosvenor Gallery as Mr. Parnell entered—apart from his new role as hero, he was a good-looking man. On the platform there was "a historic handshake" between the Liberal and the Irish leaders, and for a while "the two statesmen were engaged in earnest conversation behind Mr Gladstone's opera hat."

The vindication of Parnell had opened the road to Home Rule, to the consummation of his and Gladstone's dream with a strong mandate of popular approval. But consummation in politics is usually a slow affair, both Gladstone and Parnell were canny politicians, a great deal of opposition remained to be overcome and the details had to be agreed upon of a new Home Rule Bill which would be satisfactory to both sides; whether or not the Irish M.P.s should remain at Westminster was a particularly thorny question. Eventually, in December 1889, Parnell accepted Gladstone's invitation to visit Hawarden. The two men spent the first evening after dinner enclosed in the Temple of Peace; the next day they again engaged in earnest conversation as Gladstone showed the Irish leader the ruins of the ancient castle and walked him through the gardens. No spectacular result emerged but Gladstone wrote his customary memorandum on the discussions, noted that they had been eminently satisfactory and that he and Parnell had agreed on many issues, including the subject of the Irish M.P.s at Westminster, which should be played by ear. Parnell proceeded to Liverpool, in which city he made a speech which was, by his cool standards, fulsome in its praise of Mr. Gladstone and his devotion to Home Rule.

Personally 1889 was a year of celebration for the Gladstones, as it marked both the fiftieth anniversary of their wedding and Gladstone's eightieth birthday. On 25 July the couple were literally inundated with letters, telegrams and presents from the high and the low all over the world (some of the golden wedding presents are still stacked in the cellars at Hawarden). The actual day was spent not at their beloved Hawarden but in London, as Parliament was still in session; but Lord and Lady Aberdeen laid a special golden wedding breakfast at the house at Dollis Hill, with sprigs of orange blossom on each guest's plate, and a Millais portrait of Gladstone and his grandson Will, which had been commissioned by the Liberal Women of Great Britain, was unveiled. Mary recorded the return to Hawarden on 3 August: "The arrival of the Golden Ones was most touching and overwhelming, the feeling so deep. Village all decked with flags and arches, procession, bands, carriage dragged and arriving in front of Castle about 6. Lovely speech made many cry. Evening fireworks." The only jarring notes were a chilly telegram from Queen Victoria which merely congratulated the Gladstones on this their golden wedding day, and Her Majesty's refusal to accept Catherine's invitation to visit Hawarden while she was in north Wales. Catherine and Gladstone were deeply hurt by the refusal—surely the Queen could have spared a few hours to visit the home of the man who had served her loyally for fifty years and the wife whose friendship she professed?

The indomitable pair engaged in a fair amount of travelling themselves in 1889. At the beginning of the year they were in Naples, not returning home until the middle of February, and during September they visited Paris, where Gladstone ascended the newly constructed Eiffel Tower. He sent Mary a postcard on which he wrote that he had been "foolish enough to be inveighed into mounting to this height . . . Poor Mama who would thoroughly have enjoyed it . . . out of sorts." The only real shadow in 1889 was Willie Gladstone's health; in the summer of 1888 he had experienced several minor attacks of giddiness and numbness in one hand but at the beginning of March 1889 he suffered from severe paroxysms which left his right side paralysed and his speech slurred. There were several days of immense anxiety—though the news of the attack was kept from his parents, who were in London, until after Gladstone had made an important speech in the House of Commons—but Willie seemed to recover, his mind was unimpaired and it was thought it might have been a form of epilepsy.

The worry about Willie was counterbalanced by two happy events, the first of which was Henry's marriage in January 1890 to Maud Rendel. Henry had been engaged before in 1884, but it had been broken off by the lady. The family was delighted that this time the engagement should come to fruition and by the choice of the bride, who was the daughter of Stuart Rendel, an arms manufacturer and Liberal M.P. who had by now become a close friend of the Gladstones'. The other happy news was that Mary was again pregnant and appeared to be carrying the child satisfactorily. On 9 February 1890 Auguste Schluter noted that everybody was "anxiously awaiting the arrival of the stork," and on 11 March 1890, at the age of forty-two, Mary was safely delivered of a healthy baby girl who was christened Dorothy but known to the family as "Dossie." She grew into a sturdy child with a mass of photogenic golden curls, and the photographers had a splendid time producing pictures of the Grand Old Man and his dear little granddaughter—wisdom and innocence—which the public bought by the thousand. In November 1890 Fräulein Schluter returned to Hanover to look after her aged mother. She had been in the Gladstones' service for twenty-two years and she noted that "when I went to say Goodbye he and Mrs Gladstone were love itself." She left with a charming letter of recommendation from her sincere friend and well-wisher, W. E. Gladstone.

By 1890 "the Octagon" had been built on to Hawarden Castle. It was a strongroom to contain the mass of Gladstone's important or still secret political papers, and the family enjoyed themselves composing titles for the false spines of the books which lined the hidden entrance door; one example of the jokey titles is *An Israelite of Guile* by "Ben Disraeli." At the beginning of the year Gladstone was engaged in the monumental task of removing 27,000 of his books from the castle to two large iron rooms which had been constructed on the brow of Hawarden hill. The reason for the removal was, as Mary said, because the books were beginning to invade every part of the house like the rats in Hamelin town, and also because a vague idea was beginning to formulate at the back of Gladstone's mind as to the best use to which his vast personal library could be put. He carried thousands of the books up the hill by hand, and the further task of sorting and trying to catalogue them was conducted by him, with the occasional assistance of Helen when she was home from Cambridge.

Among the books which remained permanently by his side there was of course his Bible—in which he inscribed the births of all his children—and those written by the four men who he said had been his greatest teachers: Aristotle, St. Augustine, Dante and Bishop Butler. The last, an eighteenth-century English theologian, was always a curious choice because though he was better-known in the nineteenth century than he is today, Bishop Butler was not ranked amongst the greatest of the world's minds. But his appeal to Gladstone was understandable, as Butler's writings were immensely qualified: he too was accused of facing both ways in his search to find the meaning of things as they really were and not as they seemed or were assumed to be. Gladstone was being precise in his use of words when he said these four men had taught him more than any others—not necessarily given him the most pleasure. His choice of the world's greatest poets included Homer, Shakespeare and Dante, and possibly Goethe.

By 1890 it seemed to some close observers that Gladstone's remarkable Indian summer, during which he had displayed more vitality and enthusiasm than colleagues half his age, was drawing to its end (though nobody said the same of Catherine's). In January Lord Rosebery noted, "Mr G. changed: still wonderful but changed—walks like an old man . . . lost I think his quick snap of apprehension." However, not everybody knew Gladstone as well as Lord Rosebery did (or agreed with his opinion). At the end of January Gladstone paid his last major visit to Oxford as a guest of All Souls, of which august institution he was an honorary Fellow, and a young man who was then an undergraduate later recorded his impressions of Gladstone. They were that physically he was much taller than had been expected, that his face was extremely mobile—more so than his portraits indicated—and that his remarkable eyes were a grey-blue colour. In general conversation Gladstone did most of the talking but he did not appear to monopolise it, his manner was courteous, he had a charming habit of drawing the young or more diffident into the talk but he was also very good at ending any topic he did not wish to pursue. The young observer said, "One began to realise how much 'personal magnetism' and social skill had to do with the holding together of a miscellaneous political party in Parliament";

and he also commented that Gladstone had a strong Lancashire accent. The extant recording of Gladstone's voice which was made at the request of "Dear Mr Edison" sounded to this author's Lancastrian ear unaccented; but in 1890 it may have seemed Lancastrian because it did not possess the tight, clipped, strangulated vowel sounds which were then the common currency of the upper-class English accent. The undergraduate further commented on Catherine's arrival in Oxford for the last few days of her husband's visit and said, "We thought Mr G. somewhat resented this intrusion of the domestic," and that later Gladstone himself said of the arrival, "Yes, and I must tell you it is entirely without my countenance." At the age of eighty-one the Grand Old Man still occasionally liked to be *en garçon*, as his daughter had noted a decade earlier. Catherine's stated reason for her descent on Oxford was that she wished to ensure that her husband did not overexert himself, but one suspects that at the age of seventy-nine she also had no wish to miss the fun and activity.

Lucy Cavendish did not share Lord Rosebery's view that her uncle had lost his quick snap of apprehension and in the autumn of 1890 she described a long conversation with him at Dollis Hill. She said that he was in the finest force and spirits, that he entertained her with stories of his "old political chums and colleagues" and a discourse on Parnell, who he thought had brought the Irish question "to the astonishingly good position it now holds *by his constitutional action.*" But throughout 1890 the shadows were lengthening, personally and politically. The personal shadows were caused by the deterioration of Willie Gladstone's condition; he continued to have seizures, though none as serious as the one in 1889, but each attack left his speech slightly more slurred and his right side more paralysed. However, at the end of the year there appeared to be some improvement and Catherine wrote to Lucy, "My precious Willy at church for the whole service and none the worse."*

While Catherine was optimistic about her eldest son's health, the political shadows had blackened to an extent that brought the astonishingly good Irish position to one of near-disaster. Captain William Henry O'Shea had in fact filed suit against his wife for divorce, citing Charles Stewart Parnell as the co-respondent, at the end of 1889, but it was nearly a year before the case came into court and in the lengthy interval there had been a particularly high wall of Victorian silence about the possible outcome and implications. The suit was eventually heard on 15 November 1890 in Number One Court of the Royal Courts of Justice, the same court from which Parnell had emerged as the great British hero after the Pigott disclosures. But this time, after only two days, the Irish leader's reputation *was* shattered. The suit was undefended by him and Mrs. O'Shea, and she had entered countercharges against her husband which allowed even more damaging evidence to be introduced. With silence from both the respondent and the

---

* Members of the family now spelled the eldest son's name "Willy," but as it was originally more often spelled "Willie" I have adhered to that.

co-respondent, with witnesses being allowed to be called in refutation of Mrs. O'Shea's countercharges, with Captain O'Shea swearing on oath that he had no knowledge of the adultery until just before he filed his petition, the evidence against Parnell and his mistress appeared overwhelming and pitch-black. The judge had no hesitation in granting a decree nisi.

All the opponents of Parnell and Home Rule (notably *The Times*) enjoyed their hour of triumphant vindication, with considerable justification, it appeared, because the divorce court evidence had revealed Parnell as a treacherous, deceitful rogue. The Liberals were in a miserable situation but argued that the disgrace of one man did not invalidate the concept of Home Rule, while temporarily the Irish were suspended in disbelief, with the mass instinct being to rally round their leader. Gladstone's initial reaction has often been quoted as recorded by Mary, "It'll nae do," but he also told Lucy Cavendish that for the Irish to renounce Parnell would be like Catholics renouncing the Pope, and he remained tolerant and uncensorious about moral transgressions. Unfortunately, Parnell's lapse was not a private affair, it was a public one which threatened Home Rule, and circumstance precipitated action because the annual assembly of the National Liberal Federation was held within a few days of the divorce case and the Irish were due to re-elect their parliamentary leader for the new session. The feeling expressed at the Liberal assembly, then at countless meetings and in the correspondence which flowed upon Gladstone, was that while the grass-roots membership of the Liberal party supported him and Home Rule, it could not continue to do so if Mr. Parnell remained as the Irish leader. It was at this moment that the phrase "the Nonconformist conscience" was coined, and the Nonconformists were now the backbone of the Liberal party.

Initially, Gladstone acted with tact and consideration for Irish pride and the immense problems which faced them; his hope was that Parnell would tender his resignation—as he had after the Phoenix Park murders—which in this instance would be accepted, at least until the storm blew over. When Parnell showed no signs of resigning voluntarily, Gladstone left the comfort of Hawarden to have conclaves with his Liberal colleagues in London, then one with Justin McCarthy (the Irish party's vice-chairman), and he also wrote a letter to Parnell. In this, somewhat reluctantly and under pressure from his colleagues, he said that *his* leadership would be rendered a nullity if, in the present circumstances, Parnell retained *his*. By accident or design, Parnell failed to receive the vital message, the Irish party as a whole was not informed and on 25 November it re-elected Parnell as its leader. When Gladstone learned this news, his passion erupted in one of its volcanic outbursts and he made public his "nullity" letter, whereupon there was a violent schism in the Irish ranks and the battle of Committee Room 15 began, ending with the majority of the Nationalists rejecting Parnell's leadership. With horrible irony, Committee Room 15 of the House of Commons, which was now used by the Irish party to conduct its private business, was the room in which Joseph Chamberlain had held the meeting which was believed to have wrecked the Home Rule Bill of 1886. While this agonising internecine battle was being fought, Parnell exhibited some of the passion which was not apparent in him and issued his Manifesto to the Irish People, an extraordinary but tactically brilliant document. For it appealed over the heads of the Liberals and the dissenting Nationalists directly to the Irish people, and if Parnell could retain the people's confidence then he would triumph in the long run.

In the Manifesto Parnell played on the latent Anglo-Irish racialism by writing of the English wolves howling for his blood, and he made some wild if not downright untruthful statements. (Henry Irving, with whom Gladstone discussed the Manifesto in his dressing room at the Lyceum, considered it the finest piece of deceit since Iago had gone to work.) Lucy Cavendish recorded her uncle's reaction to the document: "On the morning when this production appeared I went to Carlton Gardens [where Gladstone was staying with the Stuart Rendels] and found Uncle William so astonished by its *owdacity* and falseness as to be almost amused." She also recorded the different levels on which her uncle's mind always operated by finishing her account: "As Spencer [Lyttleton] and I stood opposite him something in Parnell's words reminded him of *The Bride of Lammermoor* and he suspended operations for a while to look up and say to us, 'The more I read that book the more admirable do I think it.'" Catherine was unamused, in fact she was furious with Parnell, not because he had lived in sin with Katie O'Shea but because he had brought the Irish cause to the brink of ruin. The Irish cause was not just his, it was now William's too. Parnell's attitude after the divorce did not appeal to Catherine either, though it was part and parcel of the man, and under pressure Parnell's strengths and weaknesses were also becoming blacker and whiter. The attitude was summed up by Reginald Brett, who said, "He treated us all as if *we* had committed adultery with *his* wife."

Ten months after writing the Manifesto and within four months of marrying his beloved Katie O'Shea, Parnell was dead, but in the bitterness and tragedy that surrounded the last months, Gladstone was only intermittently involved. He said his heart bled for the Irish but he regarded the fierce struggles over the leadership as *their* fight, and he and Catherine were living through a more intimate tragedy. By the beginning of 1891 the doctors had come to the conclusion that Willie Gladstone was suffering from a brain tumour, and as his condition became worse, in Lucy Cavendish's words, ". . . they were satisfied that nothing could arrest the mischief, and that nothing was before him but softening of the brain, with acute pain and speechlessness, they recommended opening the head for the chance of removing the growth." On 1 July 1891 Catherine left Hawarden to travel to London, where the operation on her favourite son was to be performed. Gladstone remained at Hawarden which John Morley was visiting. The operation was performed the next day but again in Lucy's words, "Alas!

they found a tumour the size of a mandarin orange, lodged far back in the brain: non-malignant but impossible to touch." However, the resilient, ever-optimistic Catherine remained hopeful that the removal of some bone pressure would effect a temporary improvement, and she wrote to her husband, "Darling, morning brings light and hope. Our Willy goes on well. The doctors pleased—evidently the constitution is *so good* and let us hope that the operation will *help*." But Willie never recovered consciousness and he died in the early morning of 3 July before his father and Mary, who had been summoned by an urgent telegram, reached London.

The Gladstones were shattered, and Lucy remarked that it was the first sorrow of its kind that had befallen them since little Jessy's death more than forty years ago. But though Willie had been Catherine's favourite child, rather than Gladstone's, it was he who was the more upset, and Mary said that her mother's courage and bearing were astonishing. Gladstone comforted himself by reading the whole of *Pilgrim's Progress* on the day of the funeral at Hawarden, and by composing a very private memorandum of his eldest son's life and death, as he had of Jessy's forty years before. In the weeks immediately following Willie's death his mother bore up with such astonishing courage and dignity because her husband was so distraught, because she had to comfort and protect him, because his mission to pacify Ireland remained unfinished. One of the very few, touching demands Catherine made of her husband's strength—and that was towards the end of the year when he was reviving—was connected with an annual prize-giving at Hawarden: "The prize-giving would be on the 4th if you would just *stand by* me as I do it instead of dear Willy."

By the autumn of 1891 several people commented how worn and haggard Mrs. Gladstone was looking but she never faltered. Both she and her husband demonstrated "the stuff" of which Gladstone said the English were made, though without the laziness which he also attributed to his compatriots. Within a period of six months these two elderly people had suffered two grievous blows, in Parnell's disgrace and the tragic loss of their eldest son, but within three months of their son's death, as Parnell was approaching his death, they were in Newcastle-on-Tyne. There, at the beginning of October, Gladstone delivered a major speech to the annual National Liberal Federation in which he endorsed the programme which it was hoped would gain a victory for the Liberal party, under his leadership, at the next General Election.

After Willie Gladstone's death an increasing number of people began to say that it was Catherine who was now the driving force behind her husband. In October 1891 Reginald Brett wrote, "It is *she* who keeps him going in politics. He *hates* political life now." While it is doubtful that anybody, including Catherine, ever forced Gladstone to do anything against his will, or that he had completely lost his love of politics, the statement was more than half valid. Had Gladstone not been subjected to Catherine's influence in the summer and early autumn of 1891 it is possible, or even probable, that he might have finally relinquished the reins of leadership and retired to the quiet spiritual life at Hawarden of which he had dreamed for so long. Whether he would in reality have then enjoyed the retirement is another question, but if he had departed from the centre of the stage in 1891 he could not have effected another "Bulgarian" comeback, nor would his sense of propriety have allowed him to do so. But for Catherine her son's illness, followed by the sudden if merciful death, served only to reinforce her conviction that her husband's mission on earth was not yet completed and that the tragedy must be vindicated by the ultimate triumph of Home Rule for Ireland. With Catherine behind him, so assured, enthusiastic and as touchingly eager as a young girl in her belief, with many members of the Liberal party demonstrating their faith and urging him to retain the leadership, Gladstone himself became convinced that he could still serve and guide his country.

CHAPTER 19

THE FOURTH ACT

IT WAS APPROPRIATE that Gladstone should deliver his electoral rallying cry to the people in the city which had first elevated him and his wife into their position as the people's champions, Newcastle-on-Tyne. Before Parnell's disgrace, certainly since it, there had been an increasing number of people in the Liberal party insisting that Home Rule was not a sufficient platform on which the Liberals could fight the next election, and that attention must be paid to the social and economic problems in Britain itself. The result of these discussions and arguments was the programme which Gladstone endorsed in Newcastle and of which Lord Rosebery said, "It is a programme which begins by offering everything to everybody, and it will end by giving nothing to nobody." It was a Pandora's box, with Irish Home Rule still topping the list but with payment of M.P.s, one man-one vote, control of elementary education, reform of the land laws, reform of the magistracy and local government, and the disestablishment of the Welsh and Scottish churches among the goodies offered.

During the 1886 election Gladstone had stated, "All the world over, I will back the masses against the classes." In a speech made in Scotland in 1890 he showed his awareness that the twentieth century would be the century of the masses, begging and exhorting his audience, "the labouring people of this country," to remain honest and just when they had become "stronger than the capitalist, stronger than the peerage, stronger than the landed gentry, stronger than the mercantile classes—when you have become in one sense their political master." While Gladstone retained his faith in the democratic movement until the end of his life—however "vulgar and chaotic" a process it might sometimes be, as he had earlier told John Ruskin— by the early 1890s there was also a chill wind of doubt blowing round his heart. He was becoming haunted by the spectre of the masses proving to be as unjust, greedy, self-interested, tyrannical and lacking in ideals as the classes, and without the benefits of the latter's educational and cultural background. He therefore saw his continuing duty, and the Liberal party's after him, as being to convince the people *en masse* that life was a noble endeavour and that to make it such, individuals must have a moral belief and societies must have an ideal above and beyond themselves. For Gladstone, the morality was Christian and the ideal was a well-regulated Government within whose framework the individual could thrive by his own efforts and with minimum interference from that Government. It was this belief, allied to the practical problems recognised by the still canny politician, that led Gladstone to endorse the Newcastle programme, if with minimum enthusiasm. It was observed that the only times he became excited during the speech and touches of the old magic appeared were when he was speaking of Home Rule and the two other subjects about which he was passionately concerned—the reform of the House of Lords and the evacuation of the British from Egypt.

Gladstone having presented the country with a vague panacea for its problems, and as 1891 had been a terrible year for both him and his wife, they departed for a holiday in Biarritz. This visit was arranged by George (later Lord) Armitstead, another Liberal backbench M.P. who, like Stuart Rendel, had become a close friend of the Gladstones'. It was unkindly said that they used both gentlemen as their hoteliers and Armitstead as their travel agent. Lord Rosebery commented on the "low quality" of the Gladstone entourage by the early 1890s, specifically meaning the Rendels and the Armitsteads, but the quality had not entirely sunk. Dr. Döllinger had died in 1890; Cardinal Manning, with whom Catherine and Gladstone had resumed a reasonably friendly relationship, died in January 1892 while the couple were in Biarritz; but Lord Acton was still alive, John Morley was not an intellectual nonentity, nor was Lord Rosebery himself, and they were also part of the Gladstone circle.

During the sojourn in Biarritz, with John Morley as a fellow guest, Gladstone was in tremendous conversational and intellectual form. Morley gave an account in his biography of the subjects over which the Grand Old Man ranged, from Edmund Burke and de Tocqueville to the materialism of life in the United States, from Disraeli's wit to Lucretius as the greatest and sublimest of the Latin poets, from Marie Antoinette being a horribly frivolous character to verbal portraits of the British and foreign statesmen he had known in his lifetime, et cetera, et cetera. At the time Morley wrote to Sir William Harcourt, "Mr. G. has been in his most charming mood . . . not too vehement, nor preoccupied, nor over-exercised about big things, nor little ones either . . . He is a delightful comrade, and a splendid old fellow."

Of Catherine, celebrating her eightieth birthday on 6 January 1892 in Biarritz, Morley simply remarked, "What a marvel . . . !" He also recorded that Mrs. Gladstone came into his room after breakfast on the first day of the New Year and told him that she was pleased that he "had not scrupled to put unpleasant points" to her husband, as he "must not be shielded and sheltered as some great people are." To a degree he was, but one is glad to hear that even at this late stage of Gladstone's career and their mutual relationship Catherine was not entirely biased in her judgements. However, it should be added that while Morley was prepared to argue with Gladstone about Greek literature or general moral values (Morley was an agnostic), he was not as firm or definite in contradicting his leader on political matters. Although Gladstone overvalued John Morley, he was well aware that his younger colleague lacked magnetism and dynamism in the political arena.

The Gladstones returned to England invigorated, and Mary recorded her parents frisking around like three-year-olds, but before her husband faced the next General Election, Catherine had her share of political problems. These were connected with the Women's Liberal Federation and were taken seriously, not just by the women involved but by the leading male politicians too. For two years there had been a battle for control of the Federation between the militants, who were demanding that female suffrage become the main aim of the organisation, and the moderates, who, like Gladstone, thought it was now an admirable aim in theory but difficult to implement in practice, and one that could wait. In February 1892 the militants led by Rosalind, Countess of Carlisle, gained a majority vote at the general council meeting, which instructed the Executive Committee to promote the parliamentary enfranchisement of women on the same terms as men. The moderates expected Catherine to resign her presidency in protest against the decision but she did not do so, for while it is doubtful that she appreciated the issues involved, she understood that female suffrage was becoming an important matter. Of the Countess of Carlisle, Sir William Harcourt said, "You might as well try to moderate Niagara as to moderate Lady Carlisle," and Gladstone was among those who realised that moderating the actual question of votes for women was likely to prove difficult, though he had no intention of adding it to his mission in the remaining years of life. But Catherine's retention of the presidency of a Federation now devoted to promoting female suffrage was an indication of her husband's approval (or lack of disapproval) of the aim, and a recognition of the more important, individual role women were playing in the political arena. Catherine stayed at the centre of a very stormy scene until her husband became Prime Minister for the fourth time, whereupon she could feel that she had fulfilled her purpose on the female side, justly claim that the role of the Prime Minister's wife occupied most of her time and at the age of eighty-one gratefully refrain from standing for re-election to the presidency. However, the Gladstonian links with the Women's Liberal Federation were not cut, and when her mother retired in 1893 Helen Gladstone joined the Executive Committee and was an active member until her father's last illness, when she returned to Hawarden to help nurse him.

During the early months of 1892 Catherine was worried about one aspect of her husband's well-being, namely his sight. His constitution and general physical condition were as remarkable as ever, apart from deafness, but like many people whose hearing deteriorates in old age he tended to use it as a tactical weapon, hearing what he wanted, missing what he did not want to hear. His always poor eyesight was a more serious problem, and a cataract was forming on his better left eye. In March Gladstone wrote to his wife, "Your affectionate anxiety as to my eye may be fully allayed. It is I think admitted to be hardly if at all distinguishable from the other eye. It causes me no pain or inconvenience." It prevented him neither from preparing for a General Election nor from enjoying himself, and he remained a frequent theatregoer.

By 1892 his special chair at the Lyceum had been removed to the opposite side of the stage; it was now upholstered, and velvet curtains had been placed round it to protect him from draughts (it was the duty of one stagehand to see that the roller curtain did not fall on the Grand Old Man's head when he was in attendance at a show). In November 1892 Mary recorded going to the Lyceum, then backstage afterwards and seeing her father up in the "flys." Anyone who has climbed to the "flys" of a Victorian theatre will appreciate what a feat that was for Gladstone, with his failing sight, to have performed at the age of almost eighty-three; his general enthusiasm and zest for life were as vigorous as they had ever been. One theatrical venture to which Gladstone did not give his patronage was the Royal Victoria Coffee and Music Hall which Emma Cons had established in the old Coburg Theatre in the Waterloo Road and which, with its emphasis on providing entertainment and educational instruction for the people at low prices, should have appealed to him. But Lucy Cavendish repaired this omission and was a staunch, lifelong supporter of Emma Cons and later her niece Lilian Baylis, through the financial crises and vicissitudes of the venture, which became internationally renowned as the Old Vic.

By 1892 Lord Salisbury's Ministry was beginning to run out of steam, and at the end of June Parliament was dissolved and a General Election ensued. The Gladstones again campaigned in Midlothian, again staying at Dalmeny, but much was changed. Mary was not with them as she had a small daughter to look after; Gladstone was aging and the enthusiasm was not on the scale of yesteryear; Hannah Rosebery was dead and as a result Lord Rosebery was plunged into melancholia and suffered from severe insomnia. Rosebery had always been a difficult, introspective character—George Bernard Shaw said he never missed an occasion of losing an opportunity, and that he wanted the palm without the dust—but his wife's death had been a shattering blow, one which he was less temperamentally equipped to survive than were the Gladstones their tragedies. Catherine had appreciated what his wife's death had meant and had been sympathetic towards the bereaved husband and his children, and Gladstone should have appreciated what a torment almost permanent insomnia was, as he was thrown into despair after a few sleepless nights; but at Dalmeny in the summer of 1892 both of them behaved as if nothing had changed. Their tactlessness was a failure of imagination rather than actual lack of sympathy, for neither Catherine nor Gladstone had ever understood or had patience with the melancholic, the introspective or the self-pitying (as their behaviour towards Helen Gladstone and Lady Glynne indicated).

The results of the election were as disappointing for the Liberals as was the comparative failure of Gladstone's Midlothian campaign, where his majority slumped from over 4,000 to just under 700. However, the failure was merely *comparative*, to the previous monster enthusiasm and last large majority, and the G.O.M. still attracted more attention and commanded more column inches than any other British politician. The final returns were 273 Liberals, 82 Irish Home Rulers (of whom very few were now "Parnellites"), 269 Conservatives and 46 Liberal Unionists. This meant that the Liberals were in a minority against the British combination of Tories and Unionists and could only form a government with Irish support, and that Lord Salisbury had no need to resign immediately. However, the Conservatives were defeated by the Liberals and Irish on a vote of no confidence as soon as Parliament reassembled in August, and they then resigned. Queen Victoria had no alternative but to invite the Liberals to form a Government, and there was no question of a cabal forming to oust Gladstone from the leadership, even if his magic was waning and the ill-conceived Newcastle programme tied to the masthead of Home Rule had failed to stir the electorate. A concern of his close friends and colleagues was to see that what John Morley called "the last scenes of Act V" were not too sad, ignoble or Lear-like (particularly, he added later, Lear as rendered by Henry Irving).

Queen Victoria's reaction to the news that she might or would have to accept Mr. Gladstone as her Prime Minister for the fourth time was predictable. In May 1892, as Lord Salisbury first recommended the dissolution of Parliament, she noted, ". . . the GOM at 82 is a very alarming lookout"; in June she told Sir Henry Ponsonby, "The idea of a deluded excited man of 82 trying to govern England & her vast Empire with the miserable democrats under him is quite ludicrous. It is like a bad joke!"; in July, as the election results started coming in, she again told Ponsonby, "She supposes she will have that dangerous old fanatic thrust down her throat," but a fortnight later she told her secretary, "The Queen cannot make up her mind to send at once for that dreadful old man." When Lord Salisbury resigned she had to make up her mind, though she expressed her own feelings clearly by announcing in the Court Circular that she accepted the resignation "with regret" (and constitutional monarchs were supposed to be impartial and officially have no feelings). When Gladstone arrived at Osborne on 15 August 1892, Her Majesty recorded that he was "not only very much aged & walking rather bent, with a stick, but altogether his face shrunk, deadly pale, with a weird look in his eyes, a feeble expression about the mouth, & the voice altered." At the bottom of this memorandum she noted, "In the evening I was still more struck by his wild weird appearance & strange manners." After what she described to her daughter Vicky as "the Gladstone crew" had been sworn into office, Her Majesty recorded her failure to understand the democratic system: "These are trying moments, & seems to me a defect in our much famed Constitution to have to part with an admirable Govt like Lord S's for no question of any importance, or any particular reason, merely on account of the number of votes." Her Majesty's comments about Gladstone and democracy continued in similar vein, though when she saw Catherine in November 1892 she told her daughter, "She is wonderful—80! and looks like 65!"

Gladstone's impressions of Her Majesty were not much more enthusiastic than hers of him; he thought she too had aged considerably and that there was a sad deterioration in her mental powers. He told his ex-Private Secretary Sir Algernon West, who had agreed to head his secretariat for this fourth Ministry, that his meeting with the Queen at Osborne had been such as must have occurred between Marie Antoinette and her executioner.* Despite the by now mutual dislike which bordered on hatred on the Queen's side, the aged monarch and the aged Prime Minister had to work together. While Gladstone was forming his Government there were personality problems of the kind he particularly disliked, concerning Lord Rosebery and Henry Labouchere. The Gladstones' treatment of Rosebery at Dalmeny came home to roost; his lordship refused to accept the Foreign Office, and Queen Victoria was not the only person alarmed by the refusal. Eventually, with the greatest reluctance and after the personal intervention of the Prince of Wales, Rosebery agreed to serve and Sir William Harcourt told him, "Without you the Govt. would have been simply ridiculous; now it is only impossible!" Harcourt himself was being dictatorial about who should be in the Cabinet and what measures the Liberals should pursue; Gladstone said Sir William had treated him "brutally." But the Queen was not involved in this internal dispute and her only comment was that Harcourt was "rather awful looking now, like an Elephant so large & big."

In the matter of Gladstone's wish to include "Labby" in his Ministry, Her Majesty *was* involved because he was not only, in her eyes, a notorious Radical and Republican but he had for long been attacking and lampooning her and various members of her family in his magazine *Truth*. The "Labby" row was exhausting and became rather bitter. He wrote an open letter to his constitutents saying that the Queen had personally vetoed his inclusion in a Liberal Government which she had no right to do; Her Majesty became upset and said (though not of course publicly) that she had not refused him office, though she had justifiably demanded that he give up the editorship of *Truth* if he became a Minister. Caught in the cross fire and somewhat annoyed with both Her Majesty and Labouchere for their actions, Gladstone in his old age did not press the appointment and Labouchere was not included in the Government. The "Labby" problems were not finished, for having been denied office the gentleman asked to be appointed Ambassador to Washington. The Americans favoured the appointment (Mrs. Labouchere was well-known in the States from her acting days

* Eddy Hamilton was now at the Treasury but he retained close links with the Gladstones and worried a good deal about "the dear old man," though not always uncritically.

and was an excellent, extrovert hostess), but Lord Rosebery did not, for he too had been attacked and lampooned in *Truth*. As Foreign Secretary the appointment of ambassadors came under his jurisdiction, once again Labby was denied a job and Catherine said that when *she* died "Washington and Rosebery" would be found engraved on *her* heart.

Gladstone nearly failed to survive to lead his last Ministry: Catherine wrote to Her Majesty, "Dear Madam, I hasten to thank you for the kind enquiries after my husband—it has been a miraculous escape and he has quite recovered from the effects of the accident. A welsh cow which had escaped into the woods—actually rushed at him throwing him upon his back and then stood over him but he never for a moment lost his presence of mind . . . He would not tell me until after dinner when he consented to go to bed." The incident happened at Hawarden at the end of August 1892, and Gladstone was quite severely bruised and shocked. Queen Victoria's letter was charming and solicitous—even she had no desire to see the half-mad firebrand end his career under a cow's hooves—and Catherine finished her reply by informing the Queen, "The cow has been shot"; its head still adorns the walls of an hotel in Hawarden, with an appropriate plaque beneath.

The official *raison d'être* of Gladstone's fourth Ministry was the obtaining of Home Rule for Ireland but he himself displayed no urgency in tackling the subject, it was not regarded as the crucial issue by any member of the Cabinet except John Morley, and the matter which demanded immediate attention was Uganda. In 1890 Lord Salisbury had done a deal with Bismarck in which Britain ceded Heligoland (an island in the North Sea, about forty miles from the German coast) to Germany in return for larger "spheres of influence" in East Africa. "Spheres of influence," or the carving up of Africa by the European powers, had been agreed on earlier but there had been considerable tension in East Africa. In 1890 the Germans and British agreed that Tanganyika would remain a German sphere but Zanzibar and Kenya would be British, and Uganda too if the British wanted it (though if they did not the Germans—or the French—would be only too happy to step in). In fact Lord Salisbury had decided that the British should not become further involved and should withdraw support from the British East Africa Company which was already operating in Uganda. When the Liberals took office a decision on Uganda had become imperative because the British East Africa Company was in severe financial difficulties. On the one side there was Gladstone supported by Sir William Harcourt and John Morley (among others) absolutely opposed to further "grabbing of land" by Britain. On the other side there was Lord Rosebery (among others) and the formidable figure of Frederick Lugard,† who returned from Uganda to stump the country urging that Britain annex this large tract of African land.

† Lugard was an archetypal empire builder and administrator. He spent much of his adult life in Africa, East and West.

Liberal imperialism, of which Lord Rosebery was the prime exponent, was different from "jingo" imperialism in principle, if the difference was not always apparent in practice. One was not grabbing land *per se,* but rather because one recognised human greed and lust for power and sincerely believed that British influence, British civilisation and the British way of life were as good as any that had been evolved in an imperfect world. Rosebery's ideal was the eventual commonwealth of self-governing nations led by England. By 1892 an increasing number of Liberals supported his view, some for ideological reasons, some for economic ones, some for a mixture of the two. As a classicist Gladstone himself believed in the Greek concept of the spread of civilisation by the advanced races colonising the less advanced ones, and in his early days at the Colonial Office he had worked to promote happy, or happier, Englands across the world. But for him the promotion should occur only in the territories which England already possessed and he was completely out of sympathy with the current European colonial race. Even the emotional plea that if Uganda were abandoned the Christian missionaries in the country might be massacred failed to raise a flicker of Christian enthusiasm. On a telegram from Uganda which stressed the horrid dangers to the missionaries he noted, "I wonder how much the transmission of this very unimportant *jingo* paper cost."

Sir William Harcourt said he would die a thousand deaths rather than have the British remain in Uganda but Lord Rosebery and the Liberal imperialists were convinced in their beliefs and were powerful. Gladstone needed their support for his Home Rule Bill, Harcourt needed their support for the Budget he was proposing, and after some stormy Cabinet meetings a compromise on Uganda was reached. It was agreed that there should be no annexation but a temporary loan would be granted to the British East Africa Company, though if it did not improve its operations and financial position, evacuation from the territory would ensue. (The temporary loan drifted on during Gladstone's last Ministry and when he retired and Lord Rosebery became Prime Minister, Uganda was declared a British protectorate.) Similarly Gladstone said he would rather set a torch to Westminster Abbey than send more British troops to Egypt, but in 1893, again because he needed Rosebery's and the imperialist support for the Home Rule battle, the torch was not lit and the troops were sent.

In some ways Gladstone's last Ministry was a melancholy affair, with an old man capitulating over issues in which he believed and for which he would have previously fought; with his system of Cabinet government by devolution and non-interference lacking the earlier firm guiding hand; with his Ministers constantly sulking and dividing themselves into "the English bench" and "the Irish bench"; with his family in the background protecting him fiercely and dictating what he should or should not undertake. Sir Algernon West moaned in his diaries that he had to fight *all* the Gladstone family on so many issues—whether Mr. G. should attend a Cabinet or should go to Hawarden or needed a holiday or could make a public speech

—but though Herbert was in Parliament and had some influence over his ageing father, the burden of West's complaints was against the Gladstone women. He was not the only person who complained about Gladstone's "seraglio" or who flung charges of "petticoat government." Eddy Hamilton said, "The old man, and still more, the old woman, are bent on fighting *ad desperandum*," and further that Mrs. Gladstone and her daughters were "waylaying everybody, and scheming this and scheming that; intercepting letters and almost listening at keyholes."

The portrait of the ageing Liberal leader, propelled into office and sustained by the unbridled devotion of his ambitious, biased, power-seeking female relatives is only half the picture, from both his and their angles. Despite the dissensions and signs of collapse, Gladstone was holding together a Cabinet composed of particularly individualistic and able men, he could still astonish them, and Reginald Brett, who visited Hawarden in February 1893, commented how "wonderfully alert" the old man was mentally. (Brett had followed Lord Hartington into the Liberal Unionist camp and was no Gladstonian devotee.) Above all, Gladstone's handling of the second Home Rule Bill was an astonishing performance. The measure was announced in the Queen's Speech for the 1893 parliamentary session; the first reading occurred in February, the second in April and the third and final reading at the beginning of September. During these months, if the atmosphere was not quite so bitter as in 1886, it was acrimonious. There were dissensions in the Cabinet, particularly between Sir William Harcourt and John Morley (again the Chief Secretary for Ireland) on the question of what contribution the Irish should make to the imperial exchequer; there was the use of obstruction in the House of Commons; there were interminable debates about the decision to retain the Irish M.P.s at Westminster; at one point there was an actual fight in the Commons, and brawling in the chamber had not been seen for many a year. At the centre of the storm, day after day, night after night, arguing, explaining, exhorting, pleading, was the figure of a man in his eighty-fourth year whose sight had nearly gone and whose hearing was failing. It was by the sheer force of Gladstone's personality and parliamentary skill that the Home Rule Bill passed through the Commons with a majority of forty-three votes.

Catherine wrote to Lucy on 2 September 1893, "The never-to-be-forgotten birthday comes close to that tremendous evening when the 3rd Reading of Home Rule was passed with acclamation—it was a never-to-be-forgotten night the victory—you won't be surprised that my heart is overflowing that yr birthday comes just to force me to express some thoughts. Shall we not feel that your precious husband, your beloved Freddy comes vividly before us and all that you have suffered? In the excitement of last night Freddy was not fogotten." The victory was short-lived: within a week the House of Lords threw the Bill out by a massive vote of 419 to 41, as everybody had known that it would. Now, with his passion again roused, with every fibre in his being vibrating with the crisis, Gladstone wanted to challenge the power of the Lords, not only because they had thrown out the Home Rule Bill but because they had been obstructing virtually every other Bill the Liberals had got through the Commons. Gladstone had earlier penned one of his more cogent, lengthy memoranda to Her Majesty on the question of the Lords and Commons, an issue which he informed the Queen went beyond that of Home Rule and concerned "the widening of the gap, or chasm, in opinion, which more largely than heretofore separates the upper, and more powerful, from the numerous classes of the community." But he had raised the issue too late; his colleagues were in agreement that he must soon retire because he had shot his bolt over Home Rule and he was too old and unpredictable to continue as leader. Some of them concurred that the power of the Lords would have to be curtailed but they were not prepared to enter into the battle at this moment and over the subject of Home Rule. What the majority of the Liberal party wanted was to forget Ireland and to concentrate on other home and foreign issues, particularly to counter the menace on their left flank which was being presented by the Fabian and other Socialist movements.

After the Lords' rejection of the Home Rule Bill the Gladstones went on another minor stump, during which he announced in Edinburgh that this was not the end of the Irish road and that Home Rule would figure in the next session of Parliament. In October they were in Newcastle-on-Tyne and Reginald Brett recorded a touching picture of "the old couple" standing with their heads bowed while thousands of people sang "Auld Lang Syne." But the old times were gone and Gladstone was soon forced into resignation. It was not on the Irish issue that he finally went, however, but on the question of Liberal principles, which meant more to him even than his mission to pacify unhappy Erin. By November 1893 the Naval Estimates were under review and in the face of increasingly powerful German and French navies and a *rapprochement* between France and Russia which had re-tilted the European balance of power, it was in many quarters felt that Britain must increase her naval strength, the strong arm on which, as a small island with vast overseas possessions, she relied in peace and in war to maintain her life lines and those possessions. But for Gladstone the proposed increase meant militarism, jingoism and in this instance for once slightly less importantly, a waste of the taxpayers' money, and he was adamant in his refusal to sanction it. By December, when the issue had become public property and was being hotly debated in and out of Parliament, Gladstone remained firm in his refusal to consider the increase, while his Cabinet (and much of the party) were determined that Britain's navy must be strengthened.

In the middle of December, as the Naval Estimates *contretemps* continued, Catherine was at Hawarden while her husband was at Downing Street. When she returned to London he departed for the fresh sea breezes of Brighton but she was unable immediately to join him as she suffered another attack of erysipelas. The letters that passed between them are among the last extant ones, for after 1893 they were rarely separated. On 18 December Gladstone wrote to his wife, "Come back tomorrow—if you can!!" and she replied, "Yes darling I come back to you tomorrow. I have got through a good deal. How you have fed me! It has been a real pleasure being with her [Gertrude] & those darling children. As we please God shall meet so soon, no more Your Own CG." On Christmas Day she wrote to her husband, "How dear of you my own to give me such long letters & oh the wiring! . . . God bless you more & more." The letters were a fitting end to nearly fifty-five years of a correspondence which had been an invaluable safety valve for Gladstone, a link to the centres of power for Catherine, and which had, both by the absences which produced it and by the continuity, given their marriage much of its strength.

After his sojourn in Brighton, where Catherine eventually joined him, Gladstone returned to London for a Cabinet on 8 January 1894. At this he made his final offer on the Naval Estimates, saying that he would sanction half the proposed expenditure for one year only; but the Cabinet was almost unanimous in its view that the offer was unacceptable, that the full increase was required and without a time limit. The question left was when and for what official reasons Gladstone should announce his resignation. On 9 January John Morley recorded how he was detailed to break the news to Catherine, whom, for once, her husband had not kept fully in the picture. The scene occurred at Downing Street after dinner, with Gladstone and George Armitstead playing backgammon in the background, and Morley wrote, "I told her the reign was over, and the only question was whether the abdication should be now or in February. The poor lady was not in the least prepared. Would not the Cabinet change when they knew the perils with which his loss would surround them? I was obliged to keep to iron facts. What a curious scene! I breaking to her that the pride and glory of her life was at last to face eclipse, that the curtain was falling on a grand drama of fame, power, acclamation; the rattle of the dice and the laughter and chuckling of the two long-lived players sounding a strange running refrain."

The matter was not quite as simple as John Morley made it sound. Few of Gladstone's colleagues wanted him to resign on the issue of the Naval Estimates because it was one which could again split the party. They hoped that he would eventually give way on the increased expenditure, as he had over Uganda and Egypt. Nor was there unanimity about the timing of the retirement or on the question of his successor, and Gladstone himself had not actually said that he was going to retire, which could have been one reason he kept Catherine ignorant of the "iron facts." On 13 January 1894 the issue was further complicated when Gladstone and Catherine, accompanied by Mary and Dossie, Lord Acton and the faithful George Armitstead, departed for yet another holiday in Biarritz, and the Government was left in a state of suspended animation. There was a particular fear of what Gladstone might do from the distance and fastness of Biarritz, flanked by his wife and daughter, in an unpredictable state of mind and with his predilection for letter-writing (the ones he had fired from Hawarden when under stress in 1886 were remembered).

Sir Algernon West was twice sent to Biarritz to see if he could extract a decision from Gladstone on the question of the Naval Estimates and on the more vital one of his resignation. The first time he returned with Gladstone's statement on his position regarding the estimates, "You might as well try to blow up the Rock of Gibraltar. *Liberavi animam meam.*" But on the second visit towards the end of January 1894, West returned with the information that Gladstone had decided to retire and that he might be willing to do so on the grounds of his advanced age and bad eyesight rather than on the issue of the Naval Estimates. In his diary West wrote, "So the curtain is falling, and the end is not far off. God grant it may come with decency, and the great Caesar fold his robes gracefully round him as he falls!"

The final curtain had been released but it again became stuck when the news of the Prime Minister's impending resignation was leaked to the *Pall Mall Gazette*, whereupon Gladstone issued a denial (from Biarritz). When the great Caesar returned to England on 10 February he continued to swish his robes rather than to fold them around him in a graceful dying fall. He continued to suggest to his colleagues that they dissolve Parliament and appeal to the country on the issue of the House of Lords, implying that he would lead the renewed fight (he had bruited the idea from Biarritz). The reaction of his colleagues was one of dismissive hostility, and now it was a question of time. How long would Gladstone hold on in the face of the knowledge that all his colleagues wanted him to go? He made them wait until 27 February 1894 because he was now fairly angry with and contemptuous of the majority of them. His reluctance to yield power had been far from graceful but his colleagues had vacillated and they had also failed to appreciate that the Naval Estimates involved for him a real and deep principle. Lucy Cavendish recorded that her uncle "believes he is resisting what will foster & excite the war-spirit throughout the Continent, not for one year, but for an indefinite length of time; what will tend to crush people under ever-increasing unproductive expenditure, & lead to the nations vying with each other in that senseless course."

On 27 February 1894 Gladstone finally wrote to Her Majesty but the letter was in his most oblique style, and one tends to sympathise with Queen Victoria's comment, "It was about nothing more nor less than his resignation!" However, Gladstone had still not set a date—he finished his letter by saying, ". . . he reserves all explanations of particulars until the day, perhaps a very early one, when he humbly proposes to carry his intention into effect." On 28 February he travelled to Windsor, where he was greeted by an extremely cheerful Queen who thought he was looking "very old" and was "very deaf," and in her pleasure at his departure made him sit down in her presence. On 1 March he finally announced his decision to·

the Cabinet, whereupon nearly everybody became emotional and there was hardly a dry eye in the room. Whatever feelings his colleagues may have had about him in the last few months it *was* an emotional moment, the last Cabinet of the man who had been in Parliament for over sixty years, who had been four times Prime Minister, who had shaped the Liberal party in his image and who had dominated the stage, and many of their lives, like a colossus. Lord Rosebery described the very last scene of the last act to Queen Victoria: "The old man turned to go. But Harcourt, blubbering like a child, rose exclaiming, 'Stay, Mr. G, stay!' and proceeded to draw out from his inner pocket a *much corrected* manuscript, *yellow* with age, from which he read a valedictory address." In his diary Rosebery added that the only thing he could vaguely remember from the address was a long-drawn metaphor taken from the solar system! Perhaps the person least affected by the scene was Gladstone himself because, as always, once a decision was made, that was it as far as he was concerned and his mind was already turning towards other matters. At the time he said that the last Cabinet had been a really moving scene, but afterwards he referred to it as "the blubbering Cabinet" in a fairly acid tone of voice.

However, there was one area in which Gladstone himself could still be extremely affected and almost as emotional, if not as openly, as Sir William Harcourt, and that was in his relationship with Queen Victoria. On 2 March Her Majesty invited both him and Catherine to have dinner and stay overnight at Windsor. For the Queen it was the final, disagreeable but necessary courteous gesture; for Gladstone it was the moment when he officially tendered his resignation, but as Her Majesty was under the impression that he had already resigned the wires were crossed from the start. Her Majesty recorded her impressions of the visit thus: "I saw Mr. G who brought with him his letter of resignation. He went over the same ground, his eyes etc. . . . He then kissed my hand & left." Later she saw Catherine alone and noted, "She was very much upset, poor thing, & asked to be allowed to speak, as her husband 'could not speak.' This was to say, which she did with many tears, that whatever his errors might have been 'his devotion to Your Majesty & the Crown were very great.' She repeated this twice, & begged me to allow her to tell him that I believed it, which I did; for I am convinced that it is the case, though at times his actions might have made it difficult to believe. She spoke of former days and how long she had known me & dearest Albert. I kissed her when she left."

Whatever she told the Queen, the only error Catherine thought her husband was making—apart from the actual resignation which she had perforce to accept—was in stating that he was retiring because of his age and ill-health and not because of the fundamental principles raised by the question of increased naval expenditure. She thought her husband was resigning "on a lie," as she told Lucy Cavendish, but it was a tactical lie which saved the Liberal party a good deal of embarrassment and it was also a half-truth because Gladstone was now too old and infirm to lead the party. After the visit Her Majesty wrote Gladstone a letter which she thought was gracious but which he thought was abominable, for it merely stated that the Queen considered that he was right to retire after so many years of arduous labour, and trusted that he would enjoy his retirement in the company of his excellent and devoted wife and that his eyesight would improve. Almost in the way of a postscript Her Majesty added that she would have conferred a peerage on Mr. Gladstone but she knew he would not accept it (which was true). There was hardly the suggestion that any of the arduous labours had been performed in Her Majesty's service, certainly no thanks, and Gladstone commented, "The Queen's note is the only *piece* proceeding from H.M. in the process which has wound up an account reaching over 52½ years from Sept 1, 1841, when I was sworn of the Privy Council . . . The same brevity perhaps prevails in settling a tradesman's bill when it reaches over many years."

It can be said that Her Majesty did not intend to say her farewells to Mr. Gladstone "on a lie," but he was deeply and bitterly wounded. He later wrote a memorandum in which he remembered a mule he had hired in Sicily when he had toured the island in the company of Arthur Kinnaird so many years before. He wrote, "I had been on the back of the beast for many scores of hours. It had done me no wrong. It had rendered much valuable service. But it was in vain to argue. There was the fact staring me in the face. I could not get up the smallest shred of feeling for the brute. I could neither love nor like it . . . A rule-of-three sum is all that is necessary to conclude with what that Sicilian mule was to me I have been to the Queen; and the fortnight or 3 weeks are represented by 52 or 53 years." Why Her Majesty had grown to detest him so much Gladstone never understood; he could not appreciate that they were both passionate, obstinate people whose passions were not shared and whose obstinacy therefore collided; that whereas his mind was wide-ranging and always on the move, Her Majesty's was limited and became stuck in grooves; that he had treated her—as she said—as if she were a public meeting when she wanted a more personal, simple approach; and that as "the People's William" he had infringed on her divine right to the people's affection. Gladstone wondered and brooded about his relationship with Queen Victoria—had untrue stories of his associations with prostitutes reached Her Majesty's ear? Was that why their earlier, happier acquaintance had become poisoned? He dreamed of amicable meetings with Her Majesty which, even in his dreams, failed to materialise. But his reverence for the monarchy remained, and in January 1896 he wrote in his diary, "I place on record here . . . my strong desire that after my decease my family shall be most careful to keep in the background all information respecting the personal relations of the Queen and myself during these latter years down to 1894, when they died a kind of material death."‡

‡ It was Herbert Gladstone who first disrespected his father's wishes on the royal relationship, in his memoirs *After Thirty Years*, written when he had become Viscount Gladstone. His reason for breaking the silence was that several people, notably the ex-*Times* editor G. E. Buckle, who had also acted as editor for the second published series of Queen Victoria's letters, had given a view of the relations which was biased against his father and incorrect.

The only minor consolations that Gladstone received from the court as he departed from public life after half a century of service performed in the highest capacities were a personal letter from Sir Henry Ponsonby in which he said that for many people Mr. Gladstone's last audience had been a melancholy occasion, and the offer of a peerage for Mrs. Gladstone in her own right. The offer was refused. Catherine still preferred to die bearing the name which had been hers for the last fifty-five years and which was for her unquestionably the noblest in the realm, plain Mrs. Gladstone to her husband's plain Mr. Gladstone. This time Gladstone himself did not urge her to take the peerage, as he had earlier with the extinct baronetcy of Percy and Poynings. He said he looked upon the offer with no favour but would not of course press his views upon his dearest wife should she wish to accept.

Gladstone was also upset that Her Majesty did not consult him about his successor as Liberal Prime Minister (though constitutionally the monarch did not have to consult a retiring Prime Minister). Gladstone's own first choice was Lord Spencer, with Sir William Harcourt as second, but Her Majesty called upon the man whom the recent Liberal plotting and manoeuvring had driven to the forefront—Lord Rosebery. Until the last lap the favourite heir presumptive had been Sir William Harcourt but he lost the vital support of John Morley when he quarrelled with him over the Irish contribution to the imperial exchequer. It was a bitter disappointment for the volatile "Sir Bow-Wow," but an even more acrid one for his son Loulou. Reginald Brett commented that the person he felt most sorry for when Gladstone finally announced his resignation was Loulou Harcourt, who had worked unceasingly (and adroitly) for ten years to make his father Prime Minister, only to lose at the winning post. For once Lord Rosebery did not seek the occasion to lose an opportunity, and with Queen Victoria's blessing he was sworn in as Prime Minister. However, Her Majesty's mind was now firmly stuck in a non-Liberal groove and within a very short time she was writing, "I am vy much annoyed about things at home. Ld. Rosebery has pleased nobody, & has gone as far as Mr G. with the further disadvantage that he has not any conviction in what he says!"

While "Mr G." and his convictions remained a potent force, they were never again a direct one at the centre of power, and in fact Gladstone made his last speech in the House of Commons during the afternoon of 1 March 1894, after "the blubbering Cabinet." Appropriately it was on the question of the House of Lords and towards the end of the speech his voice swooped and soared with much of the old fire and passion. In his peroration he said, "The issue which is raised between a deliberative assembly, elected by the votes of more than 6,000,000 people, and a deliberative assembly occupied by many men of virtue, by many men of talent, of course with considerable diversities and varieties, is a controversy which, when once raised, must go forward to an issue." Sixteen years later his prophecy came true when one of the younger men whom he had included in his last Government, Herbert

Asquith, ranged the ranks of Gladstonian Liberalism against the Lords and finally curtailed their power. At the time, few people were aware that they were listening to Mr. Gladstone speak for the last time in the chamber in which he had exercised such dominance and magic for the better part of the century, and which he loved so much. It is curious that the two great opposing figures of nineteenth-century British history, Disraeli and Gladstone, the one a great romantic, the other imbued with the actor's sense of the dramatic, should both make their farewells in such quiet, unromantic, undramatic fashion; but Disraeli was also a cynic, and Gladstone lived in his separate compartments and the political door was finally shut.

All that remained was for the Gladstones to pack their belongings and move out of 10 Downing Street. In an answer to a query of her cousin's Mary wrote, "Yes it has been a unique time, all the love and honour and glory that Death brings without any of its terrors and horrors. The flowers without the funeral. Flowers have poured in the last fortnight 'just like funeral wreaths,' he said, and I felt they were typical of the situation . . . There has however been no flatness yet, only desperate thrill and emotion all round, and great struggles to keep the tears back, and the lump in the throat in proper order . . . there was this great old Ex-P.M. left with loads of correspondence, raining addresses, with his difficulties of sight and ill and weak from his bronchitis." On 12 March 1894, with the addresses still raining upon him and the flowers still pouring, Gladstone, accompanied by Catherine, departed from Downing Street for the last time. An informal Gladstonian domestic touch was added to the farewell scenes by little Dossie, who wandered "in and out of the various groups singing Alleluia."

CHAPTER 20

THE FINAL CURTAIN

IT WAS ON THE OCCASION of her father's final retirement that Mary remarked upon her mother's love of being inside the mainspring of history. She also commented that nobody, with the obvious exception of herself, knew what a blow the resignation had been to her mother. Temporarily Catherine held on to the belief that the Liberals could not function without her husband, and it was she who insisted that he remain in Parliament so that he would be able to answer the recall which must soon be heard. As the idea slowly penetrated Catherine's mind that her husband neither wished to nor could again hold office, there was a gradual deterioration of her faculties, and she started to slide downhill towards senility. The core and essence of her life had been the fulfillment of her ambitions, her enjoyment of power and her sense of mission through and for her husband's role as the great, guiding statesman. Her children and grandchildren she loved and they remained; her charitable activities had filled a large part of her life; but none of them was sufficient. The *raison d'être* of Catherine's existence had disappeared and with it, slowly, went the beautiful balance which had kept her spirits soaring and her optimism unquenched through tragedy, trial and tribulation. Her descent into senility was a gentle if distressing process, and for a couple of years after her husband's retirement she retained a reasonable interest in the affairs of the world. Visitors to Hawarden were chivvied into having a word with the elderly ladies at the Home in the yard, because they became so lonely if nobody spoke to them; if a particular story of distress came to her ears she was still capable of dashing off to render practical aid; and her many grandchildren and young relatives delighted in "Dan-Dan's" or "Aunt Pussy's" company. But she had lost much of her sparkle and zeal and people commented how frail Mrs. Gladstone had suddenly become. Incidentally, both her and her husband's disregard for their appearance became markedly apparent in their last years. Catherine's now frail beauty could get away with her old-fashioned and often literally very old dresses, shawls and lace caps but physically Gladstone himself had become a startling figure, with his fringe of white hair, his magnetic eyes, his prominent nose and obstinate determined mouth. In some of the numerous photographs which were taken of the Grand Old Man in his retirement, his clothes and stance are extraordinary, and Queen Victoria's description of his "weird" appearance at Osborne probably had some validity. There are photographs of Gladstone in wide-brimmed hats in which he looks as if he had just returned from the wild West at its wildest and most fictionally Western.

Shortly after his resignation the problem of Gladstone's eyesight was ameliorated by a successful operation on the cataract on the left eye; in May 1894 Catherine wrote to Lucy Cavendish to tell her that when the bandages had been removed she had asked her husband, "Can you see anything?" to which he had replied, "Yes I see your finger," and how thankful she had been. (She added that the Prince of Wales had sent a letter which had been "brimful of tenderness"). With the threat of blindness removed and some sight restored to him, Gladstone spent a fair amount of time furthering his library project. By 1894 over thirty thousand of his books had been removed from the castle to the large iron rooms on the brow of Hawarden hill (which inside were lined with pine and felt); a series of smaller buildings had been constructed, and Gladstone had finally decided what he should do with the personal library collected with such love and care over so many years. He would endow a residential library, with his books providing the basis, the two iron rooms acting as the library itself and the smaller but comfortable buildings as the studies and living quarters. The aim of the institution would be "to improve and maybe perfect our means of maintaining the harmony between Christian knowledge and all other knowledge," and though all thinking men would be welcomed to its precincts, Gladstone hoped that it would never be used "for purposes hostile to the Church of England." The idea of the residential quarters was Gladstone's own; it was to enable those who could not afford to buy many books or who had lacked the opportunity of going to university to enjoy the temporary freedom from material worries at the minimum charge which his endowment would guarantee, and to find mental or spiritual refreshment in the books and the company of their fellow students. Again Gladstone hoped that many of those who visited the library would be clergymen, but in his trust deed there were no strictures on religion or occupation, only on sex (and it is in very recent years that women have been allowed to stay at the library).

Towards the end of 1894 the first students arrived to lodge temporarily in an adjoining house and the first Warden was appointed, Mary's husband, the Reverend Harry Drew (it was he who undertook the enormous task of finally cataloguing the books, a labour which engrossed him for two years). The library was named St. Deiniol's after the patron saint of Hawarden, a Welshman who had founded the monastery at Bangor and become Bishop of the see circa A.D. 550. In his will Gladstone left £30,000 for the St. Deiniol's endowment and after his death £10,000 of the money subscribed to a memorial fund was allocated to the building of a permanent structure. In 1899 Catherine cut the first token sod for the new library—fittingly it was her last public act—and in October 1902 the building was formally opened. It remains today, its late Victorian turrets and towers comfortably overgrown with ivy, set in spacious grounds close to the parish church. St. Deiniol's is still a unique institution, a haven in which the exhausted, the world-weary, the student, the researcher, the bibliophile, the ordinand, the clergyman can rest or work, at the minimum charge envisaged by its founder. Gladstone usually marched with or ahead of his times and he would probably have approved of the widening of the terms of his trust deed to include the admittance of women. There are many who are grateful to him for the initial thought, for the time, energy and enthusiasm he devoted to the establishment of the library.

At the beginning of 1895 the Gladstones went to Cannes to stay in a villa loaned them by Stuart Rendel, now Lord Rendel, Gladstone having obtained a peerage for him in his last honours list. The visit to Cannes to escape some of the rigours of a British winter became an annual one until Gladstone's last illness. In June 1895 a family party attended the opening of the Kiel Canal, travelling in leisurely fashion on a friend's yacht via Copenhagen. In the Danish capital the yacht was opened to the public and upwards of fifteen thousand people took the opportunity of catching a glimpse of the famous Mr. Gladstone. *The Times'* manager described the Grand Old Man during the trip: "his back to the door so as to get the light, sat Mr. G. reading a Danish pamphlet, laboriously looking out words in the dictionary and writing them in the margin with a pencil . . . not a single moment of quietly doing nothing." The pomp and the ceremony of the actual opening of the Kiel Canal, with the long lines of battleships passing through, filled Gladstone with foreboding, and he told Mary, "This means war."

For him the battles were nearly over, though on his return home in August 1895, and then again in 1896, he emerged to make speeches as the news of the Armenian massacres reached England. The speech which he delivered in Liverpool on 24 September 1896 proved to be his last public one, and it was fitting that it should be on the specific subject which had generated so much passion in him—that of Turkish oppression—and that he was able to express his fundamental beliefs in personal liberty, in the freedoms to which all men were entitled and in England's role as a guiding Christian country. The speech lasted one and a half hours and Mary recorded, "The reception was striking and thrilling in the extreme, & nothing cd have been more impressive than the sight of him standing there, 86, full of wisdom & dignity, while the thunders of applause again & again echoed around. We got home by 4.30 . . . At dinner he was in unabated force, tho' slightly hoarse, having rested in bed, but without sleep. Mama slept 3 hours!"

It was during 1895 that Gladstone cut his last ties with politics. In the summer, after a tenure of office lasting little longer than a year, Lord

Rosebery dissolved Parliament and Gladstone announced that he would not recontest Midlothian. When Parliament reassembled, with a thumping victory for the Conservatives, for the first time in sixty-three years the name of William Ewart Gladstone was not listed among its members. For much of the rest of the year he devoted his attention to the editing of two massive volumes of Bishop Butler's works which were published in February 1896. During these comparatively quiet last years at Hawarden, Gladstone also translated Horace's poetry, compiled further *Gleanings* from his own past writings and contributed theological essays to various magazines. There was a steady stream of visitors, among them many foreign dignitaries. It was after a visit paid by Arthur Balfour in 1896 that he made his famous remark about Gladstone, "He is, and always was, in everything except essentials, a tremendous old Tory." It is a remark which reads or sounds well but if it is taken apart what it means is that Gladstone was *not* a tremendous old Tory. Balfour also commented that "Mr. G." was shocked by his arrival on a bicycle, though why he should have been is hard to understand. Gladstone had never been a particularly conventional man, he approved wholeheartedly of thriftiness and Mary Drew pedalled her bicycle furiously on all local errands.

Apart from the personal friends and relations who filled the rooms of Hawarden Castle with warmth, conversation and laughter, during the summer months there was the stream of sight-seers pouring through the ever-open gates of the estate. For the annual Flower Show in 1896 it was estimated that twenty-six thousand people crammed the gardens of the castle. During 1896 the family visited Penmaenmawr, which had long ago ousted Rhyl as Catherine's favourite Welsh seaside resort, and an observer commented on the party on the beach, with Gladstone absorbed in a book, apparently oblivious of the gawping crowds, while Catherine played with her grandchildren. It was at Penmaenmawr in November 1896 that Gladstone revised his last will and testament; during the 1880s he had made over fairly substantial sums of money to his children but in his final will he directed that Helen, Mary and Agnes should receive £10,000 each, Stephen and Henry £20,000 and Herbert £25,000. Henry had taken over the running of the Hawarden estate after Willie's death and he increasingly lifted financial burdens from his father's shoulders and managed his affairs for him. Until 1897 Gladstone himself kept detailed accounts; he drew up lists of his expenditures and income from 1831 until that year, noting that he had given £84,136 to charities and that he had earned from his literary output £18,836, which was not a bad sum for a strictly part-time writer.

Other than his speech on the Armenian massacres delivered in Liverpool in September, the most dramatic event of 1896 occurred the following month, when the Archbishop of Canterbury collapsed in Hawarden church and died without regaining consciousness. Gladstone commented that to die in church would be an euthanasia, as long as the other worshippers were not disturbed. At the end of 1896 he made the last entry in the diary which he had kept for seventy years. He wrote of his long and tangled life, that the basis of his political life had lain in finance and philanthropy, that the blessings of family life continued to be poured on his unworthy head, that he remembered visiting Lord Stratford de Redcliffe when he was ninety and being informed that old age was *not* a blessing. Almost at the end of this last entry he noted, "I do not enter upon interior matters. It is so easy to write, but to write honestly nearly impossible."

Early in 1897 the Gladstones paid their winter visit to Cannes, accompanied by Mary; and on this occasion there was another visitor in the town, Queen Victoria, who was accompanied by several members of her family. Gladstone said he had no wish to meet the Queen unless she wished to see him, which she did not, but Mary and Princess Louise overcame the problem and the gossip and criticism which might have arisen if two of the most famous people in the world had failed to exchange a word while they were in the same French resort at the same time. Princess Louise invited the Gladstones to tea at the royal hotel, after which it was a simple matter to extend an invitation for them to mount in the lift and enter the royal presence. The meeting was reasonably friendly; the Queen shook Mr. Gladstone's hand—for the very first time in his life, as he commented, and also the last—and kissed Catherine, and some polite desultory conversation ensued in a room which was "populated by a copious supply of Hanoverian royalties." That year was the Diamond Jubilee of Her Majesty's accession to the throne but apart from the meeting in Cannes, the only royal recognition the Gladstones received were two jubilee medals despatched to them at Hawarden.

However, in May, Her Majesty's failure to visit Hawarden and her singular lack of thanks for Mr. Gladstone's long service were somewhat compensated for when the Prince and Princess of Wales paid a visit. The preparations for the royal arrival were intense but they were undertaken by the children because Gladstone had long ceased to be involved in domestic affairs and Catherine's mind was by now disintegrating. On the journey home from Cannes Gladstone noted that his wife had broken down, though he thought the bromides she was being given were a main cause of her mental collapse. For the all-important royal luncheon a table plan was drawn up and the various ailments of the hosts and guests were noted. Somebody's good ear was placed on the correct side of the person to whom he/she was most likely to be speaking (Princess Alexandra of course suffered from deafness), while good eyes were also pointed in the right direction.

The great day, 10 May 1897, dawned cold and grey, but the Prince and Princess of Wales duly arrived at one o'clock to be greeted by the Buckley town band, with the children from the orphanage lining the route. Before the meal the royal party was conducted to the ruins of the old castle, the Princess of Wales supporting Mr. Gladstone on her arm and trying to slow him down as he struggled to mount the slope. The lunch was a success. In the afternoon, after photographs had been taken to mark the auspicious occasion, the *Daily Telegraph* recorded, "the Royal visitors took a farewell of their aged host and hostess, and drove away amid the strains of the National Anthem." Mary's version of the departure had considerably more verve: "The bands played & the sun peeped forth & the orphans cheered & the old women waved, & they all went off in a general flourish."

It was the last grand flourish that either of the Gladstones was to enjoy, but a few months of contented activity remained to him and the occasional moments of pleasure for her. By the summer of 1897 Gladstone's voracious reading and letter-writing were on the wane. One of the last letters he wrote was to Eddy Hamilton. The hand is very shaky and scrawling, particularly in contrast to Gladstone's previous beautiful firm (though extremely difficult to decipher) flow, but his mind was unimpaired and he wrote of the garden at Downing Street when he was first Chancellor of the Exchequer in 1852 and of the "disgraceful" current mania for destroying London's old buildings in the name of progress. On the envelope flap he wrote, "for disgraceful read deplorable," which in his eighty-eighth year was a nice Gladstonian touch of precision. During 1897 Mary and Harry Drew and Dossie left Hawarden Castle, as he had finally obtained his own parish, but they did not go far, merely to the adjoining parish of Buckley. Mary and Dossie made frequent visits to the castle and in the afternoons the little girl would ride with her grandparents in the ancient victoria carriage. When it was raining the hood and apron were drawn up and they played games in which each selected his/her puddle formed by the raindrops on the apron and waited to see which puddle would engulf the others first.

At the end of November the elderly couple went to stay in Cannes, this time accompanied by Herbert, and it was in Cannes that the violent, painful symptoms of the cancer which was gnawing at Gladstone's cheekbone became apparent. However, the disease was not immediately diagnosed and the doctors considered that he was suffering from a severe form of nasal catarrh. But the pain grew more agonising and by early February he and Catherine had returned home. It was decided that the slightly warmer south coast air of Bournemouth would be more beneficial than the northern chill of Hawarden; as Gladstone passed through London the Prince of Wales called on him for what was to be their last meeting. In Bournemouth the Gladstones were joined by Mary, Helen and Lucy Cavendish, as well as Herbert and Henry; Mary and Lucy were as worried about Catherine's condition as they were by Gladstone's. On 24 February 1898 Mary said that late at night her father called her into his room and told her the history of the last three months, of his terrible battle with pain and his utter collapse. Temporarily, Mary displayed a certain Gladstonian lack of sympathy with the tinge of self-pity and considered that part of her father's trouble was that he had been allowed to abandon his activities and therefore "the whole of his great unimpaired brain is turned on to his own ailments." It was Lucy Cavendish who told her uncle that he must try and pull himself together for his wife's sake because Catherine was by now very frail and feeble, and the drugs she was being given to relieve the pain of acute neuralgia or to enable her to sleep at night were further clouding her mind and slurring her speech.

The pain Gladstone himself was suffering was not diminishing, and while she remained in Bournemouth Mary played the piano to her father for two- or three-hour stretches, "softly as he could not bear it loud, & by heart as he could not bear a pause." (Mary had already performed the same service for John Ruskin as his mind flickered between sanity and madness.) In the middle of March she returned to Buckley, and on the nineteenth of the month she received a telegram from her sister Helen: "I had given her 3 words as a code, & it was the fatal one. O the nightmare of it." Gladstone himself had been told the news the previous day, that the recent swelling on his palate *was* malignant and that there was no hope of recovery. Some time earlier he had spoken to his ex-secretary, Arthur Godley, about his "excessive vitality and power of resistance" and said that one day he might have to pay for it. In the last six months of his life, from the onset of the pain in November 1897 to the final release in May 1898, he paid dearly; but once Gladstone had been told that he was facing a painful death he accepted it with the courage and fortitude which his Christian faith commanded.

On Tuesday, 22 March 1898, the Gladstones returned to Hawarden and in Mary's words, "They arrived at 7.30, the journey wonderfully accomplished. It was a blessed moment to see him come home—even though it was to die. It was most piteous, he quite under the morphia influence, she all innocent of the tragedy." But somehow, although Catherine's mind was far from lucid and none of her children actually told her that the glory of her life was dying, as the sad days and weeks went by she slowly appreciated the truth and rallied the last reserves of her strength. Towards the end, as her daughter-in-law Maud wrote, "She is perfectly her old self and talks most beautifully—the cloud of the last year completely vanished."

Gladstone did not spend the final months of his life entirely under the influence of morphine; the drug was only administered when the pain was intense, and until 9 April he insisted on struggling into the garden to sit in a shelter which his children had erected for him. On 15 April the trustees of St. Deiniol's library visited the castle and Gladstone was able to discuss its affairs with them, but after 18 April he was no longer capable of coming downstairs for his meals, and on 29 April he dictated his last letter, which, fittingly, was in reply to a message of sympathy from his beloved Oxford University. At the end of the month he asked his doctors if the release might be soon and when they replied in the affirmative he said fervently, "Thank God." To Mary, who was sitting by his bedside one evening, he said, " 'Bless you all,' then with great emphasis and deliberation 'Carry my blessing to my wife.' "

By the beginning of May Gladstone was enduring intense pain and was being heavily drugged. Catherine spent hours sitting by his bedside, and in his conscious moments Mary played his favourite music—Handel and Arne —on the piano which had been installed in the bedroom and Dossie sang his favourite hymns, "Rock of Ages" and "Praise to the Highest in the Height." (Gladstone preferred "highest" though Cardinal Newman's lines are more usually known as "holiest in the height.") Close friends and colleagues called to pay their last respects, Lord Rosebery and John Morley among them, and telegrams and letters of sympathy flooded in, including a "lovely" one from the Princess of Wales. On 12 May Mary said she heard him saying the Lord's Prayer at midnight, and three days later she said her father recognised her instantly when she called to see him before she went to church. When she told him where she was going he replied, "To Church, how nice, how charming. Pray for me, Mary dear, and for all my fellow-Christians and all the unhappy and miserable people." But not long after, he spoke his last lucid words, which were taken down by Helen: "God bless you. God bless you—may a good and silver light shine down upon your path. I am quite comfortable, quite comfortable. I am only waiting, only waiting . . . but it is a long time the end. Kindness, kindness, nothing but kindness on every side."

The end came on 19 May 1898, Ascension Day. At two o'clock in the morning the family was called to Gladstone's bedside in the small, simple room into which he had been moved. Mary, Helen, Agnes, Gertrude, Henry and his wife Maud, Stephen, Herbert and Harry Drew grouped round the bed and Catherine knelt on the right-hand side as her husband's breathing grew slower and each gasp became more laboured, until just before five o'clock in the morning, as Stephen gave the last blessing, it stopped. Mary wrote, "It was a moment full of wonder, mystery and awe, the deep and utter stillness after these long heart-aching days and hours." As the dawn spread on an early summer morning of divine beauty, the news was given to the journalists who had been keeping their vigil outside the castle for the last few days. With a single bell of Hawarden church slowly tolling, most of Gladstone's children walked through the gathering sunshine, with the leaves a soft green in the park, the summer flowers massed in colour, the sky a perfect blue, to attend the seven o'clock service and pray for the soul of their father. Gladstone's last hours were the embodiment of the Victorian Christian dream, death coming peacefully in his own home, as he lay surrounded by his family. Eddy Hamilton expressed the widespread sentiment when he wrote, "It was the ideal and noble end of an ideal and noble life."

The news of Gladstone's death reverberated in every corner of the world, and in the United States in particular there was a sense of great loss and deep mourning. In the early 1860s when he made his speech about Jefferson Davis, Gladstone had hardly been a Yankee idol but in recent years his Liberalism and his passionate defence of freedom had endeared him to many Americans, while his fight for Home Rule had won him the admiration of Irish-Americans (Eugene O'Neill, born 1888, was but one Irish-American child given the middle name of Gladstone). The New York *Tribune* said simply, "The world has lost its greatest citizen," and prayers on the death of "this grand old man" were said in the House of Representatives and in the Senate. The letters and telegrams of condolence poured in from Heads of State and Ambassadors, from Mayors and Lord Mayors, from political associations in England and abroad, from Archbishops and Cardinals and Rabbis, from the eminent and the lowly. So great was the volume of messages that scores of extra postmen had to be drafted in from Chester, Liverpool and Shrewsbury (they duly had their photograph taken—twenty-two men and one woman—standing in front of the post office in Hawarden High Street).

On 20 May both Houses of Parliament adjourned in honour of Mr. Gladstone's memory, and Arthur Balfour in the Commons and Lord Salisbury in the upper chamber introduced resolutions that he be given a state funeral and interred in Westminster Abbey. After he had learned that he was dying Gladstone himself had expressed some typically ambivalent thoughts about his funeral, namely that he wished to be buried quietly at Hawarden "unless the reasons against it are overwhelming." To Gladstone's sons the reasons against did begin to appear overwhelming and on 11 May Herbert Gladstone told Eddy Hamilton that while he half-liked the idea of the quiet funeral at Hawarden, the idea also appealed that "the most conspicuous Englishman of the 19th century be laid to rest alongside some of his greatest predecessors in what many consider the Nation's Cemetery for its great worthies." Gladstone had insisted that wherever he was buried, Catherine must be buried too, but there were no objections to his wife's body ultimately being laid to rest beside his in Westminster Abbey. The state funeral, though with minimum pomp and ceremony, was therefore agreed upon.

While a committee of management, consisting of the Duke of Norfolk (as the Earl Marshal of England, traditionally entrusted with state ceremonial), Reginald Brett and Eddy Hamilton, was set up to make the arrangements for the funeral, at Hawarden Catherine had regained her sanity, her composure, her dignity and her thought for others in distress. Four days after William's death she heard the news that a young miner had been killed in a local colliery accident, and she insisted that Mary drive her to see the widow so that she could console the young woman in their mutual hour of sorrow. On 24 May Gladstone's body was laid in the Temple of Peace robed in his Oxford gown, and some three thousand people from the neighbourhood filed through. Early in the morning of 25 May the body was placed in a simple coffin and drawn on a bier from the castle to the church where it was to lie in local state for the remainder of the day. The

Gladstone children with their wives and husbands and their own children
walked behind the bier as it was pulled by Hawarden villagers through the
park, across the High Street, into the churchyard, in the early morning
stillness of another glorious summer day. At the small medieval church
Catherine and Stephen Gladstone were waiting and Holy Communion was
celebrated as a private family affair.

Then the church was opened to the public and for the rest of the day
Hawarden became something of a bear garden or, in *The Times'* words, it
was "victimised by a devouring crowd." Thousands of people were dis-
gorged from the nearby railway stations or arrived on foot or on bicycles;
many filed through the church but more roamed through the Hawarden estate and village and, again to quote *The Times*, "it would hardly be true to
say that the scene has been solemn." At five o'clock the church was again
closed to the public while the family held the last simple service for Gladstone in the building which he had loved so dearly, and at six o'clock the
coffin on its bier, but this time drawn by horses, left for its last journey
through Hawarden. At the head of the procession a golden cross was
carried, then came the choir and clergy, followed by Catherine, her children and grandchildren, and as it reached the High Street a Volunteer Bat-
talion of the Royal Welch Fusiliers and mounted constables from Gladstone's home town of Liverpool fell in. When the procession arrived at the
gates of the estate it stopped and the bands played "Rock of Ages." As it
made its way through the park, with the evening sun dappling the grass
and glinting on the cross, the sense of occasion overcame "the somewhat
disorderly crowd" and silence fell. The procession passed in front of Hawarden Castle and rounded the ruins of the old castle before making its
way through the other side of the park to Broughton station. It made its
final halt in Hawarden beneath a splendid horse-chestnut tree whose "candles" seemed as if they were alight in the rays of the setting sun, and
"Praise to the Highest in the Height" was sung by the choir. One by one
the crowd joined in until thousands of voices were singing, and Gladstone's
favourite hymn reverberated through the beeches and elms and oaks as the
summer sun sank to its rest.

At Broughton station the crowds were again somewhat disorderly and
unmanageable, and one of the horses which had been drawing the bier
took fright as the steam engine (named *Gladstone*) belched forth, but
eventually the coffin was transferred to the train, which finally drew out of
Broughton station just before eight o'clock. Originally it had been planned
that only members of the family and mourners from the Hawarden estate
should travel on the funeral train, but Herbert Gladstone, appreciating his
father's lack of aversion to publicity and his rapport with the gentlemen of
the press, allowed the dozens of correspondents to accompany them. As the
train steamed out, somebody called "Hats off" and thousands of men
reverently obeyed, and all the way from Broughton to Chester, in the dying
light, the track was lined by men with their heads bared. *The Times'* corre-

spondent was particularly impressed by the numbers of "the labouring classes"—"rough navvies and coalheavers"—who stood with their grimy caps in their hands, and by the scores of children who had been brought by their parents to watch Mr. Gladstone's funeral train pass by. Chester was reached soon after eight o'clock; its ancient city walls were packed with people straining to catch a glimpse of the train, but by now the light was fast fading and once the train had cleared the city which Gladstone had visited on so many triumphant occasions, it gathered speed. However, at every small station and village it passed through knots of people were gathered, and on the large stations of Crewe and Stafford hundreds again lined the platforms in the darkness. It was at Rugby, the last major junction before London was reached, that the most extraordinary demonstration of affection occurred. The train arrived at nearly a quarter to eleven, yet thousands of people, young and old, packed the station and its approaches, the town band was on the main platform and as the train slowly steamed through the men removed their hats, the women bowed their heads, the band played the "Dead March" from *Saul* and Handel's solemn, majestic music echoed through the night air.

The coffin reached Westminster Hall, where it was to lie in state, soon after one o'clock on the morning of 26 May, and throughout that night and the next friends and officials stood an hourly watch. The Hall was opened to the public at 6 A.M.; the first to arrive was a woman who took up her vigil at 3 A.M., and by 5:30 A.M. the line of mourners stretched across Westminster Bridge and wound round St. Thomas's Hospital on the south side of the Thames. Throughout the day people filed past the catafalque, at the peak periods at the rate of some sixteen thousand an hour. They included the high and the low—Sir William Harcourt visited several times during the day and was observed to be deeply moved, and a party of Indians from Madras "excited no little comment." Though the Gladstone family had agreed to the public funeral, they also adhered to their vow of the minimum of pomp, and the only splash of colour in the ancient hall of Westminster was a white, blue and gold silk pall which draped the closed coffin and which had been presented to Gladstone by members of the Armenian Church after his speeches on the Armenian massacres.

Gladstone's death was not mentioned in the Court Circular and Eddy Hamilton wrote to Sir Arthur Bigge, Her Majesty's new secretary (Sir Henry Ponsonby was now dead), that it was an omission that had "given rise to a good deal of unfortunate comment. I have not heard a whisper of it in his family circles. They are probably highly gratified by the Queen's personal expression of sympathy with Mrs. G. But outside those circles invidious comparisons have been drawn between what took place at the time of Lord Beaconsfield's death and that of his rival." Hamilton was being kind and tactful in his comments; the failure even to mention Gladstone's death drew upon Queen Victoria's head some of the fiercest criticism since "the royalty crisis" of the early 1870s. The criticism came from Tory papers as much as Liberal ones, and the Leicester *Daily Mercury* summed up the feeling at its angrier levels: "While the whole world was mourning the loss of the greatest man of the century, the official record of the doings of Her Majesty never once interrupted the dreary and meaningless recital of drives and visits to express the Sovereign's sense of the loss of her oldest and most beloved statesman of her reign." The trouble was that Her Majesty did not feel *any* sense of loss. She succinctly expressed her private feelings: "I am sorry for Mrs. G: as for him, I never liked him, & I will say nothing about him." The Queen certainly carried into effect Lord Acton's strictures to Mary Gladstone about her father's behaviour on the death of Lord Beaconsfield; she did not allow herself to execute the popular wish when it contradicted her emotions and beliefs.

Her Majesty's anger at the adverse comments was exacerbated when the Prince of Wales not only stood by the catafalque in Westminster Hall but suggested that he be one of the pallbearers at the funeral. Eddy Hamilton wrote, "I doubt if the Prince of Wales ever did an act which, being so closely in accord with the national feeings, tended more to command universal approval than his taking his place by the bier." But his mother was furious and sent her son a telegram in which she said that he had no right to be a pallbearer without consulting her, and in any case it was an unconstitutional and unprecedented act for the heir apparent to perform. At the age of fifty-seven the Prince of Wales stood up to his mother for almost the first time in his life and by return telegram informed her that he had not consulted her "Owing to Mr. G being so old & knew him so well," that he could not forget how much he owed to Gladstone and that in making the offer he felt he would be "falling in with wishes & feelings of the nation." Her Majesty's verdict on Mr. Gladstone was expressed in a letter to her daughter Vicky, who had for some years been the Dowager Empress of Prussia. In the letter she told her daughter that she had been quite right to send a representative to Mr. Gladstone's funeral but she could not agree that "he was 'a great Englishman.' He was a clever man, full of talent, but he never tried to keep up the honour & prestige of Gt. Britain. He gave away the Transvaal & he abandoned Gordon, he destroyed the Irish Church & he tried to separate England from Ireland & to set class against class. The harm he did cannot easily be undone." Her Majesty obviously felt that she may have been a little hard in her judgement and allowed her disapproval to run away with her, for she added, "But he was a good & very religious man."

The interment in Westminster Abbey took place on Saturday, 28 May 1898; it was a chilly grey day. Catherine, Mary and Dossie had been staying with Lucy Cavendish at Carlton House Terrace since their arrival in London and they were at the Abbey by 10:15 A.M. The ride through the London streets was one which Dossie in her old age remembered as being frightening for a child of eight, the pavements densely packed with people but everywhere eerily silent, and hundreds of mounted and foot policemen on duty; but her mother comforted her with the thought that her beloved grandma was there so everything would be all right. At ten-thirty the Commons emerged from their chamber and walked slowly in procession to Westminster Hall, over four hundred members four abreast, led by the Speaker in full regalia and the Sergeant-at-arms bearing the mace. Shortly afterwards they were followed by the Lords temporal and spiritual, also walking four abreast and headed by Black Rod, the mace-bearer, the purse-bearer and the Lord Chancellor. Solemnly the long procession filed into Westminster Hall to pay the last respects to the man who had been one of the greatest of British parliamentarians. After the two Houses had paid their tributes the foreign and British dignitaries and the members of the royal family or their representatives joined the procession (Queen Victoria *was* represented, by the Earl of Pembroke). As Big Ben boomed eleven o'clock across a silent Westminster the cortege moved slowly from New Palace Yard on the last brief journey to the Abbey, and in the greyness of the day and the darkness of the thousands of bodies packing Parliament Square there appeared suddenly, in *The Times'* words, "a broad ribbon of rosy white," as the men in the crowd uncovered their heads.

Gladstone's simple coffin lay on a plain bier drawn by two horses, and was followed by the male family mourners, young and old, close friends and Liberal colleagues, a group of his private secretaries and a hundred villagers from Hawarden. The ceremonial was kept to the minimum, there was no military escort or bands, and again the only splash of colour was the Armenian pall draping the coffin. But the pallbearers were illustrious, including two future Kings of England—the Prince of Wales (Edward VII) and his son the Duke of York (George V)—three past, present and future Prime Ministers—the Earl of Rosebery, the Marquis of Salisbury and Arthur Balfour—two distinguished Liberals from each House—Sir William Harcourt and the Earl of Kimberley—two old friends—Lord Rendel and George Armitstead—and the Duke of Rutland. The cortege entered Westminster Abbey by the west door, passing through an escort of boys from Gladstone's "queen of all schools," Eton, and to the strains of Beethoven's *Eroica* march the coffin was borne slowly up the chancel to where Catherine was waiting.

After the service, which included Gladstone's favourite hymns and the music of his favourite composers, Catherine supported by Henry and Herbert knelt by the open graveside. (In the already well-filled confines of Westminster Abbey, the gravediggers had had problems with the new grave. At one point they hit another coffin, then they had trouble with fine sandy soil; their progress was reported with morbid interest in the newspapers.) Throughout the service Lord Rosebery described Mrs. Gladstone as "a figure of indescribable pathos," and as she knelt by the graveside and the coffin was lowered he recorded her saying, "'Once more, only once more' (I was close) with a dim idea, I think, that she was to kiss him, but the two sons gently raised her." Each member of the family had knelt in turn, including young Will Gladstone, Stephen Gladstone's three sons, Agnes Wickham's children and little Dossie, and during these scenes Lord Salisbury and Sir William Harcourt were but two members of the congregation observed to brush the tears from their eyes. The "Dead March" from *Saul* was played on the Abbey's magnificent organ, with the band joining in and the congregation standing for the last refrains; then a peal of bells rang out and, as Sir Edward Burne-Jones wrote, ". . . it was almost more than one could bear." When the ceremony was completed, Catherine asked if she could shake hands with the pallbearers to express her thanks to them, but as the Prince of Wales complied with the request he bent low and kissed her hand and the nine other gentlemen followed his example, either bending or kneeling in front of Catherine; many of them had tears in their eyes. Mary wrote of Lord Salisbury, "the great stooping figure shaken with emotion as he bent over Mama and kissed her hand, quite unable to speak."

After a brief rest at Lucy Cavendish's house, Catherine insisted on returning to Hawarden the same evening. For a while after the trauma of her husband's death she retained her dignity, composure and sanity, her sense of drama and occasion rising to its last great challenge. At the end of May she attended the dedication in Hawarden church of the stained glass window which Sir Edward Burne-Jones had designed. Burne-Jones was a great friend of Mary's, one of the artists for whom Gladstone had obtained the official recognition of a knighthood, and the window had been intended as a present to their parents from all the Gladstone children. Alas, Gladstone did not live to see the completion of the window, which many consider to be Burne-Jones' *chef d'oeuvre*, with its beautiful simple lines stretching across the four sections and its glorious predominating blues and greens. The subject is the nativity of Christ. In July 1898 Mary wrote to Eddy Hamilton to tell him that her mother was bearing up with wonderful fortitude, that her health was good and that she was still "full of interest in things . . . we go . . . near Felixstowe in August as she pines for the bracing sea. Lord Rosebery has been unremitting in his care and love for Mama."

Thereafter, Catherine drifted into the condition in which she had been for the year before her husband's death, and as with many elderly people whose faculties fail, the past became the present. She would talk to visitors as if she were the young Catherine Glynne riding her pony in Hawarden park or dancing the night through or taking exhilarating bathes in the sea, as if Lord Lincoln or Sir Robert Peel or Henry Manning were still alive. Eventually, in Eddy Hamilton's words, she became "'mindless' at times and difficult to manage," and early in May 1900 Mary wrote, "I saw Mama each day, but each time I said Goodbye she was unable to gain any self control, & we had the most disturbing scenes." As Catherine had loved and protected her husband for so many years, in turn in her decline she was loved and protected by her family. Lucy Cavendish was a frequent visitor to the castle and spent hours with her aunt, and Mary and Dossie came up every day from Buckley riding on their bicycles. On 10 May 1900 Catherine paid her last visit to the rectory at Buckley and Mary said, "her voice was strangely altered, very deep & hoarse & unlike herself." On 22 May she left Hawarden Castle for the last time to take a drive with Mary: "She was very strange & sad, & spoke so particularly of Willy."

On 26 May Catherine was taken ill with bronchitis which turned into pneumonia and the doctors informed her children that she could not survive more than a day or two; but they underestimated her stamina. For the last time she revealed her strength of character and her deep-rooted resilience. She rallied physically and mentally, and Mary wrote, "We had some very dear little chats & sometimes when I lay on the bed near her, she got quite happy. The mere sound of Dossie's name brought a smile to her lips." By 9 June Catherine was mostly unconscious and it was thought that she would not last through the night, but she hung on until 14 June 1900, when at 5:40 p.m., surrounded by her children and relations, she died peacefully. On 18 June, in accordance with her husband's wishes, Catherine's body was laid to rest beside his in Westminster Abbey. There were no mass demonstrations of affection and her body did not lie in state in Westminster Hall, but the coffin was drawn on a bier through Hawarden as his had been, and many people from the district turned out to pay their last respects. The service in the Abbey was exactly the same as his had been, with the same hymns, the same music and the same final organ solo of the "Dead March." If the roll call of mourners at her funeral was not quite as illustrious as at her husband's, it contained most of the famous names in England, and representatives were present from the Woodford Convalescent Home, the London Hospital, the Newport Market Refuge, the Hawarden Orphanage and the Women's Liberal Federation. The Prince and Princess of Wales were unable to attend but "darling Princess Alix" sent an enormous and very beautiful wreath with a handwritten inscription, "In memory of dear Mrs. Gladstone—It is but crossing with a bated breath, A white set face! a little strip of sea, To find the loved ones waiting on the shore, More beautiful, more precious, than before. Alexandra."

As had occurred after Gladstone's death, a memorial fund for Catherine was opened and Mary displayed much of her mother's unremitting determination and energy in chasing subscriptions. In August 1900 she used her daughter Dossie as a means of tugging at the heart and purse strings of the very aged Queen Victoria and extracting a subscription from her. After the Cannes encounter in 1897 Her Majesty had commanded Mrs. Drew to bring her daughter to Windsor, and Mary instructed her ten-year-old daughter to write, "Dorothy Drew's humble duty to Your Majesty: it would be a very great honour and privilege to receive a subscription towards the memorial: it is a Free Convalescent home which Dan-Dan founded in 1866 and which has received since then between thirty and forty thousand pounds and people who loved Dan-Dan want to help the Home to go on. Dorothy will never forget her visit to Your Majesty at Windsor Castle and Your Majesty's loving kindness to her, and she feels very sad now to think of the Queen's great sorrow and is her devoted subject Dorothy Drew." The royal subscription was refused on the grounds that Her Majesty never gave to individual memorials, but Mary obtained £1,000 from Andrew Carnegie (whom she had met years ago at Downing Street) and generous subscriptions from Catherine's old faithfuls such as Lord Rosebery and Sir William Harcourt. Eventually, £11,000 was raised and the Catherine Gladstone Convalescent Home was moved from Woodford into new and more spacious premises at Ravensbury House at Mitcham, which was then deep in the woods and heathland of Surrey. For years the Home remained a living memorial to a woman who had cared about the sick and needy, as the St. Deiniol's library was a living memorial to her husband's deep love for the European literary and religious inheritance.

After her father's death Mary replied to a sympathetic letter from Eddy Hamilton, "Yes the world has become a much duller place now." It seems an admirable comment on the deaths of both Catherine and William Ewart Gladstone.

EPILOGUE

On the day of Catherine's death Eddy Hamilton wrote, "She was unquestionably a very remarkable woman, and very few persons have spent a more unselfish life than she did, in actually striving to do good and doing good to others in the kindest possible way. Her first consideration was her husband—how to spare him and how to advise him to spare himself. Her second consideration were the poor and the sick; and her third consideration her friends. She had considerable capacities. People were apt to make a joke of her and term her (illegible), but she almost always attained her end . . . Her rather harum-scarum ways gave constant rise to comment: but she was much less harum-scarum herself than people gave her credit for. I remember Mr. G once saying, 'My wife has a tidiness & order of her own.' He meant that if she had lost a letter she generally knew where she had lost it . . . She would say exactly the right thing when it was wanted to be said. From no one did I receive greater or more uniform kindness."

The assessments of Gladstone started before he died and have continued ever since. The longevity of his career, the complexity of his character and the diversity of his activities have produced a tendency to focus on individual aspects, particularly in recent years as historical study has become specalised: Gladstone as financier, economist, theologian; Gladstone and Liberalism, and the Irish, and Radicalism, and the Bulgarian massacres. The area which has been least assiduously tilled either in general or in detail is his foreign policy, but there has been the occasional book about Gladstone and women. However, these were written after the celebrated Wright libel case in 1927 but before his own thoughts on his inner sexual struggles became known, and they are of the tentatively salacious variety. The 1927 libel case occurred after a journalist named Peter Wright had written an extraordinary *en passant* sentence in a book entitled *Portraits and Criticisms*. The words Captain Wright chose to throw into an essay about Lord Robert Cecil and the League of Nations stated that it was Mr. Gladstone's habit "in public to speak the language of the highest and strictest principle, and in private to pursue and possess every sort of woman." It was a comment which made the Gladstone sons decide they must take action, and as the dead cannot be libelled in English law they forced Captain Wright to sue them. During the action Wright made assertions about Mr. Gladstone's suspect relationships with Laura Thistlethwayte, Olga Novikoff, Katie O'Shea and Lillie Langtry which produced from the surviving member of the quartet, Mrs. Langtry, a strongly worded telegram insisting that the friendship had been dignified and platonic, and the comment that if she had required a lover she would not have needed to select a man in his seventies. Other assertions were easily disproven and Gladstone's name emerged from court without a stain on its high moral character. It was not stainless, and he did have the strong sexual urges which his detractors suspected, but equally he did not "pursue and possess every sort of woman."

Mary Drew read one volume of her father's diaries in 1917 and was so profoundly impressed by the portrait contained in its pages that she thought all the diaries should be published. Her brothers had reservations and considered that the difficulty of publication was that the spiritual misgivings, self-accusations and confessions of human weakness were "definitely connected with the other sex," but they did not destroy the diaries. The decision not to do so is a tribute to their integrity and to their belief that the transgressions therein revealed did not lessen Gladstone's greatness, even if they caused his sons some qualms. Mary's instant, publish-and-be-praised reaction was perhaps a feminine one—it is shared by me—but the sexual passions which Gladstone struggled to control in his unpassionate language complete the portrait of the whole man and were a part of the politician, certainly of the one who won the hearts and confidence of millions.

By the time of the Wright libel suit Gladstone's popular reputation had begun to sink. The First World War and the spectacle of the advanced nations drowning each other in mud and blood were recent history, and books such as *Eminent Victorians* had been published with their scathing reactions to what seemed the moral hypocrisy, sanctimonious self-righteousness and sheer smug naïvety of their parents. Gladstone, as one of the greatest of Victorian figures, became a major victim of anti-Victorianism, a phenomenon of his age who had little relevance for the twentieth century. He suffered in comparison with his rival Disraeli, the man for all seasons who appreciated that mankind was selfish, greedy, treacherous, deceitful as well as sometimes being kind, generous, noble and unselfish, who with a swish of the pen or a roll of the tongue encapsuled the cant and ridiculousness of life. Even Disraeli's nineteenth-century imperialism managed to retain a romantic aura, as a manifestation of his period's attitudes which in no way obviated his mordant timelessness. As a politician who in his major years operated to the left of the political spectrum, Gladstone also suffered from the criticism of what he did not attempt to achieve, for failing to tackle the social and industrial problems. Justifiably, he has been criticised for his major blind spot, science, for limiting his scientific controversies to the field of theology and unbelief, for not appreciating that scientific development was one of the wonders and threats of the nineteenth century and that the twentieth century, as well as being the century of the masses, would be the technological age. Gladstone was essentially professional in his approach to life, but his scientific block led him to support the English amateur empiricism that had helped to create the Industrial Revolution but which had also lost Britain her industrial lead long before he died, as first Germany and then the United States harnessed scientific knowledge to the inventor's flair.

Yet in some areas Gladstone was more prescient and less a man of his age than Disraeli. His latter-day conviction that Anglo-Irish relations were the urgent question and, if not settled, would fester until they burst into an open running sore has proved only too correct. His attitude towards colonial power and vast empires was untypical of late-nineteenth-century Europe, and his belief that if one possessed colonies they should be guided towards autonomy has been vindicated, though it may be added that he would have opposed the twentieth century's ideological colonialism as vehemently and passionately. The battle of unbelief which Gladstone in his later years saw as the major one is still being fought, and while religion may have been the opium of the masses, much of mankind is suffering from the withdrawal symptoms and from the problem of learning to fly without its old wings.

Gladstone helped rouse "the people," not only in Britain, by showing that he cared for them *en masse* and giving them hope for the future. In some quarters this is regarded as all he gave; in others that he was the classic example of the liberal bourgeois leader keeping the proletariat in its place by feeding it the odd lump of sugar and thereby slowing down the revolutionary process; and in yet others that clear lines can be drawn from Gladstone's Midlothian campaigns, with their torchlight processions and hysterical enthusiasm, to the Nuremberg rallies, and from his backing of the masses against the classes to the manipulation of those masses in the totalitarian states he would have denounced. For idealists in every generation who are not blinkered by the narrowness of their view and their causes, Gladstone should have a permanent appeal because of his deep-rooted belief in individual liberty, human dignity and transcendent justice. Politically, he was one of the ablest men ever to grace a democratic assembly, and the idea that he was *more* interested in the spiritual life is one that in my opinion should be quietly buried. At times he genuinely longed to escape from the toils of the world but he wrote of the *romance* of politics and until the last moment whenever he was presented with or took the opportunity of retirement, he did not accept it or it failed to satisfy him.

For the reason that Gladstone was a shining reflector rather than a great initiator—as his critics frequently pointed out—it is again difficult to accept him solely as a man of his age. It is hard to believe that the man who moved from being the rising hope of those stern, unbending Tories to being the bogeyman of high society and Tory backwoodsmen would not, had he lived in the twentieth century, with the same wide-ranging intellect, enthusiasm and physical stamina, have made an equal progression towards the needs of that century. Exactly towards what is in the realms of speculation, and historians are not supposed to speculate, but—the great pragmatic English socialist? It is not difficult to visualise Mr. Gladstone zooming across the world by jet aircraft, attending conferences to initiate détentes between nations, to curb the proliferation of nuclear weapons, to examine the problems of the monetary system and those of the Third World; and the populist in him would assuredly have accepted the media of radio and television with alacrity. It is even less difficult to picture Catherine by his side, descending from aeroplanes, gracing summit meetings, attending conferences in her own right or conducting television crews round Hawarden Castle.

Finally, there was the vital enduring relationship between the Gladstones. They were among the rare minority of human beings who find complementing partners, who have a common interest which overcomes the inevitable dissensions, whose love age does not weary, nor the years condemn. What sort of man Gladstone might have become had he not met Catherine Glynne is again speculative—a sanctimonious repressed prig? or the figure painted by Peter Wright and other detractors?—as is the person Catherine Glynne might have become had she not met the glory of her life. The portrait of a woman as eccentric as Gladstone's sister Helen and considerably more meddlesome in the lives of those who surrounded her emerges as a possibility. Together the Gladstones were a great partnership which, even with some of the suffocating wrappings removed, almost fulfilled the Victorian dream of matrimony.

John Morley ended his massive biography with lines from a speech Gladstone made to a group of Hawarden schoolboys on 19 September 1877. The choice was excellent because it was typically Gladstonian; for later generations it has a Victorian ring but its message remains inspiriting, and it expresses Catherine's vision as much as her husband's. What Gladstone said to his schoolboy audience in 1877 was, "Be inspired with the belief that life is a great and noble calling; not a mean and grovelling thing that we are to shuffle through as we can, but an elevated and lofty destiny."

SOURCES AND BIBLIOGRAPHY

The personal papers of Catherine and William Gladstone, which are known as the Glynne-Gladstone MSS, are currently lodged at the Clwyd County Record Office in the Old Rectory at Hawarden. They include the Gladstones' own correspondence 1839–93, Gladstone's letters to his parents, brothers and sisters and his wife's to her Glynne, Lyttleton and Cavendish relations. Most of Catherine's diaries are at Hawarden, there is a selection from Lord and Lady Lincoln's literally singed correspondence which Gladstone salvaged from the fire at Clumber, also the details of the Oak Farm crash, Gladstone's subsequent efforts to save the Hawarden estate and other information on his financial affairs. Among the papers are Helen Gladstone's transcripts of her father's diaries for the years 1831, 1836, 1844, 1852, 1855, 1856, 1857, 1874, 1875, 1876, 1877, 1878 and 1879. For the early years the transcripts are brief and selective, for the later ones they are much more detailed and the years 1855–56 appear to be complete. Why Miss Gladstone set herself this task or why she chose these particular years I do not know, and she abandoned the project abruptly at March 1879. As her father's diaries have been officially published only up to 1854 I would emphasise that most of my quotations after that year are from Helen Gladstone's transcripts, which I considered to be trustworthy. For the years after 1854 which her transcripts do not cover, the diary quotations are from John Morley's extracts as published in his official biography of Gladstone. Among the Glynne-Gladstone MSS there are also letters from Gladstone's female friends, such as the ones quoted from C. E. Booth, from Mr. and Mrs. Banks about Miss Housley, and about Miss Throckmorton (Chapter 8); similarly the one about Mrs. Thistlethwayte preaching in Scotland, quoted in Chapter 15, which was from Gladstone's colleague Napier Sturt. The task of cataloguing the Glynne-Gladstone MSS is now almost complete but there are no specific reference numbers.

The Glynne-Gladstone MSS remain in the possession of the Gladstone family but the W. E. Gladstone Papers in the British Library were given to the nation. They comprise the largest collection of private papers of the nineteenth century and have their own catalogue, Add mss 44086-44835. Separately catalogued are Add mss 56444-56543, a miscellaneous but interesting collection which John Morley retained after writing the official biography and which did not resurface until 1970. The bulk of the Gladstone Papers is the political and religious correspondence and memoranda over sixty years but there is more personal material, such as the Most Private memorandum on Jessy Gladstone's death (Add mss 44738), the memorandum of Gladstone's interview with Queen Victoria after the Prince Consort's death (Add mss 44752), retrospective lists of his Recorded Errors, thoughts on his early career and the final audience with the Queen (Add mss 44790 and 44791). His travel diaries are also in the British Library (Add mss 44818).

Mary Gladstone/Drew's correspondence and diaries are similarly lodged in the British Library. The unpublished diary entries from which I quote cover the years of Gladstone's retirement and Catherine's last years and death (Add mss 46264). Among the Gladstone/Drew Papers there are many unpublished letters from her mother (Add mss 46222/29); from her father (Add mss 46221); letters to her mother from various friends such as Lord Granville, Henry Manning and Lady Salisbury (Add mss 46267-69). One of her mother's later Cannes diaries is among the papers (Add mss 46269), as is the diary and correspondence of Auguste Schluter (Add mss 46271). I believe that extracts from Fräulein Schluter's diaries were edited and published in the 1920s but I was unable to trace a copy of the book.

The diaries and correspondence of Sir Edward (Eddy) Hamilton are also in the British Library. For the years 1880-85 the diaries have been edited and printed (see bibliography under Hamilton); the reference numbers for the unpublished extracts from which I quote are Add mss 48658 (May/Sept. 1892), 48673 (March/Nov. 1898) and 48678 (Jan./Aug. 1900). Little of Hamilton's correspondence has been published; the folders from which I quote are Add mss 48607, 48608 and 48609 and they include the letters to Gladstone about his night-walking in 1882 and 1886, the letters about the incident on 6 May 1882 and general letters from Mr. and Mrs. Gladstone and Mary Drew.

The Devonshire Mss at Chatsworth, Derbyshire, include the correspondence of the 8th Duke of Devonshire (Lord Hartington of the text) with his political colleagues and with the Duchess of Manchester. The correspondence with the Duchess has no specific reference numbers but those for the political correspondence from which I quote are 340/844, 855, 856, 857, 858, 886 and 922. Lucy Cavendish's diaries are also at Chatsworth and they have been edited up to 1882 but my quotations thereafter are from the largely unpublished sections.

The Harcourt Mss comprise the diaries and some correspondence of Lewis (Loulou) Harcourt, later 1st Baron Harcourt, and are in the Bodleian Library at Oxford. The reference numbers for the diary entries from which I quote are Harcourt Mss 349, 350, 351, 376 and 377.

The Ponsonby Letters are those written by Sir Henry Ponsonby to his wife Mary from 1865 to 1895 and are in the possession of Lord Ponsonby of Shulbrede. Some of these have again been published but most of my quotations are from the source material. Mary Ponsonby's letters to her husband and her journal unfortunately appear to have been lost but extracts from both have been published.

Much of Queen Victoria's voluminous correspondence has already been published. While some of my quotations are from the published sections, some are not and I append a list of the royal references. RA indicates Royal Archives; RA Q.V. Journal indicates the transcripts of Queen Victoria's Journals made by her daughter Princess Beatrice (the originals were destroyed); GV indicates George V; other letters and numerals are the Royal Archives' reference numbers; *Letters* indicates the published series; *Guedalla* the volumes of Gladstone's and Queen Victoria's correspondence edited by Philip Guedalla; and *Henry Ponsonby* his published letters (see bibliography for further details).

RA indicates Royal Archives; RA Q.V. Journal indicates the transcripts of Queen Victoria's Journals made by her daughter Princess Beatrice (the originals were destroyed); GV indicates George V; other letters and numerals are the Royal Archives' reference numbers; *Letters* indicates the published series; *Guedalla* the volumes of Gladstone's and Queen Victoria's correspondence edited by Philip Guedalla; and *Henry Ponsonby* his published letters (see bibliography for further details). Line references are to the beginning of each quotation.

Chapter 3
P. 32, l. 27. Lord John Russell to the Queen 9 April 1840; *Letters* 1st series.

Chapter 5
P. 65, l. 31. RA Y96/30; the Queen to King Leopold 12 Aug. 1851.

Chapter 6
P. 73, l. 11. Prince Albert memo. 28 Nov. 1852; *Letters* 1st series.
P. 75, l. 36. The Queen to Lord Aberdeen; copy Catherine Gladstone diary, Glynne-Gladstone Mss, Hawarden.

Chapter 7
P. 91, l. 18. RA Y102/9; the Queen to King Leopold 10 March 1857.
P. 94, l. 23. RA Add mss 24/344; letter from the Queen 3 May 1858.

Chapter 8
P. 102, l. 39. RA 27/68; Lord Derby to the Queen 8 June 1859.
P. 105, l. 14. RA 29/1; Lord Palmerston to the Queen 1 Jan. 1861.
P. 113, l. 9. RA Q.V. Journal; 19 March 1862.

Chapter 9
P. 129, l. 38. RA PP Reg Vic 23634; Catherine Gladstone to the Queen 9 April 1867.

Chapter 10
P. 134, ll. 32, 34. RA C32/153; General Grey memo. 4 Dec. 1868.

Chapter 11
P. 152, l. 21. The Queen to Lord Hatherley 10 Aug. 1871; *Guedalla* Vol. 1.
P. 154, ll. 22, 25. Mr. Gladstone to the Queen; ibid.
P. 154, l. 36. RA Add mss J/1463; Knollys to Ponsonby 8 Dec. 1872.
P. 158, ll. 18, 22. RA A43/97 & 98; the Queen to Mr. Gladstone and vice versa 13 & 16 May 1872.

Chapter 12
P. 161, l. 27. RA Q.V. Journal; 20 Feb. 1874.
P. 162, ll. 24, 27. Ibid.

Chapter 13
P. 180, ll. 14, 16, 18. RA Add U32; the Queen to Princess Royal 12 & 26 Sept. 1876 & 3 May 1877.
P. 181, ll. 1, 3. RA Add U32; ibid. to ibid. 8 Aug. & 4 Dec. 1878.
P. 185, l. 10. Quoted Robert Blake, *Disraeli*.

Chapter 14
P. 198, ll. 42, 44. RA C34/25, 2 April 1880; Add mss 12/507, 3 April 1880.

P. 199, l. 1. Ibid.; Add mss 12/518, 4 April 1880.
P. 199, l. 20. RA C34/33; Prince Leopold to the Queen 3 April 1880.
P. 199, l. 28. RA C35/133; R. J. Copley to the Queen 9 April 1880.
P. 199, l. 34. RA C35/134; Frank Hoare to the Queen 12 April 1880.

Chapter 15
P. 205, l. 19. RA GV CC50/85; Princess May of Teck to her brother Prince
      Adolphus 3 March 1883.

Chapter 16
P. 231, l. 18. The Queen's telegram to Gladstone; *Letters* 2nd series.
P. 232, l. 36. RA 025/253; Wolseley to the Queen 30 April 1885.
P. 235, ll. 7, 9. RA C36/59; Gladstone to the Queen 14 June 1885.
P. 235, l. 14. RA Q.V. Journal; 24 June 1885.

Chapter 17
P. 243, l. 19. RA Add mss C14/46; letter from the Queen 18 Feb. 1886.
P. 243, l. 34. RA Q.V. Journal; 28 Jan. 1886.
P. 244, l. 1. Ibid.; 1 Feb. 1886.
P. 246, l. 22. RA Add U32; the Queen to Princess Royal 8 July 1886.

Chapter 18
P. 255, l. 10. RA A65/48; Lord Salisbury to the Queen 4 March 1887.

Chapter 19
P. 270, l. 26. RA C39/6; royal memo. 30 May 1892.
P. 270, ll. 27, 30, 32. further royal comments; *Henry Ponsonby*.
P. 270, l. 38. RA Q.V. Journal; 15 Aug. 1892.
P. 270, l. 45. Ibid.; 18 Aug. 1892.
P. 271, l. 6. RA Add U32; the Queen to Princess Royal 30 Nov. 1892.
P. 271, l. 27. Ibid.; 4 Oct. 1892.
P. 272, l. 7. RA C39/168; Catherine Gladstone to the Queen 2 Sept. 1892.
P. 275, l. 6. Gladstone to the Queen 28 Oct. 1892; *Guedalla* Vol. 2.
P. 277, l. 40. RA Q.V. Journal; 27 Feb. 1894.
P. 277, l. 42. Ibid.; Gladstone to the Queen.
P. 278, l. 8. RA Q.V. Journal; 1 March 1894.
P. 278, ll. 27, 30. Ibid.; 3 March 1894; and *Letters* 3rd series.
P. 280, l. 31. RA Add U32; the Queen to Princess Royal 28 March 1894.

Chapter 20
P. 292, l. 37. RA L17/73; Hamilton to Bigge 25 May 1898.
P. 293, l. 16. Ibid.
P. 293, l. 24. RA L17/66; Prince of Wales to the Queen 27 May 1898.
P. 293, l. 31. RA Add U32; the Queen to Princess Royal 31 May 1898.
P. 296, l. 42. RA PP Reg Vic 8508; Dorothy Drew to the Queen 11 Aug. 1900.

Gladstone's diaries have had a chequered history. John Morley had access to all the Gladstone papers, including the original diaries, when he was commissioned to write the official biography; but he was working as a leading member of the Liberal party which was out of office and there were areas he preferred to ignore. From his day to the moment of going to press, no other Gladstonian author has had the privilege of reading the original diaries. In 1926 they, together with the bulk of the correspondence with prostitutes and professional beauties, were given into the custody of the Archbishops of Canterbury by the Gladstone sons, and then removed from Hawarden to Lambeth Palace. Eventually, it was decided to publish the diaries and four volumes have now appeared covering the years 1826–54, but access to the Lambeth Papers is withheld until the diaries have been edited and published in their entirety.

OFFICIAL PUBLICATIONS AND NEWSPAPERS

Hansard Parliamentary Debates, Third Series, Vols. 14–377; Fourth series, Vol. 58.

Newcastle Daily Chronicle	Chester Chronicle
Staffordshire Sentinel	Leicester Mercury
The Times	Morning Post
Daily Telegraph	New York Tribune
Edinburgh Review	Nineteenth Century Review

BIBLIOGRAPHY (PLACE OF PUBLICATION LONDON UNLESS OTHERWISE STATED)

SELECTIONS FROM W. E. GLADSTONE'S PUBLICATIONS

The State in Its Relations with the Church (1838)

Two Letters to Lord Aberdeen on the State Prosecutions of the Neapolitan Government (1851)

Studies of Homer and the Homeric Age 3 vols. (1858)

The Vatican Decrees in Their Bearing on Civil Allegiance: A Political Expostulation (1874)

The Bulgarian Horrors and the Question of the East (1877)

Gleanings of Past Years 7 vols. (1879–96)

Further Gleanings (1897)

EDITED DIARIES AND LETTERS OF GLADSTONE AND HIS FAMILY

The Diary of Lady Frederick Cavendish, edited John Bailey 2 vols. (1927)

Mary Gladstone (Mrs. Drew): Her Diaries and Letters, edited Lucy Masterman (1930)

Some Hawarden Letters 1878–1917 Written to Mrs. Drew (Miss Mary Gladstone), edited Lisle March-Phillips and Bertram Christian 2 vols. (1917)

W. E. Gladstone Diaries 1826–1854 vols. 1 & 2, edited M. R. D. Foot; vols. 3 & 4, edited C. H. G. Matthew (Oxford 1968 & 1975)

Gladstone to His Wife, edited A. Tilney Bassett (1936)

The Queen and Mr. Gladstone, edited Philip Guedalla 2 vols. (1933)

Gladstone and Palmerston, edited Philip Guedalla (1928)

Correspondence on Church and Religion of W. E. Gladstone, edited D. C. Lathbury
2 vols. (1910)

The Political Correspondence of Mr. Gladstone and Lord Granville 1868–76 and
1876–86, edited Agatha Ramm 4 vols. (Oxford 1952 & 1962)

The Prime Ministers' Papers: W. E. Gladstone 2 vols. (1971–72), edited John Brooke
and Mary Sorensen

BIOGRAPHIES AND SPECIFIC STUDIES OF GLADSTONE
AND HIS FAMILY

ASKWITH, BETTY, The Lyttletons: A Family Chronicle of the Nineteenth Century
(1975)

BAGEHOT, WALTER, Biographical Studies (1881)

BARKER, MICHAEL, Gladstone and Radicalism: The Reconstruction of Liberal Policy
in Britain 1885–1894 (Brighton 1976)

BATTISCOMBE, GEORGINA, Mrs. Gladstone: The Portrait of a Marriage (1954)

BIRRELL, FRANCIS, Gladstone (1932)

BURDETT, O. H., W. E. Gladstone (1927)

BUXTON, SIDNEY, Gladstone as Chancellor of the Exchequer (1901)

CHECKLAND, S. G., The Gladstones: A Family Biography (Cambridge 1971)

DEACON, RICHARD, The Private Life of Mr. Gladstone (1965)

DREW, MARY, Catherine Gladstone (1919)

——, Acton, Gladstone and Others (1924)

——, St. Deiniol's Hawarden: Mr. Gladstone's Library (1925)

EYCK, ERICH, Gladstone (translated Bernard Miall 1938)

FEUCHTWANGER, E. J., Gladstone (1975)

FLETCHER, C. R. L., Mr. Gladstone at Oxford (1908)

FRIEDERICHS, HULDA, In the Evening of His Days (1896)

GARRATT, G. T., The Two Mr. Gladstones (1936)

GLADSTONE, VISCOUNT, After Thirty Years (1928)

HAMILTON, SIR EDWARD, Mr. Gladstone: A Monograph (1898)

HAMMOND, J. L., Gladstone and the Irish Nation (1964 edition intro. M. R. D. Foot)

HAMMOND, J. L., and FOOT, M. R. D., Gladstone and Liberalism (1952)

HIRST, FRANCIS W., Gladstone as Financier and Economist (1931)

HYDE, F. E., Mr. Gladstone at the Board of Trade (1934)

KNAPLUND, D. A., Gladstone and Britain's Imperial Policy (1927)

——, Gladstone's Foreign Policy (1935)

LATHBURY, D. C., Mr. Gladstone (1907)

LYTTLETON, LORD, Glynnese Language: A Contribution Towards a Glossary (1904
edition)

MC CARTHY, JUSTIN, The Story of Gladstone's Life (1898)

MAGNUS, PHILIP, Gladstone (1954)

MALLETT, CHARLES, Herbert Gladstone: A Memoir (1932)

MORLEY, JOHN, The Life of Gladstone 3 vols. (1903 & 1905)

PRATT, EDWIN, Catherine Gladstone: Life, Good Works and Political Effort (1898)

REID, SIR T. WEMYSS (editor), The Life of William Ewart Gladstone (1899)

ROBBINS, A. F., The Early Public Life of William Ewart Gladstone (1894)

RUSSELL, G. W. E., The Rt. Hon. W. E. Gladstone (1891)

SETON WATSON, R. W., Gladstone, Disraeli and the Eastern Question (1935)

SHANNON, R. T., *Gladstone and the Bulgarian Agitation* (1963)
SMITH, GOLDWIN, *My Memory of Mr. Gladstone* (1904)
THOMAS, IVOR, *Gladstone of Hawarden* (1936)
TOLLEMACHE, LIONEL, *Talks with Mr. Gladstone* (1898)
WILLIAMS, W. E., *The Rise of Mr. Gladstone to the Leadership of the Liberal Party* (Cambridge 1934)

OTHER BIOGRAPHIES, MEMOIRS, LETTERS AND SELECTED GENERAL WORKS

ARGYLL, THE 8TH DUKE, *Autobiography and Memoirs*, edited Dowager Duchess of Argyll 2 vols. (1906)
ARNSTEIN, W. L., *The Bradlaugh Case: A Study in Late Victorian Opinion and Politics* (Oxford 1965)
ASHWELL, A. R., and WILBERFORCE, A. G., *Life of Samuel Wilberforce* 3 vols. (1880–82)
BAGEHOT, WALTER, *The English Constitution* (1963 edition intro. Richard Crossman)
BALFOUR, ARTHUR JAMES, 1ST EARL, *Chapters of Autobiography*, edited Mrs. Edgar Dugdale (1930)
BEATTIE, ALAN (editor), *English Party Politics* (1970)
BELL, H. C. F., *Lord Palmerston* 2 vols. (1936)
BLAKE, ROBERT, *Disraeli* (1966)
——, *The Conservative Party from Peel to Churchill* (1970)
CECIL, ALGERNON, *Queen Victoria and Her Prime Ministers* (1953)
CECIL, LADY GWENDOLEN, *The Life of Robert, Marquis of Salisbury* 4 vols. (1921–31)
CHADWICK, OWEN, *The Victorian Church* 2 vols. (1966 and 1970)
CHAMBERLAIN, JOSEPH, *A Political Memoir 1880–1892*, edited C. H. D. Howard (1953)
CREWE, MARQUIS OF, *Lord Rosebery* 2 vols. (1921)
DANCE, E. H., *The Victorian Illusion* (1928)
DUGDALE, BLANCHE, *Life of Arthur James Balfour* Vol. 1 1848–1905 (1936)
ESHER, REGINALD, VISCOUNT, *Journals and Letters* Vol. 1 1875–1903, edited Maurice V. Brett (1934)
EYCK, FRANK, *The Prince Consort: A Political Biography* (1954)
FITZMAURICE, LORD, *The Life of 2nd Earl Granville* 2 vols. (1905)
FRASER, PETER, *Joseph Chamberlain: Radicalism and Empire 1868–1914* (1966)
FULFORD, ROGER, *The Prince Consort* (1949)
GARDINER, A. G., *Life of Sir William Harcourt* 2 vols. (1923)
GARVIN, J. L., *Life of Joseph Chamberlain* vols. 1 & 2 (1932–33)
GASH, NORMAN, *Politics in the Age of Peel* (1953)
——, *Mr. Secretary Peel* (1961)
——, *Sir Robert Peel* (1972)
Greville Memoirs, edited Lytton Strachey and Roger Fulford 8 vols. (1938)
GWYNN, S., and TUCKWELL, G., *Life of Sir Charles Dilke* 2 vols. (1917)
HALL, NEWMAN, *Autobiography* (1898)
HAMER, D. A., *John Morley: Liberal Intellectual in Politics* (Oxford 1968)
——, *Liberal Politics in the Age of Gladstone and Rosebery* (Oxford 1972)
HAMILTON, SIR EDWARD WALTER, *Diaries 1880–1885* 2 vols., edited Dudley W. R. Bahlman (Oxford 1972)

HANHAM, H. J., *Elections and Party Management: Politics in the Time of Disraeli and Gladstone* (1959)

HARDIE, FRANK, *The Political Influence of Queen Victoria 1861–1901* (Oxford 1935)

HIRST, FRANCIS W., *In the Golden Days* (1947)

HOLLAND, BERNARD, *Life of Spencer Compton, 8th Duke of Devonshire* 2 vols. (1911)

IRVING, LAURENCE, *Henry Irving: The Actor and His World* (1951)

JAMES, ROBERT RHODES, *Lord Randolph Churchill* (1959)

———, *Rosebery: A Biography of Archibald Philip, 5th Earl of Rosebery* (1963)

JENKINS, ROY, *Sir Charles Dilke: A Victorian Tragedy* (1958)

KENNEDY, A. L., *Salisbury 1830–1903: Portrait of a Statesman* (1953)

KILBRACKEN, LORD, *Reminiscences* (1931)

KITSON CLARK, G., *The Making of Victorian England* (1962)

LESLIE, SIR SHANE, *Henry Edward Manning: His Life and Labours* (1921)

LEVESON GOWER, F., *Bygone Years* (1905)

LONGFORD, ELIZABETH, *Victoria R.I.* (1964)

LUCY, HENRY, *Diary of Two Parliaments 1874–80 and 1880–85* 2 vols. (1885)

———, *Memories of Eight Parliaments* (1908)

LYONS, F. S. L., *The Fall of Parnell 1890–91* (1960)

MARCUS, STEVEN, *The Other Victorians* (1966)

MAXWELL, SIR HERBERT, *Life and Letters of 4th Earl of Clarendon* 2 vols. (1913)

MAYHEW, HENRY, *London Labour and the London Poor* 4 vols. (1851–62)

MIALL, ARTHUR, *Life of Edward Miall* (1884)

MONEYPENNY, W. F., and BUCKLE, G. E., *The Life of Benjamin Disraeli, Earl of Beaconsfield* 6 vols. (1910–20)

MORLEY, JOHN, *Life of Richard Cobden* 2 vols. (1881)

———, *Recollections* 2 vols. (1921)

NOVIKOFF, OLGA, *The MP for Russia: Reminiscences and Correspondence*, edited W. T. Stead (1909)

NUTTING, ANTHONY, *Gordon: Martyr and Misfit* (1966)

O'BRIEN, BARRY, *Life of Charles Stewart Parnell* (1898)

O'BRIEN, CONOR CRUISE, *Parnell and His Party 1880–1891* (Oxford 1957)

O'CONNOR, T. P., *Memoirs of an Old Parliamentarian* (1929)

PEARSON, HESKETH, *Labby* (1936)

PEARSON, MICHAEL, *The Age of Consent: Victorian Prostitution and Its Enemies* (Newton Abbott 1972)

PELLING, H. M., *Popular Politics and Society in Late Victorian Britain* (1967)

PONSONBY, ARTHUR, *Henry Ponsonby: Queen Victoria's Private Secretary: His Life from His Letters* (1942)

PONSONBY, MAGDALEN, *Mary Ponsonby: A Memoir, Some Letters and a Journal* (1927)

POPE-HENNESSY, JAMES, *Monckton-Milnes* 2 vols. (1949 & 1951)

PURCELL, E. S., *Life of Cardinal Manning* 2 vols. (1896)

READ, DONALD, *Cobden and Bright: A Victorian Political Partnership* (1967)

REID, SIR T. WEMYSS, *Life of Rt. Hon. William Edward Forster* 2 vols. (1888)

———, *Memoirs 1842–1885*, edited Stuart J. Reid (1905)

RENDEL, LORD, *Personal Papers*, edited F. E. Hamer (1931)

RIDLEY, JASPER, *Palmerston* (1970)

RUSSELL, G. W. E., *One Look Back* (1912)

SOUTHGATE, DONALD, *The Passing of the Whigs 1832–1886* (1962)

ST. HELIER, LADY, *Memoirs of Fifty Years* (1909)

STANMORE, LORD, *The Earl of Aberdeen* (1893)

——, *Sidney Herbert: Lord Herbert of Lea: A Memoir* 2 vols. (1906)

TAINE, HIPPOLYTE, *Notes on England* (3rd edition 1872)

TAYLOR, A. J. P., *The Struggle for the Mastery in Europe 1848–1918* (Oxford 1954)

——, *Bismarck: The Man and the Statesman* (1955)

THOROLD, A. L., *Life of Henry Labouchere* (1913)

TREVELYAN, G. M., *Life of John Bright* (1913)

VIDLER, A. R., *The Orb and the Cross* (1945)

VINCENT, JOHN, *The Formation of the Liberal Party 1857–1868* (1966)

VINCENT, JOHN, and COOKE, A. B., *The Governing Passion: Cabinet Government and Party Politics 1885–86* (Brighton 1974)

WALPOLE, SIR SPENCER, *Life of Lord John Russell* (1889)

WEST, SIR ALGERNON, *Recollections 1832–1886* 2 vols. (1898)

——, *Private Diaries*, edited H. G. Hutchinson (1922)

YOUNG, G. M., *Portrait of an Age* (1936)   and

The Letters of Queen Victoria: A Selection from Her Majesty's Correspondence and Journal 1st Series 1837–61, edited A. C. Benson and Viscount Esher; 2nd series 1862–85, edited G. E. Buckle; 3rd series 1886–1901, edited G. E. Buckle

Dearest Mama 1861–1864 and *Your Dear Letter 1865–1871: Letters Between Queen Victoria and the Princess Royal/Crown Princess of Prussia*, edited Roger Fulford (1968 and 1971)

INDEX